Earth and Mind: How Geologists Think and Learn about the Earth

edited by

Cathryn A. Manduca
Science Education Resource Center
Carleton College
1 North College St.
Northfield, Minnesota 55057
USA

David W. Mogk
Department of Earth Sciences
Montana State University
Bozeman, Montana 59717-3480
USA

THE
GEOLOGICAL
SOCIETY
OF AMERICA

Special Paper 413

3300 Penrose Place, P.O. Box 9140 ▪ Boulder, Colorado 80301-9140, USA

2006

Published by The Geological Society of America, Inc.
3300 Penrose Place, P.O. Box 9140, Boulder, Colorado 80301-9140, USA
www.geosociety.org

Printed in U.S.A.

GSA Books Science Editors: Marion E. Bickford and Abhijit Basu

A Cataloging-in-Publication record for this volume is available from the Library of Congress.

ISBN-10 0-8137-2413-9
ISBN-13 978-0-8137-2413-3

Cover: Lena Delta, Russia. Image taken 7/27/2000. The Lena River, some 2800 miles (4400 km) long, is one of the largest rivers in the world. The Lena Delta Reserve is the most extensive protected wilderness area in Russia. It is an important refuge and breeding grounds for many species of Siberian wildlife. Image courtesy of the U.S. Geological Survey National Center for EROS and NASA Landsat Project Science Office. Graphic designed by Karin Kirk, Montana State University.

10 9 8 7 6 5 4 3 2 1

7582167

Contents

Prologue

Earth and mind: These are the substance and essence of our work as geoscientists. Earth is the focus of our work—understanding its systems and sensitivities. Mind is the most important asset we bring to this work. Geoscientists learn a body of knowledge that frames their thinking, a battery of methods that they can use to address a problem, and a sophisticated set of skills for collecting and analyzing data. But perhaps most important, geoscientists have a way of thinking about Earth that grows from a combination of their training, their scientific work, and their world experiences. While each individual is unique, geoscientists share a common core of interests, approaches, skills and knowledge that constitute geoscience expertise. This volume explores the nature of that expertise.

How we think and what we study define our discipline. Geoscience is sometimes characterized as a derivative science equal to the sum of physics, chemistry, and biology applied to Earth. One goal of this book is to illuminate how and why the thinking of geoscientists is different from that of sister disciplines. We have reached a critical juncture in the history of mankind: It is no longer possible for us to live on Earth without attending to the impacts of our actions on it and its impacts on us. The geosciences provide an important way of thinking about Earth, as well as critical tools for understanding these problems. It is difficult for others to appreciate the contributions made by geoscientists without understanding the nature of the geosciences' unique approach. Geoscientists must be able to articulate the nature of our science, its rigor, and its methods for drawing strong conclusions in understanding the complex earth system.

Understanding this expertise is also critical to our ability to teach geoscience. Geoscientists are responsible not only for developing their successors, but also for developing an understanding of geoscience in future teachers and the broader public. This is essential to a civilization that can live successfully on Earth. Teaching is difficult work. However, a better understanding of the expertise we are trying to develop and the process by which students gain this expertise can help us considerably. This book provides examples of ways in which illumination of the complex thought processes used by geoscientists to observe and interpret the world around us can be used to inform teaching and learning.

The papers presented in this book are drawn from three sources. In the first section, "Learning from the Earth," senior geoscientists reflect on how and why they do their research—how they learn. These authors are all members of the National Academy of Sciences. Their chapters make clear the diversity of thinking and learning in the field while demonstrating the importance of observation, synthesis, and integration in geoscience. In the second section, "Learning about Geoscience Thinking," geoscience educators and cognitive scientists shed their insights on the nature of geoscience thinking and particularly its relationship to fundamental cognitive processes. One leaves this section understanding that these groups have important methods and insights to share with the geoscience community. The final section, "Helping Students Learn," is the work of educators who demonstrate how understanding geoscience thinking can improve students' learning. Taken together, these sections develop an integrated picture of the special nature of the geosciences. Geoscience is a synthetic discipline whose practitioners have special skill in integrating observational, theoretical, and experimental data to understand the processes and history of the earth system; it is a discipline that requires special skill in visual and spatial thinking, in understanding deep time, and in analyzing complex systems; and it is a discipline that offers unique opportunities to study and to teach the skills that are increasingly important in our complex world.

As geoscientists, we have gained from these papers insight into what we are doing when we ponder a problem in the field, laboratory, or office. We have learned more about how leaders in our field think and learn, and thus we have improved our ability to make sound observations, draw strong conclusions, and communicate with other geoscientists. As teachers, we have a better understanding of the knowledge and skills that we would like our students to master and the challenges that they are likely to encounter in the course of this learning. Thus we are better positioned to help our students learn and practice important aspects of geoscience thinking. As researchers investigating learning, we have new insights into the interplay between the study of geoscience expertise and of more fundamental cognitive skills such as spatial thinking. We also better understand the synergy between studying expertise itself and the development of that expertise in students. By combining these approaches, we develop a more complete understanding of geoscience expertise that can be used to improve both our science and our teaching. At the same time, we contribute to the broader understanding of human cognition which informs the development of educational methods, materials and practice used in all parts of the educational enterprise. This volume is intended to help geoscientists, geoscience educators, and cognitive scientists alike see the power in bringing together these diverse and complementary sets of expertise.

This is an unusual book that spans three cultures and brings together not only their insights but also their communication styles. It requires an unusual reader with the interest to span this reach and the patience to adapt to the expository styles of each group. It also required unusual authors ready to speak to readers outside their disciplines and to clearly explain fundamental ideas. We thank those authors for accepting this bold challenge with enthusiasm. We also thank our reviewers for their excellent and timely feedback, and the GSA science editors Abhijit Basu and Pat Bickford for their willingness to undertake this experiment and for their encouragement along the way. We hope that you learn as much from *Earth and Mind* as we have in its creation and that it ushers in a new era of collaboration among geoscientists, cognitive scientists, and educators.

This book is an outgrowth of a workshop funded by the National Science Foundation and the Johnson Foundation, *Bringing Research on Learning to the Geosciences,* convened to bring together geoscientists, educators, and cognitive scientists to explore common interests focused on learning and teaching about Earth (Manduca et al., 2002). This was followed by a Pardee Symposium at the 2002 Geological Society of America Annual Meeting titled "Toward a Better Understanding of the Complicated Earth: Insights from Geologic Research, Education, and Cognitive Science." An online collection of resources related to these events and additional activities can be found at http://serc.carleton.edu/research_on_learning/. This project is based upon work supported by the National Science Foundation under Grant No. 02-13065. Any opinions, findings, and conclusions or recommendations expressed in this material are those of the author(s) and do not necessarily reflect the views of the National Science Foundation.

REFERENCE CITED

Manduca, C., Mogk, D., and Stillings, N., 2002, Bringing research on learning to the geosciences: Report from a Workshop Sponsored, by the National Science Foundation and the Johnson Foundation, July 2002, Racine Wisconsin: Northfield, Minnesota, USA, Carleton College, 34 p. (http://serc.carleton.edu/research_on_learning/workshop02/index.html).

Cathy Manduca
Dave Mogk

Learning from Earth

In this section, four senior geoscientists write about the ways in which geoscience knowledge moves forward. From their writings, we can see the range of techniques that are brought to the field as well as the processes that are used to create and test theories.

We turn first to issues of motivation and inspiration as Sue Kieffer (University of Illinois) writes about beauty and creativity in the geosciences. Drawing extensively on writings in philosophy, science, and the arts, Kieffer explores how a quest for scientific beauty characterized by harmonious integration motivates geoscientists to create and test theories. She concludes with the importance of nurturing creativity throughout the lifetime of geoscientists by exploring new ideas that challenge ones accumulating wisdom.

In the second essay, Gary Ernst from Stanford University tells how field observations and mapping shape his thinking. Ernst describes the complex interplay between observation and interpretation. One is impressed with the wide range of detailed observations that are integrated in shaping his initial hypotheses. These are tested as he looks for relationships among rocks of different types and different ages that will support or disprove his ideas. Data drawn from the physical relationships between rocks, the fabric of minerals they contain, as well as the mineralogy and chemistry of the rocks are all integrated to test theories for the rocks' origin and history. The act of mapping opens the possibilities of new hypotheses, and in turn, the mapping itself (and choice of observations) is informed by extant theories. New findings in one geographic area illuminate the processes that are possible in another. Thus, Ernst returns to make new observations in well-studied areas, finding new detail that constrains the geologic history. Ernst's approach requires an integrated synthesis across all that he has seen and learned throughout his career demonstrating that geologic understanding grows with the accumulated observations and synthesis of the entire community through time.

The thread of integration and synthesis continues as Don Anderson from the California Institute of Technology writes about the theory of plate tectonics. Anderson, a geophysicist, uses both observational data and fundamental principles of physics and chemistry to test two contrasting models for the mechanisms that drive plate tectonics. Anderson concludes that there is strong evidence that Earth behaves as a self-organizing system that evolves in response to a complex interplay of processes. His arguments demonstrate how geoscientists martial evidence from disparate sources to make arguments, as well as the way that they use simplicity to test the resulting theories. Anderson's essay points out the vigilance that is needed in testing assumptions in order to ensure that they do not assume the stature of facts over time.

Don Turcotte (University of California, Davis) is a pioneer in the use of quantitative physical arguments to test the plausibility of geologic theories. In his essay, we see how mathematical models can be used to illuminate the processes leading to geologic observations. Starting from different data and using a completely different approach, Turcotte arrives in much the same place as Anderson, recognizing the importance of interacting phenomena in yielding the complexity we observe in the natural world.

This series of four essays taken together illuminates the importance of integration and synthesis in the geosciences. Individual scientists integrate their observations and learning over their lifetimes to test and refine their understanding of Earth. The field as a whole integrates disparate types of data drawn from sites around the world and from our planetary neighbors to test theories describing the origin and evolution of Earth. Kieffer argues that it is this quest for a compelling synthesis, a type of intellectual beauty, that drives geoscientists' creative thinking. Integration and synthesis emerge as central characteristics of earth science thinking.

Geological Society of America
Special Paper 413
2006

The concepts of beauty and creativity: Earth science thinking

Susan W. Kieffer*

Department of Geology, University of Illinois, Urbana, Illinois 61801, USA

ABSTRACT

The concepts of creativity and beauty have been intertwined for centuries and have been examined by both artists and scientists. This is a personal essay reflecting on the nature of creativity, its manifestations in artists and scientists, and the challenge of maintaining creativity as we age.

Keywords: creativity, beauty, art, science.

INTRODUCTION

Like other authors in this volume, I am an earth scientist—one who came late into the earth sciences by way of a musical training in public schools, a physics and mathematics background from a liberal arts college, and a Ph.D. in planetary sciences from a technical institute. Music has been an integral part of my life since childhood: as a performer, student, and amateur composer (Fig. 1). This is a personal essay written over the past 15 years during which I have reflected variously on these elements of my life (music, physics, mathematics, earth and planetary sciences, liberal arts, science in general); on problems with identifying and preserving creativity; on the role of institutions and our working ambiance in nurturing or harming creativity; on the evolution of creativity with age; and, especially, on explaining scientific creativity to nonscientists. I have concluded that concepts of creativity and beauty are similar in the sciences and arts, but that the development of specialization and abstraction in both science and art within Euro-American cultures has made communication difficult. Recognition of similarities in our creative endeavors, in turn, and study of the long-lived composers and poets have led me to some ideas for prolonging and enhancing creativity.

The concept of beauty is often associated with creativity. For centuries, humans have thought and written about the relation between the two, and it is difficult to write about these subjects without being obvious and trivial, or pedantic and dilettantish (Chandrasekhar, 1989). My thinking is very much influenced by my life in a western, Euro-American twentieth-century culture,

and this essay should be read with that context in mind. Generalizations beyond this culture are not valid.

Much of this essay is about communication between scientists and artists, and it may read as if all scientists, artists, and people were involved in the discourse. Unfortunately, that is not true. Not all humans think about creativity and beauty. Not all think about art and science. Not all will incorporate art and science into their lives. Communication requires both eloquence in expression, and open minds in reception.

There is no "right thinking" about creativity or beauty. This essay is my thinking on this subject at this time in my life. It was begun in 1990 as I was thinking about how the major institutions in which most scientists work could nurture creativity. That thread of thinking always dead-ended in a self-serving whine. The editors of this volume redirected the focus toward examination of earth science thinking. I suspect that if I started another essay right now (mid-2006), I could not re-create the current one. A new essay would be quite different, especially if it took another 15 years to complete. Similarly, I know that if I tried to "re-create" the composition in Figure 1, I would now create something quite different...or not even feel creative about the elements that it represents at all. Such is the ephemeral, vague, whimsical, and ill-defined nature of "creativity" and "beauty," the subjects of this essay.

My thinking on these topics was crystallized by a paper "The Perception of Beauty and the Pursuit of Science" by the astrophysicist Subrahmanyan Chandrasekhar (1989). Chandrasekhar had spent approximately two decades studying the lives of poets

---

*skieffer@uiuc.edu.

Kieffer, S.W., 2006, The concepts of beauty and creativity: Earth science thinking, *in* Manduca, C.A., and Mogk, D.W., eds., Earth and Mind: How Geologists Think and Learn about the Earth: Geological Society of America Special Paper 413, p. 3–11, doi: 10.1130/2006.2413(01). For permission to copy, contact editing@ geosociety.org. ©2006 Geological Society of America. All rights reserved.

Figure 1. The score for a musical composition titled "9.77 seconds."

and scientists, and his conclusions were based not only on biographies, autobiographies, and literature on creativity, but also on personal acquaintance with famous contemporaries. His conclusion was that there is a real difference in the longevity of creativity between scientists and artists—namely, that creativity was the preserve of the young in science, but that artists preserved, or increased, their creativity with age. He felt that the difference between artists and scientists was "the apparent inability of a scientist to continuously grow and mature" (Chandrase khar, 1989, p. 27). (Interestingly, and I will assert, relevantly, he was generally comparing twentieth-century physicists and mathematicians with nineteenth-century literary and musical artists.) The social, political, and economic contexts within which much of science has been done in the twentieth century are very different from the environment of art or science in the nineteenth century. Specifically, both art and science were nearly a cottage industry in the nineteenth century—done in small clusters with a form of patronage very different from twentieth-century (and now, twenty-first century) science.

I started wondering if Chandrasekhar's discouraging conclusions were true, and, if so, how and if they applied to earth and other natural scientists. (I will restrict myself to discussing the earth sciences from here on.) Our largely inductive and tangible science is quite different from the more analytical, deductive, abstract sciences. Rather than relying purely on analysis and deduction, our thinking in the earth sciences also builds cumulatively on experience and induction. I asked myself: are earth scientists perhaps more like nineteenth-century artists than other twentieth-century scientists?

In this essay, I will (1) adopt definitions of beauty and creativity; (2) compare creativity and beauty in the arts and sciences; (3) discuss a hypothesis that the perceived schism between the arts and sciences arose in western cultures when abstraction and specialization developed and communication became difficult; (4) examine the role of aging in creativity; and (5) speculate on how individual earth scientists might prolong their creativity.

There is always risk in generalization and stereotypes—for example, regarding point 3, I have many colleagues in physics who will point to the anecdotal evidence of a correlation between physics and musical talents. Indeed, I have been the recipient of their invitations to participate in many soirées, so they might not appreciate the thoughts in this essay at all. So be it...we all understand exceptions to rules.

I came to admire the Nobel Prize–winning physicist Hideki Yukawa (1907–1981) very much as I worked on this essay. In reading Yukawa's essays, I felt as if I was sitting beside him in an easy conversation. It was a great surprise to have read the philosophic parts of his work and, only then, discover that his father was a geologist-geographer in Japan at the turn of the century. Having myself traveled in Japan with Japanese geologists, I instantly wondered about this father and his influence on Yukawa. As a young man, Yukawa perceived his father as a physically vigorous adventurer—traveling all over the country preparing geologic maps, surveying, going into the mountains

and places that were inaccessible "all involving a considerable amount of physical strain and even a certain amount of danger" (Yukawa, 1973, p. 25).

Yukawa saw none of those qualities or desires in himself. Furthermore, his father had the task of finding lodging in the mountains, a task "that required considerable contact with all kinds of people." Yukawa apparently viewed the prospect of finding and staying at a completely unfamiliar inn to be extremely frightening, and he decided that geology and geography involved the closest kinds of exchanges with human beings, and that while he was not antisocial, he was certainly asocial. Thus, he chose to go into physics by progressively eliminating the natural sciences (because they were too social), engineering (because it was both social and involved too much haggling over the prices of machines), and the social sciences ("because he had no interest in them at all"). This left him physics and mathematics. His success in these fields is perhaps a testament to his self knowledge and the elimination process by which he chose his life's work.

It is remarkable, however, that he came nearly full circle as he analyzed creativity later in his life. He emphasized the need to maintain close contact with the natural world to preserve creativity. To Yukawa, the awareness of nature, in a much more intuitive way than most westerners would accept as a part of scientific thinking, appeared to be a vital ingredient in creativity. He felt that not only his own success in moving theoretical physics a step further owed something to this way of thinking, but that an element of it can be seen in such creative acts as Heisenberg's formulation of the uncertainty principle. While accepting the fact that his later mental struggles to discern the nature of particles did not lead to any breakthrough, he expresses the conviction that "an Oriental approach" (his words)—briefly summarized by the definition of beauty used in this essay—is a better way to deeper understanding than the present pursuit of ever greater detail with an ever greater mass of facts and theories. I will conclude that it may be this contact with the natural world that allows geologists to grow and mature with age.

BEAUTY AND CREATIVITY

The concept of "beauty" is subjective, but has often been associated with creativity, and although one usually finds essays in which creativity is defined first, I found it more logical to define "beauty" and then "creativity." Much has been written for millennia about "beauty." Different scientific disciplines would probably advocate different definitions, such as "a sense of symmetry," a "theory with a minimum number of assumptions," "generality of paradigm," "predictive power," or "conformity to Occam's Razor." In this volume, Don Anderson discusses the role of simplicity and Occam's Razor in how we should evaluate the ideas of plate tectonics. Artistic disciplines would have perhaps as many other definitions, and different cultures yet others.

Of the many definitions of beauty and creativity in the literature, I chose the following:

Beauty: the "proper conformity of the parts to one another and to the whole" (an ancient definition, but possibly first explicitly given in the context of the "exact sciences" by Heisenberg, 1971).

Creativity: the ability to form or formulate something that no one else has done before, and that feels as if it has the proper conformity of the parts to the whole, i.e., the ability to formulate something that feels beautiful.

This is a personal essay, not a treatise on philosophy or aesthetics, and I do not feel compelled to define every word, including "proper," or "art," or "science," but will try to imply relations as I write. For example, it is difficult to define "proper" in this context, but it is relatively easy to define what is not proper: evil, false, forced, misleading....

By implication, Richard Feynman (as cited in Don Anderson's essay) defined "proper" in this way: "You can recognize truth[1] by its beauty and simplicity...when you get it right, it is obvious that it is right" (Feynman, 1965, p. 171).

Or, Buckminster Fuller on working on a problem "... when I have finished, if the solution is not beautiful, I know it is wrong."

The concept of beauty certainly varies from person to person and, in science, from discipline to discipline. Bodies of knowledge tend to grow and become cumbersome and complex for lack of a framework, or because the framework is wrong. Perhaps in common to all of the disciplines, beauty implies elements of simplification and unification. The concept of beauty as used in the sciences often places abstraction in a valued position, but as we examine the different scientific disciplines, we realize that the processes of abstraction, deduction, induction, and intuition all play different roles. The concept of beauty varies significantly with the proportion of these components. In mathematics, beauty may be associated with deduction and rigor; in geology, with induction and breadth. In detail, it could become as difficult to find an agreement on the concept of beauty amongst scientists as it is across the arts and sciences, but I believe there would be general agreement that in some way "beauty" is found in the relationship of parts to each other, and to the total.

How does one define creativity[2]? The lives of many creative people show evidence of internal feelings of struggle, which I feel were eloquently summarized by Yukawa (1973, p. 131–132):

"Without some contradiction within oneself, there can be no study; that, indeed, is the essential nature of study. To put it

differently, one has some place that is dark, or obscure, or vague, or puzzling within oneself, and one tries to find some light in it. Then, when one has found a ray of light, one tries to enlarge it little by little so that darkness is gradually dispelled. This, I feel, is the typical process whereby creativity shows itself."

In scientific research, a worker may get a feeling that he or she has had a creative insight, but would be at loss to describe just how that insight arose, or even why it feels creative or beautiful. Rather, one just has a feeling that something unexpected has taken place, and that it is beautiful in the above context, that is, you "get it right."

CREATIVITY IN SCIENCE AND ART

Communication of concepts, whether scientific, aesthetic, concrete or abstract, seems to be a fundamental drive of humans. The means of communication, however, differ amongst individuals, cultures, disciplines, and generations. These differences are at the root of many misunderstandings, and they present a continuing challenge to all humans.

Scientists have a goal of formulating hypotheses within the methods of science, of seeking to falsify these hypotheses, and of revising them or further testing them. Our goal is to purposely eliminate ambiguity and unclearness. To achieve this goal, scientific language has evolved almost into a new language, too commonly intelligible only to a small community of specialists.

Nevertheless, a measure of our success with science is the creation of a body of knowledge by scientists from different generations, cultures, languages, political views, and religions. The communication of the view of the world that is accessible by scientific methods is a creative feat comparable to the transmission of human aesthetics in the arts through different centuries, cultures, and languages. The mathematical sciences—math and physics—have long held prestige as the most "beautiful" of the sciences, precisely because they are the least ambiguous, most rigorous of all the sciences (see further discussion of this in chapter 8 by Dodick and Argamon). Yet we earth scientists can hold up our tremendous successes in also communicating the concepts of space, time, stratigraphy, and process through different cultures and languages. The scientific product—although very different in expression from the artistic product—resembles the arts

---

[1]This is an interesting comment from Feynman, because, taken in isolation, it implies that he believed that science could prove "truth." In fact, all we can do in science is prove something is false, which Feynman discussed extensively in this same reference. We do, however, use terms like "truth" or "laws" to refer to ideas that have withstood many tests of falsifiability. In this sense, our use of these words has different meanings from other nonscience parts of our culture. This has become increasingly obvious in the debate of the past decade within the United States over the roles of science and religion in the origin and evolution of humans. Thus, Feynman's quote is appropriate within our scientific context, but taken out of context, could be misleading about the nature of science.

[2]Creativity is difficult to define and to measure. Productivity is often used as a measure of creativity. The definition of "to produce" in (Webster's II, 1984) is rooted in the Latin words: "pro"= "forward"; "duce" = "to lead." Thus, definitions of the verb produce are: (1) to bring forth: yield; (2) to create by physical or mental effort; (3) to manufacture; (4) to give rise to; (5) to bring forward; exhibit; (6) to sponsor or present to the public (as in a musical production); (7) ...etc. Productivity in our modern world, especially the academic world, has lost some of its subtle meaning as based in the Latin roots of "to lead forward." Productivity has much more the context of "to manufacture" or "to exhibit" (i.e., "publish or perish"). I will try to distinguish between productivity and creativity in this essay.

in that it accomplishes communication between human beings across generational and cultural gaps.

When scientists are writing or conversing about their work, they ultimately aim to communicate one thought at a time clearly and unambiguously. In that particular sense, in this essay, I am striving to be linear and "scientific," even though the subject is philosophic. I am trying to communicate one thought at a time, and to progress in an orderly way toward conclusions.

The goal of communicating unambiguously and clearly does not mean that we scientists always think that way: in fact, the fundamental drive toward creativity and new ideas seems to be, as Yukawa said, ambiguities or inconsistencies in our perceptions of the world. If there were no ambiguities, we would have nothing to struggle with. Our internal struggle is to reconcile and get rid of inconsistencies. But, the processes by which scientifically creative ideas arise can often be completely different from the processes by which we test, verify, and modify these ideas.

In contrast to our scientific striving for unambiguous expression, artists seem to purposely strive for simultaneous communication on many levels. Great literature, music, dance, performance, and paintings all project out to us on many levels—direct and indirect, public and private, actual and symbolic, objective and subjective. Aldous Huxley described art as seeking to provide an experience rich in harmonics and overtones.

The short piece of music in Figure 1 is an example of artistic, rather than scientific, communication. It may mean nothing to some people, just as some scientific communications and some art works mean nothing to some people. It may, or may not, seem linear; it may or may not invoke sounds, images, color, or even, smells. It may mean more to you, or less, after you read the intent of the piece described in the appendix. It is not, however subject to any tests of falsifiability or reductionism, as would be required of a scientific figure.

If I could take some liberty and propose a generality based on my own experience, I would say that scientists live internally with fundamentals, harmonics, overtones, and dissonances, but strive to seek and sort out the fundamental from the harmonics and overtones. Artists, on the other hand, have the liberty of portraying all of these simultaneously. Because of this difference, although scientists and artists may agree on the general concepts of creativity and beauty, we have trouble recognizing this agreement in expression. I think that this difference in perception, interpretation, and communication of world views is at the root of some of the problems that we currently have in perceiving the relations among art, science, and individual lives.

It is worth reviewing briefly how and when the perceived gap between the arts and sciences arose, because it bears on the apparent difference in longevity of creativity amongst us, and on possible reasons for difficulties that both artists and scientists are having in initiating and/or prolonging their creativity in the twenty-first century. In much of western society over the past few hundred years, explicit and implicit communication between artists and scientists has become more difficult because both the sciences and the arts have become increasingly abstract and specialized. This is the so-called "schism" between the arts and sciences, the perceived "two worlds" of C.P. Snow (1959). Are earth scientists affected by this schism? Certainly yes. Are we affected as much as some other sciences? Possibly not.

If we look back to ancient Greece or to other cultures from eastern Asia, Africa, the Americas, or aboriginal Australia, we can find harmony and balance in the use of intuition and abstraction in the perception of the world. In ancient Greece, scientists appreciated poetry, poets appreciated geometry, and the world had a unity and comprehensibility to individuals. Music was perceived as organic to the soul, e.g., the Greek attribution of moods, character, and morality to their modes. Indeed, if we look back only as far as the life and philosophy of Thomas Jefferson, as reflected in the American Constitution, we can find a unity of science, philosophy, literature, and the arts that has largely disappeared in the modern western world. Until approximately the Victorian age, there was relatively little debate that creativity or the perception of the world or beauty might differ in the arts and sciences. The available science and arts were rather easily incorporated into the lives of thoughtful people.

But the roots of the schism between art and science were in place in those parts of the world where science was about to explode into abstraction and specialization. In his autobiography, Darwin tells how he became afflicted by "a curious and lamentable loss of the higher aesthetic tastes" (Darwin, August 1876). He would get so bored trying to reread Shakespeare that he would get physically ill. On the other side of the schism, the young poet Keats drank a toast (possibly after many, many other drinks!) in hopes of destruction of Newton, who had explained the "science" of the rainbow and had thus robbed it of its poetry. Even if Keats wasn't serious, his quote has not gone without serious notice; viz. Dawkins (1998) published a long book on the relationship between arts and science based on this quote of Keats.

However, in between these extremes, many have labored and written to find a middle ground, to reconcile thought processes, perceptions, and values—those general things that we believe are associated with creativity and aesthetics. T.H. Huxley, a great friend and champion of Darwin, advocated a primarily scientific education tempered with lots of humanities and classics, all of which he loved. Mathew Arnold, on the other hand, believed in a humanistic and classical education tempered with enough science to allow people to understand the world around them. Wordsworth, even though enamored with the poetry of rainbows, nevertheless was also able to admire Sir Isaac Newton.

Even the first great revolution in physics, initiated by Galileo and completed by Newton, did not complete the isolation of western science from philosophy. Abstraction began to play a more prominent role in the evolution of science with Newton's work, but concepts of space and time still accorded with intuition, and the new abstractions being introduced were directed toward problems that humans could comprehend—orbits of planets at a scale perceptible on a clear night, and the fundamental fact that we all fall down.

However, with the second revolution in physics, which included Planck's and Bohr's quantum mechanics and Einstein's theory of relativity, abstraction became a dominant process in science. In a sense, abstraction became more concrete. Einstein's four-dimensional space-time world became an intuitive reality to a new generation of physicists and became a new starting point for more abstraction. And even the physical manifestations of the theory—such as perturbations of planetary orbits—became too difficult for individuals (including many scientists) to easily understand intuitively. As a freshman entering a liberal arts college, I learned Kepler's law of planetary orbits while lying with fellow students and instructors on the grass by our small observatory watching the nightly changes in the sky. As a senior majoring in physics and mathematics, I struggled with a capstone thesis trying to understand Einstein's view of the orbit of Mercury. I did not have the same "gut-level" experience of understanding that I had with Keplerian orbits.

Atomistic concepts also became more abstract. From the time of Aristotle through the early twentieth century, scientists struggled with trying to reconcile matter versus void, atomic versus continuum properties of matter, and wave versus particle nature of light. For a long time, most scientists and intellectuals could at least intuitively relate to the problems and questions. However, in the age of new science, not only the general public, but many scientists feel estranged from a good fraction of the body of scientific knowledge. In specialization, scientists have developed their own vocabulary, and it is a vocabulary that is nonintuitive, where new words are invented as new discoveries arise (viz., quarks), or old words are given new meanings, accessible only to the inner circles (viz., charm, strings).

Not quite, but nearly, in parallel, art became more abstract. The modality of the ancient Greeks was preserved for a long time through the baroque and romantic composers, but diverged in the twentieth century, e.g., into the 12-tone patterns of Arnold Schoenberg, the chance music of John Cage, or the many forms of electronic music. Although it intermittently reconverges (e.g., into jazz), divergence has been the general trend. Poetry evolved from the classical rhythmic forms into many schools of modernism, and moved away from classical realism to the many forms of modern expression. Aesthetics became more specialized.

However, to the extent that all humans live on planet Earth, the great revolutions in geology have not isolated us from other scientists or from the public as much as the discoveries in physics and mathematics have caused isolation. Except where we adopt the most modern and complex tools of modern physics, chemistry, and biology, our earth and planetary science concepts remain relatively accessible to our colleagues and the public. Our great paradigm shifts—the invention of the map, stratigraphic concepts of time, plate tectonics—are easily appreciated by an inquiring mind, and, with the few exceptions of our time-scale nomenclature and our mineral and rock names, the concepts and words (in English) retain the general context of their origins. In this way, in spite of all of our technical sophistication, I do believe that twentieth- and twenty-first-century earth scientists are more like nineteenth-century artists than other modern scientists.

CREATIVITY, BEAUTY, AND THE EARTH SCIENCES

As a community, earth scientists do not have a historic legacy of thinking about our creativity like the mathematicians and physicists. In fact, this Geological Society of America (GSA) publication is quite unique in asking questions about earth science thinking. Furthermore, in the current intellectual climate, and with the large numbers of scientists in the world today, there are few measures of creativity. We measure productivity, not creativity. Evaluation of creativity requires a value judgment, not simple numerical counting, or even measures of "impact." In the context of this paper, it requires a judgment of beauty. Perhaps as a community, we need a new form of peer evaluation, essays that define and discuss creativity and the contributions of individuals within that context.

Take the following premise: a geologic map, well done, is certainly beautiful. William Smith did not produce the first geologic maps (George Cuvier and Alexandre Brongniart published a geologic map of the Paris Basin in 1808), but he was the first to publish a map that "got it right" (1815). Smith understood that not only was there order in the geologic strata, but that fossil contents were in the same order, and that order was preserved over a very large geographic area. This was a creative leap that introduced a dimension of time to biology and founded the historical science of life on Earth.

The concept of geologic time is beautiful. James Hutton (1726–1797) and Arthur Holmes (1890–1965), who had the ideas of relative and absolute deep geologic time, respectively, were creative. Hutton was a deeply religious man living in a time when many believed in a young Earth, and when the neptunist ideas of Werner prevailed. Driven by his theological belief that a beneficent God had put the world here for humans, Hutton developed his plutonist concepts and came to the scientific conclusions that the world was very old. His beliefs propelled him to assemble evidence about the importance of intrusions and metamorphic rocks, an interesting mix of theology and geology. Holmes, a century later, was able to take his knowledge of physics into geology to give us the first accurate ages of the Earth and our eras and, later, to give us a remarkably accurate theory of plate tectonics—~30 yr before data became available to back up the theory.

The concept of plate tectonics is beautiful. The founders of plate tectonics were creative, e.g., Holmes mentioned above, Harry Hess who was able to take his experience as a geologist and Navy submarine commander to propose seafloor spreading, and J. Tuzo Wilson (1908–1993), who proposed hotspots to account for oceanic volcanic island chains and who discovered transform faults.

The concept of geology on other planets is beautiful. Eugene Shoemaker (1928–1997), the founder of astrogeology, stole the planets from the astronomers and gave them to the geologists by advocating that terrestrial geologic mapping techniques be applied to the surfaces of other planets. Shoemaker's lifelong work on the dynamics of meteorite impact, the science of relative dating the surfaces of other planets by counting impact craters, and advocacy of "catastrophic" impact processes in the intellectual climate of uniformitarianism were creative endeavors.

Many other individuals could be cited in such an exercise. These particular examples were chosen because of the longevity of their creativity.

CREATIVITY AND AGE

Creativity tends to manifest itself in youth, but that is not the topic of this essay. Rather, it is "what happens to creativity with age?" Chandrasekhar (1989, p. 14) borrowed from T.S. Elliot to say how he was going to address this topic: "one can always save the subject by magnificent quotations." A few well-chosen quotes can illustrate the direction of Chandrasekhar's thinking:

The rule that a poet is at his best after the age of 30 might have applied as well to [Shelley] as to Shakespeare, Milton, Wordsworth, Byron, Tennyson, and indeed almost every major English poet who lived to be over 30. [Desmond King-Hele on the death of Shelley at the age of thirty.]

One of the most significant facts, for the understanding of Beethoven, is that his work shows an organic development up until the very end. The greatest music Beethoven ever wrote is to be found in the last string quartets, and the music of every decade before the final period was greater than its predecessor. [J.W.N. Sullivan]

And, then about scientists:

A person who has not made his great contribution to science before the age of thirty will never do so. [Einstein]

Age is, of course, a fever chill
that every physicist must fear.
He's better dead than living still,
when once he's past his thirtieth year!
[Dirac]

No mathematician should ever allow himself to forget that mathematics, more than any other art or science, is a young man's game....Galois died at twenty-one, Able at twenty-seven, Ramanujan at thirty-three, Riemann at forty. There have been men who have done great work later;...[but] I do not know an instance of a major mathematical advance initiated by a man past fifty...A mathematician may still be competent enough at sixty, but it is useless to expect him to have original ideas. [G.H. Hardy]

A man of science past sixty does more harm than good. [Thomas Huxley]

As Chandrasekhar says "I do not doubt that these statements will be challenged or at least subjected to qualification." However, as I searched both the literature, and my own experience, to find proof that these statements were generically wrong or had been applied to special classes of scientists (mathematicians and physicists seem especially hard on themselves!), I began to find more and more anecdotes and statistics that reinforced Chandrasekhar's conclusions given in the introduction to this paper.

Yukawa offers a reason that creativity may be the province of the young in science. Within the sciences, creativity requires a breaking down of fixed ideas—internally within a person, scientifically within a discipline, or institutionally within a community. It is not easy to break down internal frameworks.

A considerable period of preparation is necessary before a particular man can display creativity in a particular field and in a particular form. He must, in short, have acquired all kinds of knowledge and also, probably, undergo all kinds of training. It is only after many kinds of prior conditions have been satisfied that creativity can show itself. By the time that one has done research for a long continuous period and become a full-fledged research worker, one has developed within oneself a relatively stable system of knowledge. This system of knowledge has been integrated by one's own efforts into a particular, definite form. And this business of integrating by oneself is, of course, an extremely valuable experience in itself. It means that one is able to teach others, and to pass on one's own knowledge.

That state of affairs also means, conversely, that one has become set in one's way of thinking. To exaggerate a little, one has become a mass of fixed ideas.

To know a lot of things has the advantage that, in theory at least, it serves as a basis for discovering new things; but it also has a gradual immobilizing effect. Whatever happens, nothing surprises one; and the chances for a display of creativity are lost. (Yukawa, 1973, p. 125)

What about earth scientists? Referring to those whom I cited above, we find evidence of prolonged creativity. William Smith colored in the first geologic map in the world in 1799 at the age of 30 and became the founder of English, and indeed, modern geology, by publishing his famous map in 1815 at the age of 46. He developed the concepts and some of the vocabulary of the field of stratigraphy until he died. James Hutton had the idea of deep time and found evidence to support it later in his life when he was 62 (1788). Arthur Holmes pioneered geochronology at the age of 21. He is lesser known for his radical, and eventually proven, theories on continental drift. He embraced this concept because his work on radioactivity, geological time, and petrogenesis had given him an unusual insight into understanding processes in Earth's interior. He was the first to propose that slow-moving convection currents in the mantle caused continental breakup, seafloor formation, crustal assimilation, and continental drift. He had these ideas at a very young age, but developed them continuously for over 30 yr until his death. J. Tuzo Wilson, a Canadian geophysicist, had his stunning insight into the nature of plate tectonics at the age of 50, a mental leap that caused him to refute his own ideas of earlier years. From that time until his death, he contributed inspirationally and eloquently to the new paradigm. Wilson's observations of the Canadian Shield were seminal in his ideas. Eugene Shoemaker's remarkable career grew and grew and showed no signs of slowing down until he was tragically killed in an automobile accident at the age of 69.

No two careers have followed the same pattern, but there is a remarkably consistent theme that the great careers in earth sciences were grounded in a very tangible relation to Earth and observations of it. Through our profession, we are connected to the every day experience of living on this planet, and we are sustained by it in our work, as well as in our lives.

LESSONS LEARNED

Chandrasekhar (1987) pondered why Lord Rayleigh had such a prolonged career compared to Maxwell and Einstein, and he found a hint of the answer in the memorial address given by J.J. Thompson for Lord Rayleigh in Westminster Abbey, December, 1921:

> "There are some great men of science whose charm consists in having said the first word on a subject, in having introduced some new idea which has proved fruitful; there are others whose charm consists perhaps in having said the last word on the subject, and who have reduced the subject to logical consistency and clearness."

Yukawa concluded that it seems absolutely essential that in order to maintain creativity, we have to move periodically out of our own masses of fixed ideas into the unknown. Balancing newness with wisdom is a challenge. In the earth sciences, we have the opportunity to do this simply by exploring our planet, and now, other planets. We must recognize that stimulus and surprises are important. We as individuals should try to break down the barriers that our own frameworks erect and allow ourselves to be open to surprises.

Finally, we should recognize that failure does not always mean a lack of creativity. Some of the greatest and most creative of earth scientists had some major failures, e.g., J. Tuzo Wilson had to discard his old views on tectonics at the age of 50 when the new information relevant to plate tectonics became available. We should learn to reward creative failure nearly as

equally as creative success. Most people do research for about forty years. Some may go through life feeling that they have had no successes, most would hope to a few successes, and few would claim continuous success. What are we doing all of that time that we are not successful? Probably about the same thing that Beethoven or Shakespeare did when they wrote and rewrote. We are certainly not doing nothing. We are doing something (a reviewer suggested "composting," "sifting," "simmering"), even if we do not later count it as successful. We get up in the morning, work hard from dawn till dusk, and throw much of what we have done into the wastebasket in despair. The line between a beautiful success and a beautiful failure is nearly invisible.

APPENDIX: EXPLANATION OF "9,77 SECONDS, FOOTSTEPS TO A WORLD RECORD" (FIGURE 1)

The world record for the men's 100 m dash was 9.83 s when I composed this piece in 1987. At the time of submission of this manuscript in 2005, that particular men's record had been disallowed; the current world record was set in 2005 by Asafa Powell at 9.77 s. The current women's record is 10.49 s by Florence Griffith Joyner, set in 1998. Men take 44 steps to cover this distance; women take 49–50.

The piece was inspired by trying to combine the beauty of Scriabin's mystic chord, which I had just discovered (chord 1 of the piece) with the beauty of performance of the world's finest athletes. The chords, tempos, and intensities match each footstep of the race and reflect the mindset and physiology of the athlete. The notation is my own, invented for the piece; it takes at least 5 pages of notes to explain all of this in words, yet here in 4 lines, 44 notes is a representation of both a high-performance athlete and a musical wonder, Scriabin's mystical chord.

ACKNOWLEDGMENTS

The author thanks Robert Hazen and an unidentified reviewer for helpful comments and patience on an earlier, and very rough, draft, and Cathy Manduca for gently urging that I take an essay written for quite a different purpose and submit it to this volume. My thinking on this subject has been influenced over the years by many interactions with the Geological Society of America (GSA) Critical Issues Caucus.

REFERENCES CITED

Chandrasekhar, S., 1987, Truth and beauty: Aesthetics and motivations in science: Chicago, University of Chicago Press, 170 p.

Chandrasekhar, S., 1989, The perception of beauty and the pursuit of science: American Academy of Arts and Sciences Bulletin, v. XLIII, no. 3, p. 14–29; also printed in Applied Optics, 1990, v. 29, no. 16, p. 2359–2363.

Darwin, C., 1876, Recollections of the development of my mind and character, *in* Barlow, N., ed., 1958, The autobiography of Charles Darwin 1809–1882: With original omissions restored: London, Collins, 253 p.

Dawkins, R., 1998, Unweaving the rainbow: Science, delusion and the appetite for wonder: New York, Houghton Mifflin, 336 p.

Feynman, R., 1965, The character of physical law: Cambridge, MIT Press, 173 p.

Heisenberg, W., 1971, Die bedeutung des schönen in der exacten naturwissenschaft, *in Ensemble 2*, R. Oldenbourg, München, p. 228–243. [English translation, 1974: "The meaning of beauty in the exact sciences," *in* Anshen, R.N., ed. (trans. Peter Heath), Across the frontiers: New York, Harper & Row.

Snow, C.P., 1959, The two cultures and the scientific revolution: New York, Cambridge University Press, 58 p.

Webster II New Riverside University Dictionary, 1984: Boston, Riverside Publishing Company, Houghton Mifflin Company, 1536 p.

Yukawa, H., 1973, Creativity and intuition: A physicist looks at east and west (translated by John Bester): Tokyo, Kodansha International, 206 p.

MANUSCRIPT ACCEPTED BY THE SOCIETY 21 MARCH 2006

Geological Society of America
Special Paper 413
2006

Geologic mapping—Where the rubber meets the road

W.G. Ernst

Department of Geological and Environmental Sciences, Stanford University, Stanford, California 94305-2115, USA

ABSTRACT

A geologic map represents the melding of field observations with various types of analytical data and earth science concepts. Choosing features to be portrayed is a reflection of the questions posed. Some would claim that in the mapping process, theory meets reality. However, a map is a more subjective product based on the sum of the geologist's prior training, aggregate field experience, and the stage of development of scientific concepts, the complexity of the mapped units, the extent and quality of exposures, the wealth of constraining ancillary data, and the time and thought expended in the mapping. The published map also reflects accommodations to the scientific reviewers' knowledge, and to technical compromises required by the printer-publisher. Because mapping style depends on a geologist's prior experience, it is necessarily a somewhat idiosyncratic process.

My own field research has focused chiefly on the petrologic-structural development of Mesozoic and younger contractional orogenic belts, and through them, the tectonic evolution of continental margins. Mapping has been an essential step enhancing my understanding of processes that have shaped convergent portions of Earth's crust. (1) For instance, field relations combined with mineralogic analysis in the Panoche Pass area, southern Diablo Range, central California, indicated relatively high pressure–low temperature recrystallization and postmetamorphic, low-angle faulting of the Franciscan Complex. (2) Mapping of a similar Franciscan terrane in the central Diablo Range identified imbricate, subhorizontal, syn- to postmetamorphic bedding-plane thrust faults and implied accretionary growth in the Pacheco Pass quadrangle. (3) Field study of a structural inversion of high-grade metamorphic rocks tectonically overlying low-grade equivalents in the Sanbagawa belt, central Shikoku, Japan, led to the interpretation of postrecrystallization, ductile nappe emplacement and, as in California and the Western and Eastern Alps, (4) a progressive, relatively high P–low T metamorphism-exhumation subduction-zone model. (5) Mapping the interstratified distal turbidites and mafic lavas, and the discovery of pillow tops in the Sawyers Bar area, documented in situ stages of oceanic-island arc development in the North Fork terrane, central Klamath Mountains, northwestern California. Bulk-rock compositions of interlayered ocean-island basalts and island-arc tholeiites supported this interpretation. (6) Detailed geologic mapping combined with remote sensing in the central White Mountains, easternmost California, demonstrated that the Middle Jurassic Barcroft granodioritic complex is a steeply southeast-dipping slab that intruded previously deformed mid-Mesozoic arc volcanic rocks and Neoproterozoic–Lower Cambrian platform strata along a high-angle reverse fault. Conclusions derived from these studies, as well as more general plate-tectonic syntheses, depended on geologic mapping, and, for me, the field mapping was an enjoyable and scientifically fulfilling experience.

Keywords: Franciscan terrane, Sanbagawa belt, Western Alps, Klamath Mountains, White-Inyo Range.

Ernst, W.G., 2006, Geologic mapping—Where the rubber meets the road, *in* Manduca, C.A., and Mogk, D.W., eds., Earth and Mind: How Geologists Think and Learn about the Earth: Geological Society of America Special Paper 413, p. 13–28, doi: 10.1130/2006.2413(02). For permission to copy, contact editing@geosociety.org.

INTRODUCTION

Geologic study of Earth and its near-surface phenomena began in earnest with the pioneering investigations of Hutton more than two centuries ago. The nineteenth century witnessed an enormous expansion of both geologic reconnaissance and classical mapping, beginning with William Smith's remarkable field studies at the very end of the eighteenth century (Winchester, 2001). But in spite of its antiquity, geology is a derivative science. Its pursuance depends on an in-depth understanding and integrated application of the principles of mathematical, physical, chemical, and biological sciences to the products of ongoing and, by inference, ancient Earth processes. Such an approach is reasonable. But, as all geologists appreciate, our dynamic planet is a complex lithologic assemblage produced by accumulated past events that have taken place over the 4.55 b.y. sweep of Earth history. Infall of the iron-nickel core, devolatilization and compositional differentiation of the crust and mantle system, and formation of the globe-encircling hydrosphere and atmosphere, as well as early emergence and subsequent evolution of the biosphere, are fascinating histories contained in the rocks—and only in the rocks—that constitute the principal subject matter of geology. Unfortunately, the lithologic record is notoriously incomplete, and is preserved in progressively more fragmentary fashion in older units. Moreover, rocks generated during the first ~600 m.y. of Earth history appear to be missing completely.

Geologic relationships determined in the field provide an important basis (i.e., ground truth) for all earth science investigations. Relationships are most appropriately quantified and documented through the use of time slices, columnar and stratigraphic sections, multidimensional diagrams, palinspastic maps, facies maps, structure contour maps, cross sections, and, especially, geologic maps, upon which the others are based. To the extent that a researcher is able to assess the quality of such cartographic materials, his/her scientific effectiveness is enhanced. In contrast, lack of such critical abilities compromises the effectiveness of a geoscientist. Arguably the most efficient, effective way to increase one's understanding of the architecture of Earth, or at least the nature of the near-surface geologic environment, is to conduct mapping as a necessary step to subsequent investigations.

But does a geologic map really represent ground truth? At best, it provides a close approximation to actual relationships. Constructing a geologic map requires insightful, objective, and purposeful field measurements and observations coupled with a capacity to visualize relationships in three dimensions, and a good imagination as well. Also, an appreciation for the effects of geologic time is essential. Because the record is imperfectly exposed and in many cases poorly preserved, it is vitally important to carry forward a range of viable hypotheses (this is where a fertile imagination is most helpful) to be tested by spatial relationships identified during the mapping. The product reflects the practical integration of geologic principles, the scale at which the map was made, and especially, both quantitative and qualitative observations and measurements made both in the field and in the laboratory. The units to be mapped first require identification and classification (what variations are lumped together, what are separated out as distinct units, what sorts of features should be ignored?). Although cartographic representations attempt to closely approach reality, most are more subjective constructs, based on the purpose and scientific goal of the mapping, the sum of the training, prior geologic field experience, and scientific opinions of the mapper, the geologic models in vogue at the time, the extent and degree of complexity of the mapped units, the quality and extent of exposures, the amount of supporting analytical information, and the thoughtful efforts expended over time in the mapping effort. In general, the final product also reflects accommodations to the scientific reviewers' knowledge of the region, and illustrative changes and compromises required by the printer and publisher.

But just how is the mapping to be conducted? What features are to be measured in general or in great detail and geographically and/or geometrically described? What relationships can be ignored, or at least not mapped? The specific style and nature of the work depend critically on the questions to be addressed and partly or fully answered by the field work. The geologic units to be distinguished, the degree, intensity, and size of areal coverage, the systematic sample collecting program, the measurements made in the field and in the laboratory, and the scale of the mapping effort all reflect the anticipated goals of the project.

In my studies of the petrological and structural evolution of some post-Paleozoic mountain belts, mapping at scales of 1:12,000, 1:24,000, and 1:50,000 has been critical toward obtaining a better geologic understanding of each area, and of the operating earth science principles. In the following sections, I briefly describe several circum-Pacific and Alpine case studies in which my colleagues and I arrived at conclusions that were derived largely from relationships elucidated by geologic mapping. Most of the questions we have tried to answer could not even have been posed without knowledge derived through the mapping. And of course, the ultimate synthesis of plate-tectonic models in all cases must be compatible with the field relationships.

CALIFORNIA COAST RANGES

General Geology

The California Coast Ranges are underlain by two bedrock series of late Mesozoic age, the Franciscan terrane, a chaotic, largely sedimentary mélange, and the Salinian terrane, a displaced granitic block similar to the granitoid plutons of the Peninsular Ranges, the Sierra Nevada, and the Klamath Mountains (Bailey et al., 1964, 1970). We now know that, in aggregate, these granitic rocks constitute a composite batholith that formed the core of a vast Andean volcanic-plutonic arc developed along the western margin of North America; in contrast, the outboard Franciscan volcaniclastic mélange represents a largely coeval subduction complex. Detailed mapping of the Franciscan terrane by many workers has illuminated the structure, metamorphism, and accretionary architecture of this belt, thereby providing a more quantitative understanding of the westward growth of continental crust during late Mesozoic time. The Franciscan accretionary prism and its oceanic crust underpinnings floor most of western California. The Franciscan terrane consists of incipiently to thoroughly recrystallized, tectonized equivalents of medium- to fine-grained detrital rocks, chiefly graywacke, micrograywacke, and dark shale; these clastic rocks were derived largely from the Sierran volcanic-plutonic arc. Modest amounts of pillow basalt, pillow breccia, and gabbro/diabase (greenstone and blueschist, transformed from oceanic crust layers 2 and 3) overlying flow-top radiolarian chert (metachert, recrystallized hemipelagic oceanic crust layer 1) and faulted slices of serpentinized peridotite (mantle lithosphere) are tectonically interleaved with the volumetrically dominant metaclastic strata. The structural level and grade of relatively high *P*–low *T* metamorphism in the exhumed belt increase eastward toward the interior of North America (Blake et al., 1967). Although in general, stratigraphic tops are inclined toward the east, individual sedimentary packages young westward, as is typical of west-facing accretionary prisms. How did mapping help us to understand the structure, metamorphism, and assembly of this terrane?

Panoche Pass

Field relationships of the Franciscan terrane combined with petrologic analysis in the Panoche Pass area (Ernst, 1965), southern Diablo Range, western California, require relatively high *P*–low *T* recrystallization, and the presence of low-angle thrust faults, as shown in Figure 1. Large tracts of the terrane consist chiefly of metaclastic rocks that contain abundant albitic plagioclase but totally lack jadeitic pyroxene, whereas in three small areas, the metagraywacke is typified by neoblastic jadeitic pyroxene + quartz that replaced relict albite. Experimentally determined phase equilibria as well as thermochemical computations have clearly documented the relatively high *P*–low *T* nature of the jadeitic pyroxene + quartz association, requiring subduction-zone depths approaching or exceeding 25 km, with respect to the compositionally equivalent albite-bearing rock assemblage. I long puzzled over the obscure field relationships between these lower-pressure albite-bearing metagraywacke strata associated with rare blueschist blocks, and localized regions of higher-pressure jadeitic pyroxene-bearing metagraywacke ± blueschist lithologies. My initial hypothesis was that metamorphic isograds separated essentially continuous sections of metaclastic rock with or without associated metamafic boudins. More recent field observations combined with petrographic recognition of several mylonitic rocks suggest that the boundaries are actually low-angle, postmetamorphic faults, rather than isograds. Thus, the contrasting metamorphic zones bear witness to postsubduction structural discontinuities, as reflected by markedly contrasting total pressures and temperatures rather than by a gradation in attending physical conditions.

Pacheco Pass

Later geologic mapping farther north in the central Diablo Range at Pacheco Pass (Ernst, 1993) allowed the identification and documentation of syn- to postmetamorphic, imbricate, subhorizontal bedding-plane thrust faults within an apparently conformable, Franciscan stratigraphic sequence (Terabayashi et al., 1995). As presented in Figure 2, the terrane consists dominantly of quartzose jadeitic metagraywacke and finer-grained metaclastic rocks; the stratigraphy of the several units defines relatively open, gently east-plunging folds. At the base of each tectonic unit, an indistinct décollement is marked by the presence of small, discontinuous lenses of mafic blueschist capped by layers of metachert, upon which fine-grained turbidites and an upward-coarsening detrital sequence was deposited prior to relatively high *P*–low *T* metamorphism. Evidently, as oceanic crust-capped lithosphere approached the late Mesozoic margin of California, distal (and older), then progressively more proximal (and slightly younger) turbiditic sediments were laid down on the approaching paleo-Pacific plate (e.g., Matsuda and Isozaki, 1991). As this assemblage was then carried down the eastward-inclined Franciscan subduction zone, portions of the sedimentary section and the very uppermost part of the oceanic crust (layers 1 and 2) were sliced off episodically and were tectonically included in the growing accretionary prism. Decoupled from its denser lithospheric underpinnings, the deforming complex buoyantly returned to upper-crustal levels as the rest of the oceanic plate sank deeper into the upper mantle. Similar to the paragenesis at Panoche Pass, metaclastic rocks exhibit the growth of jadeitic pyroxene + quartz from preexisting albite; spatially associated mafic lenses contain sodic amphibole ± sodic pyroxene.

Structural relationships are shown in Figure 3. Five bedding-plane fault-bounded units (I –V) are present, as evident from these cross sections. Only the lowest tectonostratigraphic unit, V, in the northwestern corner of the mapped area, is characterized principally by metagraywacke totally lacking neoblastic jadeitic pyroxene. The interlayered mafic metavolcanic rocks in unit V also appear to be less intensely metamorphosed; nonetheless, the metabasalts contain scattered lawsonite ± metamorphic aragonite, indicating moderately elevated pressures during recrystallization. As indicated by the pressure discontinuity between units IV and V, unit IV must have been thrust a substantial distance up and over unit V (Fig. 3, cross-section X–X'). In fact, each tectonostratigraphic sheet shows a top-to-the-west sense of shear over the unit below. Hence, although detailed radiometric and fossil age data are not available in the Pacheco Pass area, the timing of deposition and accretion, from oldest to youngest, likely was I → V.

CENTRAL SHIKOKU

General Geology

The Sanbagawa metamorphic belt of western Honshu, Shikoku, and Kyushu, Japan, bears testament to the late Mesozoic

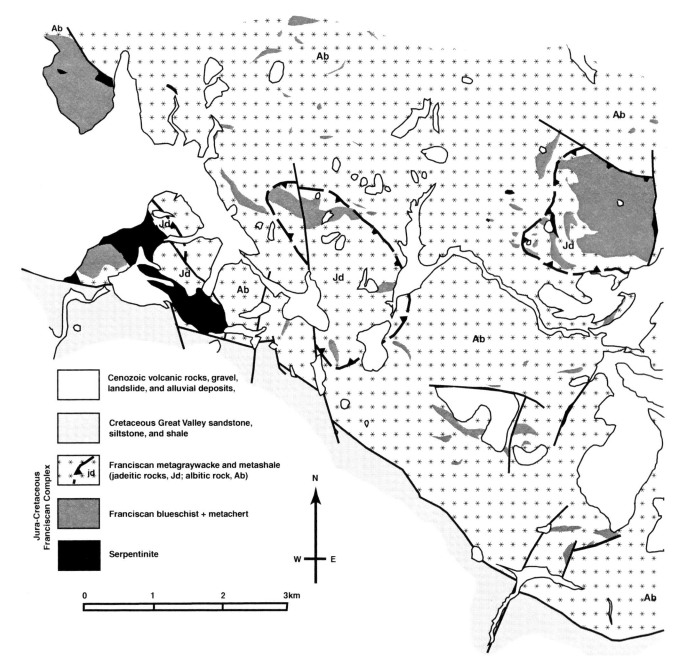

Figure 1. Geologic map of the Panoche Pass region, southern Diablo Range, central California Coast Ranges, modified after Ernst (1965). Limited areas of quartz + jadeitic pyroxene-bearing metagraywacke (Jd) are reinterpreted as representing segments of a subhorizontal thrust slice structurally overlying albite-bearing metagraywacke (Ab) rather than as the isograd boundaries originally proposed. Recrystallization and later thrust faulting took place during mid- to Late Cretaceous time.

underflow of paleo-Pacific oceanic lithosphere beneath the western limb of the Japanese island arc (Banno and Sakai, 1989). Exhumed uppermost Paleozoic and Lower Mesozoic, stratigraphically coherent sections of pelitic, psammitic, and siliceous sedimentary strata are intimately interlayered with finely laminated (tuffaceous?) mafic volcanic units. The grade of relatively high *P*–low *T* metamorphism in the belt increases continuously

northward toward the Asian mainland. The subduction complex of western Japan is similar in age and tectonic setting to that of the California Coast Ranges, but differs from the latter in two important respects. (1) The subducted prism represents the preexisting paleo-Pacific passive margin of the Japanese sector of East Asia; it consists of well-stratified superjacent units of great lateral extent. (2) The down-going section was subjected to higher tem-

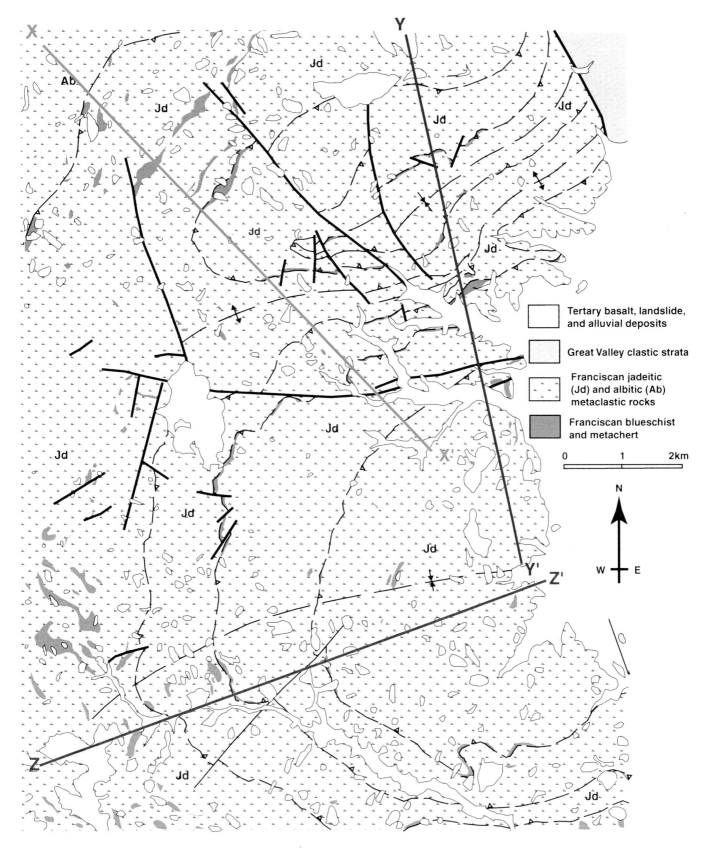

Figure 2. Simplified geologic map of the Pacheco Pass area, central Diablo Range, central California Coast Ranges (Ernst, 1993). Bedding-plane thrusts juxtapose sections composed dominantly of nearly flat-lying jadeitic pyroxene-bearing quartzose metaclastic rocks lying stratigraphically above discontinuous layers of metachert, which in turn rest on pods of blueschist. The metagraywacke unit in the lowest structural unit mapped (northwest corner) is devoid of neoblastic jadeitic pyroxene. Tectonic stacking probably took place during mid- to Late Cretaceous subduction-zone metamorphism and/or during subsequent exhumation. Cross sections of Figure 3 are indicated.

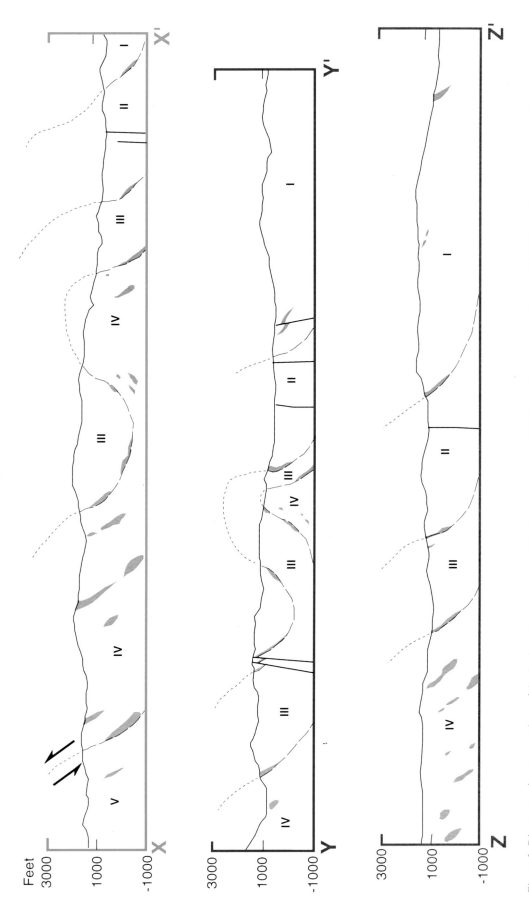

Figure 3. Diagrammatic cross sections of the Pacheco Pass area, central Diablo Range, central California Coast Ranges (Ernst, 1993). Figure 2 shows locations of the cross-sections X–X′, Y–Y′, and Z–Z′. Bedding-plane imbrication involves top-to-the-west transport (note sense of shear between units IV and V in cross-section X–X′); the sequence of deposition and time of assembly of the five recognized tectonostratigraphic units from slightly older to slightly younger is I → V.

peratures evidently accompanying slower oceanic plate descent, and hence it lost strength and deformed ductilely rather than by rupture. Consequently, the metamorphic gradation in Shikoku appears to be virtually unbroken by later faulting.

Shirataki District

In central Shikoku, meticulous geologic mapping by Hide (1961) documented a remarkable coherence of the stratigraphic section in the region surrounding the Shirataki mine, and defined a zone of lithologic bilateral symmetry. As illustrated in Figure 4,

we interpreted this zone of symmetrically paired exposures as a synclinorium typified by steeply north-dipping axial planes (Ernst et al., 1970). For Shirataki mafic igneous bulk-rock compositions, mineral assemblages include prehnite-pumpellyite and chlorite-zone greenschist facies rocks to the south, grading to a medial epidote zone of intermediate blueschist-greenschist facies, and passing by degrees yet farther northward into albite-amphibolite facies assemblages. Metashales to the south contain rare lawsonite, and are progressively transformed into porphyroblastic albite + biotite + garnet-bearing pelitic schists to the north.

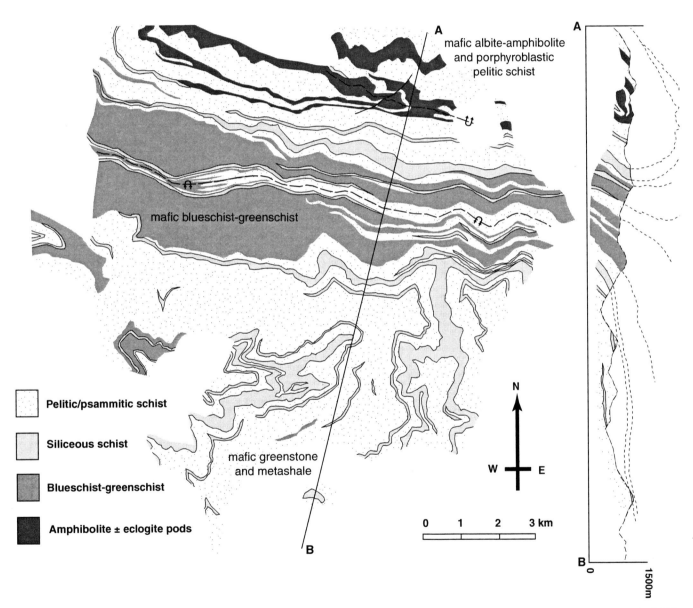

Figure 4. Simplified geologic map of the Shirataki district, central Shikoku, southwestern Japan, after Hide (1961), Sawamura et al. (1964), Kawachi (1968), and Ernst et al. (1970). A south-vergent overturned anticline-syncline pair is present in the northern and central parts of the mapped area, respectively. The northward progressive increase in metamorphic grade and the *P-T* inversion (higher-grade rocks overlying lower-grade rocks) indicate that the nearly synchronous deformation produced oceanward overturning of folds and outlasted the Late Cretaceous recrystallization.

The mapped area thus consists of south-vergent folds typified by gradual, continuous changes in metamorphic intensity; thrust faults appear to be lacking. Contiguous sections yet farther to the north of the Shirataki district include high-grade amphibolite containing lenses of eclogite, structurally overlying less intensely metamorphosed rocks (Banno, 1964; Takasu, 1984; Higashino, 1990). Recognition and mapping of this metamorphic inversion in central Shikoku led us to the interpretation of postrecrystallization, oceanward-vergent nappe emplacement (Ernst et al., 1970). Small-scale mesoscopic fold measurements supported this structural interpretation (Kawachi, 1968). Thus, more northerly sections of rock recrystallized at considerable depth in the subduction zone, lost strength but maintained stratal continuity, and ascended differentially, overriding the less deeply buried, more feebly metamorphosed units to the south.

WESTERN AND EASTERN ALPS

General Geology

The Alpine chain is remarkably well exposed, and has been investigated in detail by generations of geologists (e.g., classical work by Trümpy, 1960, 1975; Dal Piaz et al., 1972). It serves as the type section of an orogenic belt—a collisional suture juxtaposing the more northerly European foreland and the South Alpine lithospheric plates (Dewey et al., 1973, 1989). Much of the orogen has been thoroughly and repeatedly mapped at scales of 1:25,000, and the tectonic intricacies are well studied. The intimate interrelationships between metamorphism and structural geology probably are clearer in this mountain range than anywhere else on Earth. In contrast to circum-Pacific accretionary orogens, such as the California Coast Ranges and western Japan, the Western and Eastern Alps are products of continental collision and reflect Late Cretaceous–Paleogene consumption of oceanic crust-capped lithosphere during closure of Mesozoic Tethys Ocean and entrance of the southern margin of European continental crust into the south-southeast–dipping (present geographic coordinates) subduction zone. Relatively high *P*–low *T* metamorphism of Tethyan oceanic crust and the European foreland (e.g., Niggli, 1973; Frey et al., 1974) was succeeded by tectonic regurgitation of buoyant continental crustal slices along low-angle, south-southeast–rooting décollements and European foreland-vergent recumbent folds (Ernst, 1973). How does the regional tectonic-metamorphic map support such a scenario?

Subduction-Zone Metamorphism, Then Exhumation of Relatively Low-Density Complexes

Similar to geologic relationships described for the Sanbagawa and Franciscan terranes, collisional thrusting transported nonsubducted South Alpine sections of rock over the descending European lithospheric plate; the sense of shear is indicated by thrust faults that root under the Po Plain and nappes that verge toward the European foreland. A much-simplified tectonic-metamorphic map of the Alps is presented as Figure 5.

Black arrows in this illustration indicate directions of increasing Late Cretaceous–Paleogene subduction depths and prograde, relatively high *P-T* blueschist-eclogite metamorphism, now recovered. The Ticino and Tauern thermal highs represent later, pluton-invaded metamorphic culminations involving kyanite-sillimanite–grade recrystallization-annealing, which overprinted the preexisting units as a consequence of the delayed ascent of deep-seated sections of heated sialic crust, followed by thermal relaxation of the granitoids.

Comparable to circum-Pacific relatively high *P*–low *T* metamorphic belts, exhumed Alpine terranes exhibit stratigraphic tops and increasing pressures (i.e., depths) of metamorphism, and higher structural levels in the south-southeast direction of plate descent toward and beneath the nonsubducted plate, whereas metamorphic ages of imbricate sections decrease in age with the opposite polarity (Ernst, 1971). This is the now-familiar architecture of accretionary prisms. Such a tectonic model accounts for the conveyance of low-density crustal complexes to considerable depth in subduction zones, followed by episodic decoupling and ascent of slices of high *P*–low *T* recrystallized materials that remained buoyant relative to the denser mantle material they had displaced accompanying underflow. The subducted materials that return toward the surface are of uniformly lower aggregate density than the mantle; combined with increased ductility, buoyancy represents the most plausible body force capable of transporting such tectonic entities back into the upper crust.

CENTRAL KLAMATH MOUNTAINS

General Geology

The Klamath Mountains of northern California and southwestern Oregon consist of a series of subparallel, shallowly east-dipping, west-vergent thrust sheets (Irwin, 1960; Burchfiel and Davis, 1981). Each allochthon represents a separate terrane or lithostratigraphic amalgamation. Juxtaposed slabs from west to east are: the Eastern Klamath plate; the Central Metamorphic belt; the Stuart Fork terrane; the so-called Western Triassic and Paleozoic (WTrPz) belt, mostly of early Mesozoic age of formation; and the Western Jurassic belt. Depositional and recrystallization ages of the oldest rocks in each allochthon decrease toward the Pacific Ocean. Stratified units are chiefly right-side-up, and in general tops face east. Klamath terranes contain abundant mafic arc volcanic + plutonic rocks and their clastic erosional products, as well as far-traveled deep-water cherty and carbonate strata; these units rest on tectonically dismembered ophiolites, including voluminous masses of serpentinized peridotite. Similar to Franciscan, Sanbagawa, and Alpine convergent plate junctions, the Klamath Mountains exhibit the unambiguous characteristics of an accretionary margin. In contrast, however, convergence in this orogen was of substantially longer duration and involved the suturing of lithotectonic assemblages of chiefly oceanic rather than continental affinities. Individual composite terranes were juxtaposed by inferred east-descending subduction during mid-

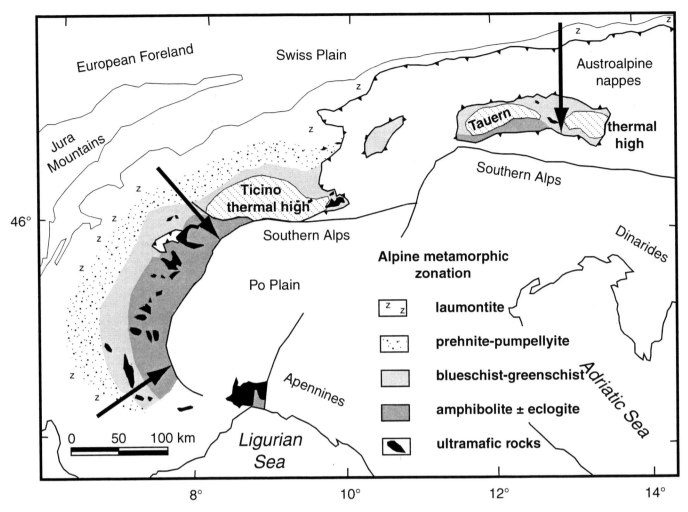

Figure 5. Generalized regional tectonic and metamorphic setting of the Western and Eastern Alps, after Ernst (1971) and Frey et al. (1974). The patterned Alpine terrane constitutes a relatively high *P*–low *T* Late Cretaceous–Paleogene metamorphic belt. In the Eastern Alps, this metamorphic terrane is structurally overlain by the southern Alpine Austroalpine nappes, and is exposed chiefly in tectonic windows. Arrows show the direction of increasing subduction depths and prograde blueschist-eclogite facies metamorphism, now recovered. Fold vergence is in the opposite sense. The Ticino and Tauern thermal highs represent early Neogene metamorphic culminations involving granitoids and kyanite-sillimanite–grade overprinting of preexisting units; these high-grade culminations may reflect deep-seated heating of crustal rocks, then diapiric exhumation following cessation of the Late Cretaceous–Paleogene subduction-zone refrigeration.

Paleozoic to mid-Mesozoic time (Irwin, 1981; Hacker et al., 1993; Wallin and Metcalf, 1998). Calc-alkaline, postkinematic plutons of Middle Jurassic to Early Cretaceous age (Lanphere et al., 1968; Barnes et al., 1992, 1996) subsequently intruded the imbricated orogen.

Sawyers Bar Area

Arcuate, eastward-dipping structural slices are defined by several distinct lithotectonic units in the central Klamath Mountains, northwestern California. Structurally beneath the Stuart Fork terrane, Irwin (1972) distinguished three north-south–trending lithostratigraphic segments of the WTrPz belt. Proceeding westward, these are: (1) the ophiolitic North Fork terrane (Ando et al., 1983); (2) the Hayfork composite terrane (Wright

and Fahan, 1988); and (3) the ophiolitic Rattlesnake Creek terrane (Wright and Wyld, 1994). Metamorphism of all three units is subgreenschist grade in the south, increasing gradually northward to amphibolite grade near the Oregon border.

Bedrock terranes in the Sawyers Bar area include the more easterly, relatively high *P*–low *T* Stuart Fork, and the relatively low-pressure–low-temperature North Fork + Eastern Hayfork allochthons, as illustrated in Figure 6. The Stuart Fork and North Fork terranes are juxtaposed along the east-dipping Soap Creek Ridge thrust fault (Hotz, 1977). The Stuart Fork terrane consists of interlayered metapelitic, metacherty, and mafic metavolcanic units. A product of Late Triassic blueschist facies metamorphism, it was sequestered at the leading edge of western North America, and was thrust over the coeval and younger outboard rocks of

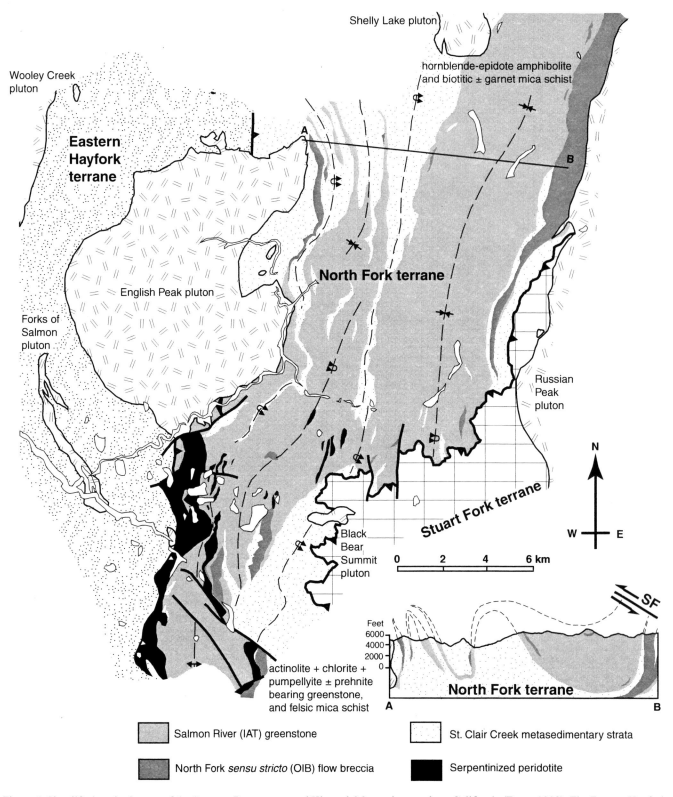

Figure 6. Simplified geologic map of the Sawyers Bar area, central Klamath Mountains, northern California (Ernst, 1998). The Eastern Hayfork, North Fork, and Stuart Fork terranes are juxtaposed along east-dipping thrust faults in the mapped area. Amalgamation, metamorphism, and exhumation were essentially completed before intrusion of the Late Jurassic granitoid plutons. The North Fork *sensu stricto*, Salmon River, and St. Clair Creek lithotectonic units of the North Fork terrane are interstratified; pillow structures are preserved locally in the metamafic rocks. As apparent from cross-section A–B, distal turbiditic metaclastic strata chiefly underlie the metavolcanic rocks in the North Fork terrane. Overturned folds in this terrane verge to the west, reflecting outboard oceanic underflow and contraction of the accreting crust at shallow subduction depths. SF—Stuart Fork terrane; IAT—island-arc tholeiitic basalt; OIB—oceanic-island basalt.

the WTrPz belt during Jurassic time (Goodge, 1990). The North Fork terrane consists of three interstratified superjacent units, now metamorphosed: (1) the St. Clair Creek distal turbidites and interlayered cherts; (2) the North Fork *sensu stricto* ocean-island basalts (OIBs) and flow breccias; and (3) the voluminous Salmon River massive to pillowed island-arc tholeiitic basalts (IATs). A fourth map unit, serpentinized peridotite, is also abundant, mainly along faults. Greenschist facies recrystallization, contraction, and thickening accompanied relatively shallow-level tectonic juxtaposition (the Siskiyou metamorphic event of Coleman et al., 1988). In the southern part of the Sawyers Bar area, the metamorphic index minerals prehnite, pumpellyite, and actinolite characterize the WTrPz units; these rocks grade imperceptibly northward to coarser-grained biotite ± garnet and hornblende-bearing lithologies. Intimate stratigraphic interlayering and pillow tops in the Sawyers Bar area reflect in situ, immature oceanic-island-arc development in the North Fork terrane, as mirrored by basalt OIB and IAT bulk-rock geochemistry (Ernst et al., 1991).

Because distal turbiditic argillite chiefly underlies the mafic volcanic pile (Fig. 6), and inasmuch as the source of the detritus appears to have been the eastern Klamath terranes, I concluded that the mafic volcanogenic North Fork arc formed in a suprasubduction zone environment near the continental margin, rather than in the open ocean (Ernst, 1998). Later arrival and docking of the outboard Eastern Hayfork mélange belt against the North Fork terrane took place along the Twin Sisters high-angle reverse fault. Individual units making up the accretionary complex evidently decoupled from the descending oceanic lithosphere at shallow depths, as indicated by low-pressure metamorphic mineral assemblages. Terrane amalgamation took place prior to the emplacement of Late Jurassic granitoid plutons, which intrude and crosscut all older lithotectonic units. Evidently contemporaneous west-vergent folding and metamorphism occurred during convergent underflow, accompanying juxtaposition of the North Fork terrane beneath the landward Stuart Fork belt; then this composite terrane collided with the yet farther outboard Eastern Hayfork terrane.

WHITE-INYO REGION

General Geology

Along the California-Nevada state line, the north-northwest–trending White-Inyo Range constitutes a well-exposed example of the transition from the Sierra Nevada to the Basin and Range Province. The White-Inyo Mountains are bounded by Cenozoic, still-active dextral strike-slip faults—on the west by the White Mountain shear zone, and on the east by the Furnace Creek fault zone. These transcurrent fault systems also have accommodated tilting and substantial uplift of the White-Inyo block (Stockli et al., 2003). North of the White-Inyo Range, this major right-lateral slip system may be responsible for the westward deflection of the Golconda and Roberts Mountain allochthons and the hairpin turn in the initial $^{87}Sr/^{86}Sr$ 0.706 isopleth marking the edge of

Precambrian basement (Kistler and Peterman, 1973; Stevens and Greene, 1999). The high-angle Barcroft structural break lies ~25 km to the southeast of these features and cuts across the mountain belt at almost 90°. Preexisting mid-Mesozoic, mildly alkaline White Mountain Peak metavolcanic rocks and interlayered volcanogenic metasedimentary units on the north were downdropped against a Neoproterozoic–Lower Cambrian well-stratified quartzite + carbonate metasedimentary platform succession on the south. Later, the Barcroft mafic granodioritic complex was emplaced along this fault. How has mapping led to a fuller appreciation of the geologic evolution of this area?

Barcroft Pluton

On the west, below ~1500 m elevation, the Middle Jurassic Barcroft granodioritic pluton disappears under thick alluvial deposits in Chalfant Valley but is exposed on the flanks and backbone of the central White Mountains at elevations ranging up to 4025 m. Figure 7 presents a digital elevation model of the mapped area. Thanks to the ruggedness of the terrane, outcrop control is good to excellent. However, in this high-alpine desert setting, coarse-grained granitoids, including the Barcroft body, weather mechanically more rapidly than the neighboring, much finer-grained superjacent volcanic units and siliciclastic strata that make up the country rock section.

The hornblende ± clinopyroxene-bearing Barcroft pluton, shown in Figure 8, consists of an intergradational comagmatic series of gabbro/diorite, granodiorite, granite, and alaskite-aplite (Ernst et al., 2002). This composite intrusive contains scattered inclusions of the superjacent section; it heated and contact-metamorphosed the wall rocks into which the magma injected several dioritic apophyses. The pluton crosscuts, deflects, and abruptly terminates preexisting folding in the adjacent country rocks—thus the Barcroft structural break invaded as an at least partly molten mass (Ernst and Hall, 1987). Detailed on-the-ground mapping along border areas of high relief, combined with remote sensing of the central White-Inyo Range, demonstrated that the complex is a steeply southeast-dipping slab that was emplaced along a high-angle reverse fault termed the Barcroft structural break. Contours on the contact are illustrated in Figure 9. Geochronologic dating of two White Mountain metavolcanic units (Hanson et al., 1987) and anisotropy of magnetic susceptibility measurements of Barcroft granodioritic rocks (Michelsen, 2003) suggest a possible truncation of the northern margin of the Barcroft pluton, apparently due to renewed, postintrusion slip. However, the Barcroft pluton is predominantly a postkinematic composite intrusion, cutting across earlier folds and faults; such structures may have been produced during the Antler, Sonoma, and/or East Sierran deformation events (Stevens and Greene, 1999; Coleman et al., 2003).

SUMMARY

Intensive training and a sturdy foundation in scientific fundamentals are obligatory prerequisites for all earth science

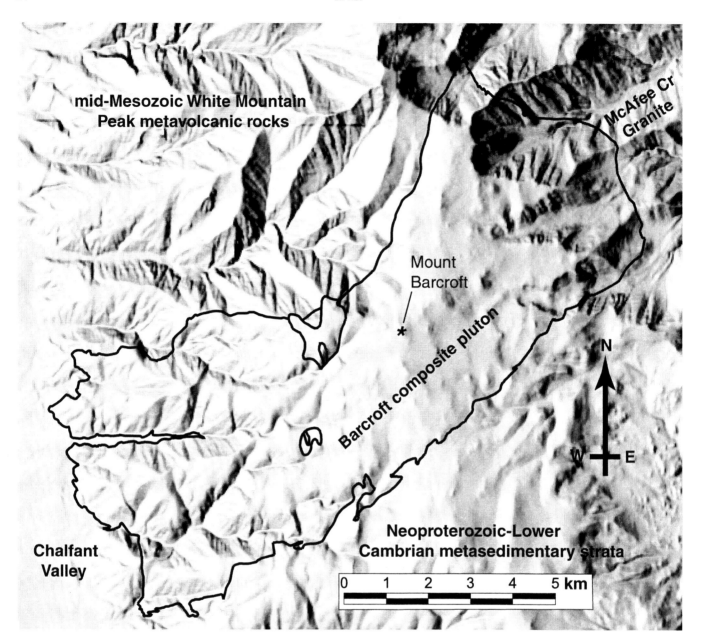

Figure 7. Digital elevation model, shaded-relief map of the central White Mountains, easternmost California, slightly modified from Ernst et al. (2003). Exposures of the Middle Jurassic Barcroft granodioritic complex range in elevation from 1500 m in Chalfant Valley to more than 4000 m at Mount Barcroft. The topography of the mafic granitoid pluton is more subdued than that of the surrounding metasedimentary and metavolcanic units.

investigations. The diverse origins of igneous, metamorphic, and sedimentary rocks cannot be quantitatively understood without adequate structural, geologic, geochronologic, and mineralogic-petrologic control. Recognition of structural and geomorphic features, as well as mineral deposits and geologic hazards, all depend on geologic field mapping. Geochemical and geophysical data provide important additional controls. Realistic plate-tectonic models and an in-depth understanding of the geologic history of a region depend on all of the above.

Reflecting my interests in metamorphic and igneous petrogenesis and the relationship of petrology to structural evolution of the crust, I have studied portions of convergent margin realms chiefly along the Pacific Rim, and in the Alpine orogenic belt (but also including continental collision suture zones typified by ultrahigh-pressure metamorphism in central and eastern Eurasia). My type of mapping has always included a major emphasis on lithologic description, structural setting, and rock sample collection in the field, followed by petrologic and geochemical

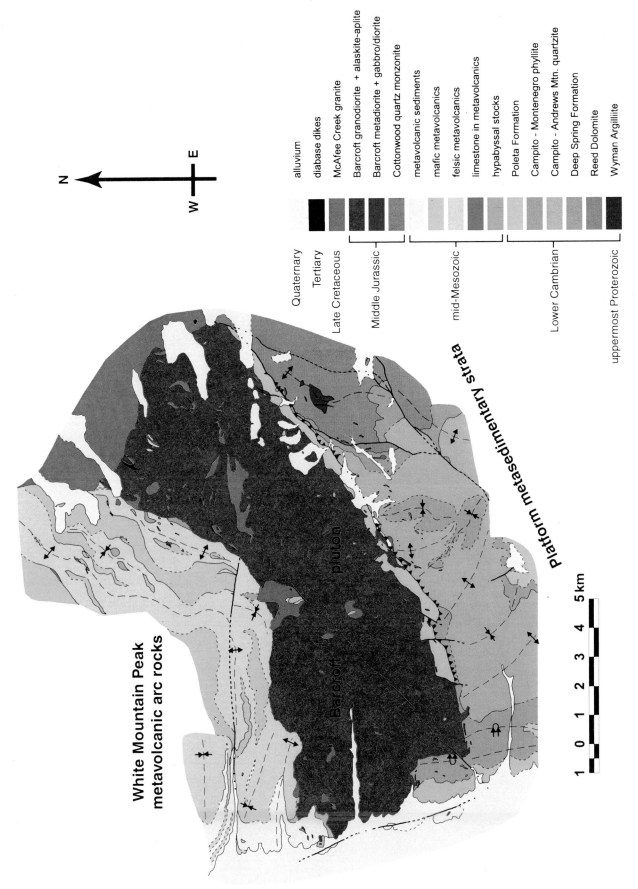

N

W—E

**White Mountain Peak
metavolcanic arc rocks**

Barcroft

Barcroft
pluton

Platform metasedimentary strata

Quaternary		alluvium
Tertiary		diabase dikes
Late Cretaceous		McAfee Creek granite
		Barcroft granodiorite + alaskite-aplite
Middle Jurassic		Barcroft metadiorite + gabbro/diorite
		Cottonwood quartz monzonite
		metavolcanic sediments
		mafic metavolcanics
mid-Mesozoic		felsic metavolcanics
		limestone in metavolcanics
		hypabyssal stocks
		Poleta Formation
		Campito - Montenegro phyllite
Lower Cambrian		Campito - Andrews Mtn. quartzite
		Deep Spring Formation
		Reed Dolomite
uppermost Proterozoic		Wyman Argilliite

1 0 1 2 3 4 5 km

Figure 8. Generalized geologic map of the central White Mountain area, after Ernst et al. (2002). The mafic granodioritic Barcroft plutonic complex was emplaced along the Barcroft structural break, crosscutting or deflecting cylindrical folds in the preexisting superjacent country rocks. Overturned folds in the southwestern corner of the mapped area suggest the possibility of contraction and transpression of the White Mountain block against the north-trending shear zone marking the eastern, alluviated edge of Owens–Chalfant Valley.

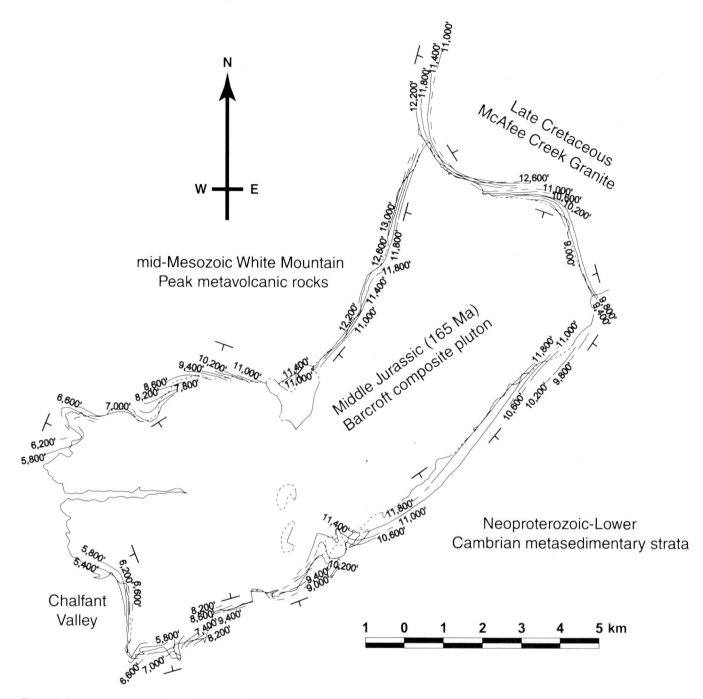

Figure 9. Structural contours (400 ft interval) defining the margins of the Barcroft granodioritic body could be drawn by Ernst et al. (2003) thanks to considerable topographic relief along the plutonic contacts. The Middle Jurassic (Ma) granitoid is a thick, steeply southeast-dipping slab, reflecting the attitude of the Barcroft structural break, a high-angle reverse fault. The pluton is covered on the west by alluvial deposits in Chalfant Valley, and is truncated on the east by the Late Cretaceous McAfee Creek Granite.

analyses in the laboratory. With the information gained, repeated return to the field in order to make additional observations and measurements has allowed the recognition of previously ignored features. For instance, the bulk-rock chemical characterization of OIB and IAT metabasaltic rocks in the North Klamath Fork terrane led to the suggestion of an island-arc setting for these

Sawyers Bar metavolcanic rocks; this interpretation was subsequently supported by the finding of pillow tops, which showed that the lava flows stratigraphically overlay distal turbiditic strata derived from eastern Klamath terranes. As another example, the change in my interpretation of structural-petrologic relationships in trench mélange units at Panoche Pass resulted from reexamination of both outcrop relationships and petrographic textural data, as well as from discussions with other workers. The recognition of bedding-plane faults in the Franciscan section exposed in the Pacheco Pass quadrangle, and of oceanward-vergent recumbent folds in central Shikoku resulted from postmapping discussions with colleagues on the outcrop as well as in the laboratory. My identification of progressive high *P*–low *T* subduction-zone metamorphism in the Alps, Shikoku, and the California Coast Ranges was made possible based on regional geologic mapping by many geologists.

Dealing with the challenges of alternative interpretations can have a salutary effect on the final product, and in my case certainly has been extremely helpful. Episodic reevaluation of a mapped area typically provides additional observational constraints and an enhanced geologic understanding. Thus, the considerable length of time required to produce a map allows for a thoughtful development and testing of interpretations. "Once over lightly" may be necessary for reconnaissance mapping, but a well-crafted, high-quality geologic map generally takes years to produce. If we hope to understand the detailed architecture of Earth as it now exists, and the evolution of our home planet, our first step must therefore include geologic mapping. This is truly where the rubber meets the road.

ACKNOWLEDGMENTS

My geologic field research was supported for 30 yr by the University of California, Los Angeles, and for the past 15 by Stanford University. C.A. Hall, Jr., Elizabeth L. Miller, Kim Kastens, and R.D. Hatcher, Jr. reviewed a first-draft manuscript. I thank these institutions and scientists for their insights and feedback. Cathryn A. Manduca and David W. Mogk invited me to participate in a Pardee Symposium entitled "Toward a Better Understanding of the Complicated Earth: Insights from Geologic Research, Education, and Cognitive Science" held at the Geological Society of America annual meeting in Denver, 29 October 2002. Original maps from which the generalized versions presented in this report were drafted may be viewed on the Web site: http://serc.carleton.edu/research_on_learning/Pardee02/talks.html.

REFERENCES CITED

Ando, C.J., Irwin, W.P., Jones, D.L., and Saleeby, J.B., 1983, The ophiolitic North Fork terrane in the Salmon River region, central Klamath Mountains, California: Geological Society of America Bulletin, v. 94, p. 236–252, doi: 10.1130/0016-7606(1983)94<236:TONFTI>2.0.CO;2.

Bailey, E.H., Irwin, W.P., and Jones, D.L., 1964, Franciscan and related rocks, and their significance in the geology of western California: California Division of Mines and Geology Bulletin 183, 171 p.

Bailey, E.H., Blake, M.C., Jr., and Jones, D.L., 1970, On-land Mesozoic oceanic crust in California Coast Ranges: U.S. Geological Survey Professional Paper 700-C, p. 70–81.

Banno, S., 1964, Petrologic studies on Sanbagawa crystalline schists in the Bessi-Ino district, central Sikoku: Journal of the Faculty of Science, University of Tokyo, Section II, v. 15, p. 213–319.

Banno, S., and Sakai, C., 1989, Geology and metamorphic evolution of the Sanbagawa belt, Japan, *in* Daly, S., Cliff, R.A., and Yardley, B.W.D., eds.,

Evolution of metamorphic belts: Geological Society of London Special Publication 43, p. 519–531.

Barnes, C.G., Peterson, S.W., Kistler, R.W., Prestvik, T., and Sundvoll, B., 1992, Tectonic implications of isotopic variation among Jurassic and Early Cretaceous plutons, Klamath Mountains: Geological Society of America Bulletin, v. 104, p. 117–126, doi: 10.1130/0016-7606(1992)104<0117:TIOIVA>2.3.CO;2.

Barnes, C.G., Peterson, S.W., Kistler, R.W., Murray, R., and Kays, M.A., 1996, Source and tectonic implications of tonalite-trondhjemite magmatism in the Klamath Mountains: Contributions to Mineralogy and Petrology, v. 123, p. 40–60, doi: 10.1007/s004100050142.

Blake, M.C., Jr., Irwin, W.P., and Coleman, R.G., 1967, Upside-down metamorphic zonation, blueschist facies, along a regional thrust in California and Oregon: U.S. Geological Survey Professional Paper 575-C, p. 1–9.

Burchfiel, B.C., and Davis, G.A., 1981, Triassic and Jurassic tectonic evolution of the Klamath Mountains—Sierra Nevada geologic terrane, *in* Ernst, W.G., ed., The geotectonic development of California: Englewood Cliffs, New Jersey, Prentice-Hall, p. 50–70.

Coleman, D.S., Briggs, S., Glazner, A.F., and Northrup, C.J., 2003, Timing of plutonism and deformation in the White Mountains of eastern California: Geological Society of America Bulletin, v. 115, p. 48–57, doi: 10.1130/0016-7606(2003)115<0048:TOPADI>2.0.CO;2.

Coleman, R.G., Mortimer, N., Donato, M.M., Manning, C.E., and Hill, L.B., 1988, Tectonic and regional metamorphic framework of the Klamath Mountains and adjacent Coast Ranges, California and Oregon, *in* Ernst, W.G., ed., Metamorphism and crustal evolution of the Western United States: Englewood Cliffs, New Jersey, Prentice-Hall, p. 1061–1097.

Dal Piaz, G.V., Hunziker, J.C., and Martinotti, G., 1972, La zona Sesia-Lanzo e l'evoluzione tettonico-metamorfica delle Alpi nordoccidentali interne: Memoire della Societa Geologica Italiani, v. 11, p. 433–460.

Dewey, J.F., Pitman, W.C., Ryan, W.B.F., and Bonnin, J., 1973, Plate tectonics and the evolution of the Alpine system: Geological Society of America Bulletin, v. 84, p. 3137–3180, doi: 10.1130/0016-7606(1973)84<3137:PTATEO>2.0.CO;2.

Dewey, J.F., Helman, M.L., Turco, E., Hutton, D.H.W., and Knott, S.D., 1989, Kinematics of the western Mediterranean, *in* Coward, M.P., Dietrich, D., and Park, R.G., eds., Alpine tectonics: Geological Society of London Special Publication 45, p. 265–283.

Ernst, W.G., 1965, Mineral paragenesis in Franciscan metamorphic rocks, Panoche Pass, California: Geological Society of America Bulletin, v. 76, p. 879–914.

Ernst, W.G., 1971, Metamorphic zonations on presumably subducted lithospheric plates from Japan, California, and the Alps: Contributions to Mineralogy and Petrology, v. 34, p. 43–59, doi: 10.1007/BF00376030.

Ernst, W.G., 1973, Interpretative synthesis of metamorphism in the Alps: Geological Society of America Bulletin, v. 84, p. 2053–2078, doi: 10.1130/0016-7606(1973)84<2053:ISOMIT>2.0.CO;2.

Ernst, W.G., 1993, Geology of the Pacheco Pass quadrangle, central California Coast Ranges: Geological Society of America Maps and Charts Series MCH078, scale 1:24,000, accompanying text 12 p.

Ernst, W.G., 1998, Geology of the Sawyers Bar area, Klamath Mountains, northern California: California Division of Mines and Geology, Map Sheet 47, scale 1:48,000, accompanying text 59 p.

Ernst, W.G., and Hall, C.A., Jr., 1987, Geology of the Mount Barcroft–Blanco Mountain area, eastern California: Geological Society of America Maps and Charts Ser. MCH066, scale 1:24,000.

Ernst, W.G., Seki, Y., Onuki, H., and Gilbert, M.C., 1970, Comparative study of low-grade metamorphism in the California Coast Ranges and the outer Metamorphic Belt of Japan: Geological Society of America Memoir 124, 276 p.

Ernst, W.G., Hacker, B.R., Barton, M.D., and Sen, G., 1991, Igneous petrogenesis of magnesian metavolcanic rocks from the central Klamath Mountains, northern California: Geological Society of America Bulletin, v. 103, p. 56–72, doi: 10.1130/0016-7606(1991)103<0056:IPOMMR>2.3.CO;2.

Ernst, W.G., Jones, R.E., and Van de Ven, C.M., 2002, Geologic map of the Mount Barcroft complex, central White Mountains, eastern California: Structure, mineral paragenesis, and tectonic evolution: California Division of Mines and Geology, Map Sheet 51, scale 1:24,000, accompanying text 85 p.

Ernst, W.G., Coleman, D.S., and Van de Ven, C.M., 2003, Petrochemistry of granitic rocks in the Mount Barcroft area—Implications for arc evolution, central White Mountains, easternmost California: Geological

Society of America Bulletin, v. 115, p. 499–512, doi: 10.1130/0016-7606(2003)115<0499:POGRIT>2.0.CO;2.

Frey, M., Hunziker, J.C., Frank, W., Bocquet, J., Dal Piaz, G.V., Jäger, E., and Niggli, E., 1974, Alpine metamorphism of the Alps: Schweizerische Mineralogisches und Petrografisches Mittelungen, v. 54, p. 248–290.

Goodge, J.W., 1990, Tectonic evolution of a coherent Late Triassic subduction complex, Stuart Fork terrane, Klamath Mountains, northern California: Geological Society of America Bulletin, v. 102, p. 86–101, doi: 10.1130/0016-7606(1990)102<0086:TEOACL>2.3.CO;2.

Hacker, B.R., Ernst, W.G., and McWilliams, M.O., 1993, Genesis and evolution of a Permian-Jurassic magmatic arc and accretionary wedge, and reevaluation of the terrane concept in the Klamath Mountains: Tectonics, v. 12, p. 387–409.

Hanson, R.B., Saleeby, J.B., and Fates, D.G., 1987, Age and tectonic setting of Mesozoic metavolcanic and metasedimentary rocks, northern White Mountains, California: Geology, v. 15, p. 1074–1078, doi: 10.1130/0091-7613(1987)15<1074:AATSOM>2.0.CO;2.

Hide, K., 1961, Geologic structure and metamorphism of the Sanbagawa crystalline schists of the Besshi-Shirataki mining district in Shikoku, southwest Japan: Hiroshima University Geological Report, no. 9, p. 1–87 (in Japanese with English abstract).

Higashino, T., 1990, The higher grade metamorphic zonation of the Sanbagawa metamorphic belt in central Shikoku, Japan: Journal of Metamorphic Geology, v. 8, p. 413–423.

Hotz, P.E., 1977, Geology of the Yreka quadrangle, Siskiyou County, California: U.S. Geological Survey Bulletin 1436, 72 p.

Irwin, W.P., 1960, Geologic reconnaissance of the northern Coast Ranges and the southern Klamath Mountains, California, with a summary of the mineral resources: California Division of Mines Bulletin 179, 80 p.

Irwin, W.P., 1972, Terranes of the western Paleozoic and Triassic belt in the southern Klamath Mountains, California: U.S. Geological Survey Professional Paper 800-C, p. 103–111.

Irwin, W.P., 1981, Tectonic accretion of the Klamath Mountains, *in* Ernst, W.G., ed., The geotectonic development of California: Englewood Cliffs, New Jersey, Prentice-Hall, p. 29–49.

Kawachi, Y., 1968, Large-scale overturned structure in the Sanbagawa metamorphic zone in central Shikoku, Japan: Geological Society of Japan Journal, v. 74, p. 607–616.

Kistler, R.W., and Peterman, Z.E., 1973, Variation in Sr, Rb, K, Na, and initial $^{87}Sr/^{86}Sr$ in Mesozoic granitic rocks and intruded wall rocks in central California: Geological Society of America Bulletin, v. 84, p. 3489–3512, doi: 10.1130/0016-7606(1973)84<3489:VISRKN>2.0.CO;2.

Lanphere, M.A., Irwin, W.P. and Hotz, P.E., 1968, Isotopic age of the Nevadan orogeny and older plutonic and metamorphic events in the Klamath Mountains, California: Geological Society of America Bulletin, v. 79, p. 1027–1052.

Matsuda, T., and Isozaki, Y., 1991, Well-documented travel history of Mesozoic pelagic chert in Japan: From remote ocean to subduction zone: Tectonics, v. 10, p. 475–499.

Michelsen, K.J., 2003, Heterogeneous internal fabric of the Mount Barcroft pluton, White Mountains, of eastern California: An anisotropy of magnetic susceptibility study [Master's of Sciences in Geological Sciences thesis]: Blacksburg, Virginia, Virginia Institute of Technology, 132 p.

Niggli, E., general coordinator, 1973, Metamorphic map of the Alps: Paris, UNESCO, scale 1:1,000,000.

Sawamura, T., Kojima, G., Mitsuno, C., and Suzuki, T., 1964, Geologic map and construction engineering map between Awaikeda and Tosayamada, Shikoku: Japan National Railway Map Series, no. 6166, scale 1:50,000.

Stevens, C.H., and Greene, D.C., 1999, Stratigraphy, depositional history, and tectonic evolution of Paleozoic continental margin rocks in roof pendants of the eastern Sierra Nevada, California: Geological Society of America Bulletin, v. 111, p. 919–933, doi: 10.1130/0016-7606(1999)111<0919:SDHATE>2.3.CO;2.

Stockli, D.F., Dumitru, T.A., McWilliams, M.O., and Farley, K.A., 2003, Cenozoic tectonic evolution of the White Mountains, California and Nevada: Geological Society of America Bulletin, v. 115, p. 788–816, doi: 10.1130/0016-7606(2003)115<0788:CTEOTW>2.0.CO;2.

Takasu, A., 1984, Prograde and retrograde eclogites in the Sanbagawa metamorphic belt, Besshi district, Japan: Journal of Petrology, v. 25, p. 619–643.

Terabayashi, M., Maruyama, S., and Liou, J.G., 1995, Thermobaric structure of the Franciscan complex in the Pacheco Pass region, Diablo Range, California: The Journal of Geology, v. 104, p. 617–636.

Trümpy, R., 1960, Paleotectonic evolution of the central and western Alps: Geological Society of America Bulletin, v. 71, p. 843–908.

Trümpy, R., 1975, Penninic-Austroalpine boundary in the Swiss Alps: A presumed former continental margin and its problems: American Journal of Science, v. 275A, p. 209–238.

Wallin, E.T., and Metcalf, R.V., 1998, Supra-subduction zone ophiolite formed in an extensional forearc: Trinity terrane, Klamath Mountains, California: The Journal of Geology, v. 106, p. 591–608.

Winchester, S., 2001, The map that changed the world: New York, HarperCollins Publishers, Inc., 329 p.

Wright, J.E., and Fahan, M.R., 1988, An expanded view of Jurassic orogenesis in the western United States Cordillera: Middle Jurassic (pre-Nevadan) regional metamorphism and thrust faulting within an active arc environment, Klamath Mountains, California: Geological Society of America Bulletin, v. 100, p. 859–876, doi: 10.1130/0016-7606(1988)100<0859:AEVOJO>2.3.CO;2.

Wright, J.E., and Wyld, S.J., 1994, The Rattlesnake Creek terrane, Klamath Mountains, California: An early Mesozoic volcanic arc and its basement of tectonically disrupted oceanic crust: Geological Society of America Bulletin, v. 106, p. 1033–1056, doi: 10.1130/0016-7606(1994)106<1033:TRCTKM>2.3.CO;2.

MANUSCRIPT ACCEPTED BY THE SOCIETY 21 MARCH 2006

Geological Society of America
Special Paper 413
2006

Plate tectonics; the general theory: Complex Earth is simpler than you think

Don L. Anderson

Seismological Laboratory, Caltech, Pasadena, California 91125, USA

"....In science, conventional wisdom is difficult to overturn. After more than 20 years some implications of plate tectonics have yet to be fully appreciated by isotope geochemists... and by geologists and geophysicists who have followed their lead.

" A myth is an invented tale, often to explain some natural phenomenon... which sometimes acquires the status of dogma... without a sound logical foundation. It is a dogma that has distorted thinking about the Earth for decades. In science this is an old story, likely to be repeated again, as the defenders of conventional wisdom are seldom treated with the same scepticism as the challengers of the status quo... the dogma has been defended with false assertions, defective data, misconceptions and misunderstandings, and with strawman arguments... The justification ... boils down to a statement of belief, an opinion, rather than a deduction from observations.

"... geochemists are reluctant to abandon cherished concepts they grew up with and have vigorously defended during their education and research careers."

—Richard L. Armstrong, 2002, The Persistent Myth of Continental Growth: Australian Journal of Earth Science, v. 38, p. 613–630.

ABSTRACT

The standard model of mantle dynamics and chemistry involves complex interactions between rigid plates and hot plumes, and exchanges of material between a homogeneous upper mantle and a "primitive" lower mantle. This model requires many assumptions and produces many paradoxes. The problems and complexities can be traced to a series of unnecessary and unfruitful assumptions. Dropping these assumptions, or assuming the opposite, removes many of the paradoxes. A theory of plate tectonics can be developed that is free from assumptions about absolute plate rigidity, hotspot fixity, mantle homogeneity, and steady-state conditions. Here, a simpler and more general hypothesis is described that is based on convective systems that are cooled and organized from the top. Plate tectonics causes thermal and fertility variations in the mantle and stress variations in the plates, thus obviating the need for extraneous assumptions about the deep mantle. The general theory of plate tectonics is more powerful than the current restricted forms that exclude incipient plate-boundary (also known as volcanic chains and hotspot tracks) and athermal (e.g., melting point, fertility, and focusing) explanations of melting anomalies. Plate tectonics,

Anderson, D.L., 2006, Plate tectonics; the general theory: Complex Earth is simpler than you think, *in* Manduca, C.A., and Mogk, D.W., eds., Earth and Mind: How Geologists Think and Learn about the Earth: Geological Society of America Special Paper 413, p. 29–38, doi: 10.1130/2006.2413(03). For permission to copy, contact editing@geosociety.org. ©2006 Geological Society of America. All rights reserved.

geology, mantle dynamics, magmatism, and recycling are upper-mantle processes, largely independent of the deep mantle. These ideas came about by examining the paradoxes and assumptions in current models of mantle structure, evolution, and chemistry. By identifying the assumptions that generate the anomalies, one can have a zero-paradox hypothesis. Eventually, new paradoxes will be identified, and a new paradigm will be introduced. This is the way science progresses.

Keywords: plate tectonics, convection, plumes, simplicity.

INTRODUCTION

The recognition that earthquakes and volcanoes delineate the boundaries of constantly moving plates at Earth's surface led to a new paradigm for understanding Earth—plate tectonics. Viewing the surface of the planet as a set of moving plates required an intellectual about-face of the first order from previous theories that viewed the surface as immobile. This is sometimes called *the plate tectonic revolution*, but Alfred Wegener is the true father of continental mobility. Plate tectonics has been one of the most successful theories in the history of the natural sciences and has revolutionized thinking in all of the earth sciences. It is a testimony to its usefulness and predictive quality that it was accepted over the course of less than a decade in spite of its descriptive nature. All geology textbooks were rewritten, with plate tectonics as the reigning paradigm. The idea of continental fixity, however, has been replaced by the idea of oceanic-island fixity—the so-called *hotspot* or *plume* hypothesis. Volcanic islands are now generally viewed as the tops of narrow hot upwellings from fixed points deep in the mantle that are independent of plate tectonics at the surface. This plume hypothesis was invented to explain some features that were apparently outside the realm of plate tectonic theory. It is generally thought—and taught—that both plates and plumes are required to explain various surface features.

Ordinarily, science progresses slowly by incremental improvements in data and theory. Science can advance, or change direction, through the testing and discarding of theories and conventional wisdom, or can stagnate by sticking too long to a dogma. Plate tectonic and plume theory are currently undergoing such an examination.

Students learn about plate tectonics and plumes from textbooks and lectures. Active researchers learn about Earth by observation and experiment. Learning about a hypothesis is different from learning how to frame or test a hypothesis. Going from an idea to a theory involves assumptions, auxiliary hypotheses, and amendments. Philosophers teach about logic, paradox, and ways of thinking; philosophers of science talk about the logic of scientific discovery, paradigms, falsification, and research programs and what it takes to evolve or overthrow established ideas. This is seldom taught to students of science. The history of science is replete with examples of scientific revolutions and paradigm shifts. The earth sciences have their share. Plate tectonics was one, and we are currently living through another.

WHAT'S THE PROBLEM?

In spite of its usefulness, there remain a number of observations that are difficult to reconcile with the standard conception of plate tectonics and mantle geochemistry, e.g., Albarede and Boyet (2003), Ballentine et al. (2002), and van Keken et al. (2002). These are known as paradoxes or even crises. Philosophers of science have identified ways that active scientists deal with crises, conflicts, and contradictions in their science (Kuhn, 1962; Popper, 1962; Armstrong, 1991; Dickinson, 2003). Currently, there are three approaches for reconciling geological, geophysical, and geochemical observations with plate tectonic theory:

1. Introduce additional features to the basic theory. This approach is taken by those who propose something outside the framework of plate tectonics; for example, plumes to break up continents and to create volcanic chains, and deep core-heat-driven thermal instabilities in deep reservoirs to explain variations in magma chemistry, bathymetry, and crustal thickness.

2. Drop various assumptions, such as the plates are uniform, permanent, and rigid, and the underlying mantle is homogeneous. This is the approach advocated in this paper.

3. Ignore conflicting evidence and live with the paradoxes.

Note that in the first approach, assumptions and auxiliary hypotheses are added to the basic framework, while in the second approach, some or all of the assumptions are pruned. I will examine the origin of these assumptions and make a case that, not only are they unnecessary, but that by eliminating them, the predictive and explanatory power of plate tectonic theory is enhanced. First, however, I examine the criteria used by scientists to evaluate theories as a foundation for comparing competing approaches.

SIMPLICITY

"You can recognize truth by its beauty and simplicity.... When you get it right, it is obvious that it is right...because usually what happens is that more comes out than goes in... truth always turns out to be simpler than you thought."

—Richard Feyman

Simplicity is a useful concept when judging the merit of alternate philosophies or deciding between cause and effect. Simplicity can be judged by looking at the assumptions, adjectives, anomalies, and auxiliary hypotheses that accompany the hypothesis. There are many criteria for judging theories. These include elegance, power, falsifiability, predictability, contradictions, and coincidences. Simplicity is one of the most useful.

OCCAM'S RAZOR

Occam's razor is a method extensively used by geologists; on the surface it is a relatively straightforward point that does not need to be belabored. However, is it the theory—the process—or the result, that should be simple? A homogeneous mantle is certainly a simple assumption. However, simple straightforward geological processes often lead to complex structures. It turns out that incredibly complex and contrived processes are needed in order to create a homogeneous planet from the debris of space, or even a homogeneous upper mantle, which is the hallmark of modern mantle geochemistry (Hofmann, 1997; Schubert et al., 2001). Yet, a set of simple physical rules can be used to predict that Earth should be a gravitationally stratified body, with a dense core, a buoyant crust, and a heterogeneous mantle. Continental fixity is a simpler idea than continental drift, but a large number of ad hoc amendments and assumptions are required to explain the observations.

Occam's razor can be used to improve, trim, simplify, and discard theories, but is most useful when it is used to test and compare theories. Quite often in the development of a hypothesis, there arises an impasse. Techniques used to overcome the difficulty include new assumptions, auxiliary hypotheses, procrustean stretching, tooth fairies, and *deux ex machina*, or a retreat to a previous stage and reconsideration of the choices that were made. The exposure of paradox, fallacy, or error may suggest that a theory is wrong. However, theories create their own inertia, and we are often tempted to add embellishments to the theory that allow it to continue to meet the requirements of the data. Advocates of a theory argue "surely we are allowed to 'complexify' models as we learn more—the current version of the model is not necessarily wrong, just because the original wasn't perfect." Occam's razor, however, encourages us, at the same time, to reconsider, with an open mind, the original theory and its assumptions. In hindsight, some of the original assumptions of a hypothesis may no longer be viable. In so doing, it is often possible to develop an even more general and simpler view that not only solves the immediate problem but solves what were thought to be unrelated problems. This is the opposite from ad hoc modifications to the original hypothesis, including modifications that do not make the hypothesis more powerful or predictive. Recognizing and discarding unuseful assumptions can be more powerful than amending an endangered idea.

The theory of plate tectonics replaced the ideas of continental fixity, permanence of the ocean basins, and Earth expansion because it provided a simpler and more general explanation of geological and geophysical observations. Although the theory has great explanatory and predictive power, it seems to fail in regions of continental deformation and breakup, large igneous provinces, and island chains; there are anomalies. Separate hypotheses have been advanced to address these phenomena, most notably, the popular plume hypothesis. The adjective rigid has been attached to plate tectonics, and fixed has been applied to oceanic-volcanic islands and the underlying mantle. Volcanoes are called hotspots, volcanic chains are called plume tracks; oceanic plateaus and large igneous provinces are called plume heads. Another term for hotspot is "mid-plate volcanism," even though most such features are on plate boundaries, or started on plate boundaries. Even the term "melting anomaly" implies that the results of plate tectonic processes should be uniform. These assumptions and definitions have diverted attention away from the true source of the phenomena.

PLATE TECTONICS—CRACKS IN THE EDIFICE

Plate tectonics is sometimes defined as a kinematic or descriptive theory that describes motions on a sphere. However, plate tectonics is much more powerful than that. The conventional statement of rigid plate tectonics with the hotspot amendment is as follows: Earth's surface is composed of about twelve—some say about 20—rigid plates that move with respect to each other. Volcanoes and earthquakes delineate the plate boundaries. Mid-plate volcanoes and volcanic islands are called hotspots; they are not related to plate tectonics; they are related to core heat and deep mantle materials. Plates and plate boundaries are mobile; hotspots are not.

This statement, short as it is, makes several unnecessary assumptions, which introduce a series of paradoxes and unneeded auxiliary hypotheses. Before accepting the amendments to the central theory, we must return to an examination of the underlying assumptions, as recommended by Occam's razor. In particular:

1. Are the plates really rigid; can they not crack and allow magma to escape?
2. Are the plates riding on a convecting mantle driven by heating from below, or do they drive themselves?
3. Is the system in a steady state; can the present plate system dissolve, to be replaced by a completely different configuration?
4. Can there be new (incipient) plate boundaries and volcanic chains that do not have their origin outside of the framework of plate tectonics? Can former and new plate boundaries look like "hotspot tracks"?

In the standard model, the homogeneous upper mantle is assumed to be the source of the homogeneous magmas that emerge at mid-ocean ridges and form the new oceanic crust. So-called hotspot magmas are assumed to be derived from a deeper part of the mantle. The upper mantle is sometimes called the convecting mantle. The convecting mantle is assumed to be well-mixed and homogeneous because mid-ocean-ridge basalts are homogeneous (e.g., Hofmann, 1997). Mid-plate volcanic chains are assumed to be the result of motions of the plates over fixed hotspots (assumed to be hot) in the mantle. These hotspots are assumed to be maintained by core heat.

Note the numerous assumptions, many more than necessary. Note also the unnecessary adjectives—homogeneous, hotspot, convecting. Sometimes one can make progress by dropping, rather than adding, adjectives and assumptions. When a theory runs into trouble with new measurements and observations, one should examine the assumptions; they may be wrong, or unnecessary. In an alternative, cooled-from-above hypothesis, plates drive and organize themselves, the mantle is hot and inhomogeneous, and the outer shell is cracked and permeable to magma, rather than absolutely rigid. Volcanic chains can reflect zones of weakness rather than zones of hotness. An isothermal, motionless and homogeneous mantle, everywhere subsolidus, and absolute plate rigidity are impossible to attain and are extraneous constraints.

After one examines the assumptions, and possible alternate assumptions, one should make sure that the definitions and words used in the theory are precise. Many of the concepts and assumptions of the standard model, which includes both plates and plumes, are ill-defined. The terms plate, mid-plate, rigid, high-temperature, anomalous, well-mixed, and fixed are ambiguous or relative terms; precise definitions, or agreed-upon usages, are necessary in order to proceed. Unfortunately, some of these concepts are statistical in nature, and statistics are seldom applied in tests of the standard model. For example, the normal temperature variations of the mantle are several hundred kelvins. These are the temperature fluctuations expected in a convecting material with the physical properties and dimensions of Earth's mantle, and the temperature variations expected from slab cooling and continental insulation. All phenomena attributed to hotspots and plumes have inferred temperatures in this range, but they are usually interpreted as manifestations of "excess" temperature, under the assumption that "excess" volumes of basalt or crust, or high elevations, require temperatures well outside the normal range (and require explanations other than plate tectonics). Thus, the plume hypothesis makes assumptions about what is normal, and what is anomalous—what is in the plate tectonic domain, and what is in the plume domain. A misapplication of Occam's razor is that plate tectonics should lead to uniform and homogeneous results, e.g., mid-ocean ridges should all be at the same elevation, the same amount of basalt should come out of ridges everywhere, the mantle should not vary in temperature, and if basalts are uniform, the source must be uniform. However, according to Occam's razor, it is the theory that should be simple, not the result.

Factors such as mantle composition, fertility, focusing of upwelling magmas, volatile content, prior history of the area, and lithospheric architecture and stress are important in determining the volume of magma produced at the surface. These are all familiar concepts in geology and volcanology. The word hotspot itself is based on assumptions, not on observations of temperature. "Melting anomaly" is a better term, but even this implies that—without plumes—there should not be regions that provide more magma than average. Bathymetric anomalies, or swells, are usually attributed to hotspots; this assumes that "normal" mantle is homogeneous in temperature, density, and composition, that all oceanic ridges should rise to exactly the same depth, and that ocean floor of a given age should always be at the same depth.

"Mid-plate" volcanoes are generally on or near plate boundaries, or were when they first formed. Regions of higher than average elevation or rates of magmatism are expected in some places since the mantle is not homogeneous or isothermal; even if it were, we expect updrafts and downdrafts. The word "midplate" implies a mechanism different than the passive upwellings or dikes associated with plate divergence, convergence, bending, or shrinking—normal plate tectonic processes.

A CONVECTING MANTLE?

The outer shell of Earth—the lithosphere—is often regarded as the top layer of mantle convection, and plate tectonics is regarded as a manifestation of this convection. Unfortunately, while this approach has yielded some important insights, it has failed to answer many first-order questions: How are plate tectonics initiated? Why are there twelve or twenty plates (instead of two or fifty)? What controls the size and shape of the plates (Anderson, 2002a)? Why are subduction zones one-sided, instead of symmetric? These problems suggest that the mantle departs from an ideal fluid in significant ways and that a different approach may be needed.

An alternative conception is that mantle convection is mainly driven by cooling from above and the negative buoyancy of the cold outer shell. The plates drive themselves, by their cooling, and they in turn organize the flow in the mantle (see Appendix). Computer simulations of mantle convection have been unable to reproduce plate tectonics, and this may be because cause and effect have been reversed.

A fluid heated from below or within will undergo a series of transitions from static equilibrium to organized cells to chaotic convection as the temperature is raised. In the absence of surface tension—or plates and continents—the fluid self-organizes itself; it is not responding to an external template, although it needs an external source of energy. However, continents and tectonic plates change the surface boundary condition; they serve as a template for mantle convection. The "fluid" mantle is no longer free to self-organize, but, given the appropriate conditions, the plates themselves may become the self-organizing system. The sizes and shapes of the coherent entities called plates, the locations of plate boundaries, and the directions and velocities of individual plates are controlled by interaction between the plates and the distribution of buoyancy (density variations) in the plates.

Just as fluctuations of temperature can drive a convecting fluid to a new state, so a fluctuation of stress (in the lithosphere, for example) can cause the plate tectonic system to completely reorganize. Such global plate reorganizations are recognized in the geological record. They are often attributed to convective overturns in the mantle, as in Rayleigh-Bénard convection. They may, however, be controlled from the top, by the interacting plate system itself, as in Bénard-Marangoni surface-tension–driven convection, or as when two continents collide. The difference between plate tectonic and surface-tension–controlled convection is that tension holds surface films together, while lateral compression, or common forces, is what holds plates together. Plates are weak in tension and fluctuations in stress can cause new plate boundaries to form. These are usually along old plate boundaries, and they are usually called hotspot tracks.

The interesting thing about convection and plate tectonics is that a few simple rules control the evolution of the system. Self-organization does not require templates or fine-tuning; it takes care of itself. It just requires that the investigator, or modeler, provide the system with enough degrees of freedom so it can self-organize. Geological examples of self-organization include mudcracks, basalt columns, salt domes, and sand dunes. Plate tectonics may be a case of self-organization. Ironically, the science that has evolved from these far-from-equilibrium considerations is called the science of complexity. It is actually an example of Occam's razor—the assumptions and parameters are minimized, and the rules are simple. Beautiful complex forms are often the result.

TWO MODES OF CONVECTION?

In systems cooled from above, the instability of the surface layer drives the motions of both the surface and the interior; this is the kind of convection involved in plate tectonics and the thermal evolution of Earth. Think of a glass of ice tea; the ice cubes and the shape of the glass control the style of convection. The ice cubes move about, constantly changing the top boundary condition. Yet it is motions of the mantle, and temperature variations in the deep mantle, independent of the surface conditions, that are often assumed to drive the plates and create volcanic chains. In one theory, the plates control their own fate, and the mantle passively follows. In the other theory, many surface features are controlled by deep convective motions and core heat; the surface passively responds or, at most, is just the surface boundary layer of a system where the bottom boundary layer is as important as the top boundary layer, in spite of the effects of pressure and sphericity.

Temperature variations in the upper mantle are caused by plate tectonic processes, such as continental insulation and absence of subduction cooling. Swells, superswells, and large-scale magmatism (so-called "anomalies") are consequences of plate tectonics rather than independent phenomena. The idea that the surface of Earth is slaved to the mantle is based on the rather obvious point that the mantle is much more massive than the plates. However, the concept of far-from-equilibrium self-organization turns this viewpoint around. This kind of organization requires a large outside source of energy and material, and a place to discard waste products. The plate system, viewed as an open thermodynamic system, requires the mantle's resources but does not need the mantle to organize it. The biosphere is one of the best known examples of this process. The biosphere is small;

it depends on the Sun and Earth for energy and matter, but it organizes itself.

It was more than fifty years after Bénard's experiments that it was realized that the hexagonal pattern did not require thermal convection in the underlying fluid. It is the other way around. The hexagonal cells in the fluid are imposed from the surface. A similar transition in thinking may be required to understand plate tectonics.

If the top and bottom faces of a tank of fluid are kept at constant temperature, and if density depends only on temperature, then thermal instabilities (plumes) form at both interfaces and serve to drive convection in the tank. This symmetry is broken if pressure is taken into account, or if other properties are functions of temperature and pressure, or if the container is a spherical shell, or if there are phase changes, or if only one surface is stress-free or isothermal. Geodynamicists speak of the plate-mode and the plume-mode of mantle convection, these being the independent responses of the top and bottom thermal boundary layers, respectively. Geochemists speak of the upper and lower boundary layers as being distinct reservoirs, and mantle in between, as the convecting mantle (the presumed—or assumed—homogeneous source of mid-ocean-ridge basalts, or MORBs).

The plate-mode must be, by far, the most important mode for the following reasons; because of secular cooling of the mantle and the distribution of radioactivity, at least an order of magnitude more heat crosses the upper thermal boundary layer than crosses the lower. That is, the mantle is more cooled from above than it is heated from below. Furthermore, because of the temperature and pressure dependence of the thermal expansion, there is much more (negative) buoyancy created at the top than positive buoyancy at the bottom. In these respects, mantle convection differs from laboratory or kitchen experiments. The other factors controlling the vigor of convection (thermal conductivity, viscosity) also favor more vigorous convection at the top. Instabilities at the base of the mantle, because of pressure, will be sluggish, immense, and long-lived, in contrast to the plate tectonic mode. Finally, the processes of gravitational differentiation during the high-temperature accretion of Earth will isolate the upper and lower mantles, even if there is only a small density contrast between them. The effects of pressure and chemical layering are almost always ignored in mantle dynamics simulations, and, often, the plates are ignored as well, or put into the calculation in an approximate way. Convection of the mantle cannot be treated as a homogeneous fluid with simple (and unchanging) boundary conditions.

Small-scale convection and stress variations and cracks in the plates are consequences of plate tectonics, and they offer alternative explanations of volcanic chains and mid-plate volcanism. Lateral variations in temperature and density (which drive mantle convection) and fertility of the upper mantle are also consequences of plate tectonics, recycling, continental insulation, and slab cooling and can explain variations in volcanic output from place to place. These options are not available if the plates are really rigid and the mantle is really isothermal and homogeneous, as often assumed. By dropping unnecessary assumptions, the plate theory becomes more powerful, plume theory becomes less plausible, and upwelling plumes become unnecessary.

FIXED RIGID PLATES

The term "plate" itself has no agreed upon formal definition but is defined operationally as a part of the outer shell that moves coherently. Plates are rigid in the sense that relative plate motions can be described by rotations about Euler poles on a sphere. We often assume therefore that plates are strong, brittle, permanent, rigid, and elastic. The word plate, in fact, implies strength, brittleness, and permanence. However, there are several possible scenarios in which plates move coherently: (1) Plates are strong and rigid (the conventional interpretation). (2) Plates are those regions defined by lateral compression since plate boundaries are formed by lateral extension. Plates may be collages, held together by stress and adjacent portions rather than by intrinsic strength. (3) Plates move coherently because the parts experience similar forces or constraints.

With the first definition, deformation and volcanism within the plate are only possible if the local tensile strength is overcome by local heating or stretching. This reasoning spawned the plume hypothesis.

With the second definition the global stress field, dictated by plate boundary and subplate conditions, controls the locations of stress conditions appropriate for the formation of dikes and volcanic chains, and incipient plate boundaries, from the underlying mantle, which is already at the melting point. Plates break at suture zones (former plate boundaries), fracture zones, and subplate boundaries, usually generating volcanic chains in the process.

With the third definition, the concept of plate almost disappears, and the concept of "plate rigidity" is replaced by "coherency of motion" as in a flock of birds or a billowing cloud.

The metaphor of a plate implies a fixed shape, and strength, but scaling relations dating back to Galileo show that large objects have essentially no strength. Plates are actually segments of spherical deformable shells or domes, aggregates of rock pushed together. Gravitational forces and lateral compression keep plates and domes and igloos together. This metaphor fails because plates do not have fixed shapes like the stones in a cathedral. Plates have higher viscosity than the underlying mantle but they are easily pulled apart, like shoals of fish. They are more akin to crystals in deforming ice—or the bubbles in a foam—constantly recrystallizing as conditions change. Volcanic-island chains and transient bursts of magmatism appear at the seams between new plates and at the sutures and cracks of old ones. These eruptions only occur because the surface has failed in tension. The lithosphere does not necessarily fail because it is pushed up, or heated, from below.

The notion that mid-plate volcanoes are "fixed" is a remnant from the early development of plate tectonic theory. Island chains

at one time were regarded as a fixed reference frame, anchored by deep motionless parts of the mantle. Originally, hotspots were thought to be rooted in the interiors of convection cells, but later they were moved down to the "non-convecting lower mantle" and ultimately to the core-mantle boundary. It is now known that these "fixed" points move relative to each by three to six centimeters per year, which is about the average relative plate velocity. Some continents move with respect to each other, or to some oceanic plates, with much smaller velocities, yet they are not regarded as fixed, or anchored to the deep mantle.

This illustrates that both definitions and assumptions should be analyzed when applying Occam's razor. It also is a reminder that sometimes our favorite ideas are based on interpretations of data that are no longer valid.

AN ALTERNATE FORMALIZATION

An alternate way of expressing plate dynamics is the following: Earth's surface is covered by a cold scum temporarily divided into ephemeral domains, called plates, which are defined by the condition that horizontal extensional stresses are minimized. Motions of the plates over the planet's interior are caused by the integral of gravitational attraction of all points in the interior, and on the surface, acting on the outer skin.

This theory has several corollaries: (1) Extension is localized at plate boundaries. (2) Plates are primarily under horizontal compression. (3) Stresses in the outer shell are superpositions of all the gravitational and thermal stresses and are not uniform. (4) Plate boundaries and volcanic chains are the locus of maximum strain.

In a planet cooled from above, the cold surface boundary is the active element (it drives plate motions and mantle convection). The mantle below responds passively. Upwellings are a consequence of mass balance, not thermal instability. The unnecessary and unfruitful adjectives—rigid, fixed, well-mixed—require auxiliary hypotheses and are candidates for trimming by Occam's razor. In fact, plates are deformable, breakable, and ephemeral, and in a convecting planet, there are no fixed or absolute reference frames, and the convecting part cannot be isothermal. Convection does not homogenize a planet; it stratifies it. Cooling plates cause mantle convection.

Plate tectonics on a sphere must be episodic; steady state and uniformity reign for only short periods of time. Earth history can be divided into supercontinent cycles. A supercontinent (or any large, slowly moving plate) insulates the mantle and isolates it from subduction cooling. The temperature increases by ~100 °C under a supercontinent and other large plates, this being added to the ±100 °C, or more, range normally available in an Earth-size convecting planet. Lateral temperature gradients and plate boundary forces break up the supercontinent—or superplate—and cause the fragments to move away from the thermal anomaly, forcing a global reorganization of plates, stress, and motions. New plate boundaries are accompanied by transient bursts of magmatism, including large igneous provinces from previously insulated regions of the mantle. There follows a period of relatively steady motion, but each time a continent overrides a ridge or a trench, or collides with or slides past another continent, the global stress pattern changes. When this happens the existing plates and plate boundaries are no longer appropriate for the new stress sate. New plates must form. An analogous situation occurs when a bubble-raft, or foam, or a bed of particles, is sheared. There are islands of little deformation, but they are transient.

Continents slow down and come to rest over cold mantle. This signals the end of a cycle. Chains of volcanic islands signal the formation of a new ridge or crack or the death of an old one. Subduction cools the mantle and introduces chemical anomalies into it. This episodic non-steady-state aspect and the creation of thermal and chemical anomalies are essential aspects of plate tectonics. Plate tectonics is thus a more general theory than generally acknowledged. The plate tectonic hypothesis is a powerful one and, if pushed hard enough, can explain phenomena that are now treated outside of the paradigm. It is the adjectives—rigid, fixed, isothermal, homogeneous—that are the suspects in suspected failures of an otherwise successful hypothesis. As usual, one can make progress by deleting adjectives and dropping assumptions. This is the essence of Occam's razor.

THE SOURCE OF MANTLE HETEROGENEITY AND RECYCLING

Most of the chemical heterogeneity of the upper mantle is due to subduction of sediments, fluids, crust, and plates of various ages, including young plates; the mantle is polluted by the processes of plate tectonics. Only thick old oceanic plates achieve enough negative buoyancy to sink rapidly through the upper mantle but even these may contribute their fluids, and even parts of their crusts, to shallow-mantle heterogeneity. Other sources of recycled material that cannot sink out of the shallow mantle include refractory products of melt extraction, backarc basins, erosion at the top, edge, and bottom of the lithosphere, delaminated crust, etc. In the standard model of mantle geochemistry, material in the asthenosphere that provides magma to oceanic islands is brought into the upper mantle by deep plumes from the core-mantle boundary, rather than by direct transfer from slabs.

The distribution of ages of subducting plates is highly variable (Rowley, 2002). There is a large amount of material of age 0–20 Ma and 40–60 Ma at subduction zones. The former is relatively hot and buoyant and will underplate continents, become flat slabs, or will thermally equilibrate in the shallow upper mantle. The rate at which this young crust enters the mantle is ~2–4 km^3/yr. The global rate of "hotspot" volcanism is ~2 km^3/yr (Phipps Morgan, 1997). This rough equality encourages us to think that "melting anomalies" may be due to fertile patches, occupied by subducted oceanic crust that was young at the time of subduction. Isotopic shifts in elements with long-lived radioactive parents document chemical variations in Earth's mantle that have been preserved for periods of at least 10^8–10^9 yr. This has been equated with the time scale of whole mantle convective overturn,

but it is also the isolation time of the upper mantle, given typical ridge migration rates. Ancient material also gets recycled into the mantle, and this, in part, is responsible for some of the apparently long isolation times.

RIDGES AND TRENCHES MOVE ABOUT

Some textbook views of mantle convection give the impression that material rises at mid-ocean ridges and is carried away on a conveyor belt that transports the plate to a trench where it subducts. This is often equated to the top of a convection cell. The real mantle is much more complex. Ridges and trenches, as well as plates, migrate about the surface of Earth. At typical ridge and trench migration rates of 1 cm/yr, relative to the underlying mantle, a section of the shallow mantle will be visited by a ridge about once every 2 b.y. and ~1 b.y. after being visited by a subduction zone. Depending on the geometry and depth of the return flow, the horizontal component of mantle convection will be on the order of 5–30 times less than the plate speeds or ~1–0.16 cm/yr. Hotspots do not need to be fixed to stationary plumes. The time available for isotopic anomalies to grow is controlled by ridge migration rates, more so than by the overturn time of the mantle, assuming whole mantle convection. The typical times of 1–2 b.y. usually quoted for the isolation times of mantle reservoirs and interpreted as whole mantle overturn times can also be understood even if plate tectonic processes such as subduction, recycling, and melting are confined to the shallow mantle.

Oxburgh and Parmentier (1977) calculated that normal oceanic lithosphere older than 8 or 10 m.y. old should have negative buoyancy and hence be subductible. Slightly thicker crust, or the presence of sediments and altered crust and lithospheric mantle, further reduce the density of the young plate. In order for a plate to be denser than the underlying mantle, and hence, subductible, there has to be enough cold deep lithosphere to counteract the buoyant crust (12% less dense than "normal" mantle) and the refractory garnet-free residue (3%–6% less dense). The "elastic" or rheological thickness of the plate is ~40 km after 80 m.y. of cooling, and the thermal boundary layer is about twice this. The bottom part of thermal boundary layer is hot, so it is the mid–thermal boundary layer that contributes most to the offset of the buoyant upper parts.

We can infer that there is likely much oceanic crust jammed into the shallow mantle. Mixing, stretching, and stirring of this recycled debris require turbulent or chaotic convection, and even in these cases, the simulations give long-lasting blobs (Bunge and Richards, 1996). The presence of plates, continents, pressure effects on physical properties, and stratification all serve to help organize mantle flow (which is mainly a passive response to plate tectonics) and keep inhomogeneities from mixing. The conventional model has a homogeneous upper mantle (convection has been confused with " stirring," "mixing," and homogenization). The real Earth likely has recycled crust and lithosphere, metasomatic bits, trapped melts, migrating fluids, subduction processed residual, and ridge processed residue in the upper mantle, and trapped young crust at collision zones. The mantle at mature ridges only appears to be homogeneous because of sampling processes. Application of the central limit theorem to volcano and ridge sampling processes eliminates the need for the large-scale isolated reservoir and box models, and narrow plumes, that form the basis of modern mantle geochemistry, and what has become known as chemical geodynamics.

THE PLUME ASSUMPTION

Plate tectonics apparently is the style of convection adopted by a hot, but cooling, planet with water, a cold atmosphere, and an interior that is buffered by the melting point of rocks containing volatile elements. In a planet as large as Earth, the effect of pressure makes the gravitational separation of different-density materials during the hot accretion process irreversible. After accretion, the planet is stratified according to volatility, melting point, chemistry, and density. The top of the mantle—since it is cooled from above—is characterized by narrow dense downwellings and broad warm passive upwellings. The warmer and more fertile regions are at or above the (variable) melting point. Most of the radioactive elements were placed in the crust and upper mantle during accretion and upward transport of melt.

A small fraction of the total surface heat flow comes from the core. The high pressure at the base of the mantle, and the low heating rate means that buoyant upwellings must be huge, long-lived, and slow to develop. Even a small intrinsic density contrast between the deep layers in the mantle will trap the upwellings, since pressure lowers the thermal expansivity of silicate rocks, and increases the viscosity and thermal conductivity.

Text books show narrow plumes of material rising from the core-mantle boundary directly to Yellowstone and Iceland and ~40 other volcanoes designated as hotspots. These cartoons are based on simple laboratory experiments involving the injection of hot fluid into a tank of stationary fluid, or the pot-on-the-stove analogy. Pressure is unimportant in these simulations. For simplicity, all the thermal properties are more-or-less constant.

Some of the more critical assumptions that have been made in developing the plume hypothesis are: (1) the mantle is below the melting point; (2) melting anomalies are due to localized high temperature (not low melting point); (3) the mantle is almost isothermal; (4) cracks in the plates will not be volcanic unless the local temperature is anomalously high; and (5) high temperatures require importation of heat from the core-mantle boundary in the form of narrow jets.

Other assumptions that motivated the plume hypothesis, such as the fixity of hotspots and the parallelism of island chains, need not concern us here. Problems with these assumptions are behind many of the paradoxes and problems associated with the standard model of mantle dynamics and chemical geodynamics. They motivated the search for alternate models, which now turns out to be plate tectonics itself, operated on by Occam's razor.

Ptolemy's scheme of planetary motion on geocentric spheres eventually collapsed because of the large number of epicycles, eccentrics, and equants introduced to patch up observational inconsistencies. William Derham (1726) appealed to the principle of economy in opposing the Ptolemaic system. He argued that the Copernican System is far more agreeable to nature, which never goes in a roundabout way but acts in the most compendious, easy, and simple method. The Ptolemaic system is "forced to invent diverse strange, unnatural, interfering eccentrics and epicycles—a hypothesis so bungling and monstrous" that a king noted that he would have advised God to mend his ways.

In the fixed plume hypothesis, it is required that the outer shell of Earth drift westwardly relative to the deep mantle, that the mantle rolls underneath the plate, that plumes feed distant islands, and that hotspots are actually large areas inside of which the volcano can move and still be regarded as fixed. Most island chains, called hotspot tracks, are not concentric circles and do not have simple age progressions as predicted and as required by Euler's equations, and many are set aside since they do not satisfy the hypothesis. Volcanoes do not define a fixed reference system. Many plumes are assumed to initiate at long-standing tectonic boundaries between plates. Alternative and simpler ideas that relate volcanoes to stress or cracks must be reevaluated.

SUMMARY

Science can often be advanced by the application of the principle of simplicity. The ultimate goal of science is unification. By removing assumptions, amendments, and auxiliary hypotheses, it is possible to make plate tectonics a simpler and at the same time a more general theory. The general theory of plate tectonics unifies plate tectonics and so-called mid-plate phenomena, and explains the diversity of magmas and other phenomena labeled as anomalies in the standard model.

This chapter has emphasized how philosophy and semantics can be applied in science. But logic and physics must also be involved. Plate tectonics is usually regarded as a kinematic theory, a theory of motions of rigid blocks or plates on a sphere. However, the creation and cooling of plates, and their ultimate subduction at trenches create forces that drive and break up the plates. This process also introduces chemical and thermal inhomogeneities into the mantle. The mantle, in a plate tectonic world, cannot be isothermal and chemically homogeneous, and plates cannot be under uniform stress. The melting points of mantle materials cannot all be the same. These assumptions have created the many amendments and paradoxes associated with current models. The forces that drive and reorganize plate tectonics, and create cracks and volcanic chains, cannot usefully be treated outside the context of plate tectonics itself. Plate forces such as ridge push, slab pull, and trench suction are basically gravitational forces generated by cooling plates. They are resisted by transform faults, bending and tearing resistance, collisional resistance, and bottom drag. The thermal and density variations introduced into the mantle by subduction also generate forces on the plates.

Plate tectonics introduces physical heterogeneities into the mantle that have dimensions typical of slabs (tens of kilometers).

The density anomalies generate a force known as slab pull. Trench migration and the time delays associated with thermal equilibration mean that this effect is not limited to current subduction areas. Density anomalies in the mantle contribute to the deformation, elevation, and motion of the lithosphere. Uplift, extensional stresses, and volcanism are most likely to occur above low-density regions of the mantle, even if these are confined to the shallow mantle. Lower-mantle density anomalies give broader uplift features, even if they are trapped in the deep mantle. Mantle flow is passive, is organized by the plates, and is not vigorous or turbulent. Slabs sink to various depths depending on their ages and other factors. These other factors serve to limit the depth of penetration, rather than allowing young slabs to sink deeper than their buoyancy limit. Young slabs and delaminated crust also warm up quickly. A large fraction of material presently at the solid surface under oceans and a substantial amount of material currently entering subduction zones, will never sink far into the mantle, and is available as ridges and incipient ridges migrate around. In principle, ridges and trenches should be much more mobile than plates or embedded mantle heterogeneities. Particularly fertile patches of mantle, due in part to ancient subducted crust, may appear to be relatively "fixed" when compared to the mobility of surface features. It was the assumption that they were absolutely fixed that led to the plume hypothesis.

The materials introduced into the mantle at subduction zones and through cracks provide part of the material subsequently reprocessed at ridges and island chains. Thus, plate tectonics is far from being just a kinematic theory that requires extraneous theories to explain its existence and so-called "mid-plate" phenomena. It is a self-contained and complete theory of geodynamics, mantle geochemistry, and mantle thermal and chemical structure and evolution. It implies the creation and migration of plate boundaries, the growth and shrinkage of plates, and global reorganizations. Magma diversity is a result of plate tectonic recycling. Mantle convection is a result of topside cooling, plate tectonics, and lithospheric architecture and motions. Lateral variations in mantle temperature, melting temperatures, melt volumes, chemistry, and "age" (i.e., anomalies) are an inevitable result of plate tectonics.

Often, new assumptions are needed to undo the damage done by the initial unnecessary assumptions, such as fixity, rigidity, elasticity, and uniformity. The general theory of plate tectonics, discussed here, drops most of the assumptions, adjectives, and limitations of the special theory and makes it evident that plate tectonics is a much more powerful concept than generally believed. The general theory is a top-down, stress- and plate-controlled, largely tectonic and athermal alternative to the bottom-up deep-thermal-plume hypothesis. Lithospheric architecture and stress, not concentrated hot jets, localize volcanism. Melting anomalies are due, in part, to fertility variations (Anderson, 1999, 2002a, 2002b; Foulger, 2002). The perceived limitations of the plate tectonic theory, which are thought to require special mechanisms to drive and break up the plates and create volcanic chains, are semantic, not real, limitations.

Pluto is the god of the underworld. His name has been applied to plutonic rocks, plutons, and plutonic processes. Hotspots, plumes, and mantle convection can be viewed as the use of plutonics in the rationalization of hotspots, plumes, and the organization of plates. In this view, the world is organized from below. Creatures of the deep include superplumes, megaplumes, hotlines, massive mantle overturns, and mantle avalanches. I distinguish this plutonic (plume) view from the point of view that plate tectonics is a self-consistent self-organized system and that mantle geodynamics is controlled from above. Platonics places emphasis on the superficial and the geometric rather than the profound, or deep (see Appendix).

APPENDIX

Dictionary

Plate tectonics: Geol., a theory the Earth's surface based on the concepts of moving plates (PLATE n.) and seafloor spreading, used to explain the distribution of earthquakes, mid-ocean ridges, deep-sea trenches, and orogenic belts; hence plate-tectonic. a., plate tectonicist.

Platonic: A. adj.

1. a. Of or pertaining to Plato, a famous philosopher of ancient Greece (ca. B.C. 429–347), or his doctrines; conceived or composed after the manner of Plato.

1. b. The Platonic philosophy says that the imagined world is more real than the actual world.

2. a. Applied to love or affection for one of the opposite sex, of a purely spiritual character, and free from sensual desire. Also applied to affection for one of the same sex; hence in various allusions. (Now use- ally with lower-case initial.) …

> A. HUXLEY in *Point Counter Point* xiii. 232 He had such a pure, childlike and platonic way of going to bed with women, that neither they nor he ever considered that the process really counted as going to bed.
> 1957 J. BRAINE *Room at Top* vii. 64 "Teddy wouldn't understand. Our relationship is strictly platonic." "Yes, I understand," Teddy said, putting his arm round June's waist. "I'm trying to take June on a platonic weekend. Of course, it'll be too bad if she has a platonic baby."

2. b. Feeling or professing platonic love.

Platonics:

1. Geol., a theory of Earth's surface based on the concept that gravitational forces in the superficial parts of Earth, such as plates, sometimes called ridge push and slab pull, move and break the plates and organize mantle flow. This is a top-down theory in contrast to the bottom-up plume hypothesis, which attributes surface phenomena to deep-mantle processes. In platonics, volcanic chains are the result of stress and fabric in the plates. Plate tectonics as a far-from-equilibrium self-organized system is a branch of plate tectonics. Platonics is to plutonics as Marangoni convection is to Rayleigh- Bénard convection. Cf. Plutonics, plumes. (Also

includes small-scale convection, edge-driven gyres and eddies [EDGE] convection, Richter rolls, diffuse plate boundaries, continental tectonics, dikes, volcanic chains, leaky transform faults, and extensional transfer.)

Pluto: The god of the underworld, King of Hades; closely linked to Satan, who resides in the solid inner core of Earth (Dante's Inferno); also, the fallen angel, who splashed up molten rock at the antipode (pr. Easter Island) as he fell to his permanent abode. Thus, the god of the plume and the profound (cf. Platonics, the shallow, superficial).

Plutonic: 1. Geol., Pertaining to or involving the action of intense heat at great depths upon the rocks forming Earth's crust; igneous; applied specifically to the theory that attributes most geological phenomena to the action of deep internal heat.

REFERENCES CITED

Albarede, F., and Boyet, M., 2003, A watered-down primordial lower mantle: American Geophysical Union, Fall meeting supplement, v. 84, no. 46, Abstract T21A-06.

Anderson, D.L., 1999, A theory of the Earth: Hutton and Humpty-Dumpty and Holmes, *in* Craig, G.Y., and Hull, J.H., eds., James Hutton—Present and future: Geological Society [London] Special Publication 150, p. 13–35.

Anderson, D.L., 2002a, How many plates?: Geology, v. 30, p. 411–414, doi: 10.1130/0091-7613(2002)030<0411:HMP>2.0.CO;2.

Anderson, D.L., 2002b, Occam's razor: Simplicity, complexity, and global geodynamics: Proceedings of the American Philosophical Society, v. 146, no. 1, p. 56–76.

Armstrong, R.L., 1991, The persistent myth of crustal growth: Australian Journal of Earth Sciences, v. 38, p. 613–630.

Ballentine, C.J., Van Keken, P.E., Porcelli, D., and Hauri, E.H., 2002, Numerical models, geochemistry and the zero-paradox noble-gas mantle: Philosophical Transactions [London], ser. A, Mathematical, Physical, and Engineering Sciences, v. 360, no. 1800, p. 2611–2631, doi: 10.1098/rsta.2002.1083.

Bunge, H.-P., and Richards, M.A., 1996, The origin of large scale structure in mantle convection: Effects of plate motions and viscosity stratification: Geophysical Research Letters, v. 23, p. 2987–2990, doi: 10.1029/96GL02522.

Derham, W., 1726, Astro-Theology: Or, a Demonstration of the Being & Attributes of God from a Survey of the Heavens, 250 p.

Dickinson, W.R., 2003, The place and power of myth in geoscience—An Associate Editor's perspective: American Journal of Science, v. 303, p. 856–864.

Foulger, G.R., 2002, Plumes, or plate tectonic processes?: Astronomy and Geophysics, v. 43, p. 6.19–6.23.

Hofmann, A.W., 1997, Mantle geochemistry: The message from oceanic volcanism: Nature, v. 385, p. 219–229, doi: 10.1038/385219a0.

Kuhn, T.S., 1962, The structure of scientific revolutions: Chicago, University of Chicago Press, 172 p.

Oxburgh, E.R., and Parmentier, E.M., 1977, Compositional and density stratification in oceanic lithosphere—Causes and consequences: Journal of the Geological Society of London, v. 133, p. 343–355.

Phipps Morgan, J., 1997, The generation of a compositional lithosphere: Earth and Planetary Science Letters, v. 146, p. 213–232, doi: 10.1016/S0012-821X(96)00207-5.

Popper, K.R., 1962, Conjectures and refutations; the growth of scientific knowledge: New York, Basic Books, 412 p.

Rowley, D.B., 2002, Rate of plate creation and destruction: 180 Ma to present: Geological Society of America Bulletin, v. 114, p. 927–933, doi: 10.1130/0016-7606(2002)114<0927:ROPCAD>2.0.CO;2.

Schubert, G., Turcotte, D.L., and Olsen, P., 2001, Mantle convection in the Earth and planets: Cambridge, Cambridge University Press, 940 p.

van Keken, P., Hauri, E.H., and Ballentine, C.J., 2002, Mantle mixing: The generation, preservation, and destruction of chemical heterogeneity: Annual Reviews of Earth and Planetary Science, v. 30, p. 493–525, doi: 10.1146/annurev.earth.30.091201.141236.

MANUSCRIPT ACCEPTED BY THE SOCIETY 21 MARCH 2006

Geological Society of America
Special Paper 413
2006

Modeling geocomplexity: "A new kind of science"

Donald L. Turcotte

Department of Geology, University of California, Davis, California 95616, USA

ABSTRACT

A major objective of science is to provide a fundamental understanding of natural phenomena. In "the old kind of science," this was done primarily by using partial differential equations. Boundary and initial value conditions were specified and solutions were obtained either analytically or numerically. However, many phenomena in geology are complex and statistical in nature and thus require alternative approaches. But the observed statistical distributions often are not Gaussian (normal) or lognormal, instead they are power laws. A power-law (fractal) distribution is a direct consequence of scale invariance, but it is now recognized to also be associated with self-organized complexity. Relatively simple cellular automata (CA) models provide explanations for a range of complex geological observations. The "sand-pile" model of Bak—the context for "self-organized criticality"—has been applied to landslides and turbidite deposits. The "forest-fire" model provides an explanation for the frequency-magnitude statistics of actual forest and wild fires. The slider-block model reproduces the Guttenberg-Richter frequency-magnitude scaling for earthquakes. Many of the patterns generated by the CA approach can be recognized in geological contexts. The use of CA models to provide an understanding of a wide range of natural phenomena has been popularized in Stephen Wolfram's bestselling book *A New Kind of Science* (2002). Since CA models are basically computer games, they are accepted enthusiastically by many students who find other approaches to the quantification of geological problems both difficult and boring.

Keywords: cellular automata, chaos, complexity, computational equivalence, drainage networks, earthquakes, forest fires, fractals, geocomplexity, landslides, seismicity, self-organized complexity, topography.

INTRODUCTION

The geosciences cover a very broad range of topics. In this paper, I will concentrate primarily on geological problems. These problems also cover a broad range of topics, i.e., the morphology of Earth's surface, the distribution and origin of rock types, the processes of sedimentation, and the distribution of earthquakes in space and time. Massive amounts of data have been collected and stored in repositories. A fundamental question is whether this data can be understood in terms of models and other approaches, such as statistical studies.

Geostatistics has played an important role in quantifying a wide range of geological processes. The Gaussian (normal) and Poisson distributions are applicable to truly random processes. Log-normal distributions have also been applied in geology; for example, to the distributions of particle sizes, thicknesses of stratigraphic units, and to mineral and petroleum reserves. A wide variety of other statistical distributions have also been used on a strictly empirical basis.

Analytic and numerical solutions to partial differential equations have been used to explain many observations in physics. In many ways, physics is a much simpler (less complex) subject

Turcotte, D.L., 2006, Modeling geocomplexity: "A new kind of science," *in* Manduca, C.A., and Mogk, D.W., eds., Earth and Mind: How Geologists Think and Learn about the Earth: Geological Society of America Special Paper 413, p. 39–50, doi: 10.1130/2006.2413(04). For permission to copy, contact editing@ geosociety.org. ©2006 Geological Society of America. All rights reserved.

than geology. The motions of particles satisfy relatively simple equations, such as Newton's equations of motion. These equations are models, and no one could imagine any introductory physics course without these equations. In the nineteenth century, a variety of models were used to explain the behavior of the solid earth. The wave equation explained the propagation of seismic waves. LaPlace's equation explained variations in surface gravity.

Our understanding of fundamental geological processes was revolutionized by the introduction of the plate tectonic model. This is a simple kinematic model that has a wide range of implications. Today, every introductory textbook in geology incorporates the fundamentals of plate tectonics.

Since the advent of plate tectonics in the late 1960s, many advances have been made in modeling and quantifying geological processes and phenomena. A focus of these studies has been "geodynamics" (Turcotte and Schubert, 2002). A variety of problems has been attacked and solved using classical physics. One example is the half-space cooling model applied to the bathymetry, heat-flow, and gravity anomalies associated with mid-ocean ridges. The hot rock introduced by volcanism at the ridge crest is cooled by conductive heat transport to the seafloor. The cooler rock is more dense and sinks to provide the morphology of ocean ridges. It would clearly be desirable for all undergraduate geology students to learn the fundamentals of elasticity, fluid-mechanics, and heat transfer. Some of this is done in every core course in structural geology and/or tectonics. However, many students who are highly motivated geologists abhor the rigors of partial differential equations, tensor analysis, etc.

It is also true that the deterministic models associated with classical physics cannot address many fundamental problems in geology, as many of these problems have a statistical component. Examples include landforms, river networks, the distributions of mineral deposits and petroleum reservoirs, and the distributions of earthquakes. Problems in this class are said to exhibit "self-organized" complexity. The classic example of self-organized complexity is fluid turbulence. Turbulence is statistical, but it is not strictly random. Turbulence is an example of deterministic chaos. The governing equations yield deterministic solutions, but these solutions are unstable to small deviations, so that the results are not predictable. A consequence is that the weather can be forecast only on a statistical basis.

A new approach to a variety of geological problems has evolved from the fundamental concepts of self-organized complexity. Many of these concepts were developed in the geological sciences in general, and in geology in particular. The first is the concept of fractals developed by Mandelbrot (1967) to explain the length of a rocky coastline. It became clear immediately that other examples of fractality included the Horton-Strahler classification of drainage networks and the Guttenberg-Richter frequency-magnitude relation for earthquakes.

The second fundamental concept in self-organized complexity is deterministic chaos. Lorenz (1963) discovered deterministic chaos while studying a simple model for thermal convection

in a fluid, the Lorenz equations. Solutions to these equations were extremely sensitive to initial conditions. Thus, the behavior of the equations was not "predictable." Only "statistical forecasts" could be made. It was then recognized that fluid turbulence is a direct consequence of deterministic chaos. The equations that govern the behavior of a fluid are well known, the Navier-Stoker equations. But fluid turbulence is a statistical phenomena consisting of fluid swirls and eddies over a wide range of scales.

A second simple model that exhibits deterministic chaos is a pair of slider blocks. If a single slider block is pulled along a surface with a spring, the frictional interaction with the surface will result in periodic slip events. These events are predictable and resemble regularly spaced earthquakes on a fault. But if two slider blocks connected with a spring are pulled along a surface with two other springs, the result can be chaotic. Although the governing equations can be specified, the frictional interactions with the surface result in deterministic chaos. The behavior of the system is not predictable. The conclusion is that tectonics and seismicity are also chaotic and therefore are not predictable in a deterministic sense. Only statistical forecasts for the occurrence of earthquakes are possible, as is the case for weather.

Although the concept of deterministic chaos was introduced in 1963 prior to the introduction of the fractal concept in 1967, the applicability of deterministic chaos to natural complex phenomena was widely questioned. The original studies of chaos were limited to "low-order" systems, the behavior of the systems was complex, but the systems themselves were not.

The third fundamental concept in self-organized complexity is self-organized criticality (SOC). Bak et al. (1988) introduced the concept in order to explain the behavior of a simple cellular automata (CA) model. In this model, a square array of boxes is considered. Particles are dropped into randomly selected boxes until a box has four particles, these particles are moved to the four adjacent boxes or are lost from the array in the case of edge blocks. Multiple redistributions often result and are referred to as "avalanches." The frequency-area distribution of avalanches is fractal. This is referred to as a cellular automata (CA) model because it consists of an array of cells (boxes) and only nearest neighbor cells (boxes) interact according to a well-defined "automata" rule, the redistribution rule.

Another simple CA model that exhibits SOC behavior is the multiple slider-block model (Carlson and Langer, 1989). Instead of the two connected slider blocks, a large array of connected slider blocks is considered. It was found that the frequency-area distribution of slip events was fractal. The progression from a pair of slider blocks that exhibited low-order deterministic chaos to a large array of slider blocks that exhibited SOC and fractal behavior related the concepts of chaos and fractality to complex systems, i.e., self-organized complexity.

Models that exhibit self-organized complexity utilize computer-based simulations. Two examples have already been given and will be considered in more detail in a later section. I will argue that the introduction of some of these simulations into undergraduate geology courses is not only possible but is also very desirable. They are basically computer games and can be very illustrative of fundamental processes in geology. Simulations that exhibit self-organized critical behavior are examples of the use of cellular automata (CA). Stephen Wolfram's recent book, *A New Kind of Science* (Wolfram, 2002), argues that CA simulations, broadly interpreted, will lead to a new scientific revolution. Topics addressed include general relativity, computability, turbulence, genetic coding, and many others. This book is a bestseller, but is also extremely controversial. There is no absolute definition of a CA model. It must be a discretized system, i.e., a one-, two-, three-, or higher-dimensional grid of points. In many applications, a square grid of points is considered. Usually, but not always, interactions are only with nearest neighbors.

FRACTALITY

The concept of fractals was introduced by Mandelbrot (1967) to quantify the length of a rocky coastline. Fractality implies the applicability of a fractal distribution

$$N \sim r^{-D}, \tag{1}$$

where N is the number of objects with a linear dimension greater than r, and D is the fractal dimension (Mandelbrot, 1982; Feder, 1988). Thus, as the size of the representative object decreases, a power-law increase in the number of objects of that size is found. Many distributions in geology satisfy this relation, examples include fragmented rocks, planetary craters, faults and joints, earthquakes, and drainage networks (Korvin, 1992; Turcotte, 1997). The applicability of a fractal distribution implies "scale invariance"; it is the only statistical distribution that is scale invariant. In other words, no characteristic length scale is needed to constrain a power-law (fractal) distribution; it applies regardless of the base unit in which r is measured. The near-universal applicability of scale invariance in geology explains the requirement that an object with a well-defined scale must be included in most geological photographs. Courses in fractality are given at many high schools, and they are often popular even with students who dislike mathematical subjects such as trigonometry and geometry. A simple way to illustrate fractality in an introductory geology laboratory is to measure the length of a closed contour on a topographic map using a fixed-length divider. In general, a plot of the number of divider steps versus the divider length satisfies equation 1.

DETERMINISTIC CHAOS

The concepts associated with deterministic chaos are very popular with students; these were set forth by Gleick (1987), Mullin (1993), and Peak and Frame (1994). Lorenz (1963) discovered deterministic chaos while studying a set of three total differential equations applicable to thermal convection. Solutions to these equations exhibit extreme sensitivity to initial conditions—their temporal evolution is not predictable. Subsequently, many other sets of nonlinear differential equations have been found to exhibit this behavior. Mantle convection and convection in Earth's core are certainly examples of chaotic convection.

From a student's point of view, the best illustration of deterministic chaos comes from the study of simple recursive formulas (maps). May (1976) showed that the logistic map illustrates all aspects of deterministic chaos very simply. The logistic map is defined by the recursion relation

$$x_{n+1} = ax_n(1 - x_n). \tag{2}$$

First, the value of the constant a must be specified. Then an initial value of x_n, designated x_0, is specified. Substitution of $x_n = x_0$ into equation 2 gives x_1; the next substitution of $x_n = x_1$ into equation 2 gives x_2, and so forth. The extreme sensitivity of solutions to initial conditions is illustrated by the following example. Take $a = 4$ and $x_0 = 0.8$, and, using equation 2, we find $x_1 = 0.64$. Using this value for x_n in equation 2, we find $x_2 = 0.9216$. After three further iterations, we find $x_5 = 0.585$. Now repeat the process taking $a = 4$ and $x_0 = 0.81$. After five iterations, we find $x_5 = 0.915...$ The initial values (0.81 and 0.80) differ by 1.25%, while the values after five iterations (0.585 and 0.915) differ by 56%. This is an illustration of the extreme sensitivity to initial conditions exhibited by deterministic chaos. Weather and seismicity are natural examples of deterministic chaos. Neither is predictable in a deterministic sense—only probabilistic forecasts can be made.

SELF-ORGANIZED CRITICALITY

The concept of self-organized criticality (SOC) (Bak, 1996; Jensen, 1998; Turcotte, 1999) was introduced by Bak et al. (1988) to explain the behavior of a simple CA model. In this model, a square array of boxes is considered. A simple example with four boxes (numbered 1–4) is shown in Figure 1. Particles are randomly dropped into the boxes. In our initial state, Figure 1A, we have two particles in box 1, three particles in box 2, one particle in box 3, and three particles in box 4. If a particle is dropped into a box with two or fewer particles, it remains in the box. However, if the randomly selected box already contains three particles, it becomes unstable, and the four particles are evenly redistributed to the four neighboring boxes. In this example, box 4 is randomly selected for the addition of a particle as shown in Figure 1B. Since the box already holds three other particles, a redistribution of the four particles is required as shown in Figure 1C. The resulting redistribution is illustrated in Figure 1D. In this state, there are now two particles in box 1, four particles in box 2, two particles in box 3, and zero particles in box 4. Two particles have been lost from the grid. Since there are now four particles in box 2, a second redistribution of particles is required as shown in Figure 1E. This redistribution of particles is illustrated in Figure 1F. There are now three particles in box 1, zero particles in box 2, two particles in box 3, and one particle in box 4. Another two particles have been lost from the grid.

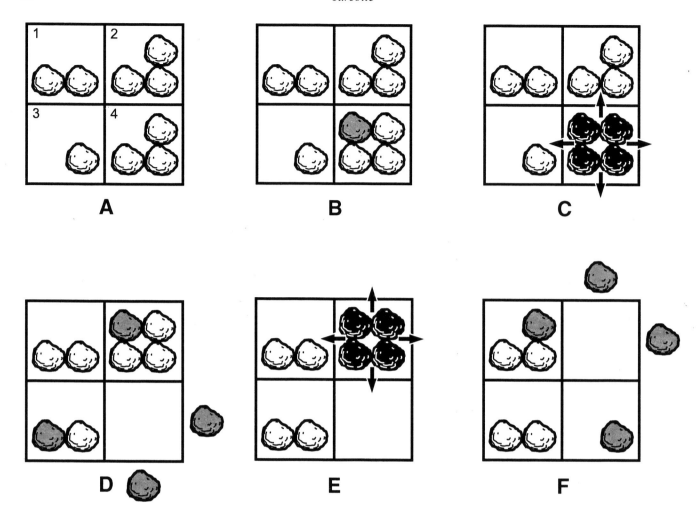

Figure 1. Illustration of the sand-pile model. Four boxes (numbered 1–4) are considered; the initial distribution of particles is given in (A). One of these boxes is selected at random, in this case box 4, and a particle is dropped into this box. As shown in (C), this box is now unstable, and the four particles are redistributed in (D). Two particles are redistributed to the adjacent boxes 2 and 3, and two particles are lost from the grid. Following this redistribution, box 2 is unstable (see E), and the four particles in this box must be redistributed as shown in (F). Two particles are redistributed to the adjacent boxes 1 and 4, and two particles are lost from the grid.

Multiple, or chain-reaction, redistributions are referred to as avalanches. Simulations with large numbers of boxes have shown that the number-area distribution of avalanches is fractal and satisfies equation 1. The area A of an avalanche, which is the number of boxes that participate in the multiple redistributions, determines the value of r in equation 1 via the relation $r = \sqrt{A}$. For this model, it is found that $D \approx 2$. Since only nearest-neighbor boxes are involved in each redistribution, this is a CA model. This model is referred to as a sand-pile model because of the relationship to the behavior of a pile of sand on a square table when individual grains of sand are added to the pile.

A simple demonstration of this behavior uses a cylindrical glass or plastic tube. The tube is half-filled with sand, glass beads, or rice and is rolled on a surface. When the flat sand surface reaches the "angle of repose," ~30°, avalanches of various sizes occur to maintain the angle. A number of published studies

have shown that in some cases a fractal distribution of laboratory avalanches is found (Nagel, 1992).

Naturally occurring avalanches are also found to satisfy fractal frequency-area statistics. It has been demonstrated convincingly that the frequency-area distribution of large landslides is fractal and satisfies equation 1 (Malamud et al., 2004). The metastable area over which a landslide spreads once triggered is analogous to the metastable region over which an avalanche spreads in the sand-pile model due to multiple redistributions. The behavior of the sand-pile model has also been associated with the fractal distribution of turbidite deposits (Rothman et al., 1994).

A second CA model that exhibits SOC is the forest-fire model (Drossel and Schwabl, 1992). In this model, a square grid of sites is considered. Each site may or may not have a tree on it (like a partially planted orchard). A simple example with 16 sites (numbered 1–16) is shown in Figure 2. Trees and matches are randomly dropped on sites. If a tree is dropped on an unoccupied (treeless) site, it is planted there. If a match is dropped on an occupied site, the tree at that site "burns." Any tree at a site adjacent to a burning tree also burns. In this way, a model forest fire spreads from site to site until no burning tree is adjacent to a nonburning tree. After the forest fire has spread to its maximum extent, any site that holds a burning tree becomes unoccupied. (The affected trees burn completely away.)

In our initial state, Figure 2A, trees are planted on sites 1, 2, 8, 9, 10, and 13. At the next step, site 15 is randomly selected, and a tree is planted at that site as shown in Figure 2B. In subsequent steps, trees are randomly planted at site 4, as illustrated in Figure 2C, and at site 5, as illustrated in Figure 2D. The tree

planted at site 5 joins a cluster of two trees and a cluster of three trees into a single cluster of six adjacent trees. At the next step, shown in Figure 2E, site 10 is randomly selected and receives a dropped match. The tree on this site ignites, and the model fire spreads through the entire six-tree cluster (sites 1, 2, 5, 9, 10, and 13), clearing those sites. The state of the model after the fire has occurred is illustrated in Figure 2F.

Simulations with large numbers of sites have shown that the number-area distribution of model fires is fractal and satisfies equation 1. The area A of a model fire, which is defined to be the number of sites on which the model trees burn, determines the value of r in equation 1 via the relation $r = \sqrt{A}$. Just as in the case of the sand-pile model, it is found that $D \approx 2$. Again, this is a CA model, since fires spread to nearest-neighbor trees. Malamud

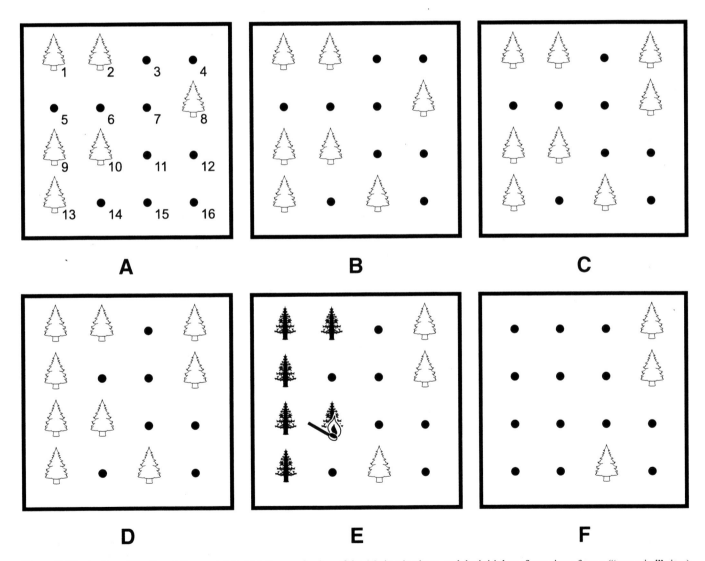

Figure 2. Illustration of the forest-fire model. In (A), the numbering of the 16 sites is given, and the initial configuration of trees ("occupied" sites) is shown. One of the unoccupied sites is selected at random, and a tree is planted on the site. In (B), (C), and (D), new trees are planted on sites 15, 4, and 5, respectively. After a specified number of tree plantings, a match is dropped on a randomly selected occupied site. The match starts a fire on that site, and the fire spreads to all adjacent occupied sites, also burning those trees. A match is dropped on site 10 in (E), and the fire spreads to five adjacent occupied sites. The burned (black) trees are removed from the grid, and the configuration after the model fire is given in (F).

et al. (1998) have shown that the frequency-area distribution of actual forest fires is fractal and satisfies equation 1.

A third CA model that exhibits SOC is the slider-block model (Carlson and Langer, 1989). This model is illustrated in Figure 3. A square array of blocks, each with mass m, is pulled across a surface by a driver plate moving at a constant speed v. The blocks are connected to the driver plate by leaf springs that have spring constant k_p. Each block is connected to its neighboring blocks by leaf or coil springs that have spring constant k_c. The blocks interact with the surface through friction, and the simplest friction law is the static-dynamic law: If the block is stationary (static), the frictional force has a maximum value F_S. If the block is slipping, the frictional force has the dynamic value F_D.

If the static value F_S is greater than the dynamic value F_D, the blocks exhibit "stick-slip behavior": A block is stationary until the force exerted by the puller spring increases the net force on the block to a value equal to F_S. At this point, the block begins to slip, and, as a result, transfers force to the adjacent blocks through the connector springs. These forces may cause one or more of the adjacent blocks to slip as well. The slip event can grow in much the same way that an avalanche grows in the sand-pile model or a forest fire spreads in the forest-fire model.

Once again, simulations with large numbers of blocks have shown that the number-area distribution of slip events is fractal and satisfies equation 1. The area A of a slip event, which is the number of blocks that slip during the event, once again determines r via $r = \sqrt{A}$. Also, as before, it is found that $D \approx 2$.

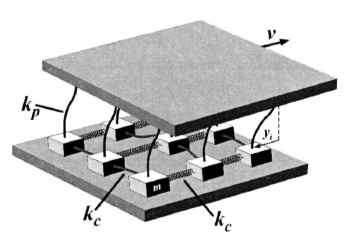

Figure 3. Illustration of the slider-block model. Blocks of mass m rest upon the lower plate (the "surface") and are attached to the upper plate (the "driver") by leaf springs (the "pullers") with spring constant k_p. Each block is also connected to its nearest neighboring blocks by either coil or leaf springs with spring constant k_c. The linear displacement y_i of each block (relative to the upper plate) is monitored over time. As the upper plate moves at velocity v with respect to the lower plate, the blocks exhibit stick-slip behavior due to the frictional interaction with the lower plate. The slip events have a fractal distribution of sizes similar to the model avalanches associated with the sand-pile model (Fig. 1) and the model forest fires associated with the forest-fire model (Fig. 2).

Slider-block models are simple analogs for repetitive earthquakes on faults (Burridge and Knopoff, 1967). Under almost all circumstances, the number N of earthquakes with magnitudes greater than M that occur in a region satisfies the Guttenberg-Richter relation

$$\log N = a - bM, \tag{3}$$

where a and b are constants. However, the earthquake magnitude M is related to the rupture area A by

$$M = \log A + c, \tag{4}$$

where c is another constant. Combining equations 3 and 4 gives

$$N = 10^{a-bc}A^{-b}. \tag{5}$$

This relation is entirely equivalent to equation 1 with a fractal dimension $D \approx 2b$. Thus, earthquakes also obey a universal fractal frequency-area distribution.

Frequency-area distributions have important practical applications. For example, the Guttenberg-Richter relation given in equation 3 is used to estimate the seismic hazard in a region. In southern California, which is seismically quite active, there are on average about ten $M = 4$ earthquakes per year. Since it is observed that $b \approx 1$ for active regions, Guttenberg-Richter extrapolates that southern California will experience one $M = 5$ earthquake each year and one $M = 6$ earthquake every ten years.

A NEW KIND OF SCIENCE

Geological problems have played an essential role in the development of a number of aspects of complexity. The concept of SOC evolved from a number of simple CA models, three of which were the sand-pile, forest-fire, and slider-block models considered in the previous section. These three models behave in remarkably similar ways. While the sand-pile and forest-fire models are stochastic (i.e., involve random selection processes), the slider-block model is completely deterministic (i.e., nonrandom).

In *A New Kind of Science*, Wolfram (2002) introduced the principle of computational equivalence. This principle implies that some fundamental problems share a basic equivalence that leads to universal behavior patterns such as those exhibited by SOC. To explore this principle, Wolfram illustrates the complexities that can be generated using a simple one-dimensional (one-row) CA model. An example of such a CA model over a progression of time steps is illustrated in Figure 4A. At every time step, each cell is either black or white. The color of each cell at the next time step is determined by a set of rules based on the cell's current color and the current colors of its two neighboring cells. In our example, we have a fifteen-cell row, and only cell x_8 is black at initial time step t_1. This model's eight required rules, illustrated in Figure 4B, specify the future cell color generated by each of the eight possible permutations of black and white cells.

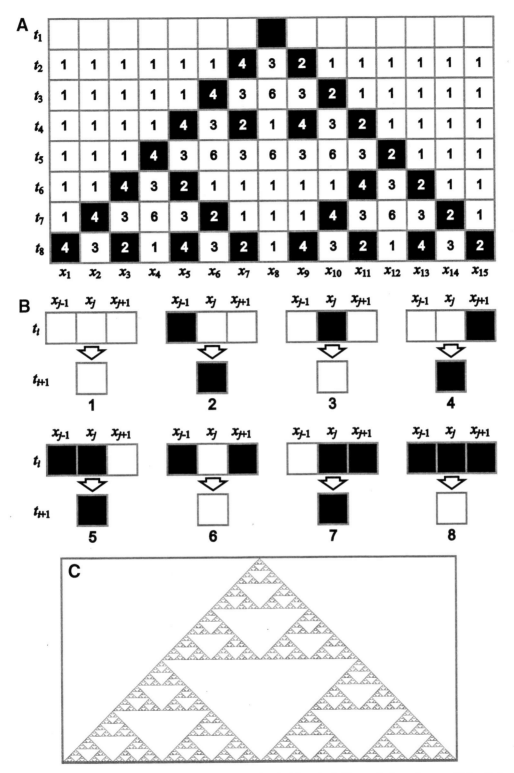

Figure 4. (A) A cellular automaton that generates a perfect fractal (the Sierpinski gasket). The evolution of a row of 15 cells (x_1, ..., x_{15}) over eight time steps (t_1, ..., t_8) is shown. For a given time step, each cell is either black or white. The color of a cell and the colors of its nearest neighbors determine the cell's color in the next time step. This determination is made according to the rule set illustrated in (B). The rule set enumerates the eight possible configurations of colors for a cell x_j, its left neighbor x_{j-1}, and its right neighbor x_{j+1} during a single time step t_i. Each configuration specifies either a black or white color for x_j at the next time step t_{i+1}. The number inside each cell in (A) indicates which of the eight configurations in (B) determined the cell's color. Note that "edge" cells are assumed to border white cells. The structure of the black and white cells in (A) is a perfect fractal construction known as a Sierpinski gasket. In (C), the CA construction given in (A) is extended to 1023 cells over 512 time steps. The fractal pattern is sharply defined at this resolution.

These rules are best understood by a specific example. Consider time step t_2 for cell x_8 in Figure 4A. At time step t_1, cell x_8 was black, and both of its neighbors, cells x_7 and x_9, were white. Looking at the rule set in Figure 4B, we see that the pattern white-black-white corresponds to rule 3. We also see that rule 3 turns the center cell white during the next time step. Thus, in Figure 4A, cell x_8 turns white at t_2. Similarly, at time step t_1, rule 4 applies to cell x_7 (and its neighbors), so cell x_7 is black at t_2. At time step t_1, rule 2 applies to cell x_9, so cell x_9 is also black at t_2. Rule 1 is applicable to the remaining cells at time step t_1, so all of them are white. Note that cells at the left and right edges are assumed to border white cells. The numbers of the applicable rules for time steps t_2 through t_8 are given for each cell in Figure 4A.

A distinct, two-dimensional pattern of black squares is formed when successive iterations of this cellular automaton are pictured "stacked" on top of one another as they are in Figure 4A. This pattern is a well-known fractal called a Sierpinski gasket. The Sierpinski gasket consists of triangular patterns of different sizes (called orders). The three black squares in time steps t_1 and t_2 are arranged in the fundamental (first-order) pattern. In time steps t_1 through t_4, three instances of the first-order pattern are arranged (triangularly) to form the second-order pattern. (In a sense, each black square in the first-order pattern is replaced by an entire first-order pattern.) The second-order pattern, plainly, consists of nine black squares. Similarly, three instances of the second-order pattern are arranged to form a third-order pattern in time steps t_1 through t_8. The third-order pattern is an arrangement of 27 black squares, or nine first-order patterns.

We now use equation 1 to calculate the fractal dimension of the Sierpinski gasket. For a pattern of a particular order n, the linear dimension r_n is defined to be the number of time steps spanned by the pattern (this span is labeled Δt). N_n is the total number of times the nth-order pattern appears in the entire figure. For the first-order pattern, we have $r_1 = 2$ (because $\Delta t_{n=1} = [t_1, t_2]$) and $N_1 = 9$ (the three-square first-order pattern appears 9 times). For the second-order pattern, we have $r_2 = 4$ ($\Delta t_{n=2} = [t_1, t_2, t_3, t_4]$) and $N_2 = 3$. For the third-order pattern, we have $r_3 = 8$ ($\Delta t_{n=3} = [t_1, \ldots, t_8]$) and $N_3 = 1$. (We may also define a single black square to be a 'zero'-order pattern with $r_0 = 1$ and $N_0 = 27$.) By manipulating equation 1, we can use the N_n and r_n values for two different pattern orders (i.e., two different values of n) to solve for the fractal dimension D of the Sierpinski gasket. We arbitrarily choose the first- and second-order patterns (i.e., $n = 1$ and $n = 2$) to get

$$D = \frac{\log(N_2 / N_1)}{\log(r_1 / r_2)}. \tag{6}$$

With the chosen values, equation 6 yields D=log(3)/log(2)≈1.585 for the Sierpinski gasket.

This fractal construction can be extended for very large rows of cells over very large numbers of time steps, and the fractal pattern will remain. Figure 4C shows the iteration of a row of 1023 cells over 512 time steps. In the initial time step, only cell 512 is black, and subsequent cell colors are chosen using the rules in Figure 4B. The Sierpinski gasket is a fantastic visual aid for the classroom because its clear depiction of scaling allows students to literally see fractal structure.

It should be noted that there are 256 distinct rule sets of the form laid out in Figure 4B. They differ in whether each rule generates a white or black cell in the next time step. The complexity of the applications of these sets is given in chapter 3 of Wolfram (2002), where the rule set illustrated in our Figure 4 is labeled "Rule 90." Wolfram (2002) goes on to relate the concepts of CA models to computational universality and a wide range of problems in mathematics, the physical, biological, and social sciences, philosophy, art, and technology. However, we will now return to applications of CA models to geological problems.

TOPOGRAPHY AND DRAINAGE NETWORKS

Topography and the associated drainage networks are examples of self-organized complexity in geology. We will first consider drainage networks (Rodriguez-Iturbe and Rinaldo, 1997). The fractal nature of drainage networks was recognized by Horton (1945) and Strahler (1957), long before the concept of fractals was introduced by Mandelbrot (1967). A typical drainage network is given in Figure 5A, and the stream ordering system is illustrated in Figure 5B. A stream with no upstream tributaries is a first-order stream. When two first-order streams combine, they form a second-order stream. When two second-order streams combine, they form a third-order stream, and so forth. When streams of unequal orders combine, the stream remains a stream of the higher of the two orders.

Horton (1945) introduced two scaling relations for river networks. The first is the bifurcation ratio R_b, defined for a particular drainage basin as the ratio of the number N_n of streams of order n to the number N_{n+1} of streams of order $n + 1$,

$$R_b = \frac{N_n}{N_{n+1}}. \tag{7}$$

The second relation is the length-order ratio R_r, defined for a particular drainage basin as the ratio of the mean length r_{n+1} of streams of order $n + 1$ to the mean length r_n of streams of order n,

$$R_r = \frac{r_{n+1}}{r_n}. \tag{8}$$

For a given drainage basin, R_b and R_r are found to be near constant over a range of stream orders. From equations 6, 7, and 8, the fractal dimension D of the drainage basin is defined by the relation

$$D = \frac{\ln(N_n / N_{n+1})}{\ln(r_{n+1} / r_n)} = \frac{\ln R_b}{\ln R_r} \tag{9}$$

Drainage basins typically satisfy fractal scaling with a fractal dimension $D \approx 1.8$ (Pelletier, 1999). A student can easily determine the orders of the streams in Figure 5A. Using the numbers of streams of each order N_1, N_1, N_2, ..., N_5, four values of the bifurcation ratio R_b can be obtained from equation 7. It will be seen that these values are nearly equal. Other drainage networks

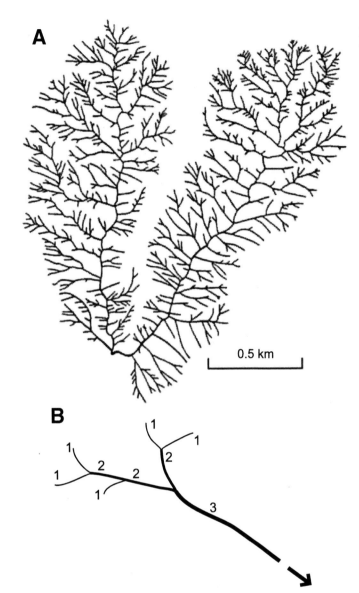

A

B

Figure 5. (A) A typical drainage network in a mountainous region. The scale is shown. Drainage networks can be obtained directly from topographic maps. (B) Illustration of the Strahler (1957) stream-ordering system. The initial streams are first order, two first-order streams merge to give a second-order stream, and so forth.

on which to carry out this exercise can be obtained by tracing them from topographic maps.

A simple CA model that generates self-similar networks is the diffusion-limited aggregation (DLA) model (Witten and Sander, 1981). In this model, a square grid of sites is considered. A seed particle is introduced at the center of the grid, and it remains in place. Moving particles are added at randomly selected sites on the boundaries of the square grid. These particles follow a random walk until either (1) the particle goes off the grid and is lost or (2) moves to a site adjacent to the growing cluster and sticks to the cluster. In a random walk, one of the four adjacent sites is selected randomly, and the particle is moved to that site. A typical DLA network (cluster) is illustrated in Figure 6A. The bifurcation ratios and length-order ratios defined in equations 7 and 8 are also found to be constant to a good approximation. Thus, DLA networks are fractal, and, by using equation 9, it has been found that $D \approx 1.56$, a value somewhat less than those of drainage networks. DLA models have been applied to understand a variety of dendritic growth patterns in igneous rocks and other minerals (Fowler, 1990).

A modification of the this DLA model does produce networks that are statistically identical to drainage networks (Masek and Turcotte, 1993). Again, a square grid of sites is considered. A number of seed particles are placed along one or more boundaries of a square region. Additional particles are added to randomly selected unoccupied sites in the interior of the grid. The particles are allowed to randomly "walk" through the grid until they reach a site adjacent to the growing network. An example of this procedure is illustrated in Figure 6B. The growth of the network is closely analogous to the headward migration of an evolving drainage network. Such a network is fractal, typically with $D \approx 1.85$.

We next examine topography along a linear, or one-dimensional, track. Let us say you are in a mountainous area. You start at a specified starting point and walk north in a straight line and record the changes in elevation relative to the starting point at equally spaced intervals, say every hundred meters. You then return to the starting point and repeat the procedure in the east, south, and west directions. The question is whether the changes in elevation are predictable, at least in a statistical sense. Of course the same data could be collected using a topographic map with much less effort.

In order to answer the question, it is necessary to introduce the concepts of a Gaussian "white noise" and a Brownian walk. Consider equally spaced points along the x-axis $x_1, x_2, x_3, \ldots x_n$. At each point a y value, $y_1, y_2, y_3, \ldots y_n$ is selected randomly from a Gaussian distribution of values. The sequence of y values is a Gaussian white noise. Adjacent points in the sequence are uncorrelated. The mean

$$\bar{y} = \frac{1}{n}(y_1 + y_2 + y_3 + \cdots + y_n),\qquad(10)$$

and standard deviation δ

$$\delta = \left[\frac{1}{n}\left[\left(y_1 - \bar{y}\right)^2 + \left(y_2 - \bar{y}\right)^2 + \left(y_3 - \bar{y}\right)^2 + \cdots + \left(y_n - \bar{y}\right)^2 \right] \right]^{\frac{1}{2}}, (11)$$

of the sequence are equal to the values for the initial Gaussian distribution.

A Brownian walk is the running sum of a Gaussian white noise. From the sequence of values $y_1, y_2, y_3, \ldots y_n$, we write $z_1 = y_1, z_2 = z_1 + y_2, z_3 = z_2 + y_3, \ldots$. A plot of these z values against x is a Brownian walk. A Brownian walk exhibits a drift. Starting out at the same point, a number of Brownian walks are carried out. The standard deviation of the values δ at a distance L from the starting point is determined using equation 11, and it is found that

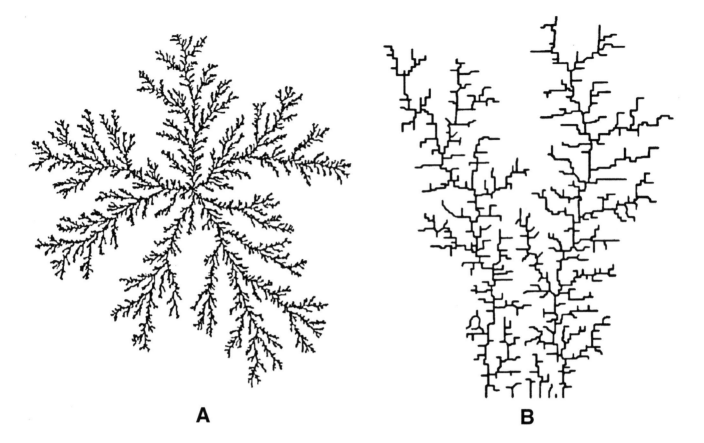

Figure 6. (A) Illustration of a typical diffusion-limited aggregation (DLA) network. The growing network started with a single seed particle at the center. The network grew by the addition of particles that followed a random-walk path until they "stuck" to the growing network. (B) Illustration of a synthetic drainage network obtained by a modification of the DLA model. Seven seed particles were placed on the lower boundary of the region. Particles were introduced at randomly selected sites within the region. These particles followed random-walk paths until they "stuck" to the growing network. The network grew from the lower boundary upward in direct analogy to the headward migration of an actual drainage network.

$$\delta(L) = C\sqrt{L} \,. \qquad (12)$$

The standard deviation of the walk increases as the square root of the length of the path from the origin.

The changes in elevation as a function of the distance from a starting point as discussed in the previous example are well approximated by a Brownian walk (Ahnert, 1984). Students can easily demonstrate this by obtaining a histogram of the changes in elevation along a series of linear tracks of length L from a common starting point in a mountainous region from a topographic map. The standard deviation of the histogram is obtained using equation 11, and the results will be well approximated by equation 12. The derived constant C is a measure of the roughness of the topography.

A simple CA model for deposition also gives this behavior (Pelletier and Turcotte, 1997). Consider a linear set of sites on which "particles" are randomly dropped. If the randomly selected site on which a particle falls is lower (has fewer "particles") than its adjacent sites, the particle remains there. If either

adjacent site is lower, the particle is moved to that site. The rules for this model are illustrated in Figure 7A, while the results of a simulation using this model are given in Figure 7B. In the latter figure, the numbers of particles (heights) are given for the 1024 sites on a linear track. The end result is entirely equivalent to elevations along a linear track. The sequence of the elevations (number of particles on each site) is a Brownian walk—the average difference in elevation Δh between two points is related to the distance L between the two points by equation 12. Again, this is a very simple model that students can analyze. This analysis is also applicable to the temporal variability of sandy coastlines. The seaward migration and recession of a sandy coastline is well approximated by a Brownian walk (Tebbens et al., 2002).

DISCUSSION

A major objective of any geology curriculum must be to provide students with the best understanding of geological phenomena possible under the circumstances. The major point of this

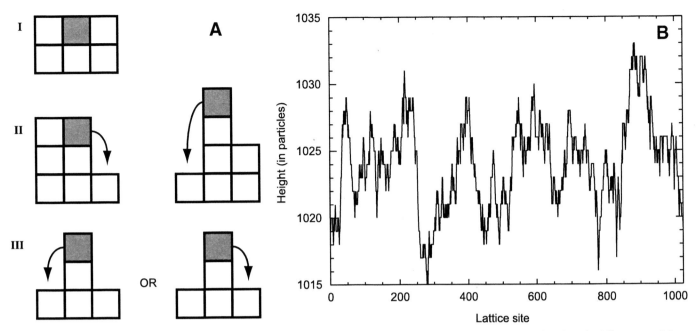

Figure 7. Illustration of the behavior of a simple cellular automata (CA) model for deposition along a one-dimensional track. A linear set of sites is considered, and a particle (square box) is dropped on a randomly selected site. (A) The CA rules are illustrated. After the particle (highlighted in gray) has dropped on a randomly selected site, it either remains on that site or is moved to an adjacent site according to the rules: (I) A particle dropped on a site lower than both neighboring sites stays. (II) A particle dropped on a site higher than at least one neighboring site migrates to the lower neighboring site. (III) Special case of (II) in which both neighboring sites have the same elevation. The particle migrates to a randomly selected neighboring site. (B) Synthetic topography (linear elevation plot) generated using this model. Particles have been dropped on 1024 sites. On average 1022 particles have been dropped on each site. The number of particles is analogous to height (elevation), and the lattice site number is analogous to horizontal distance. The horizontal variability is a Brownian walk.

paper is that the fundamental aspects of complexity are accessible to a wide range of students and that the fundamentals of complexity do provide a basic understanding of many geological observations.

The wide accessibility of high-speed desk-top and lap-top computers allows any student to carry out quite sophisticated numerical simulations. The class of numerical simulations referred to as cellular automata are basically computer games. The results obtained playing these games can be applicable to a wide range of geological phenomena.

Studies of complexity are "a new kind of science." Details for the use of cellular automata simulations in order to understand complexity in a variety of fields have been given by Wolfram (2002).

The first step toward the new science was the appreciation of the importance of fractal distributions. The concept of fractals evolved in a geological context—the length of a rocky coastline (Mandelbrot, 1967). The continuous fractal distribution given by equation 1 is not a true statistical distribution because its integral diverges to infinity. For this reason, fractal distributions are not included in courses in statistics. However, fractal distributions are essential to the understanding of many geological phenomena, such as drainage networks, landforms, and earthquakes. Fractal distributions are more widely applicable in geology than standard statistical distributions, such as the Gaussian (normal) or log-normal.

This is direct evidence that many geological observations are the consequence of self-organized complex processes such as those illustrated by simple CA simulations. It should also be emphasized that when applying fractal distributions to geological data, there are always upper and lower limits to the applicability. In terms of streams and rivers, there is always a shortest stream and longest river.

The discovery of chaos by Lorenz (1963) preceded the introduction of the fractal concept by Mandelbrot (1967). The role of deterministic chaos is certainly important in the "new" kind of science, but only with the discovery of SOC by Bak et al. (1988) did this role become clear. This evolution is clearly shown by the behavior of the slider-block model illustrated in Figure 3. A single slider block is a typical model in the "old" kind of science. A single block pulled by a spring exhibits simple harmonic motion, and periodic slip events occur. A pair of slider blocks connected to each other and to a constant velocity driver plate by springs exhibits classic deterministic chaos (Huang and Turcotte, 1990). The future behavior of the blocks is not predictable. Large numbers of connected slider blocks, on the other hand, exhibit SOC. Slip events have a fractal frequency-size distribution that is directly analogous to seismicity in a region. The association of chaos and SOC with seismicity has been interpreted as precluding earthquake prediction (Geller et al., 1997).

The basic theme of this paper is that: (1) there are many data sets in geology that exhibit fractal behavior, (2) this behavior cannot in general be obtained from the solutions of the standard partial differential equations or from standard statistical studies, and (3) in many cases, this behavior can be obtained using simple CA models. This theme is very similar to the theme set forth by Stephen Wolfram in his book, *A New Kind of Science* (2002).

ACKNOWLEDGMENTS

The author would like to thank Paul B. Rundle for his help in finalizing this paper.

REFERENCES CITED

Ahnert, F., 1984, Local relief and the height limits of mountain ranges: American Journal of Science, v. 284, p. 1035–1055.

Bak, P., 1996, How nature works: The science of self-organized criticality, New York, Copernicus, 212 p.

Bak, P., Tang, C., and Wiesenfeld, K., 1988, Self-organized criticality: Physical Review, v. A38, p. 364–374.

Burridge, R., and Knopoff, L., 1967, Model and theoretical seismicity: Bulletin of the Seismological Society of America, v. 57, p. 341–371.

Carlson, J.M., and Langer, J.S., 1989, Mechanical model of an earthquake fault: Physical Review, v. A40, p. 6470–6484.

Drossel, B., and Schwabl, F., 1992, Self-organized critical forest-fire model: Physical Review Letters, v. 69, p. 1629–1632, doi: 10.1103/PhysRevLett.69.1629.

Feder, J., 1988, Fractals: New York, Plenum Press, 283 p.

Fowler, A.D., 1990, Self-organized mineral textures of igneous rocks: The fractal approach: Earth-Science Reviews, v. 29, p. 47–55, doi: 10.1016/0012-8252(90)90027-S.

Geller, R.J., Jackson, D.D., Kagan, Y.Y., and Mulargia, F., 1997, Earthquakes cannot be predicted: Science, v. 275, p. 1616–1617, doi: 10.1126/science.275.5306.1616.

Gleick, J., 1987, Chaos: Making a new science: New York, Penguin, 352 p.

Horton, R.E., 1945, Erosional development of streams and their drainage basins; hydrophysical approach to quantitative morphology: Geological Society of America Bulletin, v. 56, p. 275–370.

Huang, J., and Turcotte, D.L., 1990, Are earthquakes an example of deterministic chaos?: Geophysical Research Letters, v. 17, p. 223–226.

Jensen, H.J., 1998, Self-organized criticality: Emergent complex behavior in physical and biological sciences: Cambridge, Cambridge University Press, 153 p.

Korvin, G., 1992, Fractal models in the earth sciences: Amsterdam, Elsevier, 396 p..

Lorenz, E.N., 1963, Deterministic nonperiodic flow: Journal of Atmospheric Sciences, v. 20, p. 130–141, doi: 10.1175/1520-0469(1963)020<0130:DNF>2.0.CO;2.

Malamud, B.D., Morein, G., and Turcotte, D.L., 1998, Forest fires: An example of self-organized critical behavior: Science, v. 281, p. 1840–1842, doi: 10.1126/science.281.5384.1840.

Malamud, B.D., Turcotte, D.L., Guzzetti, F., and Reichenbach, P., 2004, Landslide inventories and their statistical properties: Earth Surface Processes and Landforms, v. 29, p. 687–711, doi: 10.1002/esp.1064.

Mandelbrot, B., 1967, How long is the coast of Britain? Statistical self-similarity and fractional dimension: Science, v. 156, p. 636–638.

Mandelbrot, B., 1982, The fractal geometry of nature: San Francisco, Freeman, 468 p.

Masek, J.G., and Turcotte, D.L., 1993, A diffusion-limited aggregation model for the evolution of drainage networks: Earth and Planetary Science Letters, v. 119, p. 379–386, doi: 10.1016/0012-821X(93)90145-Y.

May, R.M., 1976, Simple mathematical models with very complicated dynamics: Nature, v. 261, p. 459–467, doi: 10.1038/261459a0.

Mullin, T., ed., 1993, The nature of chaos: Oxford, Oxford University Press, 314 p.

Nagel, S.R., 1992, Instabilities in a sandpile: Reviews of Modern Physics, v. 64, p. 321–325, doi: 10.1103/RevModPhys.64.321.

Peak, D., and Frame, M., 1994, Chaos under control: New York, W.H. Freeman, 408 p.

Pelletier, J.D., 1999, Self-organization and scaling relationships of evolving river networks: Journal of Geophysical Research, v. 104, p. 7359–7375, doi: 10.1029/1998JB900110.

Pelletier, J.D., and Turcotte, D.L., 1997, Synthetic stratigraphy with a stochastic diffusion model of fluvial sedimentation: Journal of Sedimentary Research, v. 67, p. 1060–1067.

Rodriguez-Iturbe, I., and Rinaldo, A., 1997, Fractal river basins: Cambridge, Cambridge University Press, 547 p.

Rothman, D.H., Grotzinger, J.P., and Flemings, P., 1994, Scaling in turbidite deposition: Journal of Sedimentary Petrology, v. A64, p. 59–67.

Strahler, A.N., 1957, Quantitative analysis of watershed geomorphology: American Geophysical Union Transactions, v. 38, p. 913–920.

Tebbens, S.F., Burroughs, S.M., and Nelson, E.E., 2002, Wavelet analysis of shoreline change on the Outer Banks of North Carolina: An example of complexity in the marine sciences: Proceedings of the National Academy of Sciences of the United States of America, v. 99, p. 2554–2560, doi: 10.1073/pnas.012582699.

Turcotte, D.L., 1997, Fractals and chaos in geology and geophysics (2nd edition): Cambridge, Cambridge University Press, 398 p.

Turcotte, D.L., 1999, Self organized criticality: Reports on Progress in Physics, v. 62, p. 1377–1429, doi: 10.1088/0034-4885/62/10/201.

Turcotte, D.L., and Schubert, G., 2002, Geodynamics (2nd edition): Cambridge, Cambridge University Press, 456 p.

Witten, T.A., and Sander, L.M., 1981, Diffusion-limited aggregation, a kinetic critical phenomenon: Physical Review Letters, v. 47, p. 1400–1403, doi: 10.1103/PhysRevLett.47.1400.

Wolfram, S., 2002, A new kind of science: Champaign, Wolfram Media, 1197 p.

Manuscript Accepted by the Society 21 March 2006

Learning about Geoscience Thinking

Having heard from senior geoscientists reflecting upon their own thinking and learning, we turn to cognitive scientists and educators who study thinking and learning itself for their perceptions of how geoscientists think and learn about the Earth. These chapters explore the relationship between key conceptual understanding in geosciences and cognitive science research while illuminating the approach and methods used by cognitive science.

We start with the work of a professional geoscientist who is now also recognized as a cognitive science researcher. Kim Kastens (Columbia University) and her colleague Toru Ishikawa characterize the work of geoscientists in the spatial realm and link it to relevant insights from cognitive science. This chapter will help geoscientists and cognitive scientists alike understand the linkages between these fields. The cataloging of spatial tasks in the geosciences will resonate with geoscientists. Its detail enables both geoscientists and cognitive scientists to see the relevance of cognitive science research to understanding geoscience expertise. Kastens and Ishikawa also outline the research questions and implications for education that come from this unique synthesis of geoscience and cognitive science expertise.

Turning from space to time, Jeff Dodick (The Hebrew University of Jerusalem) and Nir Orion (Weizmann Institute of Science) use a study of student learning to illuminate how geoscientists think about geologic time. Again a parsing of the types of thinking that fall in this realm is fundamental to understanding this aspect of cognition. Understanding deep time requires different cognitive skills than assigning relative ages. The detailed description of the research design will help geoscientists understand the design of cognitive and educational experiments, while providing cognitive scientists an example of research design bridging from fundamental issues in cognitive science to their application in specialized skills in the geosciences. This chapter in particular addresses the relationships between cognitive development and the development of geoscience expertise with important implications for the design and timing of curriculum in elementary and middle school.

Building on the discussion of complex systems by Turcotte, Bruce Herbert, a geoscience educator at Texas A&M, describes the challenges of teaching and learning about complex systems for both geoscience students and policy makers seeking to apply this understanding to decision making. Herbert uses examples to demonstrate the relationships between scientific problems and methods and three primary challenges to learners. He then draws on educational and cognitive research to recommend educational strategies that may effectively address these challenges.

Having addressed three of the most fundamental characteristics of geoscience thinking, space, time, and complex systems, we turn to an analysis of the discipline as a whole, its philosophy, and its methods as revealed through analysis of language and discourse in the geosciences. Jeff Dodick and Shlomo Argamon (Illinois Institute of Technology) describe the distinctions between the goals, questions, and methods of geoscience, which they term a historical science, and the experimental approach typified by physics and chemistry. This chapter presents a history of the field and its development as the foundation for testable hypotheses regarding the distinctions between historical and experimental approaches. An analysis of language patterns in published papers provides a first level of validation for this theory, which speaks directly to the importance and value of geoscience thinking and learning.

Lastly, we hear from two cognitive scientists David Rapp (University of Minnesota) and David Uttal (Northwestern University) about the value of collaborations between geoscientists and cognitive scientists.

Choosing examples from the study of visualization, they illustrate the power of such collaborations for making fundamental contributions in both fields.

Taken together, these chapters build important bridges between the two disciplines by delineating the types of thinking undertaken by geoscientists in terms that are both of interest and amenable to study by cognitive scientists. The chapters demonstrate the breadth of insights and methods that cognitive science brings to understanding geoscience learning and the value of those insights in developing stronger supports for geoscience learning in both education and research. The potential for collaborative work is clear, as are the similarities between geoscience and cognitive science, which both study complex systems through a combination of observational and experimental methods. The reader leaves with an understanding of the role of observational experiments in determining the important paradigms and variables in geoscience thinking and learning, and the synergies that come from studying learning, i.e., the development of expertise, and the expertise itself.

Geological Society of America
Special Paper 413
2006

Spatial thinking in the geosciences and cognitive sciences: A cross-disciplinary look at the intersection of the two fields

Kim A. Kastens[†]

Lamont-Doherty Earth Observatory and Department of Earth & Environmental Sciences, Columbia University, Palisades, New York 10964, USA

Toru Ishikawa[‡]

Lamont-Doherty Earth Observatory, Columbia University, Palisades, New York 10964, USA

ABSTRACT

Learning geoscience and becoming a professional geoscientist require high-level spatial thinking. Thus, geoscience offers an intriguing context for studying people's mental representations and processes as they pertain to large-scale, three-dimensional spatial cognition and learning, from both cognitive science and geoscience perspectives. This paper discusses major tasks that professional geoscientists and geoscience learners deal with, focusing on the spatial nature of the tasks and underlying cognitive processes. The specific tasks include recognizing, describing, and classifying the shape of an object; describing the position and orientation of objects; making and using maps; envisioning processes in three dimensions; and using spatial-thinking strategies to think about nonspatial phenomena. Findings and implications from cognitive science literature that could be incorporated into geoscience teaching and some questions for future research are also discussed.

Keywords: spatial cognition, geoscience education.

INTRODUCTION

In this paper, we look for common ground within the domain of spatial thinking between the fields of geosciences and cognitive sciences. Learning geoscience and becoming a professional geoscientist require extensive high-level spatial thinking. Thus, from a cognitive science perspective, geoscience offers an intriguing context for studying people's mental representations and processes as they pertain to three-dimensional spatial cognition and learning. From a geoscience perspective, cognitive science may be able to shed light on why many geoscience learners have difficulty with certain spatially intensive tasks, how expert geoscientists' thought processes differ from novices', and how students' progress toward expert thought processes can be fostered.

We begin by identifying and describing some of the geoscientist's tasks that require thinking about objects or processes or phenomena in space, the kind of thought processes that we broadly call spatial thinking. Then we look for insights and lines of inquiry in the cognitive science literature that could shed light on how expert geoscientists and geoscience learners accomplish those tasks. This paper's mapping of the connections between geoscientists' mental processes and cognitive scientists' research findings is not exhaustive; it is merely an early step in what we hope will be an ongoing dialog between these two fields. Our intended audience is both

[†]E-mail: kastens@ldeo.columbia.edu.
[‡]E-mail: ishikawa@ldeo.columbia.edu. Ishikawa now at the Center for Spatial Information Science, University of Tokyo, Japan.

Kastens, K.A., and Ishikawa, T., 2006, Spatial thinking in the geosciences and cognitive sciences: A cross-disciplinary look at the intersection of the two fields, *in* Manduca, C.A., and Mogk, D.W., eds., Earth and Mind: How Geologists Think and Learn about the Earth: Geological Society of America Special Paper 413, p. 53–76, doi: 10.1130/2006.2413(05). For permission to copy, contact editing@geosociety.org. ©2006 Geological Society of America. All rights reserved.

geoscientists and cognitive scientists. We hope that geoscientists and geoscience educators find insights that will sharpen their own thought processes or enable them to better understand their students' difficulties. We hope that cognitive scientists find questions that trigger new lines of inquiry.

We consider three groups of geoscience tasks: (1) describing and interpreting objects, (2) comprehending spatial properties and processes, and (3) metaphorical usage of spatial thinking. The first group of tasks includes:

- describing the shape of an object, rigorously and unambiguously;
- identifying or classifying an object by its shape;
- ascribing meaning to the shape of a natural object; and
- recognizing a shape or pattern amid a noisy background.

The second group of tasks includes:

- recalling the location and appearance of previously seen objects;
- describing the position and orientation of objects;
- making and using maps;
- synthesizing one- or two-dimensional observations into a three-dimensional mental image; and
- envisioning the processes by which materials or objects change position or shape.

And the third group of tasks includes:

- using spatial-thinking strategies and techniques to think about nonspatial phenomena.

Collectively, such thought processes are at the heart of virtually all fields of geosciences. Furthermore, researchers have shown that spatial ability and thinking play important roles in many fields of science and engineering, including physics, chemistry, mathematics, engineering, geoscience, and medicine (Carter et al., 1987; Downs and Liben, 1991; Mathewson, 1999; Pallrand and Seeber, 1984; Piburn, 1980; Rochford, 1985; Russell-Gebbett, 1984; Tuckey and Selvaratnam, 1993). Therefore, space is a unifying theme across many disciplines. Spatial thinking in geosciences spans a huge range of scales, from the atomic (e.g., the crystalline structure of minerals) to the global (e.g., atmospheric circulation patterns).

In articulating those geoscience tasks, we focus on two end-member categories of thinkers: (1) pioneering geoscientists, at the frontiers of science, undertaking a spatial challenge for the very first time that it has ever been done; and (2) beginning students, undertaking a spatial challenge for the first time it has been done by them.

For additional insights into spatial thinking by geoscience learners in an educational context, we refer the reader to Kastens and Ishikawa (2004) and Ishikawa and Kastens (2005). For additional insights into spatial thinking across a range of disciplines, we recommend National Research Council (2006).

DESCRIBING AND INTERPRETING OBJECTS

Describing the Shape of an Object, Rigorously and Unambiguously

The Geoscientist's Task—Describing the Richness of Nature

Faced with the huge range of objects found in nature, early mineralogists, petrologists, geomorphologists, structural geologists, sedimentologists, zoologists, and botanists had to begin by agreeing upon words and measurements with which to describe these natural objects. Given a collection of objects that intuitively seem related in some way, what should one observe, and what should one measure, in order to capture the shape of each object in a way that is rigorous, unambiguous, and includes all of the important observable parameters?

After much spatial thinking, crystallographers decided that they should observe how many planes of symmetry the crystal has and the angles between those planes of symmetry. Size and color of the crystal are not so important. After much spatial thinking, structural geologists decided that they should describe a fold in a sedimentary layer by imaging a plane of symmetry of the fold, and then measuring the orientation of this axial plane, and how much the fold axis departs from the horizontal.

The mental processes of pioneering observers of nature as they develop a new description methodology include (1) careful observation of the shape of a large number of objects; (2) integrating these observations into a mental model of what constitutes the shared characteristics among this group of objects; (3) identifying ways in which individual objects can differ while still remaining within the group; and (4) developing a methodical, reproducible set of observation parameters that describes the range of natural variability within the group. Step 4 may include developing a lexicon or taxonomy of terms, developing new measurement instruments, developing new units of measurement, or developing two-dimensional graphical representations of some aspect of the three-dimensional objects (Fig. 1).

Geoscience novices learning to describe objects of nature professionally must first become facile with the terms and techniques used by specialists who have previously studied this class of objects. In some cases, these descriptive techniques may call upon spatial skills that many learners find extremely difficult. Examples include the technique by which structural geologists capture the shape of a folded sedimentary layer by projecting vectors perpendicular to the fold onto a lower-hemisphere equal-area projection diagram (Fig. 1A), and the system of Miller indices by which mineralogists describe the angular relationships between the faces of a crystal (Fig. 1B).

Insights from the Cognitive Science Literature—Topological, Projective, and Euclidean Spatial Concepts

In the cognitive science literature, Piaget's developmental theory has been very influential. Piaget and Inhelder (1948

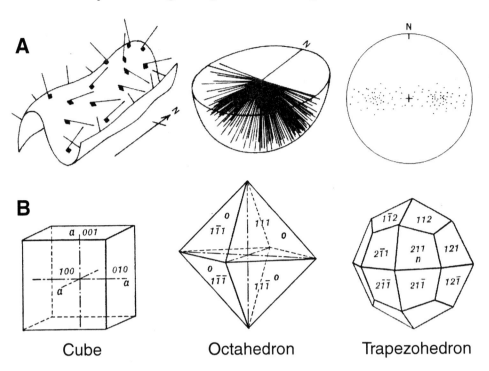

Figure 1. Examples of the specialized representational techniques that geoscientists have developed to describe the shape of natural objects. (A) The lower-hemisphere equal-area projection that structural geologists use to describe the shape of a folded sedimentary stratum. Left: The lines represent vectors that are locally perpendicular to a rock surface, in this case a folded rock surface. Middle: These vectors are projected downward from a common origin until they intersect an imaginary hemisphere. Right: This hemisphere is then projected onto a plane by an equal-area projection. The general trend of points in this representation records and conveys the overall shape and orientation of the rock surface, while the scatter of the points conveys the irregularity of the surface (reproduced with permission from Hobbs et al. [1976, Fig. A11]). (B) The system of Miller indices with which mineralogists describe the angular relationships between the faces of a crystal. A set of three coordinate axes is defined, with its origin in the center of the crystal, and a vector is drawn from the origin perpendicular to each crystal face. The Miller index of a crystal face is the *a-b-c* coordinates of the point where the vector intersects the crystal face, normalized to a unit length. For example, in the cube, the vector from the origin intersects the front face of the crystal at point (1, 0, 0), so the Miller index of this face is 1 0 0. A number with a bar on top is negative (reproduced with permission from Hurlbut [1971, Figures 66, 67, and 75]). In Piaget and Inhelder's (1948 [1967]) classification scheme of three spatial concepts (topological, projective, and Euclidean), the fold-description task requires the projective spatial concept, while the crystal-faces task draws heavily on the Euclidean spatial concept.

[1967]) classified spatial concepts into three categories: topological, projective, and Euclidean. Topological spatial concepts involve only qualitative relationships such as separation, order, and continuity (e.g., "next to," "between," "inside/outside"). Projective spatial concepts encompass understanding of spatial relations tied to a specific viewpoint and differentiation of various viewpoints; for example, the ability to imagine (1) the shape of a shadow that would be cast onto a screen by a geometric shape held at various angles to a light source or (2) what a scene would look like if viewed from several different vantage points. Euclidean spatial concepts contain metric information, such as distance, direction, and angle, coordinated in a fixed frame of reference. Piaget and Inhelder argued that children understand topological space before projective and Euclidean spaces. Understanding of projective and Euclidean spaces emerges in parallel at approximately the same developmental stage, but the Euclidean spatial concept takes longer to be fully comprehended.

When we look back at the geoscientist's tasks from this perspective, we find that many of the descriptive tasks that geoscience learners find most difficult have a strong projective or Euclidean component. For example, the structural geologist's lower-hemisphere equal-area representation of the shape of a fold (Fig. 1A) requires use of the projective spatial concept to envision the outcome of projecting multiple vectors onto a surface simultaneously. The mineralogist's Miller indices (Fig. 1B) require use of the Euclidean spatial concept to compare the crystal faces against a hypothetical three-dimensional coordinate system. This suggests that expert geoscientists have more sophisticated projective and Euclidean spatial concepts, gained through repeated practice, than (even adult) geoscience novices do. In fact, Downs and Liben (1991) found that a significant portion of college students performed poorly on tasks that required accurate understanding of projective and Euclidean spatial concepts.

IDENTIFYING OR CLASSIFYING AN OBJECT BY ITS SHAPE

The Geoscientist's Task—Classifying a Newly Described Object

Having described a natural object using the professionally arrived-at vocabulary and techniques discussed in the previous section, the geoscientist then classifies the object into a group or category. Paleontologists or micropaleontologists classify fossils or microfossils according to their morphology; geomorphologists do the same with landforms. Traditionally, mineralogists or petrologists (scientists who study rocks) identify minerals in a hand sample or photomicrograph by shape, color (including color changes under different lighting conditions), and texture (e.g., Does it have stripes? Does it have a shiny surface?) (Fig. 2A).

Geoscience novices learn this skill by comparing unknown fossils, minerals, or geomorphological features against a catalog, using the descriptive terms and measurements mentioned above. To become experts, students must construct their own mental catalog of the properties of dozens to hundreds of fossils or minerals, and then develop facility at comparing each unknown new mineral or fossil against this mental catalog.

Insights from the Cognitive Science Literature— Categorization

Such a task has been studied in cognitive psychology under the heading *categorization*. Categorization is one of the most basic characteristics of human thinking; in fact, it has been of interest since the era of Aristotle. Linguist George Lakoff said, "There is nothing more basic than categorization to our thought, perception, action, and speech. . . . Without the ability to categorize, we could not function at all, either in the physical world or in our social and intellectual lives. An understanding of how we categorize is central to any understanding of how we think and how we function, and therefore central to an understanding of what makes us human" (Lakoff, 1987, p. 5–6).

How do people categorize? The traditional view maintains that a list of attributes, individually necessary and jointly sufficient, defines what is or is not a member of a category (defining-attribute theory). One of the earliest and most famous examples of this theory is Collins and Quillian's (1969) semantic network model, in which concepts are represented as hierarchies of interconnected nodes (Fig. 2B). Each node, or concept, has associated defining attributes (e.g., a bird has wings, can fly, has feathers). Subordinate concepts share the defining attributes of their superordinate concepts (e.g., a bird breathes, eats, has skin). Collins and Quillian predicted that, if knowledge is mentally represented as such a network, it should take more time to verify a sentence that relates two concepts farther apart in the network than to verify a sentence with concepts near each other. For example, people should take more time to verify the sentence "a canary is an animal" (the two concepts are two links apart in the hierarchy) than

the sentence "a canary is a bird" (one link apart). They found that people's verification times were consistent with this prediction.

Later, it was pointed out that categories are often not clearly defined by a finite set of defining attributes; rather, categories have fuzzy boundaries. In the face of such criticism, some researchers proposed prototype theory (e.g., Rosch, 1978). This theory maintains that members of a concept vary in their typicality (e.g., a robin is a more typical member of the concept *bird* than an ostrich), and that category membership is determined by the degree of similarity (or family resemblance) to the category's prototype (i.e., the best example).

Geoscientists use classification schemes that resemble the cognitive scientist's defining-attribute theory, semantic network model, and prototype theory. A geoscience example of the defining-attribute strategy for classifying objects is the venerable Udden-Wentworth scale (Blatt et al., 1972) for classifying sedimentary grain sizes, in which all grains between 2 mm and 62 µm in diameter are classified as sand, grains between 62 µm and 4 µm are classified as silt, and so on. The hierarchies of Collins and Quillian's semantic network model resemble Carolus Linnaeus taxonomic hierarchies (Farber, 2000). A geoscience example of the prototype strategy for classifying objects is the manner in which a species of fossil (or living organism) is defined by reference to a specific individual of that species preserved in a museum; other individuals are classified as members or nonmembers of that species based on their resemblance to the so-called type specimen (International Commission on Zoological Nomenclature, 1985; Simpson, 1940). Each of these classification schemes was developed in the earliest days of natural history, and remains in use today.

Most geoscientists would probably argue that the early natural scientists developed different kinds of classification schemes for different types of natural objects because the relationships among those objects do, in fact, vary in nature. Sedimentary grain sizes vary along a continuum from extremely fine to extremely coarse, so the "obviously sensible" way to categorize clastic sediments is to define attributes that mark the boundary between one category and the next. Fossils usually do not fall along a continuum of physical characteristics; instead they tend to display clusters of characteristics, so the "obviously sensible" way to categorize them is by resemblance or nonresemblance to an ideal or prototype. But faced with the cognitive science finding that the human brain may inherently favor certain ways of forming categories, geoscientists have to ask whether our classification schemes truly reflect what is out there in nature. Do we use "sand/silt/clay" because these terms represent natural categories of sediment that differ in their depositional and erosional processes? To what extent are our classification schemes a product of our brains' facility for categorizing? Do we use "sand/silt/clay" because these categorical labels are easier for our brains to think about than the fairly arbitrary numerical values that have been chosen to subdivide the natural continuum? A resolution of this question may lie in evolutionary psychology (see e.g., Tooby and Cosmides, 1992). The lives of ancestral humans were domi-

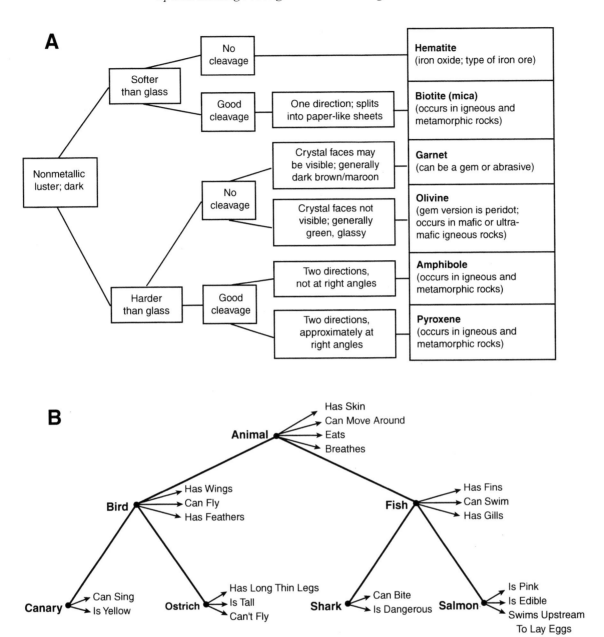

Figure 2. Classification of objects according to their shapes. (A) Example of a hierarchical system for classifying Earth objects, in this case minerals, according to shape and other visible characteristics (adapted with permission from Marshak [2001, app. B-2]). (B) Collins and Quillian (1969) hypothesized that concepts are represented mentally as hierarchies of interconnected nodes (adapted with permission from Collins and Quillian [1969, Fig. 1]).

nated by the same natural objects that concern today's geologists and ecologists: plants, animals, rocks, and landforms. Thus the human brain may have evolved the ability to organize concepts into categories according to patterns common in nature. Then natural scientists exploited that mental capacity to develop formal and intricate classification schemes (see also the discussion about object location memory in a following section).

Ascribing Meaning to the Shape of a Natural Object

The Geoscientist's Task—Inferring History and Formative Processes

The shape of a natural object (including its size and orientation) carries clues about its history and formative processes. To begin with the most famous examples of ascribing meaning to the shape of natural objects in the history of geosciences, Alfred Wegener (Wegener, 1929) noted the jigsaw fit of the coastlines of Africa and South America, and inferred that the continents had previously been connected (Fig. 3A). James Hutton (Hutton, 1788) noted the contrast in tilt and texture of underlying and overlying rocks at Siccar Point in Scotland, and inferred the existence of unconformities and the immensity of geologic time (Fig. 3B).

Among modern geoscientists, micropaleontologists use morphologic clues to infer both the geologic age and the paleoenvironment within which planktonic microfossils lived and died (Fig. 3C). If one sample of diatom (a form of phytoplankton) fossils has thick silicate shells, whereas another group has delicate,

thin shells, this could be attributed to the latter group growing in a water mass impoverished in dissolved silica. If the carbonate-shelled microfossils (foraminifera) in a sediment sample are pitted and lacking delicate protuberances, this could be attributed to the sediment sample being deposited near the calcite compensation depth, the depth in the ocean below which carbonate dissolves. The observation that a group of microfossils is much smaller than typical for their species could be attributed to their living in a stressed environment, for example a marine species living in brackish water (Kennett, 1982).

Structural geologists look at distortions in the shapes of crystals and fossils to infer the strain (and thereby the stress) that a body of rock has undergone (Ramsay and Huber, 1983). Sedi-

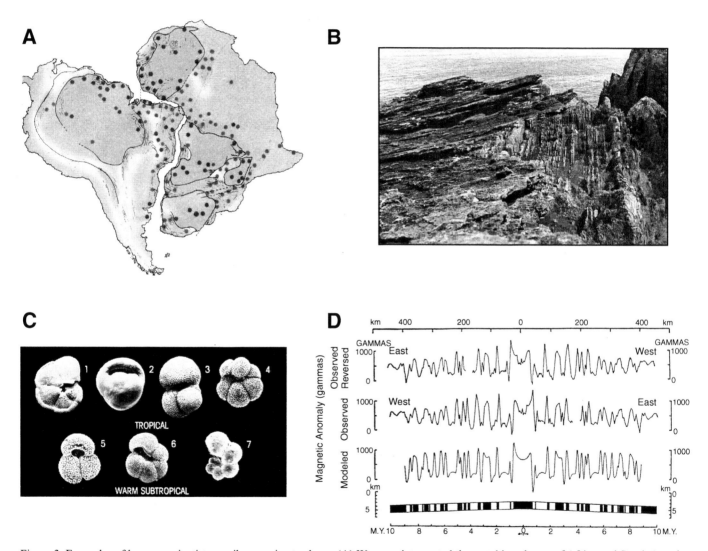

Figure 3. Examples of how geoscientists ascribe meaning to shape. (A) Wegener interpreted the matching shapes of Africa and South America as evidence of continental drift (reproduced with permission from Hamblin [1994, Figure 16.2]). (B) Hutton interpreted the geometry of this and similar unconformities as evidence that there had been a long gap of time during which erosion had occurred (from http://www.geos.ed.ac. uk/undergraduate/field/siccarpoint/closer.html, downloaded October 2002.). (C) Micropaleontologists interpret the shapes of these planktonic microfossils as evidence of the water temperature in which the fossils grew (reproduced with permission from Kennett [1982, Figure 16.1]). (D) Pitman interpreted the shape of this Eltanin-19 magnetic anomaly profile across the Pacific-Antarctic Ridge as evidence of seafloor spreading (adapted with permission from Pitman and Heirtzler [1966, Fig. 3]).

mentologists use the presence of ripples and certain other sedimentary structures to infer that a sedimentary stratum was deposited under flowing water, and use the orientation and asymmetry of the ripples to determine which way the current was flowing in the ancient body of water (Blatt et al., 1972). Whether a river is meandering, straight, or braided speaks to a geomorphologist about the energy regime, discharge, and slope of the river (Allen, 1970). Similarly, the grain size distribution of sedimentary particles tells a sedimentologist about the velocity of an ancient river; it takes a higher energy flow to carry gravel than sand. Sedimentary stratigraphers infer whether sea level was rising or falling on a continental margin from the shape of the sedimentary "packets" in seismic-reflection profiles acquired perpendicular to the margin (Vail et al., 1977).

The symmetry or lack of symmetry of an object of nature can be attributed to either the properties of its constituents or to the circumstances under which it formed or evolved. The symmetry of crystals emerges from the packing geometry of their constituent molecules. Animals that move are likely to have evolved bilateral symmetry, with sensors (e.g., eyes, nose) located on the side that first encounters new stimuli, whereas organisms with radial symmetry are more likely to be attached to the seafloor, equally ready to cope with threats or opportunities coming from any direction.

To summarize from these examples, the shape of a natural object can be influenced by its strain history, the energy regime under which it was formed, the chemical environment under which it formed, and changes in the physical or chemical environments that it experienced after its initial formation. Geoscientists seek to reason backward from observing the morphology to inferring the influencing processes, guided by observations of current-day processes that are thought to be analogous. Key questions involved in this task are: What processes or forces could have acted upon this mineral or landform or fossil or organism (the fossil before it died) to cause it to have this shape? What function could this form have served in the life of the organism?

Geoscience novices, like novice learners in other disciplines (e.g., Chi et al., 1981), generally begin by applying learned rules of thumb, without necessarily understanding the underlying causal relationship. At the expert level, the process of inferring history and formative processes involves reasoning from first principles about the connections among form, function, and history, on the basis of an expert knowledge base about the normal characteristics of the class of objects under study.

Insights from the Cognitive Science Literature—Schema Theory

To explain the organization of knowledge of more complex relations and structures, beyond simple object concepts, schema theory was proposed. A schema is a general knowledge structure that is composed of various relations, events, agents, actions, and so on. People apply a schema to a specific situation to guide their behavior and understanding. In other words, open "slots" in a generic schema are filled out according to specific situations.

One of the earliest concepts of schema can be found in Bartlett's (1932) study of the role of expectations in remembering. He told a North American Indian folk tale, which was not familiar to people in the European culture, to English participants, and asked them to recall it later. He found that they did not remember the story as it was, but changed or "reconstructed" it so that it became more consistent with traditional European folk stories. That is, their interpretation of the story was influenced by their expectations, or schemata.

Thus if a geoscientist or geoscience student has a schema that says "sedimentary rocks are deposited in layers," that person will tend to see layers when observing sedimentary rocks in the field, and will tend to recall layers when describing that outcrop at a later time.

It should be noted that cognitive scientists consider the process of understanding to be a two-way, constructive process; that is, understanding is influenced by existing knowledge structures, and at the same time, the knowledge structures undergo changes in interaction with the world. Piaget called these processes assimilation and accommodation, where assimilation refers to integrating new information into one's existing schema, and accommodation refers to modifying one's schema in light of new information. He argued that knowledge was acquired in interaction between the self and the world, and "the progressive equilibrium between assimilation and accommodation is an instance of a fundamental process in cognitive development" (Piaget, 1983, p. 109).

How do geoscientists develop expert schemata for ascribing meaning to the shape of natural objects? This is a very interesting but underinvestigated issue. We offer two generalizations. A first generalization is that a new explanatory schema in geosciences may originate by observing instances when the formative process and the resulting objects can be observed simultaneously, either in a modern environment or in an experiment. For example, the schema for inferring paleocurrent directions in ancient sedimentary rocks from the shape and orientation of preserved sedimentary structures, was constructed by observing ripples and other bedforms in modern bodies of water where the current speed and direction can be measured directly. Similarly, schemata for interpreting metamorphic rocks are informed by laboratory experiments in which rocks are deformed under elevated temperatures and pressures. This method of developing new schemata is enshrined in the geologist's slogan: "the present is the key to the past."

A second generalization is that a new explanatory schema in geosciences may originate by observing fortuitous instances in which the shape of the natural object is a nearly pure result of one formative process. For example, the schema for interpreting the shapes of wiggles in profiles of the magnetic signature of the oceanic crust in terms of seafloor spreading, was clinched by Walter Pitman's interpretation of the Eltanin-19 profile (Glen, 1982; Pitman and Heirtzler, 1966). This beautifully symmetrical profile has a high-latitude position, E-W orientation, and location away from ridge jumps and transform offsets, which lead to a simple, clear profile shaped only by seafloor spreading (Fig. 3D). Later workers expanded the schema to cover situations where the magnetic signal was weaker or obscured by other processes. This second anecdote illustrates something else about the development of schemata in science: Piaget's cyclical process of assimilation and accommodation can be shared across a community of investigators rather than occurring entirely within one brain.

Recognizing a Shape or Pattern amid a Noisy Background

The Geoscientist's Task—Finding Meaningful Patterns or Shapes in Image Data and Outcrops

Quantitative, digital geophysical data are often displayed as images rather than numbers. Examples include seismic-reflection profiles, side-looking sonar data, and satellite remote-sensing data. This strategy of transforming the numbers of quantitative data into something that looks like a picture is a matter of preference. For example, bathymetric and topographic data have historically been shown as contour maps, a form of data display that preserves the numerical depth or elevation (Fig. 4A). With the availability of increased computer processing power, marine geologists and geomorphologists now often choose to display bathymetric and topographic data as shaded-relief images, a form of display that looks somewhat like a photograph and does not present the absolute depth or elevation as a number (Fig. 4B).

Why should the developers of geophysical instruments strive to acquire the most accurate and precise digital data, but then transform these numbers into picture-like data displays before interpretation? It seems that image displays allow the data interpreter's eye and brain to tap into a powerful ability to recognize significant patterns amid noise. The eye can "see" erosional or faulted fabric in the shaded-relief display more easily than in a contour map or other numerical display. This ability to detect geologically significant patterns improves through training and practice. An experienced interpreter of seismic-reflection data can confidently and reproducibly trace seismic reflectors across a profile that looks like uniform gray noise to the untrained eye.

The ability to spot subtle but significant patterns amid a visually complex background is crucial on the outcrop as well. A talented paleontologist can stand at an outcrop with a bus-full of other geologists and spot fossils where the others see nothing.

In recognizing a shape or pattern amid a noisy background, the expert geoscientist's eye is guided by experience of what might be important. For example, in spectroscopic studies, an expert would recognize significance in asymmetry of peaks, for example, a "shoulder" on a peak that might indicate absorption of a given wavelength or overlapping peaks that have to be deconvolved. Geoscience novices describing the same data set might not even notice the asymmetry, because it conveyed no significance to them.

Insights from the Cognitive Science Literature—Expert Problem Solving

Although the geoscientist interpreting an outcrop or image may be tapping into a universal human ability to see patterns amid

visual clutter, it seems that expert geoscientists can see significant patterns where novices do not. What differentiates experts from novices? It has been found that experts do not simply have more factual knowledge, but they also store and use knowledge in more meaningful and efficient ways than do novices. For example, Chase and Simon (1973) found that chess masters recalled briefly presented board positions from actual games better than novice players, whereas the two groups of players did not differ in the accuracy of recall when the pieces were randomly arranged on the board. Gilhooly et al. (1988) found that undergraduate students skilled in reading topographic contour maps showed better memory for contour maps than low-skill students, whereas the two groups of students did not differ in accuracy of memory for ordinary town maps. Lesgold et al. (1988) found that, in diagnosing X-ray films, expert radiologists were superior to novices in clustering observed abnormalities into a single medical problem and generating diagnostic hypotheses. In each case, the experts were attuned to patterns in visually perceived information because those patterns had significance for them, significance that the novices were not aware of. In such expert problem solving, past experience and existing knowledge should play an important role (as discussed in the section on schemata).

Insights from the Cognitive Science Literature—The Embedded Figures Test

The embedded figures test is a classic psychometric test, often given as one of a battery of tests designed to assess people's spatial abilities. In this test, the participant is shown a simple shape, and then asked to find and trace that simple shape where it occurs within a more complex configuration (Fig. 5A). The specific ability required by this test is to perceive and keep an image in memory and then detect it among complex configurations by ignoring irrelevant or distracting information (called flexibility of closure; Carroll, 1993).

Although the embedded figures test resembles the geoscientist's task of finding reflectors in a seismic profile or fossils in an outcrop or structures in a geologic map (Fig. 5B), there are significant differences that make the geoscientist's task harder. First, in the embedded figures test, the example simple figure and the embedded simple figure are exact duplicates with respect to size, shape, and orientation; in contrast, the simple figure in the geoscientist's tasks can be regarded as an archetype or model, which could differ in size or orientation or details of morphology from the embedded figure. Second, in some variants of the embedded figures test, one can look back at the simple figure while searching within the complex figure; whereas the geoscientist is typically comparing against a mental picture of the sought-after shape rather than against a physical object or external representation. Also, in the embedded figures test, one knows that the simple shape is, in fact, present in the complex shape, but the geoscientist has no such assurance. Finally, the background within which the geoscientist is searching is often much more complicated and noisy than the "complex" figure of the embedded figures test.

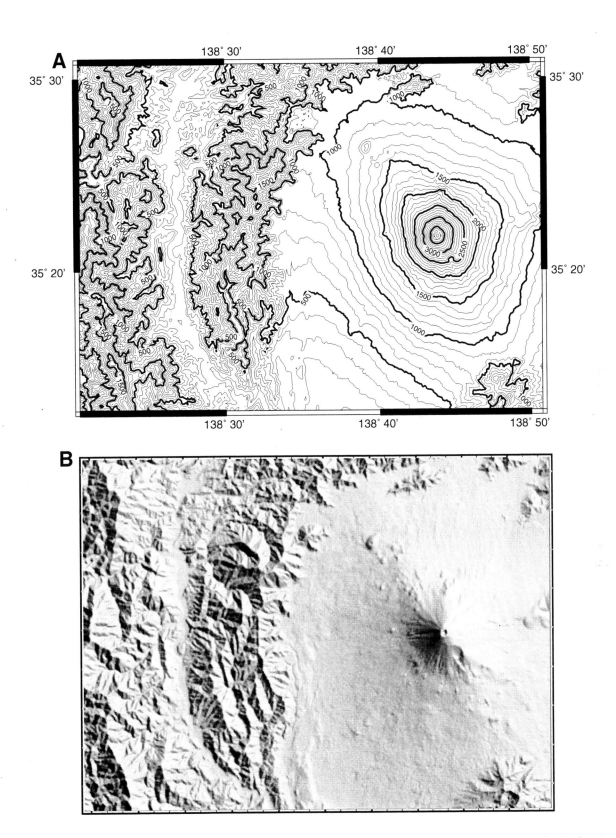

Figure 4. For certain types of data, a numerical, quantitative display may be less informative than a display that mimics what the human eye is used to seeing in the world around us. (A) Topography in the region of Mt. Fuji, Japan, shown as contours in meters. (B) The same elevation data, shown as a shaded-relief image. The topographic contours retain the quantitative information about the elevation of each point on the map. However, most geoscientists find it easier to infer the erosional and volcanic processes that shaped the landscape by examining the shaded-relief image display. (Images created by William Haxby using GeoMapApp.)

A

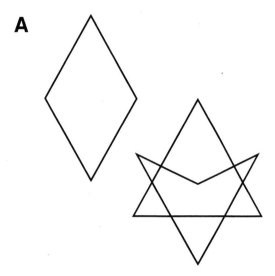

"Find and trace the simple figure on the left,
within the complex figure on the right."

B

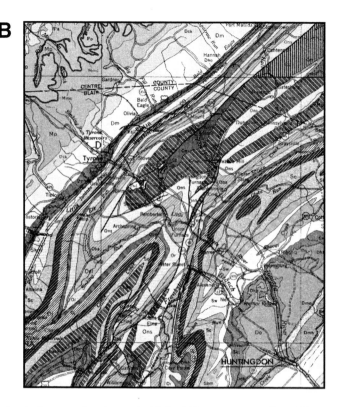

Figure 5. (A) The embedded figures test requires the participant to find a simple figure or drawing embedded within a more complicated figure (reproduced with permission from Eliot and Smith [1983, p. 409]). (B) The geoscientist exercises a similar skill looking for significant shapes or patterns in a complex geologic map or in image data. On such a geologic map (original in color), the color bands represent rock units of different ages. The zigzag pattern of the rock units in the SW quadrant of this map is characteristic of folded rock strata that have been partially eroded (reproduced with permission from Owen et al. [2001]).

The relative ease with which experts "see" fossils or seismic reflectors leads us to wonder whether embedded-figures performance would be dependent on the familiarity of the shape being sought. Are arbitrary shapes harder for people to find than familiar shapes, such as the household objects and items of clothing typically found in children's "find-the-hidden-objects" puzzles? If so, that might suggest that the progression from novice to expert in geoscience tasks that involve recognizing a significant pattern or shape amid a complex or noisy background is driven by the progression from unfamiliarity to familiarity with the sought-after shapes or patterns. In fact, there have been research findings that show the effects of familiarity on the speed of detecting embedded figures: Hock et al. (1974) found that, within embedded complex figures, uppercase alphabet letters in their normal orientation were detected faster than letters in unfamiliar orientation (rotated 180°). Hanawalt (1942) also found that practice facilitated people's detection of embedded figures.

Questions for Future Research

What steps are involved in the progression from novice to expert in the task of finding significant patterns or shapes in a visually complex background, such as an outcrop, geophysical image, or geologic map? How important is exactness/inexactness of fit between the embedded shape and the example shape? How important is being able to see the example shape while looking for the embedded shape? How important is familiarity/unfamiliarity with the sought-after shape?

COMPREHENDING SPATIAL PROPERTIES AND PROCESSES

Recalling the Location and Appearance of Previously Seen Items

The Geoscientist's Task—Remembering Geological Observations

The great Appalachian field geologist John Rodgers (Rodgers, 2001) knew the location of every outcrop and every ice cream stand from Maine to Georgia. Students recall that he remembered the salient sedimentary and structural characteristics of every outcrop he had ever seen in any mountain range in the world, and where it was located. His ability to remember the relationships among the rock bodies at those outcrops allowed him to construct, over a long lifetime in the field, a mental catalog of occurrences of geologic structures, which he drew upon to create a masterful synthesis of how fold-and-faulted mountain ranges form (Rodgers, 1990).

William Smith [1769–1839] made the world's first geologic map, a map of England and Wales showing rocks of different ages in different colors (Winchester, 2001). When Smith began his field work, it was not understood that rocks occurred on Earth's surface in organized spatial patterns; he figured out that the organizing principle was the age of the rocks as recorded in their fossils. Many spatial skills must have contributed to Smith's effort, but among them was his ability to remember and organize, aided only by the simplest of paper-and-pencil recording aids, a huge body of spatially referenced observations. His nephew, John Phillips, wrote of William Smith: "A fine specimen of this ammonite was here laid by a particular tree on the roads side, as it was large and inconvenient for the pocket, according to the custom often observed by Mr. Smith, *whose memory for localities was so exact* that he has often, after many years, gone direct to some hoard of nature to recover his fossils" (cited in Winchester, 2001, p. 270; emphasis added). The ammonite example focuses on memory for the location of a discrete object, but geologists must also have a memory for recurring patterns or configurations, for example, a distinctive sequence of rock types.

Insights from the Cognitive Science Literature—Object Location Memory

In the psychometric literature, males have been found to perform better than females on some spatial tests, including the mental rotations test, which will be described later (see Linn and Petersen, 1985; Voyer et al., 1995). However, performance on one spatial task has been found to favor females: object location memory task. In this task, the participant is shown an array of objects and, after removal of the array, asked to recall what objects were located where. For example, Silverman and Eals (1992) showed participants an array of objects; after removing the array, they showed the participants a new array of objects, saying that the two arrays contained the same objects. The participants' task was to identify which items were in the same location and which were not. Whether the learning was incidental or intentional (i.e., whether they were explicitly instructed to remember the array or not), females recalled more objects correctly than males did. Another test for this ability is the board game Memory, where people have to remember under which card a specific picture occurred when a matching picture is overturned on another card (McBurney et al., 1997). Some researchers have interpreted these findings from an evolutionary perspective, arguing that in a hunter-gatherer society, object location memory was important for female foragers, who needed to remember the location of medicinal and edible plants so as to be able to harvest them at a later date. For a discussion about the rationale of evolutionary psychology, see Tooby and Cosmides (1992).

Siegel and White (1975) described a special kind of figurative memory, called "recognition-in-context" memory, which allows one to remember not merely "I have seen that before," but also what the landmark was next to, when it last occurred, and what its connection was to other landmarks. Siegel and White state that the clarity of a recognition-in-context memory depends in part on the degree of meaningfulness of the event for that person at that moment. This suggests that, within an individual's education and career in geosciences, spatial memory for Earth features should strengthen as he or she develops the contextual and theoretical framework to establish "meaningfulness" for isolated observations. However, it does not explain the person-to-person variability between spatial geniuses, such as Rodgers or Smith, and ordinary geoscientists.

Describing the Position and Orientation of Objects

The Geoscientist's Task—Describing the Position and Orientation of Real-World Objects Relative to the Earth

Learning to measure strike and dip of sedimentary strata or other planar surfaces is a well-known stumbling block for introductory geoscience students (Fig. 6A). Strike is the compass azimuth of the line defining the intersection between the surface to be described and the horizontal plane. Dip is the angle between the horizontal plane and the surface to be described, measured within a vertical plane perpendicular to the strike line. Strike and dip measurements can be made in the field with a geologist's compass. These two measurements together uniquely define the orientation of a planar surface relative to the Earth. Many students seem to have trouble grasping this technique at any kind of deep or intuitive level.

Until the advent of full-time-available global positioning system (GPS), navigation was a huge issue for seagoing oceanographers. The quality of field work at sea depends on oceanographers' ability to accurately determine the latitude and longitude of ships, sampling devices, and instruments. Every navigation technique—dead reckoning, sextant, Loran, transit satellite navigation, seafloor-based acoustic transponders, or GPS—requires thinking about how angles and/or distances change as a function of relative motions between objects. By knowing the positions of several objects (e.g., satellites, stars, seafloor acoustic transponders) in an frame of reference fixed onto the rotating Earth, the navigator can determine the unknown position of the object of interest. Seismologists face a similar problem when using information about the distance of an earthquake from known seismograph stations to triangulate the unknown location of the earthquake.

Insights from the Cognitive Science Literature—The Water-Level Task

Piaget and Inhelder (1948 [1967]) developed the water-level task and plumb-line task to investigate children's understanding of vertical and horizontal axes, which they considered to be a Euclidean spatial concept (Fig. 6B). The water-level task asks the participant to draw the surface of water inside a drawing of a bottle tilted at various angles from the tabletop; the plumb-line task asks the participant to draw a weighted string (i.e., a plumb

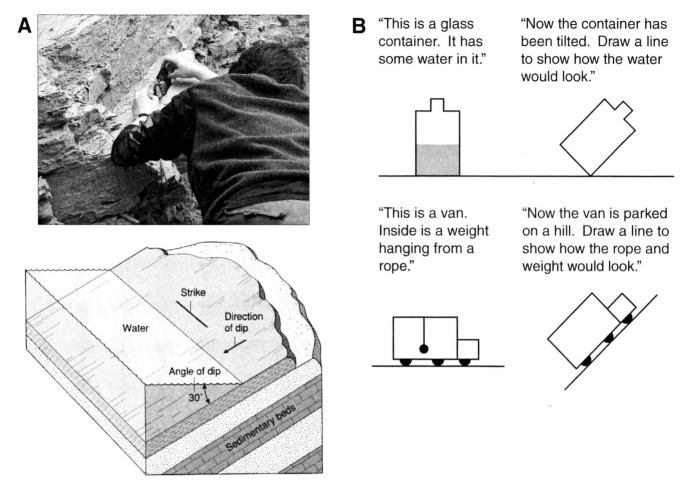

Figure 6. (A) Geologists record the orientation of a sloping planar surface by measuring the strike and dip of the surface, which requires measuring relative to an imaginary horizontal plane and within an imaginary vertical plane (photo by Kim Kastens; figure reproduced with permission from McGeary and Plummer [1998, Figure 6.8]). (B) Psychologists use the water-level and plumb-line tasks to assess people's understanding of the horizontal and vertical axes (adapted with permission from Vasta et al. [1996, Figures 1 and 3]).

line) hanging from the top of the tilted bottle (or, in later investigators' versions, from the roof of a van on a hillside). These tasks resemble the geologist's measurement of strike and dip. In fact, one introductory textbook illustration (McGeary and Plummer, 1998) seeks to clarify the meaning of the term strike by showing imaginary water lapping against the planar surface to be described; the imaginary shoreline defines the line of intersection between the horizontal surface and the surface to be described, that is, the strike line (Fig. 6A). Piaget and Inhelder found that, at an early developmental stage, children did not grasp the notion of horizontal/vertical at all, then, as they got older, began to draw straight lines that were parallel to the base of a bottle, and finally came to understand that the water level should be horizontal and the plumb line should be vertical at any degree of tilt.

More recent investigators have reported that a significant portion of college students, particularly female students, have trouble with these tasks (e.g., Liben, 1978; Liben and Golbeck, 1984; Thomas and Jamison, 1975; Thomas et al., 1973). It has also been pointed out that the relevant physical knowledge about the behavior of water in the real world and a fully developed conceptual framework of space are important for these tasks (e.g., Liben, 1991; Merriwether and Liben, 1997; Vasta et al., 1996). It seems likely that a college student who struggles with the water-level task would be bewildered by dip and strike.

Insights from the Cognitive Science Literature—Frames of Reference

To describe an object's position or orientation, one needs to specify it with respect to something else; that is, one needs to define location in a frame of reference. Levinson (1996) identified three kinds of frames of reference (Fig. 7A). In a relative frame of reference, positions are specified in terms of directions relative to a viewer (e.g., the cat is to the left of the tree; the coarse-grained sediments are at the right end of the outcrop). Distance from a viewer is also a form of relative positional information (e.g., the cat is near to me; the earthquake is 152 km from the seismograph). In the latter example, the "viewer" is not a human being, but rather a scientific instrument that observes Earth on

A

RELATIVE

"He's to the left of the house."

INTRINSIC

"He's in front of the house."

ABSOLUTE

"He's north of the house."

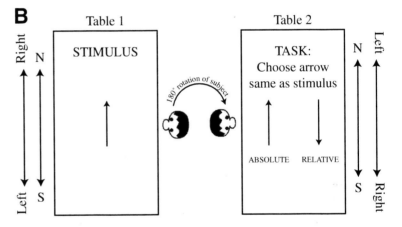

Figure 7. (A) Levinson (1996) discussed three types of frames of reference: relative, intrinsic, and absolute (F—figure; G—ground; V—viewpoint; X—origin of the coordinate system). The coordinate axes are attached to the viewer (V) in the relative frame of reference, to the house (G) in the intrinsic, and to the Earth in the absolute. Seismologists locating earthquakes and oceanographers navigating remotely operated vehicles and submersibles must translate between measurements relative to the observation point (e.g., distance from earthquake to seismograph or distance from bottom-moored navigation beacon to submersible) and positions in an absolute frame of reference (latitude, longitude, depth). (B) Dutch and Tenejapan participants were shown a stimulus arranged in a specific direction on one table, and then asked to rotate 180° and choose on another table the one which they thought was the "same" as the one seen before (reproduced with permission from Levinson [1996, Figures 4.2 and 4.9]).

behalf of the human scientist. In an intrinsic frame of reference, positions are specified in terms of inherent properties of an object within the system under consideration (e.g., the cat is in front of the car; the cracks are along the axis of the fold). Oceanographers and other seafarers use port and starboard to establish an unambiguous intrinsic frame of reference to replace the ambiguous relative terms left and right. An absolute frame of reference is an arbitrary frame fixed onto the surroundings, outside of the system under consideration. Cardinal directions (north, south, east, and west) and latitude and longitude are absolute frames of reference fixed onto rotating Earth.

Developmentally, it has been shown that the frame of reference that children use progresses from an egocentric (or self-centered) frame of reference to an absolute (allocentric or environment-centered) frame of reference (see e.g., Hart and Moore, 1973). Children first orient objects in space with respect to their bodies, namely, they use an egocentric frame of reference. The egocentric frame of reference is a special case of the relative

frame of reference, in which the viewer and the speaker coincide. Children at a later stage of development are able to interrelate objects in space in a coordinated frame of reference. Acredolo (1976, 1977), in a series of experiments, showed that younger children (three-year-olds) relied on the relationship with their own bodies in locating an object in space. For example, once trained to find an object to their left, they went to the wrong location—to their left—after being rotated 180° and starting from the opposite side of a room. In contrast, older children (five-year-olds) comprehended the reversal with respect to their bodies and also used landmarks to locate an object in a fixed, larger frame of reference.

One interesting and important finding about the use of different frames of reference is that they are not equally accessible to humans. When the relative and absolute frames of reference are compared, many people find the latter more difficult to use. A major reason for the difficulty is that, to use the absolute frame of reference, one needs to constantly update one's own orientation relative to the surroundings (e.g., if you head to the north and make a right turn, your right becomes south, not east). In contrast, in the relative frame of reference, one's right is always right regardless of rotation. Also, Levinson (1996) found cultural influences on the choice of frame of reference: the characteristics of language that people use affect the use of different frames of reference in nonlinguistic tasks. He compared two groups of people, Dutch and Tenejapan. Dutch speakers predominantly use relative terms in referring to directions, such as front, back, left, and right; whereas Tenejapan speakers use absolute terms, such as downhill (corresponding to north in their local terrain) and uphill (corresponding to south) in conversation. Levinson presented them a stimulus arranged in a specific direction on one table, and then asked them to rotate 180° and choose on another table the one that they thought was the "same" as the one seen before (Fig. 7B). If they encode the stimulus in the relative sense, they should choose the one heading to their right as the same; if they encode the stimulus in the absolute sense, they should choose the one heading to the north as the same. Dutch participants predominantly showed the former response pattern, whereas the Tenejapan participants tended to show the latter response pattern.

The oceanographer's navigation tasks require conversions between relative and absolute frames of reference. Most navigation techniques generate observables in a relative frame of reference: celestial navigation measures the angle between a star and the horizon as seen from the navigator's vantage point; dead reckoning measures (or estimates) the distance that the navigator has traveled relative to a previous navigation fix; GPS measures the distance between the satellite and the receiving antenna; acoustic transponder navigation measures the distance between a ship or instrument and the transponder, and so on. But what the navigator desires is a position in an absolute frame of reference: latitude, longitude, and in the case of a submerged vehicle, depth. Similarly, seismologists who seek the location of an earthquake work initially in relative frames of reference, as they calculate the distance from epicenter to several seismographs, and then translate this data to an absolute frame of reference to report their findings as latitude, longitude, and depth.

Question for Future Research

What are the mental processes involved in visualizing the transformation of positions and orientations from one spatial frame of reference to another, as for example triangulating to convert earthquake location data out of the relative distances from seismic stations into the absolute framework of latitude, longitude, and depth?

Using and Making Maps

The Geoscientist's Task—Using Maps to Record and Convey Spatial Information

Almost all subdisciplines of geosciences use maps to record and convey information about the Earth. Maps are used to document the locations of discrete phenomena such as ore deposits or volcanoes, or the distribution of properties such as the geologic age of rocks, the salinity of seawater, or the temperature of the atmosphere. Maps capture a record of ephemeral phenomena such as earthquakes or weather systems. Geoscientists use maps to show the past (e.g., reconstructions of previous plate tectonic geometries), the present (e.g., geologic maps), and the future (e.g., climate forecast maps). Maps are most often used to record and convey information that the map maker considers to be factual or at least consistent with available data, but they can also be used to convey a hypothesis, for example Wegener's (1929) hypothesis of continental drift.

For generations of geology students, the field-mapping course has been a rite of passage. In such a course, students observe rock outcrops in the field, make measurements of characteristic attributes, record information about the age, lithology, and structure of observed rocks onto a topographic base map, and then interpret their observations in terms of buried structures and their formative processes. Because the spatial relationship among observations is crucial in inferring buried structures, students must become proficient in locating themselves on the topographic base map by comparing observed features of the terrain with features on the map. Many students find this task difficult.

Learning how to figure where you are on a topographic map has a counterpart in ordinary life in figuring out where you are on a road map or walking map. The mental process involves making connections between the three-dimensional, horizontally viewed, infinitely detailed, ever-changing landscape that surrounds you, and the two-dimensional, vertically viewed, schematic, unchanging representation of that landscape on a piece of paper (Kastens et al., 2001). Although navigating through an unfamiliar terrain by referring to a map is probably the most common map-using task for nonprofessionals, this map skill is rarely taught in school; for example, it is not mentioned in the National Geography Standards (Geography Education Standards Project, 1994).

Insights from the Cognitive Science Literature—The Efficacy of Maps as Tools for Conveying Information

Maps represent information pertaining to space in a schematic and simultaneous fashion. There have been research findings that indicate that the effectiveness of maps and other spatial representations depends on the kind of spatial information being conveyed, the goals or purposes of using such representations, and the spatial ability of users.

Research has shown that maps help people learn the spatial layout of their environment, compared to direct navigation in the space. Thorndyke and Hayes-Roth (1982) examined how two groups of participants' knowledge about a building differed after one group learned the building only by direct navigation and the other group only learned a map of the building. The navigation-learners did better in estimating along-route distances and pointing to unseen landmarks standing at several locations in the building, whereas the map-learners did better in estimating straight-line distances and locating landmarks on a map in relation to each other. Thus, map-learners comprehended the layout of landmarks in the building better than navigation-learners, who had difficulty interrelating separate views into an integrated whole.

More broadly, the effectiveness of spatial representations, such as pictures, diagrams, and animations, has also been studied. Hegarty and Sims (1994) examined how well people comprehend the motion of a mechanical system (a system of belts and pulleys) from a pictorial diagram of the system. They found that people who were poor at mentally visualizing shapes and motions tended to make inaccurate inferences about the motion. Mayer and Sims (1994) gave people visual and verbal explanations of a mechanical system (e.g., a bicycle tire pump), either concurrently (animation and narration together) or successively (animation followed by narration, or vice versa); they then examined the degree of transfer of such acquired knowledge to a new situation. The results showed

that people with high spatial ability benefited from the concurrent visual and verbal representations, whereas low-spatial-ability people had trouble connecting the two different modes of representations. In a geoscience education context, these findings suggest that a spatial representation, such as a complex map, that communicates well with other geoscientists and with high-spatial-ability students might not communicate well with low-spatial-ability students.

Insights from the Cognitive Science Literature—Perspective Taking

The field-geology students' task of locating themselves on a topographic map bears some resemblance to Piaget and Inhelder's (1948 [1967]) three-mountain problem (Fig. 8A). Piaget and Inhelder developed this test to examine children's ability

A "Here is a view of a landscape."

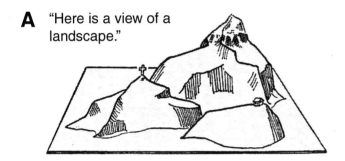

"Here is a map of the same landscape seen from above. Would you see the view above if you were standing at position A, B, C, or D on the map?"

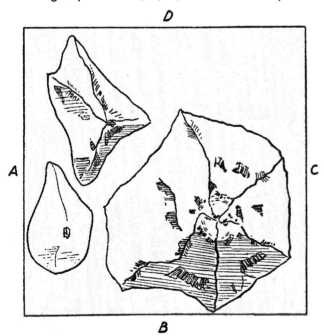

B "Look at the object on the top. Two of the four drawings below it show the same object. Can you find those two?"

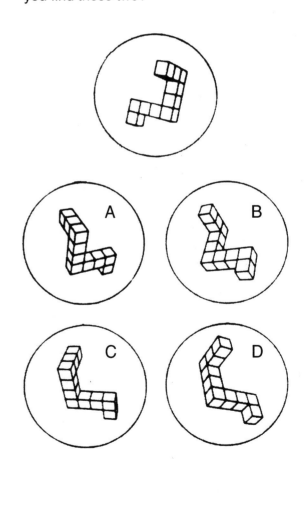

Figure 8. (A) Piaget and Inhelder (1948 [1967]) developed the three-mountain problem to examine children's ability to envision a space from different viewpoints (reproduced with permission from Piaget and Inhelder [1967, Fig. 21]). (B) The mental rotation test examines the participant's ability to envision what an object would look like if rotated to a different position (adapted with permission from Eliot and Smith [1983, p. 322]). Both of these skills seem related to the field geologist's task of using a map in a field area. Answers: (A), correct answer is A; (B) correct answers are A and C.

to coordinate spatial relationships from different viewpoints (i.e., the acquisition of projective spatial concepts). They had children view a tabletop three-dimensional (3-D) model of three mountains, which differed in color, size, and an object located at the top (a house, a cross, or snow). In one variant of this task, the children were shown a picture of the mountains as seen from a position around the perimeter of the model. They were then asked to indicate which of the four positions around the model (A–D in Fig. 8A) a wooden doll would have to occupy to take a photograph similar to the view in the picture. To accomplish this task, children had to imagine how the three mountains would look from different viewpoints and compare their imagined view with the picture. Similarly, field-geology students must imagine how the terrain would look from different positions within a two-dimensional map, and then compare the imagined view with the actual three-dimensional terrain surrounding them. Piaget and Inhelder's results showed that children's responses were confined to their own perspectives at first, but as they matured they improved in their ability to discriminate views from different positions.

Geoscience educators have observed that many students have difficulty positioning themselves accurately on a topographic base map, which suggests that perspective taking remains difficult even for many college-age people. The geology student's task is more difficult than the three-mountain problem because the geology student must consider an infinite number of possible positions within the map, whereas the three-mountain study has only four possible positions, all located around the periphery of the tabletop model. As an indication that perspective-taking ability is related to map-use ability, Liben and Downs (1993), using a variant of the three-mountain problem, showed that perspective-taking ability was correlated (about 0.30) with children's ability to show on a map the location and direction of a person standing in a classroom.

Insights from the Cognitive Science Literature—Mental Rotation

The ability to mentally rotate objects has been identified as one of the major spatial abilities (see e.g., McGee, 1979). For example, a standard psychometric test called the mental rotations test asks the participant to compare pairs of object drawings (Fig. 8B) and answer if they are the same except for rotation (Vandenberg and Kuse, 1978). People take more time to respond as the angular disparity in orientation between the pairs of object drawings increases from 0° to 180°, indicating that people in fact mentally rotate the drawings as if they were rotating physical objects in space (Shepard and Metzler, 1971). Performance on this test has been found to show wide person-to-person variability (with males outperforming females on average), and to correlate moderately (correlation of about 0.30) with the ability to learn spatial layout of a large-scale environment (e.g., Bryant, 1982). Kail and Park (1990) found that, after receiving training on the mental rotations test, which consisted of hundreds of tri-

als with feedback on correctness, people came to respond much faster, compared to people without training.

Mental rotation ability should be related to the use of maps in the field, inasmuch as one needs to align a map with the surrounds, either mentally or physically. Kastens and Liben (unpublished data) found that the mental rotations test is a good predictor of fourth graders' ability to place colored stickers on a map to indicate the location of colored flags in a field-based test of map skills. Students with poor mental rotation ability made a characteristic error in which they consistently placed stickers on the east side of the map that should have been on the west side, and vice versa, as though they had gotten turned around. Similar findings have been observed with respect to "you-are-here" maps, located on campus, in a shopping mall, inside an airport, and so on: when the map is posted out of alignment with the surrounding space, for example upside down, people often go in the wrong direction, by erroneously thinking that the upward direction on the map corresponds with the forward direction in the space (e.g., Levine et al., 1982, 1984). These "map alignment" effects have also been found when a map is held horizontally by a traveler's hand (e.g., Warren and Scott, 1993).

Questions for Future Research

Why are maps such a powerful tool for recording, organizing, and conveying information about the Earth? Do maps reflect one of the brain's methods for organizing information? Given that maps are such powerful thought-aids for geoscience experts, why is it that a significant number of geoscience novices have trouble using maps and other spatial representations?

Synthesizing 1- or 2-D Observations into a 3-D Mental Image

The Geoscientist's Task—Visualizing 3-D Structures and Processes from 1-D or 2-D Data

Many geoscience subdisciplines share the problem that observations are collected in one or two dimensions and then must be interpreted in terms of three-dimensional (or four-dimensional, including time) objects or structures or processes. For example, physical oceanographers measure the temperature and salinity of seawater by lowering an instrument package on a wire vertically down from a ship and recording the temperature, conductivity, and pressure at the instrument. Thousands of such vertical CTD profiles have been combined to create our current understanding of the three-dimensional interfingering of the water masses of the world's oceans. Field geologists examine rock layers and structures exposed above Earth's surface in outcrop, taking advantage of differently oriented road cuts or stream cuts or wave cuts to glimpse the third dimension. From this surficial view, they construct a mental view, or more commonly multiple possible views, of the interior of the rock body.

Seismographs record the acceleration of Earth separately in three directions (up/down, north/south, east/west) as a function of time (Fig. 9A, upper panel). Seismograph records from all over the world are examined to see whether the first motion was toward or away from the site of the earthquake, and this information is combined to define four quadrants of Earth with the same sense of first motion (Fig. 9A, lower-left panel). The results are expressed on a "beach ball" diagram, in which quadrants experiencing first motion away from the earthquake are dark and quadrants experiencing first motion toward the earthquake are white (Fig. 9A, lower-right panel). The geometry of the beach ball conveys the two possible orientations of the fault plane and the two possible directions of fault slip (Anderson, 1986). Although much of this process is now automated, students are still expected to understand this progression from one-dimensional observables to three-dimensional sense of motion, and to interpret the resulting spatial representations.

Marie Tharp, pioneer cartographer of the seafloor, visualized the Mid-Atlantic Ridge rift valley from primitive echosounder records (Fig. 9B). Although the data were collected as water depth versus distance along a ship track, the scale and display technique did not allow the raw data to be directly viewed as profiles. Tharp and her assistants measured thousands of water depths by hand, plotted them by hand onto table-sized plotting sheets, combined ship's tracks to draw profiles, and then contoured in map view by hand, or sketched physiographic diagrams. Her vision of a crack running down the middle of the Atlantic became one of the early compelling pieces of evidence in favor of the theory of seafloor spreading and continental drift (Lawrence, 1999, 2002).

The expert's visualization of the parts of the structure that cannot be seen is guided by more than a simple mechanical interpolation between the observed sections or profiles. The physical oceanographer's visualization is shaped by an understanding of gravity and buoyancy, which require that low density water masses will not ordinarily underlie higher-density water masses. The field geologist's visualization is shaped by the understanding that marine sedimentation processes tend to produce layers that are roughly horizontal and roughly uniform in thickness before deformation. The seismologist's interpretation of the beach ball diagram is guided by an understanding of the regional tectonics that may make one of the two possible fault planes more plausible. Marie Tharp's case is interesting because the early Heezen and Tharp maps were published before they or anyone else knew any details about the tectonic and volcanic processes that form the seafloor geomorphology. Their maps in areas of sparse data (the Southern Oceans, for example) are far better than would have been possible by interpolating from data alone (Lamont-Doherty Earth Observatory, 2001). The physical oceanographer and the field geologist in our examples are guided by knowledge of the processes that shaped the unseen parts of the puzzle, but in Tharp's case, she seems to have developed an intuition or "feel" for the seafloor before the formative processes were well-understood, perhaps analogous to the "feel for the organism" ascribed to Barbara McClintock (Keller, 1983).

Insights from the Cognitive Science Literature—Visual Processing from an Image on the Retina

David Marr (1982) offered a computational theory of visual processing that begins with an image on the retina (Fig. 9C). From intensity changes and local geometric structure in the image, a representation of the two-dimensional image, called the primal sketch, is constructed. The next step is to indicate the geometry and depth of the visible surfaces in the primal sketch, in order to construct a representation called the 2½-D sketch. The primal sketch and the 2½-D sketch are viewer-centered representations. The final step of Marr's sequence is to construct a representation of 3-D shape and spatial arrangement of an object in an object-centered frame of reference. The resulting representation is called the 3-D model representation.

Marr's work points out that each one of us has vast experience of converting (probably in most cases unconsciously) two-dimensional retinal images into mental representations that capture the three-dimensional shape of the objects around us, the objects that we successfully pick up, drive around, and otherwise interact with all day long. It seems likely that this life-long practice of 2-D to 3-D conversion comes into play as geoscientists convert 2-D data displays into 3-D mental representations.

Question for Future Research

How can we capitalize on this experience to smooth the transition from geoscience novice to expert, with respect to tasks involving the synthesis of 2-D observations into mental images of 3-D structures, and then to interpretations of 3-D processes?

Envisioning the Processes by which Objects Change Position or Shape

The Geoscientist's Task—Envisioning Deformation within the Solid Earth

Solid parts of the Earth system may respond to imposed forces by changing their shape, by deforming, by folding and faulting. After struggling to visualize the internal three-dimensional structure of a rock body, the geologist's next step is often to try to figure out the sequence of folding and faulting events that has created the observed structures (Fig. 10A). This task may be tackled either forward or backward: backward, by "unfolding" the folds and "unfaulting" the faults; or forward, by applying various combinations of folds and faults to an initially undeformed sequence of rock layers until a combination that resembles the observed structure is found.

Elements of the solid Earth also change their shape through erosion, through the uneven removal of parts of the whole. Thinking about eroded terrains requires the ability to envision negative spaces, the shape and internal structure of the stuff that is not there any more.

Insights from the Cognitive Science Literature—Envisioning Folding and Unfolding of Paper

The geoscientist's mental folding and unfolding of rock strata resembles the paper folding test used by psychologists to

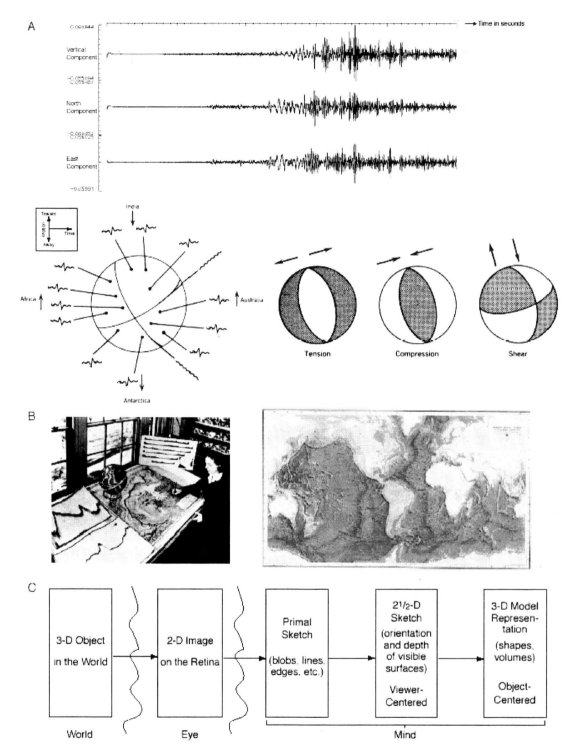

Figure 9. Raw geoscience data, as collected, is often one-dimensional or two-dimensional; it must be integrated to visualize a three-dimensional structure or think about a three-dimensional process. (A) Top: seismograph record showing the acceleration of Earth in three directions (up/down, north/south, and east/west) as a function of time (from Lamont Cooperative Seismic Network Web site, http://www.ldeo.columbia.edu/LCSN/). Lower left: diagram showing Earth divided into four quadrants, each with the same sense of first motion for a specific earthquake. Lower right: "beach ball" diagram, in which quadrants experiencing initial compression are dark and quadrants experiencing initial rarefaction are white (reproduced with permission from Anderson [1986, Figures 3–18 and 3–19]). (B) Pioneering marine cartographer Marie Tharp combined echo-sounder profiles of the seafloor to create physiographic models of the seafloor that allowed both geologists and the general public to visualize the seafloor mountains and valleys as though the water had been removed (photo and map available online at, or linked from, http://www.earthinstitute.columbia.edu/library/MarieTharp.html). (C) David Marr's (1982) model of visual processing illustrates that we all have vast experience transforming information from a two-dimensional image on the retina into a mental representation that captures the three-dimensional nature of a viewed object or landscape.

A

"Show how the present geometry could have been derived by folding and faulting."

0   10 m

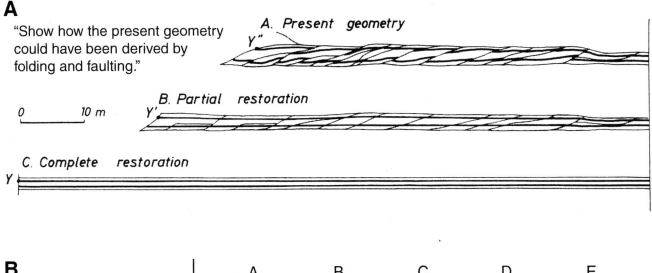

B

"The two figures on the left represent a square piece of paper being folded. In the second figure a small circle shows where a hole has been punched through all of the thicknesses of paper. Choose a drawing on the right that shows where the holes are after the paper has been unfolded."

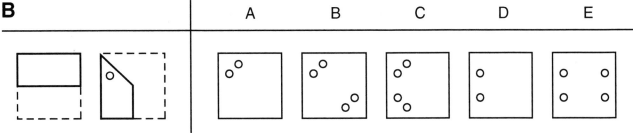

C

"Which of the lettered edges on the object at the right are the same as the numbered edges on the piece of paper at the left?"

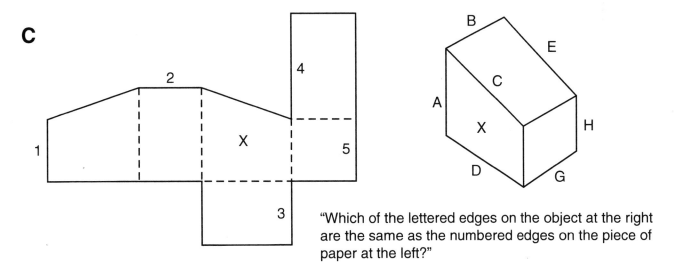

Figure 10. (A) Geoscientists need to envision how Earth materials change shape through deformation and removal of parts of the whole. In this example, initially flat-lying sedimentary strata have been deformed by folding and faulting (reproduced with permission from Ramsay and Huber [1987, Figure 24.13]). (B, C) The paper folding test and surface development test assess an aspect of spatial ability having to do with ability to mentally envision the outcome of manipulating an object by folding and unfolding (reproduced with permission from Eliot and Smith [1983, p. 331 and 341]). Answers: (B), correct answer is C; (C), correct answers are 1 = H; 2 = B; 3 = G; 4 = C; 5 = H.

study people's spatial visualization ability (Fig. 10B). This test shows the participant a piece of paper that has been folded and had holes punched through all the thicknesses of the paper, and then asks how the paper would look when unfolded. Shepard and Feng (1972) found that people took more time to respond as the total number of squares that would be involved in each fold increased. Kyllonen et al. (1984) showed that performance on the paper folding test can be improved by training, and that the effectiveness of different types of training methods (verbal or visual training, or self-directed practice) depended on both spatial and verbal ability of their participants.

Another related spatial test is the surface development test. In this test, the participant is shown a flat piece of paper and an object drawing. The object can be formed by folding the flat paper on dotted lines (Fig. 10C). The participant is then asked to indicate which edges of the flat paper correspond to which edges of the object drawing. Piburn et al. (2005) found that good performers on this test tended to score high on a geology content exam containing spatial items. Students who took laboratory sessions that emphasized spatial skills in geological contexts using computer-based learning materials (e.g., topographic map reading, sequencing geologic events such as layer deposition, folding, faulting, intrusions, and erosion) scored higher on the surface development test after the laboratory sessions than before. That is, spatial visualization ability seems to be important for geology learning, and also can be improved by spatially demanding geology exercises.

METAPHORICAL USE OF SPATIAL THINKING

Using Spatial-Thinking Strategies and Techniques to Think about Nonspatial Phenomena

The Geoscientist's Task—Using Space as a Proxy for Time

It is fairly common in thinking about the Earth to find that variation or progression through space is closely connected with variation or progression through time. For example, within a basin of undeformed sedimentary rocks, the downward direction corresponds to increasing time since deposition. On the seafloor, distance away from the mid-ocean-ridge spreading center corresponds to increasing time since formation of that strip of seafloor.

As a consequence, geologists often think about distance in space when they really want to be thinking about duration of geologic time. Distance in space is easy to measure, in vertical meters of stratal thickness, or horizontal kilometers of distance from ridge crest. Duration of geologic time is hard to measure and subject to ongoing revision, involving complicated forays into seafloor magnetic anomalies, radiometric dating, stable isotope ratios, or biostratigraphy.

In ordinary life, people also confound lengths in distance and lengths in time, but the asymmetry is the opposite direction. One asks, "How far to New Haven?" and the other answers, "about an hour and a half." In modern society, time is

the easy observable; people have more experience at estimating time than distance, and most people wear a time measuring device on their wrists. Therefore, the answer is given in time even though the question is posed in space ("how far?").

Time is important in geosciences because it constrains causal patterns. The sequence in which events happened constrains causality (if A happened before B, then A can have caused or influenced B, but not vice versa). The rate at which events happened constrains the power required (deposition at a rate of meters per thousand years requires different causal processes than deposition at centimeters per thousand years). Using a spatial dimension of a data display as a visual analogy to represent time allows the geoscientist to reveal or highlight causal relationships. For example, Sclater et al.'s (1971) depiction of seafloor age versus depth in oceans of different spreading rates (Fig. 11A) helped reveal the process of lithospheric cooling.

The Geoscientist's Task—Using Space as a Proxy for Other Quantifiable Properties

Specialists within different branches of geosciences have a tendency to use space as a metaphor for variation in observable but nonspatial parameters of natural systems. For example, petrologists visualize a tetrahedron, in which each corner is occupied by a chemical element or by a mineral of pure composition (e.g., one end member of a solid solution). Any given rock can be placed at a point within the tetrahedron according to the concentration of each of the components in the rock. To communicate this tetrahedron to colleagues, the data are projected down onto one of the sides of the tetrahedron, where it appears on the page as a triangle, with each rock sample appearing as a dot.

Igneous and metamorphic petrologists use pressure-temperature space. The pressure dimension of this space is something like distance beneath Earth's surface, but denominated in units of downward-increasing pressure rather than in units of distance. The temperature dimension is also related to distance beneath Earth's surface, with temperature increasing downward. The chemical composition of an igneous rock depends, in part, on where in pressure-temperature space the initial melt separated out of the mantle.

Physical oceanographers use T-S diagrams, where T is temperature and S is salinity of a water mass (Fig. 11B). Temperature and salinity together control the density of the water mass, and density in turn controls whether the water mass will sink relative to other water masses in the same ocean. Water samples that share a common history will likely cluster together in T-S space, and water masses with different histories of formation will usually occupy different areas of T-S space.

The mental processes for thinking about these non-distance-denominated "geospaces" feel similar to the thought processes for thinking about distribution of, and movement through, regular distance-space. A clue is that the vocabulary is the same. A body of rock in the mantle "moves" through pressure-temperature space on a "trajectory." Two water masses are "close together" or "far apart" in T-S space.

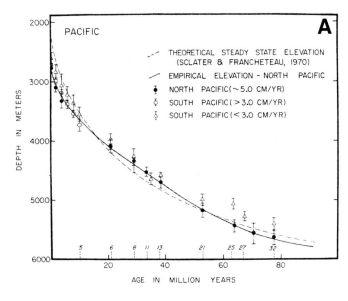

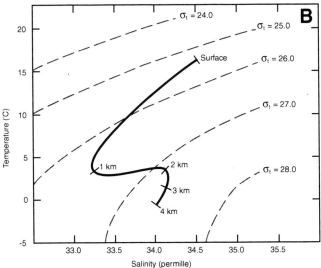

Figure 11. Geoscientists use spatial thinking as a metaphor or mental aid for thinking about nonspatial properties. (A) In this plot of ocean water depth, the horizontal axis represents time, in millions of years, that a patch of the seafloor has spent spreading away from its parent mid-ocean spreading center. When displayed this way, data points from various parts of the world's oceans fall neatly on an exponential curve. If the horizontal axis had been plotted as distance rather than time, the data from oceans with different spreading rates would have been scattered. This spatial-thinking insight helped Sclater et al. (1971) to demonstrate that the oceanic lithosphere cools as it ages, and subsides as it cools (reproduced with permission from Sclater et al. [1971, Fig. 2a]). (B) In this example, spatial dimensions of the graph are used to show temperature and salinity of an oceanic water mass. The dashed lines show contours of constant density, and the solid line shows an idealized vertical profile from sea surface to seafloor, at one spot in the ocean. At this locality, temperature and salinity decrease from the surface down to 1 km depth, temperature stays constant while salinity increases from 1 to 2 km, and then both decrease from 2 to 4 km. Water samples that fall close to each other in temperature-salinity space often share a common history (from online course notes for Climate System, Columbia University, http://eesc.columbia.edu/courses/ees/climate/lectures/o_strat.html).

Insights from the Cognitive Science Literature— Spatialization

Lakoff and Johnson (2003) offered an experientialist account of human understanding, as an alternative to objectivism and subjectivism. They argued that the human conceptual system is metaphorical in nature; in other words, we tend to understand something new in terms of something else, something grounded in our experiences in the physical and cultural environments. We constantly interact with space, and so, according to Lakoff and Johnson, spatialization metaphors are one of our essential ways of understanding. For example, the "more is up" metaphor (e.g., my income rose/fell last year) builds upon the physical basis that "if you add more of a substance or of physical objects to a container or pile, the level goes up" (p. 16). Related "up" metaphors are "future is up" (e.g., What's coming *up* this week?), "good is up" (e.g., he does *high*-quality work), and "virtue is up" (e.g., she has *high* standards), which are based on different aspects of physical and cultural experiences. In this view, use of space for depicting nonspatial parameters, such as those discussed in the previous section, is in line with human understanding of phenomena in general. Using a geoscience example, the geologic time scale, which shows the chronological history of Earth starting from the bottom (pre-Archean) to the top (present), may be conceived of as an analogy of rock layers, as younger strata settled on top of older strata through time.

Siegel and White (1975) discuss humans' tendency to transform nonspatial domains of human experience into a pattern or picture by a spatial interpretation or representation. They provide examples where this spatialization of nonspatial information seems to facilitate memory, retrieval of remembered information, and solution of reasoning problems. In Siegel and White's discussion and examples, the spatialization of nonspatial information is entirely a mental operation, whereas in our geoscience examples, the geoscientist often makes an external representation (e.g., a graph or sketch) in which the two dimensions of the paper or computer screen parallel the inherently nonspatial "dimensions" of the data.

CONCLUDING REMARKS

Synthesis: What is "Thinking Spatially" in the Geosciences?

From our discussion of geoscientists' tasks, spatial thinking in the geosciences can be summarized as follows:

1. observing, describing, recording, classifying, recognizing, remembering, and communicating the two- or three-dimensional shape, internal structure, orientation and/or position of objects, properties, or processes;

2. mentally manipulating those shapes, structures, orientations, or positions, for example, by rotation, translation, deformation, or partial removal;

3. making interpretations about what caused the objects, properties, or processes to have those particular shapes, structures, orientations, or positions;

4. making predictions about the consequences or implications of the observed shapes, internal structures, orientations, and positions; and

5. using spatial-thinking strategies as a shortcut, metaphor, or mental crutch to think about processes or properties that are distributed across some dimension other than distance-space.

Questions for Future Work

Although we have found many fascinating areas of overlapping interests between the domains of geoscience and cognitive science, there are many questions that remain incompletely answered or completely unaddressed. In addition to the finer-granularity questions we discussed above, broader questions include:

1. *Concerning explanatory schemata:* By what steps do geoscience novices learn to use the schemata that will enable them to ascribe meaning to spatial patterns, and how can that process be facilitated by geoscience educators? By what process do geoscientists working at the frontiers of knowledge develop new schemata? How are erroneous schemata replaced?

2. *Concerning evolutionary psychology:* The objects of interest to earth and environmental scientists are the same objects that were of life-and-death importance in the lives of ancestral humans (landforms, bodies of water, rocks, plants, animals). How has the way that the human brain thinks about the Earth and environment been shaped by the evolutionary pressures on our Pleistocene hunter-gatherer ancestors?

3. *Concerning synthesis:* How does the expert geoscientist integrate and synthesize spatial observations into a coherent whole, going from often fragmentary and ambiguous local observations, to a regional or global synthesis of observations, and then to a testable hypothesis about formative processes?

ACKNOWLEDGMENTS

Kastens originally developed some of the geosciences ideas in this paper for the National Research Committee on "Learning to Think Spatially: GIS as a Support System in the K–12 Curriculum"; she thanks the National Academies staff and the committee members for their encouragement and insights. Some of these ideas were presented at a Pardee Symposium held at the Annual Meeting of the Geological Society of America in Denver, Colorado, in October 2002; we thank Cathryn Manduca and David Mogk for organizing the symposium and all the participants for stimulating discussions. We are grateful to Gary Ernst, Cathy Manduca, Dave Mogk, and two anonymous reviewers for their valuable comments on an earlier draft of the manuscript. We thank Maureen Anders, Linda Pistolesi, and Margaret Turrin for their assistance with illustrations. This research was supported by the National Science Foundation under grant no. GEO 01-22001, GEO 03-31212, and REC 04-11823. This is Lamont-Doherty Earth Observatory contribution number 6926.

REFERENCES CITED

Acredolo, L.P., 1976, Frames of reference used by children for orientation in unfamiliar spaces, *in* Moore, G.T., and Golledge, R.G., eds., Environmental knowing: Theories, research, and methods: Stroudsburg, Pennsylvania, Dowden, Hutchinson and Ross, p. 165–172.

Acredolo, L.P., 1977, Developmental changes in the ability to coordinate perspectives of a large-scale space: Developmental Psychology, v. 13, p. 1–8, doi: 10.1037//0012-1649.13.1.1.

Allen, J.R.L., 1970, Physical processes of sedimentation: New York, American Elsevier, 248 p.

Anderson, R.N., 1986, Marine geology: A planet Earth perspective: New York, Wiley, 336 p.

Bartlett, F.C., 1932, Remembering: A study in experimental and social psychology: Cambridge, Cambridge University Press, 337 p.

Blatt, H., Middleton, G., and Murray, R., 1972, Origin of sedimentary rocks: Englewood Cliffs, New Jersey, Prentice-Hall, 634 p.

Bryant, K.J., 1982, Personality correlates of sense of direction and geographical orientation: Journal of Personality and Social Psychology, v. 43, p. 1318–1324, doi: 10.1037//0022-3514.43.6.1318.

Carroll, J.B., 1993, Human cognitive abilities: A survey of factor-analytic studies: Cambridge, Cambridge University Press, 829 p.

Carter, C., LaRussa, M., and Bodner, G., 1987, A study of two measures of spatial ability as predictors of success in different levels of general chemistry: Journal of Research in Science Teaching, v. 24, p. 645–657.

Chase, W.G., and Simon, H.A., 1973, Perception in chess: Cognitive Psychology, v. 4, p. 55–81, doi: 10.1016/0010-0285(73)90004-2.

Chi, M.T.H., Feltovich, P.J., and Glaser, R., 1981, Categorization and representation of physics problems by experts and novices: Cognitive Science, v. 5, p. 121–152.

Collins, A.M., and Quillian, M.R., 1969, Retrieval time from semantic memory: Journal of Verbal Learning and Verbal Behavior, v. 8, p. 240–248, doi: 10.1016/S0022-5371(69)80069-1.

Downs, R.M., and Liben, L.S., 1991, The development of expertise in geography: A cognitive-developmental approach to geographic education: Annals of the Association of American Geographers, v. 81, p. 304–327, doi: 10.1111/j.1467-8306.1991.tb01692.x.

Eliot, J., and Smith, I.M., 1983, An international directory of spatial tests: Windsor, UK, NFER-Nelson, 458 p.

Farber, P.L., 2000, Finding order in nature: The naturalist tradition from Linnaeus to E.O. Wilson: Baltimore, Johns Hopkins University Press, 152 p.

Geography Education Standards Project, 1994, Geography for life: National Geography Standards 1994: Washington, D.C., National Geographic Research and Exploration, 272 p.

Gilhooly, K.J., Wood, M., Kinnear, P.R., and Green, C., 1988, Skill in map reading and memory for maps: The Quarterly Journal of Experimental Psychology, v. 40A, p. 87–107.

Glen, W., 1982, The road to Jaramillo: Critical years of the revolution in earth science: Stanford, California, Stanford University Press, 459 p.

Hamblin, W.K., 1994, Introduction to physical geology (2nd edition): New York, Macmillan, 400 p.

Hanawalt, N.G., 1942, The effect of practice upon the perception of simple designs masked by more complex designs: Journal of Experimental Psychology, v. 31, p. 134–148.

Hart, R.A., and Moore, G.T., 1973, The development of spatial cognition: A review, *in* Downs, R.M., and Stea, D., eds., Image and environment: Cognitive mapping and spatial behavior: Chicago, Aldine, p. 246–288.

Hegarty, M., and Sims, V.K., 1994, Individual differences in mental animation during mechanical reasoning: Memory & Cognition, v. 22, p. 411–430.

Hobbs, B.E., Means, W.D., and Williams, P.F., 1976, An outline of structural geology: New York, Wiley, 512 p.

Hock, H.S., Gordon, G.P., and Marcus, N., 1974, Individual differences in the detection of embedded figures: Perception & Psychophysics, v. 15, p. 47–52.

Hurlbut, C.S., Jr., 1971, Dana's manual of mineralogy (18th edition): New York, Wiley, 530 p.

Hutton, J., 1788, Theory of the earth; or an investigation of the laws observable in the composition, dissolution, and restoration of land upon the globe: Transactions of the Royal Society of Edinburgh, v. 1, pt. 2, p. 209–304 (available online at http://www.uwmc.uwc.edu/geography/hutton/hutton.htm).

International Commission on Zoological Nomenclature, 1985, International code of zoological nomenclature (3rd edition): Berkeley, University of California Press, 338 p.

Ishikawa, T., and Kastens, K.A., 2005, Why some students have trouble with maps and other spatial representations: Journal of Geoscience Education, v. 53, p. 184–197.

Kail, R., and Park, Y., 1990, Impact of practice on speeded mental rotation: Journal of Experimental Child Psychology, v. 49, p. 227–244, doi: 10.1016/0022-0965(90)90056-E.

Kastens, K.A., and Ishikawa, T., 2004, Why some students have trouble with maps and spatial representations: An on-line tutorial for geoscience faculty: http://www.ldeo.columbia.edu/edu/DLESE/maptutorial.

Kastens, K.A., Kaplan, D., and Christie-Blick, K., 2001, Development and evaluation of a technology-supported map-skills curriculum, *Where are We?*: Journal of Geoscience Education, v. 49, p. 249–266.

Keller, E.F., 1983, A feeling for the organism: The life and work of Barbara McClintock: New York, Freeman, 272 p.

Kennett, J.P., 1982, Marine geology: Englewood Cliffs, New Jersey, Prentice-Hall, 813 p.

Kyllonen, P.C., Lohman, D.F., and Snow, R.E., 1984, Effects of aptitudes, strategy training, and task facets on spatial task performance: Journal of Educational Psychology, v. 76, p. 130–145, doi: 10.1037//0022-0663.76.1.130.

Lakoff, G., 1987, Women, fire, and dangerous things: What categories reveal about the mind: Chicago, University of Chicago Press, 632 p.

Lakoff, G., and Johnson, M., 2003, Metaphors we live by: Chicago, University of Chicago Press, 2nd edition, 256 p.

Lamont-Doherty Earth Observatory, 2001, Citation for award of first Lamont-Doherty Heritage Award: http://www.earthinstitute.columbia.edu/news/aboutStory/about7_1_01.html (accessed October 2002).

Lawrence, D.M., 1999, Mountains under the sea: Mercator's World, Nov/Dec issue, p. 36–43.

Lawrence, D.M., 2002, Upheaval from the abyss: Ocean floor mapping and the earth science revolution: New Brunswick, New Jersey, Rutgers University Press, 248 p.

Lesgold, A.M., Rubinson, H., Feltovich, P.J., Glaser, R., Klopfer, D., and Wang, Y., 1988, Expertise in a complex skill: Diagnosing X-ray pictures, *in* Chi, M.T.H., Glaser, R., and Farr, M., eds., The nature of expertise: Hillsdale, New Jersey, Erlbaum, p. 311–342.

Levine, M., Jankovic, I.N., and Palij, M., 1982, Principles of spatial problem solving: Journal of Experimental Psychology, General, v. 111, p. 157–175, doi: 10.1037//0096-3445.111.2.157.

Levine, M., Marchon, I., and Hanley, G., 1984, The placement and misplacement of you-are-here maps: Environment and Behavior, v. 16, p. 139–157.

Levinson, S.C., 1996, Frames of reference and Molyneux's question: Cross-linguistic evidence, *in* Bloom, P., Peterson, M.A., Nadel, L., and Garrett, M.F., eds., Language and space: Cambridge, Massachusetts, Massachusetts Institute of Technology (MIT) Press, p. 109–169.

Liben, L.S., 1978, Performance on Piagetian spatial tasks as a function of sex, field dependence, and training: Merrill-Palmer Quarterly, v. 24, p. 97–110.

Liben, L.S., 1991, Adults' performance on horizontality tasks: Conflicting frames of reference: Developmental Psychology, v. 27, p. 285–294, doi: 10.1037/0012-1649.27.2.285.

Liben, L.S., and Downs, R.M., 1993, Understanding person-space-map relations: Cartographic and developmental perspectives: Developmental Psychology, v. 29, p. 739–752, doi: 10.1037/0012-1649.29.4.739.

Liben, L.S., and Golbeck, S.L., 1984, Performance on Piagetian horizontality and verticality tasks: Sex-related differences in knowledge of relevant physical phenomena: Developmental Psychology, v. 20, p. 595–606, doi: 10.1037//0012-1649.20.4.595.

Linn, M.C., and Petersen, A.C., 1985, Emergence and characterization of sex differences in spatial ability: A meta-analysis: Child Development, v. 56, p. 1479–1498.

Marr, D., 1982, Vision: A computational investigation into the human representation and processing of visual information: New York, Freeman, 397 p.

Marshak, S., 2001, Earth: Portrait of a planet: New York, Norton, 735 p.

Mathewson, J.H., 1999, Visual-spatial thinking: An aspect of science overlooked by educators: Science & Education, v. 83, p. 33–54, doi: 10.1002/(SICI)1098-237X(199901)83:1<33::AID-SCE2>3.0.CO;2-Z.

Mayer, R.E., and Sims, V.K., 1994, For whom is a picture worth a thousand words? Extensions of a dual-coding theory of multimedia learning: Journal of Educational Psychology, v. 86, p. 389–401, doi: 10.1037/0022-0663.86.3.389.

McBurney, D.H., Gaulin, S.J.C., Devineni, T., and Adams, C., 1997, Superior spatial memory of women: Stronger evidence for the gathering hypothesis: Evolution and Human Behavior, v. 18, p. 165–174, doi: 10.1016/S1090-5138(97)00001-9.

McGeary, D., and Plummer, C.C., 1998, Physical geology: Earth revealed (3rd edition): Boston, McGraw-Hill, 592 p.

McGee, M.G., 1979, Human spatial abilities: Psychometric studies and environmental, genetic, hormonal, and neurological influences: Psychological Bulletin, v. 86, p. 889–918, doi: 10.1037//0033-2909.86.5.889.

Merriwether, A.M., and Liben, L.S., 1997, Adults' failures on Euclidean and projective spatial tasks: Implications for characterizing spatial cognition: Journal of Adult Development, v. 4, p. 57–69.

National Research Council, 2006, Learning to think spatially: Washington, D.C., The National Academies Press, 313 p.

Owen, C., Pirie, D., and Draper, G., 2001, Earth lab: Exploring the earth sciences: Pacific Grove, California, Brooks/Cole, 432 p.

Pallrand, G., and Seeber, F., 1984, Spatial ability and achievement in introductory physics: Journal of Research in Science Teaching, v. 21, p. 507–516.

Piaget, J., 1983, Piaget's theory, *in* Kessen, W., ed., Handbook of child psychology. Volume 1: History, theory, and methods (4th edition): New York, Wiley, p. 103–128.

Piaget, J., and Inhelder, B., 1967, The child's conception of space (trans. F.J. Langdon and J.L. Lunzer): New York, Norton (original work published 1948, 512 p.).

Piburn, M., 1980, Spatial reasoning as a correlate of formal thought and science achievement for New Zealand students: Journal of Research in Science Teaching, v. 17, p. 443–448.

Piburn, M., Reynolds, S.J., McAuliffe, C., Leedy, D.E., Birk, J.P., and Johnson, J.K., 2005, The role of visualization in learning from computer-based images. International Journal of Science Education, v. 27, p. 513–527.

Pitman, W.C., III, and Heirtzler, J.R., 1966, Magnetic anomalies over the Pacific-Antarctic Ridge: Science, v. 154, p. 1164–1171.

Ramsay, J.G., and Huber, M.I., 1983, The techniques of modern structural geology. Volume 1: Strain analysis: London, Academic Press, 307 p.

Ramsay, J.G., and Huber, M.I., 1987, The techniques of modern structural geology. Volume 2: Folds and fractures: London, Academic Press, 391 p.

Rochford, K., 1985, Spatial learning disabilities and underachievement among university anatomy students: Medical Education, v. 19, p. 13–26.

Rodgers, J., 1990, Fold-and-thrust belts in sedimentary rocks. Part 1: Typical examples: American Journal of Science, v. 290, p. 321–359.

Rodgers, J., 2001, The company I kept; autobiography of a geologist: Transactions of the Connecticut Academy of Arts and Sciences, v. 58, p. 224.

Rosch, E., 1978, Principles of categorization, *in* Rosch, E., and Lloyd, B.B., eds., Cognition and categorization: Hillsdale, New Jersey, Erlbaum, p. 27–48.

Russell-Gebbett, J., 1984, Pupils' perceptions of three-dimensional structures in biology lessons: Journal of Biological Education, v. 18, p. 220–226.

Sclater, J., and J. Francheteau, 1970, The implications of terrestrial heat flow observations on current tectonic and geochemical models of the crust and upper mantle of the Earth: Geophysical Journal of the Royal Astronomical Society, v. 20, p. 493–509.

Sclater, J.G., Anderson, R.N., and Bell, M.L., 1971, Elevation of ridges and evolution of the central eastern Pacific: Journal of Geophysical Research, v. 76, p. 7888–7915.

Shepard, R.N., and Feng, C., 1972, A chronometric study of mental paper folding: Cognitive Psychology, v. 3, p. 228–243, doi: 10.1016/0010-0285(72)90005-9.

Shepard, R.N., and Metzler, J., 1971, Mental rotation of three-dimensional objects: Science, v. 171, p. 701–703.

Siegel, A.W., and White, S.H., 1975, The development of spatial representations of large-scale environments, *in* Reese, H.W., ed., Advances in child development and behavior, vol. 10: New York, Academic Press, p. 9–55.

Silverman, I., and Eals, M., 1992, Sex differences in spatial abilities: Evolutionary theory and data, *in* Barkow, J.H., Cosmides, L., and Tooby, J., eds., The adapted mind: Evolutionary psychology and the generation of culture: New York, Oxford University Press, p. 533–549.

Simpson, G.G., 1940, Types in modern taxonomy: American Journal of Science, v. 238, p. 413–431.

Thomas, H., and Jamison, W., 1975, On the acquisition of understanding that still water is horizontal: Merrill-Palmer Quarterly, v. 21, p. 31–44.

Thomas, H., Jamison, W., and Hummel, D.D., 1973, Observation is insufficient for discovering that the surface of still water is invariably horizontal: Science, v. 181, p. 173–174.

Thorndyke, P.W., and Hayes-Roth, B., 1982, Differences in spatial knowledge acquired from maps and navigation: Cognitive Psychology, v. 14, p. 560–589, doi: 10.1016/0010-0285(82)90019-6.

Tooby, J., and Cosmides, L., 1992, The psychological foundations of culture, *in* Barkow, J.H., Cosmides, L., and Tooby, J., eds., The adapted mind: Evolutionary psychology and the generation of culture: New York, Oxford University Press, p. 19–136.

Tuckey, H., and Selvaratnam, M., 1993, Studies involving three-dimensional visualization skills in chemistry: A review: Studies in Science Education, v. 21, p. 99–121.

Vail, P.R., Mitchum, R.M., Jr., Todd, R.G., Widmier, J.M., Thompson, S., III, Sangree, J.B., Bubb, J.N., and Hatlelid, W.G., 1977, Seismic stratigraphy and global changes of sea level, *in* Payton, C.E., ed., Seismic stratigraphy: Applications to hydrocarbon exploration: Tulsa, Oklahoma, American Association of Petroleum Geologists, p. 49–212.

Vandenberg, S.G., and Kuse, A.R., 1978, Mental rotations, a group test of three-dimensional spatial visualization: Perceptual and Motor Skills, v. 47, p. 599–604.

Vasta, R., Knott, J.A., and Gaze, C.E., 1996, Can spatial training erase the gender differences on the water-level task?: Psychology of Women Quarterly, v. 20, p. 549–567.

Voyer, D., Voyer, S., and Bryden, M.P., 1995, Magnitude of sex differences in spatial abilities: A meta-analysis and consideration of critical variables: Psychological Bulletin, v. 117, p. 250–270, doi: 10.1037/0033-2909.117.2.250.

Warren, D.H., and Scott, T.E., 1993, Map alignment in traveling multisegment routes: Environment and Behavior, v. 25, p. 643–666.

Wegener, A.L., 1929, The origin of continents and oceans (3rd edition) (trans. J. Biram 1966): New York, Dover, 246 p.

Winchester, S., 2001, The map that changed the world: William Smith and the birth of modern geology: New York, HarperCollins, 352 p.

MANUSCRIPT ACCEPTED BY THE SOCIETY 21 MARCH 2006

Geological Society of America
Special Paper 413
2006

Building an understanding of geological time: A cognitive synthesis of the "macro" and "micro" scales of time

Jeff Dodick

Science Teaching Center, The Hebrew University of Jerusalem, Givat Ram, Jerusalem 91904, Israel

Nir Orion

Department of Science Teaching, Weizmann Institute of Science, Rehovot 76100, Israel

ABSTRACT

Few discoveries in geology are more important than geological time. However, for most people, it is impossible to grasp because of its massive scale. In this chapter, we offer a solution to this problem based on our research in cognition and education. Our strategy involves the decoupling of geological time between the macroscale of deep time, which includes the major features of Earth history, and the study of which we call event-based studies, and the microscale of relative time, represented by strata, the study of which we term logic-based studies. Our event-based study focuses on the problem of learning about macroevolution within the massive time scale of the fossil record. We approached this problem by creating a four-stage learning model in which the students manipulated a series of increasingly complex visual representations of evolution in time. Postprogram results indicate that students had a better understanding of macroevolution as seen in the fossil record; moreover, they appreciated that different events in absolute time required different scales of time to occur. Our logic-based studies used Montangero's diachronic thinking model as a basis for describing how students reconstruct geological systems in time. Using this model, we designed three specialized instruments to test a sample of middle and high school students. Our findings indicated that there were significant differences between students in grade 9–12 and grade 7–8 in their ability to reconstruct geological systems. Moreover, grade 11–12 geology majors in Israel had a significant advantage over their nongeological counterparts in such reconstruction tasks.

Keywords: geological time, relative time, diachronic thinking, absolute time, scale.

INTRODUCTION

Geology has provided science with two paradigms, which rival the revolutionary discoveries of the quanta in physics and the uncoiling of the DNA (deoxyribonucleic acid) helix in biology—plate tectonics and geological time. The former, a discovery of the late nineteenth and twentieth centuries, forever banished the picture of a static earth, replacing it with a vision of a world composed of drifting continents. It is discussed in detail in another chapter of this book (Anderson, this volume, chapter 3). The second paradigm, the discovery of geological time, has scientific roots that extend back to the eighteenth century, in the work of James Hutton, who discarded the "comforting" image of a world that was separated by a mere 6000 yr from its creation (and creator) to one in which "we find no vestige of a beginning and no prospect of an end" (Hutton, 1788, p. 304).

Dodick, J., and Orion, N., 2006, Building an understanding of geological time: A cognitive synthesis of the "macro" and "micro" scales of time, *in* Manduca, C.A., and Mogk, D.W., eds., Earth and Mind: How Geologists Think and Learn about the Earth: Geological Society of America Special Paper 413, p. 77–93, doi: 10.1130/2006.2413(06). For permission to copy, contact editing@geosociety.org. ©2006 Geological Society of America. All rights reserved.

The revolution of geological time is important to science because of its influence not only upon geology, but many scientific disciplines, including paleontology, evolutionary biology, and cosmology, all of which are constrained by large-scale temporal processes. Thus, any student or practitioner that wants to build an understanding of such fields must do so within a framework of geological time.

Yet to grasp what John McPhee (1980) poetically termed "deep time" is no easy task. Human beings are limited to a lifetime that will allow them to see (with good health) the passage of three generations, not nearly the time needed to psychologically encompass 4.6 billion years of Earth history. Thus, the question remains as to how it might be possible to understand (and accept) the vastness of geological time and the events that have shaped our planet. The purpose of this chapter, therefore, is to offer solutions to this problem, based on our experiences as both scientists and researchers in science education. Using the tools of cognition and education, we present a series of studies that define the factors affecting students' ability to understand changes that shape the Earth in the framework of "deep time," as well as possible directions for future research. By doing this, we hope to contribute to a better understanding about some of the reasoning processes used in geology, and thus, provide conceptual tools that might help geoscience educators improve their practice.

Previous Research on the Understanding of Geological Time

Despite the critical importance of geological time, there has been relatively little attention given to it by researchers in the field of cognition or science education. The small amount of research that has been completed was previously reviewed by Dodick and Orion (2003a, 2003b, 2003c) and is updated here to provide structure to the ensuing discussion; it includes two types of research: event-based studies and logic-based studies.

Event-based studies include research that surveys student understanding of the entirety of "deep time" (beginning with the formation of Earth or the universe) and usually involves sequencing a series of biological-geological events. This is done relatively, using card-sorting tasks, or lists of such events, and sometimes includes reference to absolute time, using questionnaires and/or interviews that rely on time lines or response time scales divided into numerical intervals. Often in such sequencing tasks, the subject is asked to justify his reasons for his proposed temporal order. Using such responses, the subjects are often profiled into categories, which represent their knowledge and misconceptions about relative and absolute time. The small number of event-based studies can be classified according to their demographic breakdown and include:

Noonan and Good's (1999) research on middle school students' understanding about the origins of Earth and life; a similar study by Marques and Thompson (1997) with Portuguese students in elementary and middle schools; and Trends' studies on the conception of geological time amongst 10–11-yr-old children (Trend, 1997, 1998, 2001c, 2002), 17 yr olds (Trend, 2001b, 2001c, 2002), as well as amongst primary teacher trainees (Trend, 2000, 2001c, 2002), and teachers (Trend, 2001a, 2001c, 2002). Most recently, research has focused on university students and includes White et al.'s (2004) time-line study with 63 students from four U.S. colleges, as well as the work of Libarkin and Kurdziel (2004) and Libarkin et al. (2005), which classifies college students' ontological perspectives toward geological time.

Although it is difficult to compare such studies, as most used different research protocols, the findings do show that all of the samples tested had difficulties with sequence, assigning absolute dates, as well as scaling events on a time line. Qualitatively, however, these difficulties do appear to lessen with the increasing age of the subjects who participated in these studies.

The second type of research, the logic-based study, is based on the logical decisions that students apply to the ordering of geological-biological events as seen in stratigraphic layers (using basic principles of relative dating). Two studies of this type are found in the literature: Chang and Barufaldi (1999) examined the effects of a problem-solving–based instructional model on their subjects' (ninth-grade students in Taiwan) achievements and alternative frameworks in the geosciences. In their research, they used a questionnaire that contained visual problems testing the ability to reconstruct depositional environments. In contrast, Ault (1981) interviewed a group of students (grades K–6) using a series of puzzles designed to test how they reconstructed geological strata. Based on Zwart's (1976) suggestion that the development of temporal understanding lies in the "before and after" relationship, Ault (1981, 1982) theorized that young children organize geological time relationally. Using these results, Ault (1981) claimed that the young child's concept of conventional time was no impediment toward his or her understanding of the geologic past. Nonetheless, although many of the children in Ault's (1981) study were successful at solving his interview problems, these same subjects had difficulties in solving similar problems in the field, indicating that there was little transfer from the classroom to authentic geological settings.

These difficulties can be traced to Ault's (1981) research design, which, influenced as it was by Piaget's (1969) previous work, included physics-based problems, which associate time conception with the understanding of velocity, motion, and distance. However, geology largely builds its knowledge of time through visual interpretation of static entities, such as strata (Frodeman, 1995, 1996), which represent previously dynamic systems. Ault's (1981) design multiplied the variables that he needed to explain, as he admitted in a later work (Ault, 1982). Further, it did not focus its efforts on the special qualities of geological time (such as its enormous scale) that might complicate a young child's thinking.

This argument is supported by research in psychology. Both Friedman (1978) and Harner (1982) noted that it is not until around age 14 that children begin using time concepts such as century, generation, and forefather. Thus, it is unlikely that the children studied by Ault (1981, 1982) would have had a deep understanding of absolute geological time.

Indeed, there is no reason to suggest that understanding the relationships amongst strata should necessarily allow one to conceptualize the massive scale of geological time. Thus, we argue that the understanding of relative and absolute time can be studied, and taught, respectively, as separate entities (Dodick and Orion, 2003a, 2003c). In the earth sciences, this is common, as geologists do not necessarily need to apply both relative and numerical dating methods to a given collection of strata in order to date them.

In addition to the studies previously mentioned, we note the small body of research that catalogues general ideas about Earth, including problems related to geological time (Happs, 1982; Marques, 1988; Oversby, 1996; Schoon, 1989, 1992). The problem with such studies is that they do not provide a cognitive model of student understanding of geological time.

Finally, one might mention those works within geological education that have concentrated on the practical elements of teaching geological time (Everitt et al., 1996; Hume, 1978; Metzger, 1992; Miller, 2005; Nieto-Obregon, 2005; Reuss and Gardulski, 2001; Ritger and Cummins, 1991; Rowland, 1983; Spencer-Cervato and Daly, 2000; Thomas, 2005). Unfortunately, most of these teaching models have never been formally evaluated, so it is difficult to attest to their effectiveness. Nonetheless, Ritger and Cummins' (1991) approach does show promise because it emphasizes a constructivistic approach in which the student builds a "personal metaphor" of geological time permitting him to structure this abstract concept based on his own criteria. Moreover, the interactive game approach designed by Reuss and Gardulski (2001) for their course in historical geology received very high ratings by the undergraduates who participated in this course.

In this chapter, we discuss our research (Dodick and Orion, 2003a, 2003b, 2003c) in which we define some of the problems faced by middle and high school students in understanding geological time. The goal of this work was to devise effective strategies for helping students interpret the fossil record. Thus, our research focused on the cognitive skills that are required for understanding evolution and environmental change over time. Rather than a concept in of itself, geological time is often referenced within the context of historical sciences such as paleontology, archaeology, or geology, so it was felt that contextualizing geological time would provide a better indication of the students' understanding of this concept, while also permitting us to apply the results toward improving our curriculum development efforts. Indeed, much research supports such situated cognition in learning environments.

This research followed the taxonomy of event-based and logic-based studies proposed in the previous sections. In doing this, we hoped to build a synthesis of the larger "macro" (event-based studies) and smaller "micro" (logic-based studies) scales of geological time.

PART 1: UNDERSTANDING EVOLUTIONARY CHANGE WITHIN THE FRAMEWORK OF "DEEP TIME"—AN EVENT-BASED STUDY

Macroevolution (i.e., evolution above the taxonomic level of species) takes place in geological time. However, as Dodick and Orion (2003b) have shown, most curricula, as well as education research connected to evolutionary biology, ignore macroevolution and have largely concentrated on the mechanisms of microevolution. Thus, in this study, we focused on a learning strategy that was designed to overcome students' difficulty in understanding the massive absolute scale of geological time as it applies to macroevolution as witnessed in the fossil record. This strategy was employed in the Israeli high school program *From Dinosaurs to Darwin: Evolution from the Perspective of Time* (Dodick and Orion, 2000).

METHOD

To evaluate this learning strategy, we focused on an in-depth case study involving the implementation of this program amongst a single high school class, consisting of 22 earth sciences students with little background in biology, in an urban high school in Israel. (Our intention is to expand this research with a larger sample of high school students.) This class was chosen for implementation because the subject of this curriculum expanded on a required element of their earth sciences program, "History of Earth" (focusing on the physical changes affecting the development of Earth over the vast span of geological time).

The subjects of this study were evaluated both prior to and following the learning of the program with two questionnaires:
1.   Geological Time Assessment Test (*GeoTAT*): a validated questionnaire containing a series of cognitive puzzles testing the students' ability to reconstruct depositional systems in time.
2.   Macroevolution knowledge questionnaire, which tested both the students' understanding of (macro) evolution, as well as absolute time. Thus, one of the tasks was for students to sequence major events in the fossil record on a numerical time line similar to the work of White et al. (2004).

In addition, the first author was present at all sessions of this program to observe the students and interview them as they proceeded through the activities.

EVALUATION

Briefly, the program *From Dinosaurs to Darwin* was divided into three units:
1.   *Materials in time.* This unit dealt with the basic materials of the fossil record and the principles of relative dating that permit scientists to understand their temporal relationships. This unit included field work in which the students reconstructed the depositional history of Mahktesh Hatira, a natural crater in the north-central Negev region of Israel.

2. *Evolution and the fossil record.* This unit was concerned with modeling the adaptive radiation of organisms in the context of absolute geological time.
3. *Independent project.* This unit enabled the students to investigate evolutionary aspects of the fossil record (e.g., the evolution of flight).

It is in the second unit that we employed the strategy of fusing evolution and the massive scale of geological time. This consisted of four activities in which the guiding principle was to shape the students ability to manipulate multiple (iconographic) representations of evolution in time, while at the same time introducing the concept of absolute time. According to Kozma et al. (2000), the ability to interpret (scientific) representations is critical to professional scientists because it allows them to organize information into conceptually meaningful patterns. Further, they argued that if science students are to pursue inquiry-based problems, a fundamental goal of science education (American Association for the Advancement of Science, 1990, 1993; National Research Council, 1996, 2000), they must also obtain such interpretation skills. In their research, they showed that chemists have a set of representational skills central to their research. These skills allow them to move flexibly between different types of representations so that they may better understand their domain. Similarly, paleontologists must mediate between different sets of representations, including phylogenetic trees, cross sections, and anatomical figures to solve specific problems.

In the second unit, students experimented with some of these representations to learn how professional scientists transform concrete field-based information to a three-dimensional picture of evolution. As the material was conceptually new, we have scaffolded the investigations into a four-stage model linked by a series of bridging questions. These questions were worded so that the students could critique the models that they designed at each stage of the unit, while linking them to the next iconographic model. Thus, they built parallel conceptions of macroevolution that were nested within the scale of absolute time.

Stage 1: The "Infamous Ladder of Progress" (Gould, 1989, 1995)

Although most biology and earth science textbooks deal with evolution, they sometimes unintentionally mislead students by using representations that treat evolution as a linear progression in time from prokaryotes to man, and thus, perpetuate the misconception that the history of life represents progress from primitive to complex. Moreover, because they isolate single groups of life (for example, fish, which evolve prior to amphibians) in this temporal progression, students inadvertently construct a second misconception, that one form of life replaces another in time. (Indeed our research confirms this assertion.)

Gould (1995, p. 252) in his essay "Evolution by Walking" noted a similar trend in the way fossils are displayed in many museums of natural history:

In other words, temporal order is not construed as a set of representative samples for all animal groups through time, but as a sequential tale of the most progressive at any moment, with superseded groups dropped forever once a new "ruler" emerges, even though the old groups may continue to flourish and diversify.

Possibly, this misconception is enhanced by the iconography of geology itself. A predominant representation in earth science textbooks is the cross section. If fossils are illustrated within the section, they often show supposed progression from "primitive" (at the bottom) to "complex" (at the top) life forms. Moreover, many students who understand the principle of superposition will naturally assume this progressive trend. Thus, it was important that we design activities that would counteract this misunderstanding. In the first activity of this unit, students participate in an investigation titled, "Fossils and Rocks: A Detective Puzzle." This investigation is a large-scale problem in biostratigraphic correlation, in which the students constructed a cross section consisting of 27 events representing the key evolutionary features of Earth history (which were based on a survey of textbooks and interviews with earth scientists and biologists). At the beginning of this investigation, they received a set of nine cross sections (representing geographically distinct sites) divided into five strata, each containing a different assemblage of fossils representing a key feature of the fossil record. After completing the correlation, the students listed the key features of the fossil record (from oldest to youngest), based on their position relative to other key features, and place them into a table containing absolute dates for each of the key features. After completing this unit, the students significantly improved their ability to correlate strata. Preprogram, they scored 67.8%; postprogram, their scores improved to 81.1%, indicating that they had grasped the mechanics of stratigraphic correlation. Note, that the student-built cross section indeed anticipates the misconception of "the ladder of progress." Thus, immediately after completing this activity, the students were confronted by two bridging questions that challenged this misconception. The first asked for a critique of this representation as an "image of evolution in time," whereas the second asked them to suggest a better representation. To the former question, students noted many of the difficulties previously mentioned. In fact, some noticed these problems without being prompted. To the latter question, most suggested a branching tree-like icon, as it better represents evolutionary relationships, parallel development of different lineages, and extinction. Postprogram, students recognized the superiority of this icon (prescores = 22.2% and postscores = 55.6%); more importantly, they could also cite reasons for its superiority (prescores = 16.7% and postscores = 58.3%).

Stage 2: Evolutionary Relationships in Time

The second stage was connected to the first by requiring the students to build the preferred icon of evolution in time, the evolutionary tree. To complete this activity, the students completed group reports on a select number of key features of the fossil record (using MacDonald's [1989] method of small-group oral presentations), the result of which was the construction of a simple phylogenetic tree.

Our strategy was that while building their phylogenetic tree, the students constructed an association between biological events and geological time periods. This strategy was based on research in psychology, which indicates that one of the symbolic modes involved in representing conventional time systems (such as days of the week) is the associational network (Collins and Loftus, 1975). For example, Friedman (1982, p. 182) argued that individual months are recognized by their linkage with "numerous personal or shared propositions (e.g., my birthday, cold, Halloween, etc.)." So, we thought it possible to understand geological time by associating specific time periods with key evolutionary events.

Central to this learning strategy is that fossils are rich visual evidence for evolutionary change in time. In their studies of historical understanding amongst grade 5 children, Barton and Levstik (1996) and Levstik and Barton (1996) concluded that using visual images with a variety of chronological clues stimulated a greater depth of historical understanding than mere verbal description. So too, fossil materials, representing key events in life's history, act as a concrete organizer to bridge over the abstract difficulties of evolutionary change in time.

Stage 3: The Scales of Time

A critical element in this unit was developing a sense of "deep time,"—the understanding that human dominion is confined to the last microseconds of the metaphorical geologic clock. Previous efforts at teaching this concept have focused on constructing a single metaphor that might help the student build a perspective of the scale of geological time (Everitt et al., 1996; Hume, 1978; Metzger, 1992; Nieto-Obregon, 2005; Ritger and Cummins, 1991; Rowland, 1983; Spencer-Cervato and Daly, 2000).

The difficulty with these approaches is that by scaling all biological-geological events to the same time line, students lose site of humankind's relation to geological time. Instead, we had the students compare six different time scales, geological time (4.6 Ga), biological time (3.8 Ga), fossil time (530 Ma), human evolution (2 Ma), civilization (5000 yr), and personal time (75 yr). The advantage is that students realize that different (historically constrained) disciplines, including the earth sciences, archaeology, and history, by necessity, operate on different scales of absolute time, which at the same time often dwarf the human life span.

Postprogram, most students improved their ability to assign absolute dates to a variety of (well-known) evolutionary events, such as the beginning of life. More difficult was plotting these events on a scaled time line, especially at its terminal end, as represented by events such as the appearance of dinosaurs or hominids. As with White et al.'s (2004) study of undergraduates, as well as Noonan and Good's (1999) work on middle school

students, the tendency here was for the students to strongly overestimate the absolute age of these events on a time line.

Nonetheless, although the students did not accurately date these events on the time line, they did get closer to the correct figures, postprogram; simply put, they reduced their overestimation. This suggests that the strategy of associating evolutionary events and their chronology is fundamentally sound. Moreover, students were more successful in understanding the chronology of events they had personally researched in their group projects.

Stage 4: The Rates of Evolution

Having completed the third stage, the students had a better understanding of the enormous scale of geological time, although problems remained. For this reason, we added a further representation of time. As this curriculum's focus was evolution, we thought it best to add another temporal criterion: that much of the development of life, as seen in the fossil record, has occurred in the last 530 million years of the geological time scale, beginning with the "Cambrian explosion" (Gould, 1989). This represents a mere 11% of all geological time. (In fact, cellular life appears to have evolved approximately 3.8 billion years ago; however, the fossil record is biased toward Cambrian events because it was only then that hard skeletons evolved.)

Thus, in this stage, students returned to the phylogenetic tree completed in stage two and added a scale of absolute time. As a result, they saw that much of evolution was squeezed into the upper reaches of their branching diagrams (Figs. 1A and 1B). Moreover, they gained a newfound perspective into the antiquity (and diversity) of unicellular life, echoing the sentiments

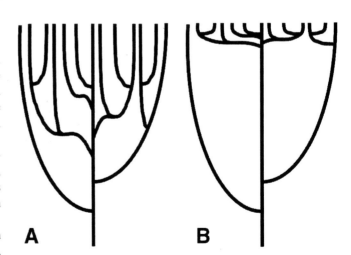

Figure 1. Illustrations of evolutionary relationships often do not add a scale of time (A). By adding a temporal scale, students see that much of the evolution of organisms with skeletons is compacted into the last 11% of time (B). (These figures are schematic in nature and do not replicate any known phylogeny.)

of Gould (1995, p. 252): "bacteria continue to rule the world today, as they have since life's beginnings (and will until the sun explodes)." Finally, this activity demonstrated that different organisms evolve at different rates.

Our experience has shown that linking evolution with geological time is a sound method of building an understanding of absolute time. The key to this process is in exposing students to a variety of visual representations, each of which symbolizes a different aspect of evolution in time. In this way, students have the ability to critique the representations they see, as well as build a more sophisticated understanding of an abstract subject.

PART 2: RECONSTRUCTING GEOLOGICAL AND BIOLOGICAL PROCESSES IN TIME-LOGIC-BASED STUDIES

Of the literature that does deal with geological time, most of it focuses on the difficulties associated with encompassing the vast scale of deep time. This is usually associated with the huge time spans provided by radiometric dating techniques in the geosciences. However, geology also builds its understanding of temporal changes through individual rock layers exposed on Earth's surface. Such layers can be logically ordered using relative dating principles, many of which were formulated in Europe between the seventeenth and nineteenth centuries. Thus, in this section, we discuss the research we undertook to cognitively model the strategies that middle school and high school students use to reconstruct depositional sequences over time (Dodick and Orion, 2003a, 2003c).

BACKGROUND

Scientific skills are usually acquired after a long process of study and use of such skills that are situated in their natural environment. However, our research has shown that even students untutored in geology can apply some of its formal principles for reconstructing sequences of strata. They can do this because the structure of such principles is similar to Montangero's (1992, 1996) model of diachronic thinking, which is the capacity to represent transformations over time. Montangero's (1996) model defined the structural and functional entities that are activated when diachronic thinking is used. He tested this model by asking children aged 7–11 to reconstruct the time-based changes that affected phenomena they recognized from their daily lives, such as a tree's life cycle. Based on these arguments, we thought that students might also be able to transfer this natural talent in diachronic thinking to the more specialized scenarios of a depositional system (Dodick and Orion, 2003a, 2003c).

Montangero's (1996) model consists of four schemes that permit a subject to think diachronically. As part of our research, these schemes were translated into the specific principles that geologists use to reconstruct stratigraphic sequences. This correlation between Montangero's schemes and geologic principles was first presented in Dodick and Orion (2003a, 2003c) and is repeated here for clarity (Table 1).

The factor limiting a subject's ability to activate these schemes is his or her knowledge of the phenomenon; in his work, Montangero (1996) delineated three different types of knowledge that are important for activating the diachronic schemes. The following two knowledge factors are most important for understanding geological transformations:

1. *Empirical knowledge.* This is knowledge of transformations derived from personal experience or from the influence of specific cultural representations. Thus, if students do not know that limestone is composed of reef-dwelling organisms that lived in shallow water, they may not be able to reconstruct its full depositional history.

TABLE 1. DIACHRONIC SCHEMES AND THEIR GEOLOGICAL CORRELATES

Diachronic schemes and their Explanation (Montangero, 1996)	Geological Correlate
Transformation: This scheme defines a principle of change, whether qualitative or quantitative. Quantitative transformation implies an increase or a decrease in the number of elements comprising an object, for example, the changing number of a tree's leaves during different seasons. Qualitative transformations are concerned with the complexity of objects, such as the change in shape of a growing tree.	In geology, such transformations are understood through the principle of "actualism" ("the present as a key to the past"), in which geological or biological change is reconstructed through comparison with contemporary fossil and depositional environments.
Temporal Organization: This scheme defines the sequential order of stages in a transformational process, as well as the general form of the sequence of stages, for example, linear, cyclical, etc.	In geology, principles, such as superposition, correlation, and original horizontality, all of which are based on the three-dimensional relationship amongst strata, are used as a means of determining temporal organization.
Interstage Linkage: The connections between the successive stages of transformation phenomena. Such connections are built in two ways: 1. Relations between necessary prerequisite and its sequel. 2. Cause and effect relationships.	In geology, such stages of interstage linkage are reconstructed via the combination of actualism (as defined above) and (scientific) causal reasoning.
Dynamic Synthesis: Forming a whole from a set of successive stages which are thus conceived of as manifestations of a single process of change.	In geology, such a dynamic synthesis is not a separate scheme but is rather a result of correctly activating the principles discussed previously. For this reason, this element was not emphasized in our study.

2. *Organizational knowledge.* This is an understanding of dimensions (numbers, space, and time) as well as causal relations. Unlike novices, experienced geologists understand that the numbers of layers and outcrop size are not usually related to their absolute age.

METHOD

We used a combination of qualitative (interviews, observations in class and field) and quantitative (open questionnaires) methods to fully expose the strategies that our research sample used to temporally reconstruct depositional systems. The quantitative instruments included three questionnaires:

1. *GeoTAT* (Geological Time Aptitude Test):

The *GeoTAT* served a twofold purpose in this research: (i) to determine the factors that affect students' ability to temporally reconstruct a depositional system; and (ii) to test how learning geology contributes to a student's ability in reconstructing depositional systems. The former study relied on a cross-sectional sample of 285 students in grades 7–12, none of whom had studied geology (designated NGS). The latter study compared two samples of grade 11–12 students: 54 who were studying geology (designated GS) and 98 NGS. (Note that in grades 11–12 in Israeli schools, students "major" in different subjects such as geology.)

The *GeoTAT* can be divided into three sections. (Please see the Appendix for the complete *GeoTAT* questionnaire):

A. Puzzles (6a and 6b) that require the use of the single diachronic scheme of transformation (without reference to the other two diachronic schemes). This corresponds to the geologist's use of "actualism."

B. Puzzles (1a, 4, 5) that require the use of the single diachronic scheme of temporal organization (again, without reference to the other two diachronic schemes) These puzzles rely on the geological skills of superposition, correlation, and bracketing.

C. Puzzles (1b, 2, 3a, 3b, 6c) that entail an integrated use of three diachronic schemes (transformation, temporal organization, and interstage linkage). Geologically, these puzzles require the use of a combination of skills including actualism, superposition, and causal thinking.

2. *TST* (Temporal-Spatial Test):

This instrument combined four selected puzzles of the *GeoTAT* and seventeen selected puzzles from the MGMP (Middle Grades Mathematics Project) Spatial visualization test (Ben-Chaim et al., 1986, 1988). Its purpose was to determine if the ability to temporally order strata is influenced by spatial-visual ability. Product moment correlation coefficients were calculated for the entire *GeoTAT* and its individual puzzles against the MGMP. It was distributed to 172 NGS in grades 10–11.

3. *SFT* (Stratigraphic Factors Test):

This test consisted of three pairs of three-dimensional representations of outcrops that differed in overall size and/or numbers of layers. The test subjects were required to estimate which outcrop in a pair was older and justify their reasons. It was distributed to 52 GS in grades 11–12.

RESULTS AND DISCUSSION

Table 2 presents a cross-sectional comparison of the grade 7–12 NGS sample on the *GeoTAT*. The numbers of the puzzles can be matched with the test that is presented in the Appendix. Note that Table 2 lists the diachronic schemes, as well as the corresponding geological skill required to solve each puzzle. One-way ANOVA (analysis of variance) was used to determine if there was any difference whatsoever amongst any of the grade's mean scores for each *GeoTAT* puzzle. If such a difference did exist, then Duncan's new multiple range test was used to determine (post-priori) how each of the six grades (7–12) differed specifically for each of the puzzles (Huck et al., 1974). In other words, Ducan's test checks all possible combinations of differences (whether significant or not) amongst the different grades. All differences in the Duncan's test were evaluated at a significance level of $p < 0.05$. In reading Duncan's new multiple range test in Table 2, the mean grade scores were arranged in order of the size of the means. Moreover, all grade levels that come before a "greater than" sign ($>$) achieved scores that were significantly larger than the scores achieved by the grades that come after this sign, whereas all grade levels separated by commas did not achieve scores that were significantly different.

Generally, these data show an age trend: 6 of 10 puzzles of the *GeoTAT* show a significant difference ($p < 0.05$) between

TABLE 2. CROSS-SECTIONAL COMPARISSON OF THE NGS SAMPLE ON THE GEOTAT ($N = 285$)

Puzzle	Geological skill(s) required	Diachronic schemes required	Duncan ($p < .05$)
1a	Superposition, original horizontality	Isolated temporal organization	11 > 10, 9, 12, 7, 8, 10, 9 > 8
1b	Superposition, actualistic thinking, and causal thinking	Integrated use of diachronic schemes	11, 12 > 10, 9, 8, 7
2	Superposition, actualistic thinking, and causal thinking	Integrated use of diachronic schemes	12, 10 > 8, 7
3a	Superposition, actualistic thinking, and causal thinking	Integrated use of diachronic schemes	12, 9, 10, 11 > 7, 8
3b	Superposition, actualistic thinking, and causal thinking	Integrated use of diachronic schemes	12, 11, 10, 9 > 8, 7
4	Superposition, bracketing	Isolated temporal organization	N.A. (98% failure rate by NGS)
5	Superposition, correlation	Isolated temporal organization	12, 9, 10, 11 > 8, 7
6a	Actualistic thinking	Isolated transformation	12, 11, 9, 10 > 8, 7; 8 > 7
6b	Actualistic thinking	Isolated transformation	11, 12, 9, 10 > 8, 7
6c	Superposition, actualistic thinking, and causal thinking	Integrated use of diachronic schemes	12 > 9, 8, 7; 11, 10, 9 > 8, 7

NGS—designation for students in grades 7–12 who have not studied geology. GEOTAT—Geological Time Assessment Test.

grade 9–12 students and grade 7–8 students. In other words, the grade 9–12 students were significantly better at activating the diachronic schemes when confronted by problems in depositional history. Thus, to improve middle school students' abilities in reconstructing geological systems, programs in earth sciences should focus on enhancing their natural ability to think diachronically.

In addition, when comparing the grade 11–12 GS against their NGS counterparts, we found that the former group held a significant advantage over the latter group in solving temporally constrained problems in stratigraphy (Dodick and Orion, 2003c). This advantage was strengthened in grade 12, by which time the GS had accumulated many hours in the field.

We will now present a more detailed analysis of the specific factors that were critical for students of differing grade (7–12) and skill level (GS versus NGS) in solving the *GeoTAT* puzzles. The framework that was used to analyze the results of this research is rooted in Montangero's (1996) diachronic thinking model, which was modified by the authors (Dodick and Orion, 2003a) for this research and is presented here to aid in this discussion (Fig. 2).

Transformation Scheme

The transformation scheme was a key element for both GS and NGS in solving the *GeoTAT* puzzles. This is due to the fact that if the subject does not recognize that a change has taken place, such as the alteration of rock or fossil types in adjacent strata, he will not activate the other diachronic schemes. In turn, to activate the transformation scheme, the subject must be able to link his empirical knowledge of present-day phenomena with the past, based on the geological principle of actualism (see Table 1).

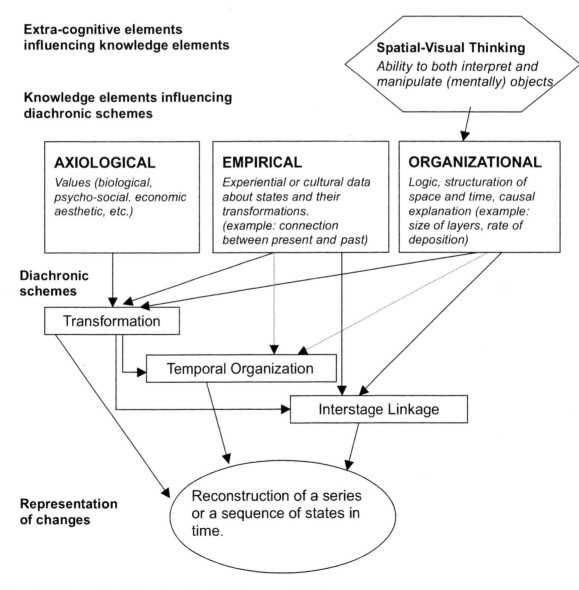

Figure 2. A model of temporal logic in geology (based on Montangero, 1996).

Even the youngest subjects (grade 7) in our studies were able to use this principle, given the proper trigger (even if they could not articulate this principle). Thus, a question for future research is the age limit for applying actualistic thinking. This is significant for science education since this form of analogy is a basic reasoning pattern of many sciences.

Temporal Organization Scheme

The most easily applied diachronic scheme for all subjects (GS and NGS) in this research was temporal organization. This result is somewhat misleading, however, in that four of the five integrated diachronic puzzles in the *GeoTAT* contained undisturbed, horizontal strata that permitted temporal ordering using superposition. In fact, Ault (1981) demonstrated that young children in grade 2 could reliably order strata using this principle, so this result was not surprising.

The one integrated diachronic puzzle in the *GeoTAT* (1b) that contained folded layers received the lowest scores amongst the NGS because many of the subjects could not apply a necessary second principle of geology, original horizontality (even when it was provided as a direct clue), which would have helped them solve this puzzle's depositional history. In other words, the students were unable to reconstruct how the originally horizontal layers became folded. This therefore inhibited their ability to solve the other diachronic schemes in this puzzle. The GS with their experience in both class and field had a clear advantage and did significantly better on this question than the NGS at both the grade 11 and 12 levels ($F = 15.43$, degrees of freedom [df] = 99, $p < 0.001$) based on a two-way ANOVA (Dodick and Orion, 2003c).

This leads to the question of the origin of a young student's understanding of geological superposition. Based on Zwart's (1976) argument that a child's temporal understanding is derived from the "before and after" relationship, Ault (1981) suggested that ordering geological layers via superposition is an advanced application of this relationship, serially applied to outcrops. Research has shown that children as young as three years in age verbally understand "before and after" (Stevenson and Pollitt, 1986; Harner, 1982); nonetheless, does this verbal understanding translate to a visual interpretation of strata?

A further question concerns students' ability to reconstruct tilted, folded, or crosscutting strata. Three lines of evidence suggest that this can be learned in the middle school years. Our research has shown that students in grade 9 with no background in geology could spontaneously order the fossil contents of folded strata. In other words, they ignored the misleading clues of relative height of fossil contents and instead relied on the relationship of the strata itself. Moreover, observations of middle school children (grade 7–8) participating in the Israeli curriculum *The Rock Cycle* have shown that they can reconstruct tilted strata (although this ability has not been tested formally). Finally, Chang and Barufaldi (1999) indicated that grade 9 students in Taiwan (after completing a problem-solving unit in the earth sciences) could

solve stratigraphic problems involving crosscutting relationships. However, the question remains whether even younger students could handle such material. Moreover, will such ability on written tests be transferred to the field?

Turning to stratigraphic correlation, we found that it was more difficult to do than superposition because it requires a three-dimensional strategy incorporating both superposition and translation between different localities. This difference in difficulty is mirrored in history; the principle of superposition was elucidated by the Danish natural philosopher Steno in the seventeenth century, whereas English geological surveyor William Smith only established correlation in the 1790s. This enhanced level of complexity is reflected in the fact that the scores of all of the NGS (grade 9–12) were lower on the correlation puzzle (5) in comparison to scores obtained on the superposition puzzle (1a). Moreover, on this same puzzle, most of the grade 7–8 NGS failed to translate across outcrops and relied strictly on a strategy of superposition, and hence received lower scores.

Our research shows that it is possible to teach correlation effectively in both class and field in both middle and high schools. This is due to the fact that we found significant differences favoring the grade 12 GS over the grade 12 NGS ($t = 2.86$, df = 142, $p < 0.01$). Moreover, two grade 9 middle school classes saw their scores on the correlation puzzle increase significantly ($p < 0.05$) after completing the program *From Dinosaurs to Darwin*, which includes an in-depth activity in correlation.

Ault (1981), however, maintains that even younger subjects can correlate strata. In five of ten interviews with grade 6 students, the subjects were able to solve a simulated problem in correlation. However, this problem was easier than the example used in the *GeoTAT*, and did not fully refer to geological correlation. Moreover, Ault (1981) noted that it was rare for students to be able to transfer such understanding to similar problems in the field.

Spatial Visual Thinking

As noted above, stratigraphic correlation employs a strategy mixing superposition and translation across different localities in search of matching fossils. This suggests that correlation places a heavier premium on spatial visual perception, as opposed to problems involving superposition alone (which only requires vertical ordering along a single outcrop).

This conjecture was tested with the *TST* in which product-moment correlations were calculated for four puzzles of the *GeoTAT* against puzzles of the MGMP spatial visualization test. The results indicated the strongest correlation between the stratigraphic correlation puzzle and the MGMP puzzles ($r = 0.41$, $p < 0.0001$) (Table 3). In other words, stratigraphic correlation seems to require the highest level of spatial visual thinking in order to temporally order its contents.

This suggestion, that there is a correlation between spatial visualization and temporal reasoning, has a long history extending back to Kant's *Critique of Pure Reason*. More recently,

TABLE 3. PRODUCT MOMENT CORRELATIONS BETWEEN SELECT PUZZLES OF THE GEOTAT AND MGMP SPATIAL VISUALIZATION TEST WITH NGS (*N* = 172)

GeoTaT puzzle	Geological skills	Correlation (*r*) with MGMP	*p*
1a	Superposition, original horizontality	0.09	0.24
2	Superposition, actualistic thinking and causal thinking	0.14	0.13
6c	Superposition, actualistic thinking and causal thinking	0.21	0.02
5	Superposition, correlation	0.41	0.0001

GEOTAT—Geological Time Assessment Test. MGMP—Middle Grades Mathematics Project. NGS—designation for students in grades 7–12 who have not studied geology.

Friedman (1983, 1989, 1992) proposed that conventional time systems containing cycles, such as the days of the week are represented and manipulated by subjects older than 12 years in age as three-dimensional positions in space. However, our research is the first to show this relationship in earth science. Nonetheless, this work has only scratched the surface of this complex connection between these two cognitive abilities; future research should investigate this effect with more complex depositional systems (such as those containing crosscutting relationships), as well as the effect of field conditions in which geological structures are often hidden. Such work could be conducted with novice geological students in high school and university, as well as with expert geoscientists.

Organizational Knowledge (Layer Size; Rate of Deposition)

A single puzzle (4) of the *GeoTAT* tested the students' ability to absolutely date a series of sedimentary rock exposures bracketed by horizontal layers of igneous rock. As noted in Table 2, 98% of the NGS failed this question, while even the majority of the **GS** had major difficulties, with only 33% of the grade 12 and 14.2% of the grade 11 GS successfully solving this puzzle. Surprisingly, the same mistake appeared amongst most of the incorrect solutions: the apportioning of equal amounts of time to each of the sedimentary layers. As each of the layers was equal in height on the *GeoTAT* puzzle, this led to the hypothesis that the students believed that the absolute age of the strata was connected to its proportional size. In turn, this suggested the additional hypothesis that students mistakenly see the process of sedimentary deposition as a linear process. These hypotheses were tested with the *SFT* (Stratigraphic Factors Test).

The *SFT* consists of three pairs of three-dimensional representations of outcrops that differ in overall size and/or numbers of layers. The task of the subjects was to estimate which outcrop in a pair was older and provide their reasoning. The results showed that in general, the effect of size, both of the entire outcrop, and the individual layers, as well as the total number of layers strongly influenced the GS subjects' understanding of absolute age. This is supported by the fact that no more than 35% of the students in any of the three *SFT* questions chose the correct answer for these puzzles, which is that it is (usually) impossible to estimate the age of an outcrop based on its size, or numbers of layers. Further,

even when choosing this correct answer, it was rare (8%) for the subjects to give a correct reason, such as the fact that they were missing critical information, such as deposition rate.

When combined with the fact that in the *GeoTAT*, many of the same students apportioned equal amounts of time to strata of the same height, this provides strong evidence that most students misunderstand the concept of rate in geological systems. At most, they see deposition as a process that occurs at a uniform or linear rate. In contrast, geologists know that different environmental conditions over time can significantly alter the rate of deposition. Moreover, sedimentation can cease, and erosional processes can take over, leaving large temporal gaps (such as unconformities) in the rock record.

Obviously, varying rates of sedimentation complicate the understanding of deposition. However, it is a critical element that students should master if they are to have a complete understanding of deposition, and, through it, geological time. Rates of change are a basic concept of many scientific disciplines, both as a concrete methodological problem (measurement of rates) and as a more abstract philosophical concept (discrete versus continuous rates of change). Thus, exposing students to rates within the earth sciences provides them with a chance to explore a scientifically universal concept.

To date, research on student understanding of rates has largely been associated with mathematics and physics education, with much of this research focused on the physical dynamics in real time of bodies in motion (Karpus et al., 1983; Thompson, 1991, 1994). However historical sciences, such as geology, add another level of complexity, as noted in another chapter of this book by Dodick and Argamon (chapter 8), in that its practitioners cannot directly manipulate the systems they study. Instead, the geological method permits one to reconstruct dynamic processes, such as deposition, by interpreting largely static clues, such as strata and fossils, from the past. Such clues are combined with evidence measured and observed from active earth systems today (provided that the present-day conditions sufficiently match those that built the structures of the past); accordingly, geologists are then able to reconstruct geological history. This methodology differs tremendously from experimental sciences that rely on a real-time strategy of manipulating independent variables and measuring such changes in dependent variables. Thus, any well-thought-out curriculum that teaches rates in earth systems should also include a discussion of the nature of the historical sciences.

SUMMARY: BUILDING A SYNTHESIS

Geological time is one of the foundational elements of the earth sciences because it provides a framework for organizing the events that have shaped our planet. Even the other most important paradigm in geology, plate tectonics, is only known through the changes that it has wrought upon our globe over the span of geological time. Indeed, many other fields in science are influenced by the massive temporal span provided by geological time. Nonetheless, geological time can be intimidating because it reduces one's personal (and even our own species') history to the metaphorical blink of an eye. How then is it possible to rationally accept this temporal framework that is so necessary to learning earth science?

Cognitively, our strategy involves the decoupling of geological time between the macroscale of deep time, including as it does, the major events of Earth history, and the microscale of relative time, represented by individual strata. Nonetheless, pedagogically, there is a commonality to our method, in that we try to reduce the abstract nature of these scales by contextualizing them within the concrete visual images of the earth sciences. Indeed, this method is common to many scientific concepts constrained by very large or very small scales.

In the case of the entirety of geological time, this is done via a series of increasingly complex iconographic representations of evolution in time. Using this method, students learn that different time scales are appropriate for representing different phenomena, from our planet's birth to the evolution of humans. Moreover, they also discover that different events develop at different rates. Such insight into differing scale and rate are not confined to geology alone; thus, investigating deep time serves as a starting point for discussing many other sciences influenced by time spans of varying magnitudes.

Our strategy of reducing the abstract nature of deep time shows potential for helping students visualize the unseen. Nonetheless, research questions do remain, many associated with the age limits of the learner. Previous research indicates that it is unlikely that elementary school students could develop a strong understanding of deep time. Both Friedman (1978) and Harner (1982) showed that it is not until around age 14 that children develop the verbal concepts for dealing with long time spans. Thus, even when deep time is taught in middle school, caution must be exercised because of its enormous scale, and the numbers used to measure it. As we have noted, one way to avoid such problems is through the use of visual images containing a variety of chronological clues, as it permits students to relatively sequence such phenomena using their own knowledge, a task that is cognitively easier than simply relying on absolute dates; as we have seen, even university students when asked to provide absolute dates for events, such as the appearance of dinosaurs, on a geological time line, greatly overestimate the age of such events (White, 2004).

A further solution is through basic research on students understanding of absolute or geochronological time. There have only been a limited number of studies concerning how students of different ages understand absolute geological time. Moreover, comparing studies is difficult because of differing research methodologies. Thus, a comprehensive survey of students from middle schools to university is required. At least one of the probes used in such research should be the student-generated time line as used in Noonan and Good's (1999) and White et al.'s (2004) respective studies. Unlike verbal response scales, time lines have the advantage in that they represent sequence, scale, and rate of geological time in one graphic package; thus, they more thoroughly expose underlying misconceptions. Such research can be combined with studies on students' worldview or ontological perspectives similar to those done by Noonan and Good (1999) and Libarkin et al. (2005). The purpose of such research is to classify students' explanations about events in geological time, which can then be used to refine cognitive baselines for designing learning materials.

A related problem connected to the time-line issue concerns student understanding of exponential numbers. The problem of greatly overestimating the absolute age of features in the fossil record maybe derived from the fact that massively large numbers simply have no meaning for students. Students in Israel first learn about exponents in grades 7–8, but this is no guarantee that they understand massively large exponential numbers, as seen in geological time. A survey of the research shows that there is very little research that is focused on this issue. Confrey (1991) interviewed a single undergraduate on her developing understanding of exponents using a geological time line. More recently, M. Tabach (2005, personal commun.) submitted a paper on the related issue of middle school students' understanding of exponential growth. Thus, there is certainly room for research on the development of the understanding of exponents and their significance for geological time.

In the case of relative time, our learning strategy is to decompose the temporal complexity of geological structures via the use of diachronic schemes. Consequently, students acquire the ability to translate the static image of strata into their true nature—a transforming dynamic system. This methodology agrees with the vision of many earth science educators who have emphasized the systemic nature of geology (Mayer et al., 1992). An important component of systemic thinking is the understanding of how a system changes over time; in other words, systemic thinking demands an understanding of geological time, and diachronic thinking provides a cognitive skill that helps students reconstruct the unseen changes that affect such a system.

Diachronic thinking takes advantage of a general cognitive ability that seems to develop early in life. For this reason, this natural ability can reduce the cognitive load of students of all ages when learning about the transformation of geological systems. Moreover, since diachronic thinking is a general cognitive ability, it can be applied to a variety of time-constrained systems; exposure to it within geology could better prepare students for learning about other systems in other sciences. Thus, again, the earth sciences can serve as an entry point to other sciences.

An important question for future research is the age limit for learning about relative geological time. Our work has shown that middle school students do develop some of the diachronic skills needed to understand some of the principles of relative dating (Dodick and Orion, 2003a, 2003c); but what about younger children in elementary school?

Montangero's (1992, 1996) studies suggest that children acquire the ability to understand transformations early in life (between ages 7 and 11). Moreover, Ault's (1981) research indicates that some young children (K–6) do understand principles of relative time, such as superposition. However, this question, concerning elementary students, needs further study before it is validated. Ault's (1981) research was an important start, but it had methodological problems, complicating its results. Moreover, it was limited by a small sample size (40 interviews in total from a single school). To build a large statistical sample will require a quantitative instrument similar to the *GeoTAT*, but with less-complex puzzles.

This interest in younger students is not simply academic curiosity. Although a staple of many middle school curricula, the earth sciences are rarely taught in elementary schools. This is unfortunate as the earth sciences address some of the most pressing scientific problems that we face in the modern world, many of them connected to the environment. Fixing such problems can only come through an intelligent change in attitudes, and the sooner this process starts, the more likely that it will have an impact. Giving students the conceptual tools to be able to interpret how Earth changes over time could lead to better environmental awareness.

Moreover, exposing young students to earth science and its historical methodology is important for broadening their understanding of science. Most young children, when surveyed about science, usually identify a scientist as "someone working in a laboratory who does experiments." Teaching about the historical, field-based methods of the geosciences, including the basic principles of stratigraphy, would counter this stereotype, while also providing children with an appreciation of their environment by participating in field work.

Aside from age limits, another research question concerns the pedagogical effect of learning the earth sciences on students' understanding of geological time. Our research shows that experienced high school geology majors do have a significant advantage in their ability to reconstruct geological systems over their counterparts who lack such experience (Dodick and Orion, 2003c). We suggest that the primary reason for this difference was the geological students' field work experience. This is based on our observation that field work provides students with a three-dimensional understanding of how depositional systems change over time, in contrast to the static, flat images of textbooks. Moreover, field work teaches a student about what types of evidence must be sought (and also ignored) in reconstructing a geological system. Such observations might be validated through an in-depth study of students as they solve problems in the field.

As Frodeman (1995, 2000) noted, geology has unfortunately been treated by many philosophers and scientists as a derivative science, the methodology and logic of which are provided by the physical sciences. This is partly due to the fact that geology is considered by its critics to have theoretical limitations, such as the nature of geological time itself, which cannot be directly observed. This view is limited in that geological time provides a temporal framework that is critical for understanding many physical, chemical, and biological processes. Moreover, many of the skills required for understanding geological time, such as spatial visualization, reasoning with number, size, and rate, and systemic thinking, are general (cognitive) skills that can be applied by a student to other sciences as well. Thus, ignoring geological time not only prevents students from appreciating the nature of the earth system, but could also impede their progress in learning other sciences as well.

APPENDIX

The following is a complete copy of the *GeoTAT* questionnaire.

1.   The geologist in the diagram below is standing on a column of marine sedimentary rock containing fossils:

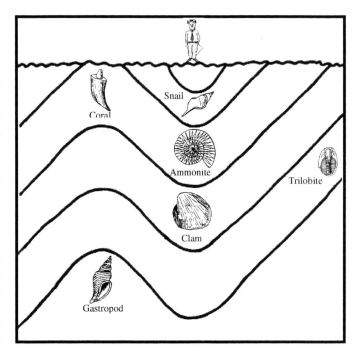

1a.   Attempt to order the fossils according to their age, from the oldest fossil to the youngest fossil. (**Clue:** marine sedimentary rock is originally deposited in horizontally lying layers.)

1b.   Try to reconstruct the processes in the order that leads to the creation of the rock exposure in the picture above.

2. The illustration below represents a series of rock layers from a specific locality in the world. Try to reconstruct the stages that created this sequence of layers based on their order of formation.

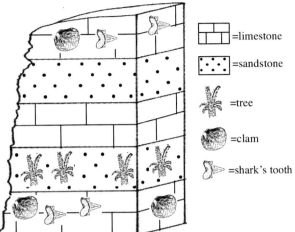

☐ =limestone

▢ =sandstone

🌿 =tree

🦪 =clam

🦷 =shark's tooth

4. The following picture represents a rock exposure that contains three types of fossils (snail, coral, and clam). Two layers of igneous rocks (represented by the v symbol) lie between the layers containing the fossils. The ages of the igneous rock layers have been determined in the lab by scientists. Try to determine the absolute age (in years) of the three different fossils (snail, coral, and clam).

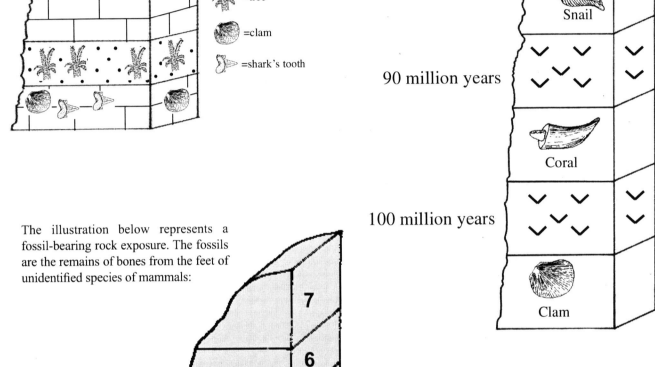

90 million years

100 million years

3. The illustration below represents a fossil-bearing rock exposure. The fossils are the remains of bones from the feet of unidentified species of mammals:

3a. Try and describe the process that took place between rock layer 1 and rock layer 4.

3b. Try to suggest two possible reasons for the absence of fossils after rock layer 4.

5.   The illustration below represents three rock exposures containing fossils: Try to order the fossils according to their implied age, from the oldest fossil to the youngest fossil.

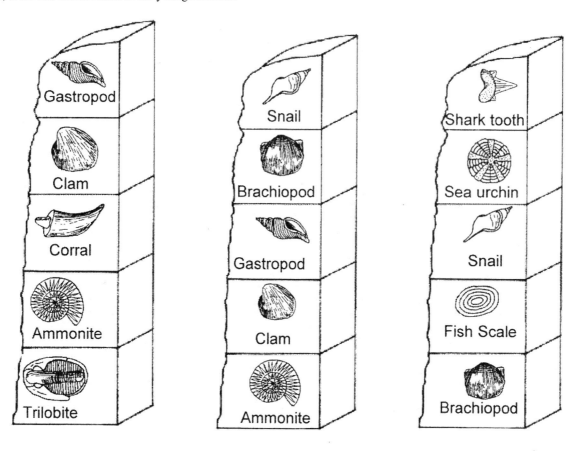

6.   The following illustration represents a dinosaur excavation site. This excavation can be broken down into two areas:

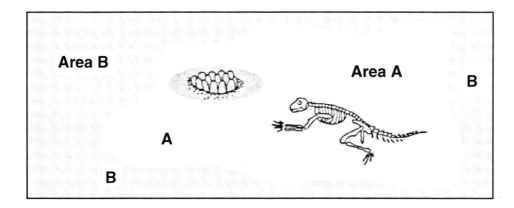

Area A. This site is built of terrestrial sedimentary rock containing the skeletons of dinosaurs. Two important points can be noted about this area:

1.   The dinosaur skeletons excavated in this area range in size from very tiny to very large. This suggests that in this one area, the age range of the dinosaurs was broad, ranging from newly hatched babies to fully grown adults.

2.   In this site, a large series of nests containing fossilized eggs was discovered.

Area B. This area surrounds area A and is built of marine sedimentary rock containing fish.

   6a. Try to reconstruct how this looked when the dinosaurs were alive. What did areas A and B comprise?

   6b. What in your opinion might be the significance that in one single area scientists found a species of dinosaur ranging in size and age from egg to adult?

   6c. When scientists excavated this area deeply, they found an alternating arrangement of layers consisting of marine sedimentary rock containing no fossils and terrestrial sedimentary rock containing fossils of dinosaurs (in the illustration below). What is the significance of this alternating arrangement of layers containing terrestrial sedimentary rock containing dinosaurs, and marine sedimentary rock without dinosaurs?

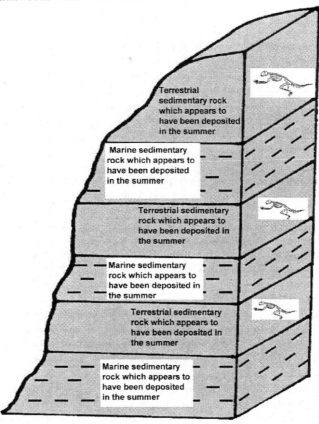

REFERENCES CITED

American Association for the Advancement of Science, 1990, Science for all Americans: New York, Oxford University Press, 418 p.

American Association for the Advancement of Science, 1993, Benchmarks for science literacy: New York, Oxford University Press, 272 p.

Anderson, D.L., this volume, 2006, Plate tectonics; the general theory: Complex Earth is simpler than you think, *in* Manduca, C., and Mogk, D., eds., Earth and Mind: How Geologists Think and Learn about the Earth: Geological Society of America Special Paper 413, doi: 10.1130/2006.2413(03).

Ault, C.R., 1981, Children's concepts about time no barrier to understanding the geologic past [Ph.D. thesis]: Ithaca, Cornell University, 280 p.

Ault, C.R., 1982, Time in geological explanations as perceived by elementary school students: Journal of Geological Education, v. 30, p. 304–309.

Barton, K.C., and Levstik, L.S., 1996, "Back when God was around and everything": Elementary children's understanding of historical time: American Educational Research Journal, v. 33, p. 419–454.

Ben-Chaim, D., Lappan, G., and Houang, R.T., 1986, Development of a spatial visualizaton test for middle school boys and girls: Perceptual and Motor Skills, v. 63, p. 659–669.

Ben-Chaim, D., Lappan, G., and Houang, R.T., 1988, The effect on spatial visualization skills of middle school boys and girls: American Educational Research Journal, v. 25, p. 51–71.

Chang, C.Y., and Barufaldi, J.P., 1999, The use of problem solving based instructional model in initiating change in students' achievement and alternative frameworks: International Journal of Science Education, v. 21, p. 373–388, doi: 10.1080/095006999290606.

Collins, A.M., and Loftus, E.F., 1975, A spreading activation theory of semantic processing: Psychological Review, v. 82, p. 407–428, doi: 10.1037//0033-295X.82.6.407.

Confrey, J., 1991, Learning to listen: A student's understanding of powers of ten, *in* von Glassesfeld, E., ed., Radical constructivism in mathematics education: Amsterdam, Kluwer Academic Publishers, p. 111–138.

Dodick, J.T., and Orion, N., 2000, From dinosaurs to Darwin: Evolution from the perspective of "deep time": Rehovot, Israel, Weizmann Institute of Science, 128 p.

Dodick, J.T., and Orion, N., 2003a, Cognitive factors affecting student understanding of geological time: Journal of Research in Science Teaching, v. 40, p. 415–442, doi: 10.1002/tea.10083.

Dodick, J.T., and Orion, N., 2003b, Introducing evolution to non-biology majors via the fossil record: A case study from the Israeli high school system: The American Biology Teacher, v. 65, p. 185–190.

Dodick, J.T., and Orion, N., 2003c, Measuring student understanding of "deep time": Science & Education, v. 87, p. 708–731, doi: 10.1002/sce.1057.

Dodick, J., and Argamon, S., this volume, 2006, Rediscovering the historical methodology of the earth sciences by analyzing scientific communication styles, *in* Manduca, C., and Mogk, D., eds., Earth and Mind: How Geologists Think and Learn about the Earth: Geological Society of America Special Paper 413, doi: 10.1130/2006.2413(08).

Everitt, C.L., Good, S.C., and Pankiewicz, P.R., 1996, Conceptualizing the inconceivable by depicting the magnitude of geological time with a yearly planning calendar: Journal of Geoscience Education, v. 44, p. 290–293.

Friedman, W., 1978, Development of time concepts in children, *in* Reese, H., and Lipsett, L.P., eds., Advances in child development and behaviour, Volume 12: New York, Academic Press, p. 267–298.

Friedman, W., 1982, Conventional time concepts and children's structuring of time, *in* Friedman, W., ed., The developmental psychology of time: New York, Academic Press, p. 174–205.

Friedman, W., 1983, Image and verbal processes in reasoning about the months of the year: Journal of Experimental Psychology: Learning, Memory, and Cognition, v. 9, p. 650–666, doi: 10.1037//0278-7393.9.4.650.

Friedman, W., 1989, The representation of temporal structure in children, adolescents, and adults, *in* Levin, I., and Zakay, D., eds., Time and human cognition: A life span perspective: Amsterdam, North-Holland Publishing, p. 259–304.

Friedman, W., 1992, The development of children's representations of temporal structure, *in* Macar, F., ed., Time action and cognition: Amsterdam, Kluwer Academic Publishers, p. 67–75.

Frodeman, R.L., 1995, Geological reasoning: Geology as an interpretive and historical science: Geological Society of America Bulletin, v. 107, p. 960–968, doi: 10.1130/0016-7606(1995)107<0960:GRGAAI>2.3.CO;2.

Frodeman, R.L., 1996, Envisioning the outcrop: Journal of Geoscience Education, v. 44, p. 417–427.

Frodeman, R.L., 2000, Shifting plates, *in* Frodeman, R.L., ed., Earth matters: The earth sciences, philosophy and the claims of the community: Upper Saddle River, New Jersey, Prentice Hall, vii–xiii.

Gould, S.J., 1995, Dinosaur in a haystack: Reflections in natural history: New York, Harmony Books, 496 p.

Gould, S.J., 1989, Wonderful life: The Burgess Shale and the nature of history: London, W.W. Norton and Company, 256 p.

Happs, J.C., 1982, Some aspects of student understanding of two New Zealand landforms: New Zealand Science Teacher, v. 32, p. 4–12.

Harner, L., 1982, Talking about the past and the future, *in* Friedman, W., ed., The developmental psychology of time: New York, Academic Press, p. 141–169.

Huck, S.C., Cormier, W.H., and Bounds, W.G., 1974, Reading statistics and research: New York, Harper and Row, 377 p.

Hume, J.D., 1978, An understanding of geological time: Journal of Geological Education, v. 26, p. 141–143.

Hutton, J., 1788, Theory of the earth: Transactions of the Royal Society of Edinburgh, v. 1(2), p. 209–304.

Karplus, R., Pulos, S., and Stage, E., 1983, Early adolescents' proportional reasoning on 'rate' problems: Educational Studies in Mathematics, v. 14, p. 219–234, doi: 10.1007/BF00410539.

Kozma, R., Chin, E., Russell, J., and Marx, N., 2000, The roles of representations and tools in the chemistry laboratory and their implications for chemistry learning: The Journal of the Learning Sciences, v. 9, p. 105–143, doi: 10.1207/s15327809jls0902_1.

Levstik, L.S., and Barton, K.C., 1996, 'They still use some of their past': Historical salience in elementary children's chronological thinking: Journal of Curriculum Studies, v. 28, p. 531–576.

Libarkin, J.C., and Kurdziel, J.P., 2004, Time is everything: Geologic time as a linchpin to a complete understanding of the Earth, *in* Proceedings, 77th National Association of Research in Science Teaching Annual Meeting, Vancouver, British Columbia.

Libarkin, J.C., Anderson, S.W., Science, J.D., Beilfuss, M., and Boone, W., 2005, Qualitative analysis of college students' ideas about the Earth: Interviews and open-ended questionnaires: Journal of Geoscience Education, v. 53, p. 17–26.

MacDonald, H., 1989, Small-group oral presentations in historical geology: Journal of Geoscience Education, v. 37, p. 49–52.

Marques, L.F., 1988, Alternative frameworks for urban Portuguese pupils age 10/11 and 14/15 with respect to Earth, life, and volcanoes [M.S. dissertation]: Keele, UK, Keele University,, 385 p.

Marques, L.F., and Thompson, D.B., 1997, Portuguese students' understanding at age 10/11 and 14/15 of the origin and nature of the Earth and the development of life: Research in Science and Technology Education, v. 15, p. 29–51.

Mayer, V.J., Armstrong, R.E., Barrow, L.H., Brown, S.M., Crowder, J.N., Fortner, R.W., Graham, M., Hoyt, W.H., Humphris, S.E., Jax, D.W., Shay, E.L., and Shropshire, K.L, 1992, The role of planet Earth in the new science curriculum: Journal of Geological Education, v. 40, p. 66–73.

McPhee, J.A., 1980, Basin and range: New York, Farrar, Straus, and Giroux, 216 p.

Metzger, E.P., 1992, The strategy column for pre-college science teachers: Lessons on time: Journal of Geological Education, v. 40, p. 261–264.

Miller, M.G., 2005, Regional geology as a unifying theme and springboard to deep time: Journal of Geoscience Education, v. 49, p. 10–17.

Montangero, J., 1992, The development of the diachronic perspective in children, *in* Macar, F., ed., Time action and cognition: Amsterdam, Kluwer Academic Publishers, p. 55–65.

Montangero, J., 1996, Understanding changes in time: London, Taylor and Francis, 195 p.

National Research Council, 1996, The National Science Education Standards: Washington, D.C., National Academy, 262 p.

National Research Council, 2000, Inquiry and the National Science Education Standards: Washington, D.C., National Academy Press, 202 p.

Nieto-Obregon, J., 2005, Geologic time scales, maps and the chronoscalimeter: Journal of Geoscience Education, v. 49, p. 25–29.

Noonan, L.C., and Good, R.G., 1999, Deep time: Middle school students' ideas on the origins of Earth and life on Earth, *in* Proceedings, 72nd National Association of Research in Science Teaching Annual Meeting, Boston, Massachusetts.

Oversby, J., 1996, Knowledge of earth science and the potential for development: The School Science Review, v. 78, p. 91–97.

Piaget, J., 1969, The child's conception of time: London, Routledge and Kegan Paul Publishing, 285 p.

Reuss, R.L., and Gardulski, A.F., 2001, An interactive game approach to learning in historical geology and paleontology: Journal of Geoscience Education, v. 49, p. 120–129.

Ritger, S.D., and Cummins, R.H., 1991, Using student created metaphors to comprehend geological time: Journal of Geological Education, v. 39, p. 9–11.

Rowland, S.M., 1983, Fingernail growth and time-distance rates in geology: Journal of Geological Education, v. 31, p. 176–178.

Schoon, K.J., 1989, Misconceptions in the earth sciences: A cross-age study, *in* Proceedings, 62nd Meeting of the National Association for Research in Science Teaching: San Francisco, California.

Schoon, K.J., 1992, Students' alternative conceptions of Earth and space: Journal of Geological Education, v. 40, p. 209–214.

Spencer-Cervato, C., and Daly, J.F., 2000, Geological time: An interactive team-oriented introductory geology laboratory: Teaching Earth Sciences, v. 25, p. 19–22.

Stevenson, R.J., and Pollitt, C., 1986, The acquisition of temporal terms: Journal of Child Language, v. 14, p. 533–545.

Thomas, R.C., 2005, Learning geologic time in the field: Journal of Geoscience Education, v. 49, p. 18–21.

Thompson, P.W., 1991, The development of the concept of speed and its relationship to concepts of rate, *in* Harel, G., and Confrey, J., eds., The development of multiplicative reasoning in the learning of mathematics: Albany, New York, State University of New York (SUNY) Press, 179–234

Thompson, P.W., 1994, Images of rate and operational understanding of the fundamental theorem of calculus. Educational Studies in Mathematics, v. 26, no. 2-3, p. 229–274.

Trend, R.D., 1997, An investigation into understanding of geological time among 10- and 11-year old children, with a discussion of implications for learning of other geological concepts, *in* Proceedings, Second International Conference on Geoscience Education and Training, Hilo, Hawaii.

Trend, R.D., 1998, An investigation into understanding of geological time among 10- and 11-year old children: International Journal of Science Education, v. 20, p. 973–988.

Trend, R.D., 2000, Conceptions of geological time among primary teacher trainees, with reference to their engagement with geosciences, history and science: International Journal of Science Education, v. 22, p. 539–555, doi: 10.1080/095006900289778.

Trend, R.D., 2001a, Deep time framework: A preliminary study of UK primary teachers' conceptions of geological time and perceptions of geoscience: Journal of Research in Science Teaching, v. 38, p. 191–221, doi: 10.1002/1098-2736(200102)38:2<191::AID-TEA1003>3.0.CO;2-C.

Trend, R.D., 2001b, An investigation into the understanding of geological time among 17-year-old students, with implications for the subject matter knowledge of future teachers: International Research in Geographical and Environmental Education, v. 10, p. 298–321.

Trend, R.D., 2001c, Perceptions of the planet: Deep time: Teaching Earth Science, v. 26, p. 30–38.

Trend, R.D., 2002, Developing the concept of deep time, *in* Mayer, M.J., ed., Global science literacy: London, Kluwer Academic Publishers, p. 187–202.

White, O.L., Beilfuss, M., Boone, W., and Libarkin, J., 2004, Analyzing student perceptions of geological time through the use of graphic timelines, Paper presented at the National Association for Research in Science Teaching Annual Conference (Vancouver, British Columbia, 1–4 April 2004).

Zwart, P.J., 1976, About time: A philosophical inquiry into the origin and nature of time: Amsterdam, North-Holland Publishing Company, 266 p.

Manuscript Accepted by the Society 21 March 2006

Geological Society of America
Special Paper 413
2006

Student understanding of complex earth systems

Bruce E. Herbert[†]

Department of Geology and Geophysics, Texas A&M University, College Station, Texas 77843-3115, USA

ABSTRACT

Most environmental issues involve near-surface earth systems that often exhibit complex spatial characteristics and dynamics. Conceptual understanding of complex earth systems influences the development of effective policy and management strategies. Students, like all people, organize knowledge and reason about environmental issues through manipulation of mental models. A mental model is a relatively enduring and accessible, but limited, cognitive representation of an external natural phenomenon. The nature of near-surface earth systems may present major cognitive difficulties to students in their development of authentic, accurate mental models of earth systems. These cognitive difficulties include conceptualization of natural earth environments as systems, understanding the complex characteristics of these systems, and the application of conceptual models of complex earth systems to support environmental problem solving. This paper reviews the nature of near-surface earth systems that exhibit complex behavior and the cognitive and epistemological issues that students may experience in understanding these systems. Finally, I suggest that the same learning issues that students face in the classroom also are encountered by experts, policy managers, and stakeholders while they develop solutions to environmental problems. Therefore, educational research of student learning in earth science may not only support the development of improved pedagogical practices and learning environments, but this research may also support improved environmental decision making.

Keywords: student learning, complex systems, system science, environmental problems.

INTRODUCTION

Understanding near-surface earth systems is central to the development of solutions to important environmental issues arising from the growth of human populations and economic activities (Lubchenco, 1998). A recent report from the National Research Council (NRC, 2000), *Grand Challenges in Environmental Sciences,* outlined eight major challenges facing human society: biogeochemical cycles, biological diversity and ecosystem functioning, climate variability, hydrologic forecasting, infectious disease and the environment, institutions and resource use, land-use dynamics, and reinventing the use of materials. The NRC report also highlighted the need for new models of sci-

ence education and training that focus on developing expertise in problem-orientated science (Stokes, 1997). In particular, the report cited the need for expertise that can address interdisciplinary problems through the efforts of collaborative groups that integrate the natural sciences, social sciences, and engineering around common research problems. Restoration of the Florida Everglades, for example, involves the close collaboration of teams of experts including civil engineers, hydrogeologists, restoration ecologists, and economists.

Most environmental issues involve complex earth systems, which are defined as near-surface earth systems that exhibit complex spatial characteristics and dynamics. There are three fundamental challenges in understanding complex earth systems. The

[†]E-mail: herbert@geo.tamu.edu.

Herbert, B.E., 2006, Student understanding of complex earth systems, *in* Manduca, C.A., and Mogk, D.W., eds., Earth and Mind: How Geologists Think and Learn about the Earth: Geological Society of America Special Paper 413, p. 95–104, doi: 10.1130/2006.2413(07). For permission to copy, contact editing@geosociety.org. ©2006 Geological Society of America. All rights reserved.

first challenge is the conceptualization of natural earth environments as systems, with accurate definitions of boundaries and the nature of interactions between the elements of the system. Descriptions of the processes that transfer and manipulate matter and energy within the systems and across system boundaries, as well as relations between one system and other systems, should also be included in an accurate conceptualization. The second challenge is the characterization and explanation of the complex nature of earth systems through a description of the system's state over space and time, self-organization, or emergence of structure or patterns. A system's state encompasses a description of the all the important variables of the system and how they change under both steady-state and nonequilibrium conditions. The third major challenge is the application of conceptual and scientific models of earth systems to support problem solving and the development of effective environmental policy (Oreskes et al., 1994).

Experts, policy managers, and stakeholders have been found to commit cognitive errors when reasoning about environmental issues. The behavior and dynamics of earth systems are often complex enough to make prediction of future behavior difficult (Doyle and Ford, 1998). Differences in the conceptualizations of systems by stakeholders have contributed to conflict concerning ecosystem (Hurley et al., 2003) and water resources management (Sneddon et al., 2002), through differences in assumed cause and effect mechanisms and average characteristics of the systems. People's conceptualizations of earth systems, when applied to risk perception, are also often ill-structured, which leads to incorrect perceptions of risk due to global warming (Kempton, 1991), radon (Bostrom et al., 1993), and electric fields (Morgan et al., 1990).

Environmental decision making can present policy managers and stakeholders with serious behavioral, cognitive, or technical demands (Schofield, 2004). As a result, innovative decision-making processes have directly incorporated learning and adaptive management within the processes to identify and minimize cognitive errors (Allen et al., 2001; McDaniels and Gregory, 2004; Schofield, 2004). Adaptive management techniques utilize cycles of implementation, evaluation, and improvement to develop more effective environmental management strategies. I propose that a better understanding of the cognitive and epistemological issues students have in understanding and reasoning about complex earth systems, along with teaching methods that directly address these learning issues, are needed to support reform in both earth science education and the management of major environmental issues facing human society.

THE NATURE OF COMPLEX EARTH SYSTEMS

Systems that exhibit complex behavior, often labeled "complex systems," consist of a large number of mutually interacting and interwoven parts, entities, or agents. They are woven out of many parts, the Latin *complexus* comes from the Greek *pleko* or *plektos*, meaning "to plait or twine." The concept that systems can exhibit complex behavior spans almost every scientific, engineering, and social science discipline. Systems in physics (Bak et al., 1987; Bar-Yam, 1997), chemistry (Prigogine, 1978; Whitesides and Ismagilov, 1999), biology (Kitano, 2002), ecology (Scheffer et al., 2001), earth sciences (Phillips, 1999), and engineering (Fisk, 2004; Tomlin and Axelrod, 2005) all have been found to exhibit complex behavior.

Systems are defined by the nature of their boundaries, the types of interactions between system elements, and the structure of the system. Complex systems are open systems due to the constant import and export of energy across system boundaries (Goldenfeld and Kadanoff, 1999; Katchalsky and Curan, 1967; Nicolis and Progigine, 1977). Complex systems also typically exhibit nonlinear relationships between system elements, with both negative and positive feedbacks. Finally, complex systems are also commonly structured in a hierarchy, where the components of the system are themselves complex adaptive systems or scale-independent networks (Strogatz, 2001). These features have both deterministic and stochastic components that are essential to system stability.

Though complex systems are usually far from equilibrium, they often exhibit the appearance of stability through the generation of spatiotemporal patterns through self-organization, and bifurcations to new stable states (Bak, 1996; Bak et al., 1987; Bar-Yam, 1997; Barabási and Albert, 1999; Carlson et al., 1990), such as the cloud structure in a hurricane or tornado. Self-organization refers to a process in which the internal organization of a system, normally an open system, increases automatically without being guided or managed by an outside source. Self-organizing systems typically (though not always) display emergent properties. What distinguishes a complex system from a merely complicated system? In a complex system, some behaviors emerge as a result of the patterns of relationship or interactions between the elements or components of the system, not through some external agent that imposes order.

Other complex systems can exhibit chaotic dynamics, where the state of the system is sensitive to initial conditions. This type of complex system is typified by highly turbulent flow in fluids, among others (Eckmann and Ruelle, 1985; Goldenfeld and Kadanoff, 1999). In some cases, nature can produce complex structures in simple systems, while other systems obey simple laws in complex situations; therefore, nature is both complex and chaotic (Goldenfeld and Kadanoff, 1999). Chaotic systems often exhibit exponential or other distributions (Gheorghiu and Coppens, 2004), where improbable event are orders of magnitude more likely than events that follow the Gaussian distribution. Estimates and predictions of system future behavior, particularly Gaussian estimates, formed by observations collected over short time periods provide an incorrect picture of large-scale fluctuations. Exceptional events in complex systems are often not that rare (Goldenfeld and Kadanoff, 1999). These observations have interesting implications for the traditional uniformitarianism versus catastrophism debate in the geosciences.

Since each complex system is different, fundamental laws describing nonequilibrium, complex systems are likely to remain elusive. Instead, heuristics developed through study of one complex system can be applied to develop understanding of other systems (Goldenfeld and Kadanoff, 1999), mirroring the role of analogy in classic geologic inquiry. Fundamental laws describing complex systems may not be possible because of difficulties in upscaling, which Anderson (1972) defined as the constructivist hypothesis (Anderson, 1972; Goldenfeld and Kadanoff, 1999). The constructivist hypothesis fails when confronted with the twin difficulties of scale and complexity. At each level of complexity, entirely new properties can arise in complex systems, requiring the development of insight and understanding through research of fundamental questions appropriate to that scale. These authors, on the other hand, suggested that common analysis techniques and methods may result in knowledge about certain types of complex systems that can be transferable to other situations, an example of analogous reasoning.

The earth system perspective developed in the 1980s in response to the growing understanding that large-scale environmental change required an integrated view of the mutual interactions between the biosphere, human society, and Earth. Earth system science focuses on the key processes that link the physical, chemical, biological, and human dimensions of the earth system, and employs relevant problem solving methods and system modeling concepts. Earth systems are defined based upon the transfer of matter and energy across real or imaginary boundaries, which separate the system from the rest of the universe, and the cycle and storage of matter and energy within the system. Characterization of earth systems is typically focused on the nature of the boundaries and structure of the system, feedbacks, and other connections within and between systems, and the dynamics of systems variables, which define the phase space of a system. For instance, the watershed or drainage basin has become the default system conceptualization to examine many questions concerning pollutants and water quality and water resources. Figure 1 shows maps of the Guadalupe and San Antonio River watersheds, the systems of interest for the proposed Texas Hydrologic Observatory. Complex earth systems typically operate across a wide range of time and spatial scales. Complex spatial structures, such as those found in fluvial sediments along the Mississippi River (Fig. 2) or phytoplankton blooms off of the coast of Japan (Fig. 3), can control the movement of matter and energy through the systems, controlling the overall state of the systems. Complex system dynamics have been observed in species interaction in ecological systems (Brown et al., 2001), catastrophic shifts in ecosystems (Scheffer, 1991; Scheffer et al., 1993, 2001), stability of food webs (Neutel et al., 2002), and geologic systems (Aki, 1995; Culling, 1988; Meijer, 1990; Phillips, 1992, 1999; Ravelo et al., 2004; Thomas, 2001; Triantafyllou et al., 1995; Turcotte, 1995; Valentine et al., 2002).

Current scientific inquiry seeking to address pressing environmental issues involving global, regional, and local earth or environmental systems is focused on building mechanistic understanding of the complex system and the impact that anthropogenic and geogenic perturbations have on the stability and functioning of earth systems. Examples include the restoration

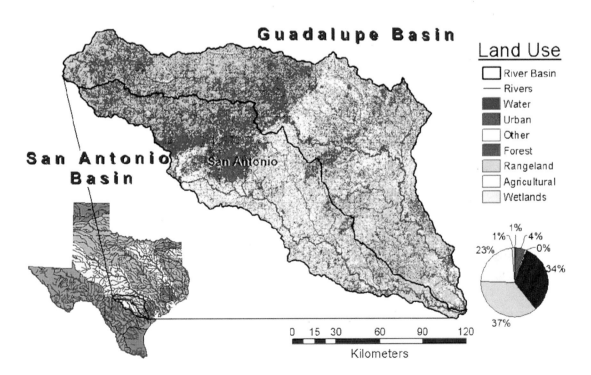

Figure 1. Two adjacent watersheds—the Guadalupe and San Antonio—and major underlying aquifers—the Edwards and Carrizo-Wilcox—are the focus of the proposed Texas Hydrologic Observatory (http://www.txh2o.org/). Watersheds are examples of regional complex earth systems.

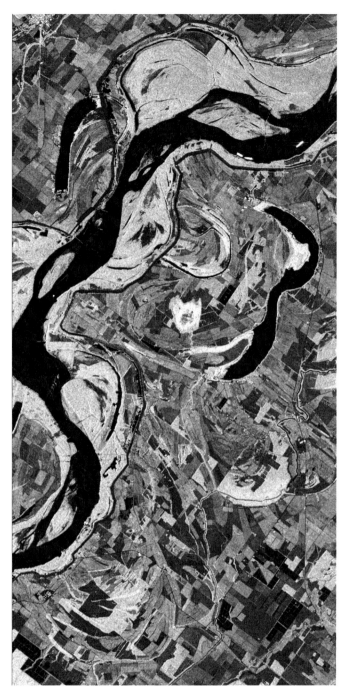

Figure 2. National Aeronautics and Space Administration (NASA) Spaceborne Imaging Radar–C/X-Band Synthetic Aperture Imaging Radar image of the Mississippi River in Mississippi, Arkansas, and Louisiana. The image highlights the spatial patterns of fluvial sediments along the river, which influence the dynamics of groundwater–surface water interactions.

Figure 3. The Moderate Resolution Imaging Spectroradiometer (MODIS) on NASA's Aqua satellite captured this image of phytoplankton blooms off of the coast of Honshu, Japan's main island, on 4 May 2005. The complex spatial patterns of the phytoplankton reflect both biological growth and transport of the organisms and nutrients by ocean currents.

of natural ecosystems such as the Everglades, the dynamics of water cycling as a function of hydrology, or the impact of nitrogen loading from fertilizer on phytoplankton population dynamics in lakes and estuaries. It is typical that there is a large amount of uncertainty concerning system characteristics, which makes the accurate prediction of complex earth systems and the development of effective environmental policy difficult.

Three major inquiry methods have been adopted to address these challenges: simulations, characterization of the properties and dynamics of natural systems over a range of spatial and temporal scales, and experiments on model systems where conditions can be controlled and causal relationships established (Scheffer et al., 2001). The results of these different types of inquiry must be carefully synthesized because each is limited in important ways. Simulations can only represent a small amount of the complexity of natural systems due to incomplete knowledge of initial conditions and phase space over time and space, though the development of new modeling techniques coupled with increased computing power have dramatically increased our ability to simulate complex systems. Recent developments in modeling techniques include the application of Bayesian statistics (Brooks, 2004), fractal analysis (Neuman and Di Federico, 2003; Strogatz, 1994; Turcotte, 1994, 1995), cellular automata, neural networks, or other hierarchical techniques (Guermond et al., 2004; Mitchell et al., 1996; Peak et al., 2004; Wu and David, 2002), and fractional calculus (Benson et al., 2001; Clarke et al., 2005; Schumer et al., 2003).

Direct observation of the characteristics and dynamics of natural earth systems is possible due to the development of new sensor technologies, including remote sensing (Donoghue, 2002; Power et al., 2005; Schmidt, 2005) or chemical sensors that can directly characterize water chemistry (Bakker, 2004; Vo-Dinh et al., 2000; Wolfbeis, 2004). At other scales, particularly characterizing earth systems over geologic time scales, earth scientists use data proxies to characterize other variables of interest, such as $O16/O18$ ratios found in Artic and Antarctic ice cores as a means to study temperature conditions and changes in paleoclimates.

Scientists have only limited control of conditions in natural experiments, making establishment of casual relationships difficult. Laboratory experiments are frequently employed for purposes of evaluating the validity and reliability of the data proxies or understanding system mechanisms (Daehler and Strong, 1996; Drake et al., 1996; Ives et al., 1996), especially where casual relationships between a limited number of variables need to be established. Laboratory-scale experiments, however, can lack the complexity of real systems thereby limiting the usefulness of this reductionist approach (Carpenter, 1996).

Scientific exploration of the nature and dynamics of complex earth systems is relatively new and evolving, and the challenge is in creating inquiry that adapts traditional modes of geologic inquiry to new questions and techniques (Baker, 2000; Frodeman, 2000, 2003; Sarewitz, 2000; Schrader-Frechette, 2000).

SUPPORTING CONCEPTUAL CHANGE THROUGH MODEL-BASED LEARNING AND AUTHENTIC INQUIRY

Supporting student development of meaningful conceptual understandings of science and its ways of describing, explaining, predicting, and controlling natural phenomena remains one of the core goals of science education. In order to meet this important goal, we need to understand the major learning difficulties that a particular knowledge domain presents to students. We are just beginning to be able to articulate the specific cognitive, epistemological, and learning difficulties students have in understanding complex earth systems. While some of these characteristics are shared by other, more traditional scientific disciplines, taken together they form a set of characteristics that likely affect learning about complex systems. There are three cognitive difficulties that people are likely to have in reasoning about complex systems. The first issue is that many earth processes occur at spatial and temporal scales beyond human experience (Dodick and Orion, 2003; Giorgi, 1997). The second issue entails the difficulty people have in developing accurate conceptual models of complex systems when there are a number of variables control-

ling system behavior, especially when the interactions between variables are nonlinear (Berger, 1998). It is likely that in most cases, student's assumptions about causality default to simple, linear, casual relationships between a small number of variables (Grotzer, 1993). The final cognitive issue involves the tendency to focus on average properties of a system, often discarding data far from the average as noise (Petrosino et al., 2003). In most systems far from equilibrium, average properties are rarely relevant because it is the extreme events or characteristics that dominate the nature of the system (Goldenfeld and Kadanoff, 1999).

Epistemologically, there are major challenges in the nature of inquiry methods and evidence that can be used to describe complex systems, a characteristic that has important implications for environmental policy (Palumbi, 2005). Applying standards of scientific inquiry that are used to assess the link between evidence and explanation common in reductionist studies may be too restrictive given the nature and our current understanding of complex systems. Because of the difficulties in both the study and modeling of complex systems, it is likely that relaxed standards of scientific evidence and inquiry are going to have to be adopted when science is needed to inform policy instead of adopting a policy of inaction. The final issue concerns the social nature of complex earth systems and environmental issues. Most environmental issues are value-laden and strongly socially constructed. Secondly, the study of complex earth systems and environmental issues requires an interdisciplinary approach (Brewer, 1999; Hansson, 1999; Karlqvist, 1999; Wijkman, 1999), an approach that is counter to the more common specialization of knowledge.

This brings us to consider appropriate educational strategies that best develop student conceptual understanding about the nature of complex earth systems. The specific cognitive and epistemological issues described here can be incorporated into the larger learning challenges discussed in the introduction, namely student conceptualization of earth systems, understanding the complex behavior of these systems, and applying this knowledge toward the development of environmental policy. Conceptual change related to these three challenges is directly related to student development of, manipulation of, and reasoning with internal or mental models (Clement, 1989, 2000; Gobert and Buckley, 2000). A mental model (Doyle and Ford, 1998) is defined as a relatively enduring and accessible, but limited, cognitive representation of an external natural phenomenon (Table 1). The structure of a mental model maintains the perceived structure of the external system (Johnson-Laird, 1983). The theory of mental models has been extended to explain deductive reasoning (Johnson-Laird and Shafir, 1993) and learning (Bransford et al., 2000). Mental models can be expressed through words, drawings, objects, or other symbols, allowing social comment and criticism. Those expressed models adopted by groups are defined as conceptual models (Greca and Moreira, 2002; Libarkin et al., 2003). Scientific models, then are a special type of conceptual model, adopted and used by scientists as cognitive tools to aid in experimental design, develop understanding of complex systems

TABLE 1. CLASSIFICATION OF CONCEPTUAL MODELS

Model	Description
Mental model	Personal cognitive representation formed alone or while interacting within a group
Expressed model	A mental model placed in the public domain by an individual or group through the use of one or more modes of representation
Scientific model	An expressed model developed through scientific inquiry and formal testing. The utility of scientific models is often judged by their ability to make empirically supported predictions
Historical model	Models that have a utility that has been agreed upon by a community in some historical context, but now has been superseded by other models

Note: from Gilbert et al. (2000).

through comparisons with observations, or to make qualitative and quantitative predictions concerning system behaviors under specified conditions.

Though the research is limited, it is likely that many students have difficulty in understanding earth systems of even modest complexity, predicting future system behavior in a variety of scenarios, and reasoning correctly about complex environmental issues because of misconceptions, inaccuracies, or incompleteness in their mental models of these systems (Ekborg, 2003; Forrester, 1992). Instructional sequences and learning environments that stress model-based teaching and learning may address student development of more accurate mental models of complex earth systems (Boulter and Gilbert, 2000).

Modeling as a pedagogical tool involves cycles of model construction, characterization, application to specific problems, evaluation, and revision. Modeling emphasizes forms of knowledge representation and topics including visualization, data structures, and measurement and uncertainty (Table 2). Model-based learning also supports student understanding about the nature of science because model-based learning typically stresses the relationship between mental models and scientific models. Scientific models are major outcomes and products of scientific inquiry, and understanding the nature of science requires an understanding of these models within a philosophical, scientific, and historical context (Gilbert et al., 2000; Grandy, 2003).

Student manipulation of mental, conceptual, or scientific models is only one aspect of effective instructional sequences. Educational research has shown that learning by authentic inquiry is the most appropriate method of instruction to instill scientific understanding and reasoning in students, such that the instructional technique has become embedded in almost all national and state science standards (National Research Council, 2000). Authentic (i.e., scientific) inquiry is defined by educators as the

activities that scientists engage in while conducting research (Dunbar, 1995; Latour and Woolgar, 1986).

Because scientific inquiry is a complex process that varies across disciplines in terms of required cognitive and metacognitive processes, epistemology, and methods, there is significant debate in the science education literature about the nature of authentic inquiry and how it should be implemented in different educational settings (Chinn and Malhotra, 2002; Minstrell, 2000). Recent analyses show that authentic inquiry has not been incorporated into most classroom activities in secondary schools and universities (Chinn and Malhotra, 2002). A host of reasons have been cited to explain why authentic inquiry is uncommon in classrooms, including the characteristics of the students and/or teachers and the constraints of the learning environment.

Inquiry-based learning is a student-centered, active learning approach focusing on engaging students in questioning, critical thinking, and problem solving. For instance, the Legacy Learning Cycle, developed at the Learning Technology Center at Vanderbilt University conceptualizes authentic inquiry as cycles of challenge, thoughts, perspectives and resources, assessment, and wrap-up (http://iris.peabody.vanderbilt.edu/slm.html). In most cases, student manipulation of models is not conceptualized as a major component in inquiry-based learning. Authentic inquiry could be reconceptualized to place manipulation of conceptual models as its core activity, an idea supported by the analysis of potential learning issues connected with student understanding of complex earth systems presented here and the importance of modeling in scientific research (Fig. 4).

Students show evidence of being able to reason scientifically and engage in scientific inquiry (American Association for the Advancement of Science Project 2061, 1989) when learning is focused on challenging scientific problems with personal significance, efforts are scaffolded, and evidenced-based reasoning is

TABLE 2. CLASSIFICATION OF REPRESENTATIONS

Modes of representations	Description
Concrete	Physical models made of materials
Verbal	Descriptions composed of metaphors and analogies expressed in oral and written forms
Mathematical	Mathematical expressions
Visual	Graphical or pictorial forms in graphs or diagrams
Symbolic	A mixed mode representation

Note: from Gilbert et al. (2000).

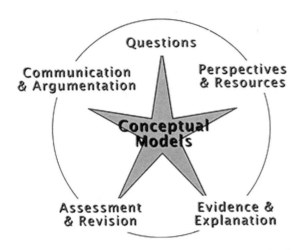

Figure 4. Conceptualization of scientific inquiry as a set of activities focused on the scientific exploration of a question or theme with the development and manipulation of conceptual models as the central cognitive activity.

developed from personal observation and experiences. The role of authentic inquiry in developing student's "scientific habit of mind" (Duschl and Gitomer, 1997) assumes students can learn the cognitive and manipulative methods of science exploration that generate data and evidence. It also assumes that students can use the reasoning and argumentation skills needed for model development and evaluation that link evidence to explanations. A scientific habit of mind is an example of a cognitive strand, which we define as a set of interdependent cognitive and metacognitive skills and strategies (e.g., developing mental models, connecting multiple representations, visualization, using iterative processes, and critical thinking), that allows students to engage in scientific inquiry. Jim Minstrell has used a strand analogy to describe the nature of preconceptions in physics students and the role of effective instruction in developing understanding (Minstrell, 1989, p. 130–131):

> Students initial ideas about mechanics are like strands of yarn, some unconnected, some loosely interwoven. The act of instruction can be viewed as helping the students unravel individual strands of belief, label them, and then weave them into a fabric of more complete understanding. Rather than denying the relevancy of a belief, teachers might do better by helping students differentiate their ideas from and integrate them into conceptual beliefs like those of scientists.

Serious questions remain on how best to implement instructional sequences that embed model-based reasoning about complex earth systems within inquiry-based learning. Information technology remains one of most promising strategies to meet these educational goals. The use of information technology to support student understanding of complex earth systems through authentic-inquiry learning should employ learner manipulation of complex data sets and physical models, the development and

testing of conceptual models based on available evidence, exposure to authentic, complex, and ill-constrained problems, and it should contain explicit instruction in cognitive and metacognitive strategies. Because of these characteristics, the design and development of information technology–based learning environments are directly supported by research activities conducted by university, government, and industry, and supports the integration of research and education.

There is a need to enhance earth and environmental science instruction at all levels through the further development and incorporation of effective and innovative information technology–based learning materials in ways that build on the strengths of the Internet and distributed networks, and the availability of large environmental data sets. Given the individuality of instructional style and curricula, the development of information technology–based instructional materials should be highly modular in nature to foster dissemination, where each module emphasizes the development of specific cognitive strands (e.g., connecting multiple representations, visualization, using iterative processes, critical thinking) and competencies in learners. In addition, further efforts need to be placed on assessment of design and implementation strategies using authentic assessment methodologies.

SUPPORTING REFORM OF EARTH SCIENCE EDUCATION

In the discourse above, I outline major learning challenges, cognitive errors, and epistemological issues surrounding student learning about complex earth systems. I also describe potentially effective instructional strategies, namely model-based learning, authentic inquiry, and the role of information technology to support learning within classroom contexts, which may address these learning challenges. The question remains about the relationship among these rather specific conclusions and larger issues of tertiary science education reform. Several major issues have guided reform efforts in the United States, including the poor retention of scientific knowledge and lack of cognitive skill development in students, the low retention of students in science, especially those from underrepresented minorities, and the limited scientific literacy among the American public.

In a series of reports, national committees have focused on the state of science education in higher education institutions (George, 1996; Ireton et al., 1997; Resnick, 1987; Stout et al., 1994; The Boyer Commission on Educating Undergraduates in the Research University, 1998). Calls for reform of science education, including earth and environmental science, at the university and college level are not new. Passivity in students, often ascribed to the prevalent lecture format of science classes, the lack of dialogue with instructors, a focus on grades, and the need to develop thinking and reasoning in students, has been acknowledged for more than a century (Dutch, 1996; Howe, 1892; Smith, 1955). These reports are quite uniform in their critique of the current situation and recommendations. These recommendations focus on five general areas: content and curriculum; pedagogy and assessment; development of student skills in written and spoken communications, interpersonal skills, and problem solving and critical analysis; scientific literacy in citizens; and the potential of computer-aided instruction to support important educational goals. Reforms are particularly important for introductory courses, which are typically terminal science classes for many undergraduates (Stout et al., 1994). The perceived dullness or complexity of the material, a lack of concrete applications, and preconceptions among both students and instructors can make introductory science classes difficult for nonscience majors and can lead to lower retention rates of science majors (Delaughter et al., 1998). Introductory sciences are our best chance to increase scientific literacy of college students (Abd-El-Khalick and Lederman, 2000; Laugksch and Spargo, 1996; Miller, 1998). Scientific literacy is important for the health of a democracy in an increasingly technological society, where citizens are being asked to participate in important issues such as developing solutions to pressing environmental problems (Miller, 1998).

While many of these reports suggest the potential of authentic inquiry to support student learning, there remains a great need for additional research on learning issues (e.g., misconceptions, poor mental models, reasoning errors) associated with learning about complex earth systems. Likewise, there is a need to assess the implementation of authentic inquiry in various classroom contexts, and develop additional assessment techniques and instructional materials that support learning. Finally, there is a need to establish whether student learning issues concerning complex earth systems are an adequate model of similar cognitive issues expressed by experts, policy managers, or stakeholders involved in developing solutions to environmental problems. If the two groups exhibit similar reasoning errors and misconceptions, then educational research in the earth science has an important new application.

IMPLICATIONS

Development and implementation of effective environmental policy that addresses the most pressing issues involving the relationship between human society and Earth will require direct involvement by all stakeholders. It is likely that these people will face serious difficulty in understanding the complex nature of earth systems. Educational research focused on undergraduate student learning about complex earth systems will likely develop important insights that can be used to serve two distinct goals: improve undergraduate earth science education and address stakeholder learning issues during environmental problem solving.

ACKNOWLEDGMENTS

The National Science Foundation generously supported this work through grant ESI 0353377 and through support from the Information Technology in Science (ITS) Center for Learning and Teaching at Texas A&M University (ESI-0083336). Any opinions, findings, and conclusions or recommendations expressed in this material are those of the author(s) and do not necessarily reflect the views of the National Science Foundation. The author would also like to acknowledge the efforts of two anonymous reviewers.

REFERENCES CITED

Abd-El-Khalick, F., and Lederman, N.G., 2000, The influence of history of science courses on students' views of nature of science: Journal of Research in Science Teaching, v. 37, no. 10, p. 1057–1095, doi: 10.1002/1098-2736(200012)37:10<1057::AID-TEA3>3.0.CO;2-C.

Aki, K., 1995, Earthquake prediction, societal implications, 1995: Reviews of Geophysics, v. 33, Supplement, p. S243–S247.

Allen, W., Bosch, O., Kilvington, M., Oliver, J., and Gilbert, M., 2001, Benefits of collaborative learning for environmental management: Applying the integrated systems for knowledge management approach to support animal pest control: Environmental Management, v. 27, no. 2, p. 215–223, doi: 10.1007/s002670010144.

American Association for the Advancement of Science Project 2061, 1989, Science for all Americans: A project 2061 report on literacy goals in science, mathematics, and technology: Washington, D.C., American Association for the Advancement of Science, 217 p.

Anderson, P.W., 1972, More is different: Science, v. 177, no. 4047, p. 393–396.

Bak, P., 1996, How nature works: The science of self-organized criticality: New York, Copernicus, 212 p.

Bak, P., Tang, C., and Wiesenfeld, K., 1987, Self-organized criticality: An explanation of the 1/f noise: Physical Review Letters, v. 59, no. 4, p. 381, doi: 10.1103/PhysRevLett.59.381.

Baker, V.R., 2000, Conversing with the Earth: The geological approach to understanding, *in* Frodeman, R., ed., Earth matters: The earth sciences, philosophy, and the claims of community: Upper Saddle River, New Jersey, Prentice-Hall, p. 2–10.

Bakker, E., 2004, Electrochemical sensors: Analytical Chemistry, v. 76, no. 12, p. 3285–3298, doi: 10.1021/ac049580z.

Barabási, A., and Albert, R., 1999, Emergence of scaling in random networks: Science, v. 286, p. 509–512, doi: 10.1126/science.286.5439.509.

Bar-Yam, Y., 1997, Dynamics of complex systems: Reading, Massachusetts, Addison-Wesley, 848 p.

Benson, D.A., Schumer, R., Meerschaert, M.M., and Wheatcraft, S.W., 2001, Fractional dispersion, Levy motions, and the MADE tracer tests: Transport in Porous Media, v. 42, p. 211–240, doi: 10.1023/A:1006733002131.

Berger, R., 1998, Understanding science: Why causes are not enough: Philosophy of Science, v. 65, no. 2, p. 306–333, doi: 10.1086/392641.

Bostrom, A., Fischhoff, B., and Morgan, M.G., 1993, Characterizing mental models of hazardous processes: A methodology and an application to radon: The Journal of Social Issues, v. 48, no. 4, p. 85–100.

Boulter, C.J., and Gilbert, J.K., 2000, Challenges and opportunities of developing models in science education, *in* Gilbert, J.K., and Boulter, C.J., eds., Developing models in science education: Netherlands, Kluwer Academic Publishing, p. 343–362.

Bransford, J.D., Brown, A., and Cocking, R.R., eds., 2000, How people learn: Brain, mind, experience, and school: Expanded edition: Washington, D.C., National Academy Press, 374 p.

Brewer, G.D., 1999, The challenges of interdisciplinarity: Policy Sciences, v. 32, p. 327–337, doi: 10.1023/A:1004706019826.

Brooks, S.P., 2004, Bayesian computation: A statistical revolution: Philosophical Transactions of the Royal Society, ser. A, Mathematical Physical and Engineering Sciences, v. 362, no. 1813, p. 2681–2697.

Brown, J.H., Whitham, T.G., Ernest, S.K.M., and Gehring, C.A., 2001, Complex species interactions and the dynamics of ecological systems: Long-term experiments: Science, v. 293, no. 5530, p. 643–650, doi: 10.1126/science.293.5530.643.

Carlson, J.M., Chayes, J.T., Grannan, E.R., and Swindle, G.H., 1990, Self-organized criticality and singular diffusion: Physical Review Letters, v. 65, no. 20, p. 2547–2550, doi: 10.1103/PhysRevLett.65.2547.

Carpenter, S.R., 1996, Microcosm experiments have limited relevance for community and ecosystem ecology: Ecology, v. 77, no. 3, p. 677–680.

Chinn, C.A., and Malhotra, B.A., 2002, Epistemologically authentic inquiry in schools: A theoretical framework for evaluating inquiry tasks: Science and Education, v. 86, no. 2, p. 175–218, doi: 10.1002/sce.10001.

Clarke, D., Meerschaert, M.M., and Wheatcraft, S.W., 2005, Fractal travel time estimates for dispersive contaminants: Ground Water, v. 43, no. 3, p. 401–407, doi: 10.1111/j.1745–6584.2005.0025.x.

Clement, J., 1989, Learning via model construction and criticism, *in* Glover, G., Ronning, R., and Reynolds, C., eds., Handbook of creativity: Assessment, theory, and research: New York, Plenum Press, p. 341–381.

Clement, J., 2000, Model based learning as a key research area for science education: International Journal of Science Education, v. 22, no. 9, p. 1041–1053.

Culling, W.E.H., 1988, Dimension and entropy in the soil covered landscape: Earth Surface Processes and Landforms, v. 13, p. 619–648.

Daehler, C.C., and Strong, D.R., 1996, Can you bottle nature? The roles of microcosms in ecological research: Ecology, v. 77, no. 3, p. 663–664.

Delaughter, J.E., Stein, S., Stein, C.A., and Bain, K.R., 1998, Preconceptions abound among students in an introductory earth science course: Eos (Transactions, American Geophysical Union), v. 79, no. 36, p. 429–432.

Dodick, J., and Orion, N., 2003, Measuring student understanding of geological time: Science and Education, v. 87, no. 5, p. 708–731, doi: 10.1002/sce.1057.

Donoghue, D.N.M., 2002, Remote sensing: Environmental change: Progress in Physical Geography, v. 26, no. 1, p. 144–152, doi: 10.1191/0309133302pp329pr.

Doyle, J.K., and Ford, D.N., 1998, Mental models concepts for system dynamics research: System Dynamics Review, v. 14, no. 1, p. 3–29, doi: 10.1002/(SICI)1099–1727(199821)14:1<3::AID-SDR140>3.0.CO;2-K.

Drake, J.A., Huxel, G.R., and Hewitt, C.L., 1996, Microcosms as models for generating and testing community theory: Ecology, v. 77, no. 3, p. 670–677.

Dunbar, K., 1995, How scientists really reason: Scientific reasoning in real-world laboratories, *in* Sternberg, R.J., and Davidson, J.E., ed., The nature of insight: Cambridge, Massachusetts, Massachusetts Institute of Technology Press, p. 365–395.

Duschl, R.A., and Gitomer, D.H., 1997, Strategies and challenges to changing the focus of assessment and instruction in science classrooms: Educational Assessment, v. 4, no. 1, p. 37–74.

Dutch, S.I., 1996, The standard model for reform in science education does not work: Journal of Geoscience Education, v. 44, p. 245–249.

Eckmann, J.-P., and Ruelle, D., 1985, Ergodic theory of chaos and strange attractors: Reviews of Modern Physics, v. 54, p. 617–656, doi: 10.1103/RevModPhys.57.617.

Ekborg, M., 2003, How student teachers use scientific conceptions to discuss a complex environmental issue: Journal of Biological Education, v. 37, no. 3, p. 126–132.

Fisk, D., 2004, Engineering complexity: Interdisciplinary Science Reviews, v. 29, no. 2, p. 151–161.

Forrester, J.W., 1992, Policies, decisions, and information sources for modeling: European Journal of Operational Research, v. 59, no. 1, p. 52–68.

Frodeman, R., 2000, Preface: Shifting plate: The new earth sciences, *in* Frodeman, R., ed., Earth matters: The earth sciences, philosophy, and the claims of community: Upper Saddle River, New Jersey, Prentice-Hal, p. vii–xiii.

Frodeman, R., 2003, Geo-logic: Breaking ground between philosophy and the earth sciences: Ithaca, New York, State University of New York Press, 192 p.

George, M.D.C., 1996, Shaping the future: New expectation for undergraduate education in science, mathematics, engineering and technology: Washington, D.C., National Science Foundation: http://www.nsf.gov/publications/pub_summ.jsp?ods_key=nsf96139 (accessed September 2006).

Gheorghiu, S., and Coppens, M.-O., 2004, Heterogeneity explains features of "anomalous" thermodynamics and statistics: Proceedings of the National Academy of Sciences of the United States of America, v. 101, p. 15,852–15,856, doi: 10.1073/pnas.0407191101.

Gilbert, J.K., Boulter, C.J., and Elmer, R., 2000, Positioning models in science education and in design and technology education, *in* Gilbert, J.K., and Boulter, C.J., eds., Developing models in science education: Netherlands, Kluwer Academic Publishing, p. 3–17.

Giorgi, F.A.R., 1997, Representation of heterogeneity effects in earth system modeling: Experience from land surface modeling: Reviews of Geophysics, v. 35, no. 4, p. 413, doi: 10.1029/97RG01754.

Gobert, J.D., and Buckley, B.C., 2000, Introduction to model-based teaching and learning in science education: International Journal of Science Education, v. 22, no. 9, p. 891–894.

Goldenfeld, N., and Kadanoff, L.P., 1999, Simple lessons from complexity: Science, v. 284, no. 5411, p. 87–89, doi: 10.1126/science.284.5411.87.

Grandy, R.E., 2003, What are models and why do we need them?: Science and Education, v. 12, no. 8, p. 773–777, doi: 10.1023/B:SCED.0000004572.67859.43.

Greca, I.M., and Moreira, M.A., 2002, Mental, physical, and mathematical models in the teaching and learning of physics: Science and Education, v. 86, no. 1, p. 106–121.

Grotzer, T.A., 1993, Children's understanding of complex causal relationships in natural systems: A research study [PhD. dissertation]: Boston, Massachusetts, Harvard University, 319 p.

Guermond, Y., Delahaye, D., Dubos-Paillard, E., and Langlois, P., 2004, From modelling to experiment: GeoJournal, v. 59, no. 3, p. 171–176, doi: 10.1023/B:GEJO.0000026687.80908.59.

Hansson, B., 1999, Interdisciplinarity: For what purpose?: Policy Sciences, v. 32, p. 339–343, doi: 10.1023/A:1004718320735.

Howe, J.L., 1892, The teaching of science: Science, v. 19, no. 481, p. 233–235.

Hurley, J.M., Ginger, C., and Capen, D.E., 2003, Property concepts, ecological thought, and ecosystem management: A case of conservation policymaking in Vermont: Society and Natural Resources, v. 15, no. 4, p. 295–312, doi: 10.1080/089419202753570792.

Ireton, F.W., Manduca, C.A., and Mogk, D.W., 1997, Towards a coherent plan for undergraduate earth science education: A systems approach: Journal of College Science Teaching, v. 26, p. 304–308.

Ives, A.R., Foufopoulos, J., Klopfer, E.D., Klug, J.L., and Palmer, T.M., 1996, Bottle or big-scale studies: How do we do ecology?: Ecology, v. 77, no. 3, p. 681–685.

Johnson-Laird, P.N., 1983, Mental models: Towards a cognitive science of language, inference and consciousness: Cambridge, Massachusetts, Harvard University Press, 513 p.

Johnson-Laird, P.N., and Shafir, E., 1993, The interaction between reasoning and decision making: An introduction: Cognition, v. 49, no. 1–2, p. 1–9.

Karlqvist, A., 1999, Going beyond disciplines: Policy Sciences, v. 32, p. 379–383, doi: 10.1023/A:1004736204322.

Katchalsky, A., and Curan, P.F., 1967, Nonequilibrium processes in biophysics: Cambridge, Massachusetts, Harvard University Press, 248 p.

Kempton, W., 1991, Public understanding of global warming: Society and Natural Resources, v. 4, p. 331–345.

Kitano, H., 2002, Systems biology: A brief overview: Science, v. 295, p. 1662–1664, doi: 10.1126/science.1069492.

Latour, B., and Woolgar, S., 1986, Laboratory life: The construction of scientific fact (2nd edition): Princeton, New Jersey, Princeton University Press, 294 p.

Laugksch, R.C., and Spargo, P.E., 1996, Development of a pool of scientific literacy test-items based on selected AAAS literacy goals: Science and Education, v. 80, no. 2, p. 121–143, doi: 10.1002/(SICI)1098–237X(199604)80:2<121::AID-SCE1>3.0, v. 2-I.

Libarkin, J.C., Beilfuss, M., and Kurdziel, J.P., 2003, Research methodologies in science education: Mental models and cognition in education: Journal of Geoscience Education, v. 51, January, p. 121–126.

Lubchenco, J., 1998, Entering the century of the environment: A new social contract for science: Science, v. 279, p. 491–497, doi: 10.1126/science.279.5350.491.

McDaniels, T., and Gregory, R., 2004, Learning as an objective within a structured risk management decision process: Environmental Science and Technology, v. 38, no. 7, p. 1921–1926, doi: 10.1021/es0264246.

Meijer, E.L., 1990, Modelling of non-linear equilibrium relations in the soil-water system: Chemical Geology, v. 84, p. 279–280.

Miller, J.D., 1998, The measurement of civic scientific literacy: Public Understanding of Science, v. 7, p. 203–223, doi: 10.1088/0963–6625/7/3/001.

Minstrell, J.A., 1989, Teaching science for understanding, *in* Resnick, L.B., and Klopfer, L.E., eds., Toward the thinking curriculum: Current cognitive research: Alexandria, Virginia, Association for Supervision and Curriculum Development, p. 130–131.

Minstrell, J.A., 2000, Implications for teaching and learning inquiry: A summary, *in* Zee, J.M.E.V., ed., Inquiring into inquiry learning and teaching in science: Washington, D.C., American Association for the Advancement of Science (AAAS), p. 471–496.

Mitchell, N., Crutchfield, J.P., and Das, R., 1996, Evolving cellular automata with genetic algorithms: A review of recent works, *in* Proceedings of the First International Conference on Evolutionary Computation and Its Applications (EvCA'96): Moscow, Russia, Russian Academy of Sciences, 15 p. (Available at http://www.cs.pdx.edu/~mm/evca-review.pdf.)

Morgan, M.G., Florig, H.K., Nair, I., Cortes, C., and Marsh, K., 1990, Lay understanding of low-frequency electric and magnetic fields: Bioelectromagnetics, v. 11, no. 4, p. 313, doi: 10.1002/bem.2250110407.

National Research Council, 2000, Inquiry and the National Science Education Standards: A guide for teaching and learning: Washington, D.C., National Academy Press, 224 p.

Neuman, S.P., and Di Federico, V., 2003, Multifaceted nature of hydrogeologic scaling and its interpretation: Reviews of Geophysics, v. 41, no. 3, p. 1014.

Neutel, A.-M., Heesterbeek, J.A.P., and de Ruiter, P.C., 2002, Stability in real food webs: Weak links in long loops: Science, v. 296, no. 5570, p. 1120–1123, doi: 10.1126/science.1068326.

Nicolis, G., and Progigine, I., 1977, Self-organization in nonequilibrium systems: New York, Wiley, 512 p.

Oreskes, N., Shrader-Frechette, K., and Belitz, K., 1994, Verification, validation, and confirmation of numerical models in the earth sciences: Science, v. 263, no. 4, p. 641–646.

Palumbi, S.R., 2005, Environmental science: Germ theory for ailing corals: Nature, v. 434, p. 713–715, doi: 10.1038/434713a.

Peak, D., West, J.D., Messinger, S.M., and Mott, K.A., 2004, Evidence for complex, collective dynamics and emergent, distributed computation in plants: Proceedings of the National Academy of Sciences of the United States of America, v. 101, p. 918–922, doi: 10.1073/pnas.0307811100.

Petrosino, A.J., Lehrer, R., and Schauble, L., 2003, Structuring error and experimental variation as distribution in the fourth grade: Journal of Mathematical Thinking and Learning, v. 5, no. 2 and 3, p. 131–156, doi: 10.1207/S15327833MTL0502&3_02.

Phillips, J.D., 1992, Qualitative chaos in geomorphic systems, with an example from wetland response to sea level rise: The Journal of Geology, v. 100, p. 365–374.

Phillips, J.D., 1999, Earth surface systems: Complexity, order, and scale: New York, Blackwell Publishers, 180 p.

Power, M.E., Brozovi, N., Bode, C., and Zilberman, D., 2005, Spatially explicit tools for understanding and sustaining inland water ecosystems: Frontiers in Ecology and the Environment, v. 3, no. 1, p. 47–55.

Prigogine, I., 1978, Time, structure, and fluctuations: Science, v. 201, no. 4358, p. 777–782.

Ravelo, A.C., Andreasen, D.H., Lyle, M., Lyle, A.O., and Wara, M.W., 2004, Regional climate shifts caused by gradual global cooling in the Pliocene epoch: Nature, v. 429, p. 263–267, doi: 10.1038/nature02567.

Resnick, L.B., 1987, Education and learning to think: Washington, D.C., National Academy Press, 62 p.

Sarewitz, D., 2000, Science and environmental policy: An excess of objectivity, *in* Frodeman, R., ed., Earth matters: The earth sciences, philosophy, and the claims of community: Upper Saddle River, New Jersey, Prentice-Hall, p. 79–98.

Scheffer, M., 1991, Should we expect strange attractors behind plankton dynamics—and if so, should we bother?: Journal of Plankton Research, v. 13, no. 6, p. 1291–1305.

Scheffer, M., Hosper, S.H., Meijer, M.L., Moss, B., and Jeppesen, E., 1993, Alternative equilibria in shallow lakes: Trends in Ecology and Evolution, v. 8, p. 275–279, doi: 10.1016/0169-5347(93)90254-M.

Scheffer, M., Carpenter, S., Foley, J.A., Folke, C., and Walkerk, B., 2001, Catastrophic shifts in ecosystems: Nature, v. 413, p. 591–596, doi: 10.1038/35098000.

Schmidt, C.W., 2005, Terra cognita: Using Earth observing systems to understand our world: Environmental Health Perspectives, v. 113, no. 2, p. A98–A104.

Schofield, J., 2004, A model of learned implementation: Public Administration, v. 82, no. 2, p. 283–308, doi: 10.1111/j.0033-3298.2004.00395.x.

Schrader-Frechette, K., 2000, Reading the riddle of nuclear waste: Idealized geological models and positivist epistemology, *in* Frodeman, R., ed., Earth matters: The earth sciences, philosophy, and the claims of community: Upper Saddle River, New Jersey, Prentice-Hall, p. 11–24.

Schumer, R., Benson, D.A., Meerschaert, M.M., and Baeumer, B., 2003, Multiscaling fractional advection-dispersion equations and their solutions: Water Resources Research, v. 39, no. 1, p. 1022–1032, doi: 10.1029/2001WR001229.

Smith, C.P., 1955, The sins of higher education: Education should replace instruction: The Journal of Higher Education, v. 26, no. 1, p. 31–36, 58.

Sneddon, C., Harris, L., Dimitrov, R., and Özesmi, U., 2002, Contested waters: Conflict, scale, and sustainability in aquatic socioecological systems: Society and Natural Resources, v. 15, no. 8, p. 663–675, doi: 10.1080/08941920290069272.

Stokes, D.E., 1997, Pasteur's quadrant: Basic science and technological innovation: Washington, D.C., Brookings Institution Press, 180 p.

Stout, D.L., Bierly, E.W., and Snow, J.T., 1994, Scrutiny of undergraduate geoscience education: Is the viability of the geosciences in jeopardy?: Washington, D.C., American Geophysical Union Chapman Conference, 55 p.

Strogatz, S.H., 1994, Nonlinear dynamics and chaos: With applications to physics, biology, chemistry, and engineering: Cambridge, Massachusetts, Perseus Books, 498 p.

Strogatz, S.H., 2001, Exploring complex networks: Nature, v. 410, p. 268–276, doi: 10.1038/35065725.

The Boyer Commission on Educating Undergraduates in the Research University, 1998, Reinventing undergraduate education: A blueprint for America's research universities: New York, Carnegie Foundation for the Advancement of Teaching, 54 p.

Thomas, M.F., 2001, Landscape sensitivity in time and space—An introduction: CATENA, v. 42, no. 2–4, p. 83–98, doi: 10.1016/S0341–8162(00)00133–8.

Tomlin, C.J., and Axelrod, J.D., 2005, Understanding biology by reverse engineering the control: Proceedings of the National Academy of Sciences of the United States of America, v. 102, no. 12, p. 4219–4220, doi: 10.1073/pnas.0500276102.

Triantafyllou, G.N., Elsner, J.B., Lascaratos, A., Koutitas, C., and Tsonis, A.A., 1995, Structure and properties of the attractor of a marine dynamical system: Mathematical and Computer Modelling, v. 21, no. 6, p. 73–86, doi: 10.1016/0895–7177(95)00024-V.

Turcotte, D.L., 1994, Modeling geomorphic processes: Physica D, Nonlinear Phenomena, v. 77, no. 1–3, p. 229–237, doi: 10.1016/0167–2789(94)90136–8.

Turcotte, D.L., 1995, Chaos, fractals, nonlinear phenomena in earth sciences: Reviews of Geophysics, v. 33, supplement, p. 341–344.

Valentine, G.A., Zhang, D., and Robinson, B.A., 2002, Modeling complex, nonlinear geological processes: Annual Review of Earth and Planetary Sciences, v. 30, p. 35–64, doi: 10.1146/annurev.earth.30.082801.150140.

Vo-Dinh, T., Griffin, G.D., Alarie, J.P., Cullum, B., Sumpter, B., and Noid, D., 2000, Development of nanosensors and bioprobes: Journal of Nanoparticle Research, v. 2, no. 1, p. 17–27, doi: 10.1023/A:1010005908586.

Whitesides, G.M., and Ismagilov, R.F., 1999, Complexity in chemistry: Science, v. 284, p. 89–92, doi: 10.1126/science.284.5411.89.

Wijkman, A., 1999, Sustainable development requires integrated approaches: Policy Sciences, v. 32, p. 345–350, doi: 10.1023/A:1004722400687.

Wolfbeis, O.S., 2004, Fiber-optic chemical sensors and biosensors: Analytical Chemistry, v. 76, no. 12, p. 3269–3284, doi: 10.1021/ac040049d.

Wu, J., and David, J.L., 2002, A spatially explicit hierarchical approach to modeling complex ecological systems: Theory and applications: Ecological Modelling, v. 153, p. 7–26, doi: 10.1016/S0304–3800(01)00499–9.

MANUSCRIPT ACCEPTED BY THE SOCIETY 21 MARCH 2006

Geological Society of America
Special Paper 413
2006

Rediscovering the historical methodology of the earth sciences by analyzing scientific communication styles

Jeff Dodick[†]

Science Teaching Center, Hebrew University of Jerusalem, Givat Ram, Jerusalem 91904, Israel

Shlomo Argamon[‡]

Department of Computer Science, Illinois Institute of Technology, 10 W. 31st Street, Chicago, Illinois 60616, USA

ABSTRACT

Despite the still-reigning concept of science proceeding by a monolithic "scientific method," philosophers and historians of science are increasingly recognizing that the scientific methodologies of the historical sciences (e.g., geology, paleontology) differ fundamentally from those of the experimental sciences (e.g., physics, chemistry). This new understanding promises to aid education, where currently, students are usually limited to the dominant paradigm of the experimental sciences, with little chance to experience the unique retrospective logic of the historical sciences. A clear understanding of these methodological differences and how they are expressed in the practice of the earth sciences is thus essential to developing effective educational curricula that cover the diversity of scientific methods. This chapter reviews the question of historical scientific methodology (focusing on geology), as it has been addressed by historians, philosophers, science educators, and working scientists. We present results of a novel linguistic analysis of scientific texts, which shows that such posited methodological differences are indeed reflected in scientific language use. Characteristic features of historical scientists' language can be directly connected to aspects of historical scientific methodology, as explicated by philosophers and historians of science. This shows that the same methodological concerns are reflected in working scientists' conceptualizations of their discipline. These results give guidance to science educators, in the light of the recent emphasis on teaching language skills, such as "Writing across the Curriculum," in order to focus on teaching and evaluating language and discourse skills within the methodological conceptual framework of the historical sciences.

Keywords: scientific methodology, experimental science, historical science, language, philosophy of science.

INTRODUCTION

There is a widely held misconception that scientists make use of a single, universal scientific method in their work (Cartwright, 1999; Cleland, 2001, 2002; Hacking, 1983, 1999). According

to many modern science textbooks at both the high school and even university level, this method involves conducting experiments under controlled conditions in a laboratory to test hypotheses. Indeed, this belief was so strong at one time, that as Hacking (1983, p. 149) noted the "experimental method used to be

[†]E-mail: jdodick@vms.huji.ac.il.
[‡]E-mail: argamon@iit.edu.

Dodick, J., and Argamon, S., 2006, Rediscovering the historical methodology of the earth sciences by analyzing scientific communication styles, *in* Manduca, C.A., and Mogk, D.W., eds., Earth and Mind: How Geologists Think and Learn about the Earth: Geological Society of America Special Paper 413, p. 105–120, doi: 10.1130/2006.2413(08). For permission to copy, contact editing@geosociety.org. ©2006 Geological Society of America. All rights reserved.

just another name for the scientific method." However, not all hypotheses can be tested in the laboratory. Historical hypotheses postulate particular causes for currently observable phenomena based on the (uncontrolled) traces that they leave behind. Such historical hypotheses are connected to the earth sciences, but also play a role in fields as disparate as evolutionary biology, astronomy, and archaeology.

As Cleland (2001, 2002) noted, scientists are well aware of the differences between experimental and historical sciences with regard to the difference in testing hypotheses. Indeed, scientists in experimental fields have often disparaged the claims of their colleagues in the historical sciences, contending that the support offered by the evidence in such fields is too weak to count as "good science" (Cleland, 2001, 2002; Gould, 1986).

Such criticism has had a profound effect on science education, especially at the pre-college level (Dodick and Orion, 2003). To a large degree, the earth sciences are not represented as a standard part of the core science curriculum across the United States. In part, this may be due to the thinking that since geology does not conform to the supposed universal scientific methodology, it does not represent the type of science that should be taught in the pre-college curriculum. One example of this prejudice at the pre-college level can be seen in the letter of protest distributed by the American Geological Institute assailing the January 25, 2002, *Draft California Science Framework for K–12 Public Schools.* Under this plan, all students in California were mandated to take 2 yr of laboratory science. Earth science was acceptable only "if they have as a prerequisite (or provide basic knowledge in) physics, chemistry and biology." (See Dodick and Orion [2003] for the full text.)

In the case of the university, it cannot be said that historical sciences such as geology are missing from its science curriculum. Nonetheless, Gould (1986, p. 74) still saw subtle prejudice acting against such fields as he noted:

> Harvard organizes its core curriculum and breaks conceptual ground by dividing sciences into two major styles experimental-predictive and historical, rather than traditionally by discipline. But guess which domain becomes 'Science A' and which 'Science B'?

The overall effect of such discrimination both at the high school and university level is that students often lose the chance to gain scientific literacy not only in earth science, but in many historically based subjects, which, by definition, require an understanding of temporally related changes.

However, things are changing on the education front. The recent national standards documents (American Association for the Advancement of Science, 1990, 1993; National Research Council, 1996) have called upon teachers to convey the diversity of scientific methods, including the historical method. To support this goal, it will be necessary to create new learning materials that more accurately represent the different methodologies of science. More importantly, it will be necessary to change the philosophi-

cal mind set of teachers so that they understand how science can accurately investigate the past using methodologies provided by the historical sciences.

As part of this effort, there is growing interest in examining the nature of the methodological differences between the experimental and historical sciences. Recently, philosophers of science as well as science educators have started to examine such differences (Cleland, 2001, 2002; Cooper, 2002, 2004; Diamond, 1999; Frodeman, 1995; Gould, 1986; Raab and Frodeman, 2002; Rudolph and Stewart, 1998). Such work is an important first step in that it establishes the fact that indeed there is no single logically superior method in science, and hence historical methods are not inherently inferior to those used in experimental science. More importantly, efforts are under way to elucidate more precisely what the historical methods are, and how such methods logically follow from the kinds of questions upon which historical scientists work.

In this chapter, we review the question of methodology in the historical sciences (with a focus on geology) as it has been addressed by philosophers, science educators, and working scientists. We then present a logical next step, which is the empirical investigation of these methodological questions. This is addressed here via the analysis of scientists' language, in the light of the recent emphasis on improving language skills in various disciplines, as in the "Writing across the Curriculum" program (Emig, 1988; Locke, 1992; Klein and Aller, 1998; Moore, 1993).

Our contention, borne out by our research results, is that methodological differences between scientific fields are reflected in related differences in language use in scientific communication. Educators should therefore be aware of the features characterizing such language use, both to be able to draw students' attention to those features, as well as for evaluating student writing about the sciences. By thus elucidating linguistic features that are specifically associated with the earth sciences, we hope to point the way toward new language-oriented foci for earth science education.

We have begun this work by analyzing stylistic variation in language use between scientists in different fields. Our initial results from comparing writing style in peer-reviewed articles from paleontology, evolutionary biology, geology, physics, and physical and organic chemistry give promising results that show how stylistic analysis of the ways in which different kinds of scientists organize their communication can provide empirical evidence supporting the existence and importance of the methodological distinctions between fields posited by philosophers and historians of science.

PERSPECTIVES FROM THE HISTORY AND PHILOSOPHY OF SCIENCE

As noted, some scientists (mistakenly) disparage the method of historical science as being less scientific than the experimental method. In part, this attitude can be traced to developments in the philosophy of science during the nineteenth and early twentieth centuries (Rudolph and Stewart, 1998). Based on the success of Newtonian physics, philosophers took physics as the model of how proper science should be done. Indeed, the views of the nineteenth-century philosophers on science reflected a strong bias toward direct observations made during (controlled) experimental manipulation of nature (Mayr, 1985; Kitcher, 1993; Rudolph and Stewart, 1998). It was mistakenly believed at the time that by using experimental methods, that is, by manipulating independent variables and measuring changes in dependent variables, scientific conclusions could be established with greater certainty.

Citing the case of Charles Darwin, Rudolph and Stewart (1998) and Gould (1986) noted that many in the British scientific community who accepted Darwin's conclusions concerning evolution by natural selection still had deep misgivings about the historical-comparative method he used to arrive at such conclusions. In part, as Rudolph and Stewart (1998) noted, such misgivings were based on the philosophical backdrop to this period. Earlier in the nineteenth century, philosophers including John Herschel in his *Preliminary Discourses on the Study of Natural Philosophy* (1830) and John Stuart Mill's *System of Logic* (1843) were establishing the supposed foundations of scientific methodology (Hull, 1973). According to them, it was firmly associated with the empirical, inductive methods of Newton (and other physicists).

This restrictive account of science, however, ignored the scientific basis of evolutionary biology up to the time of Darwin. Naturalists of the time described and classified the phenomena of the past and present, which might explain general patterns of development. However, it was not until Darwin that someone was able to provide an evolutionary mechanism that was accepted by the scientific public. In contrast to the complex diversity of life that naturalists tried to explain, with their systemic methodology, the methods of Newton attempted to reduce the world to its simplest forces. The success that Newton had with such reductionist methods provided the model for science that many in the philosophical community of the nineteenth century used as their standard for producing certain knowledge.

This bias of philosophers toward Newtonian physics as the model of science continued well into the twentieth century, and was reinforced by the development of the school of thought known as "logical empiricism." Based upon this view, the goal of inquiry in science was the establishment of laws or universal mathematical statements (Sober, 1993). In turn, such sciences produced theories that lent themselves well to experimental confirmation (Rudolph and Stewart, 1998). While such a methodology can be, and is, generally applied in the physical sciences, attempts at reconfiguring historical sciences, such as evolutionary biology and geology, toward this methodology have largely failed (as we shall see).

As a result of this bias against historical sciences in general, some scientists and philosophers of science have mistakenly labeled geology as a "derivative science" (see Schumm [1991] as an example of this "derivative" claim). In this view, geology is seen as a synthetic science, the reasoning of which could lit-erally be reduced to elements supplied by physics and chemistry. Moreover, in contrast to experimental sciences, in which all variables could be controlled, geology was said to have a series of problems (including its great expanse of geological time and gaps in the stratigraphic record) that undercut its claim to knowledge. Indeed, this situation is reflected by the meager attention that the earth sciences have received by historians and philosophers of science, themselves. This neglect was based largely on the assumption that since geology is a synthetic science, which is easily subsumed under the (experimentally based) physical sciences, there is little need to study its historical development.

Paralleling these developments in philosophy, we also find that the geological community has itself sometimes contributed to the understanding that geology (as a historical science) is subservient to (the experimental science of) physics. To better understand this claim, we will briefly review the history of the "founders" of (British) geology, James Hutton and Charles Lyell. (This history has been detailed elsewhere, including Dodick and Orion [2003], and so, by necessity, this review will be brief.) The salient point here is that this history has greatly influenced the way modern geology (as an historical science) is both practiced and perceived both within and outside of the field.

James Hutton (1726–1797) is sometimes portrayed as the "father of geology," largely due to his logical deduction of the nature of geological time. Before Hutton, it was understood that Earth's landmasses would ultimately wear away due to erosional processes. However, this understanding clashed with Hutton's belief in a purposeful world created by God, which might sustain favorable living conditions for man (Toulmin and Goodfield, 1965; Albritton, 1980; Gould, 1987; Burchfield, 1998). Based on this belief, Hutton viewed the Earth as a self-maintaining machine, continuously cycling through processes of deposition and uplift so as to counter the effects of erosion and thus maintain environmental stability. With such continuous cycles, geological time was deemed by Hutton to be an endless, immeasurable entity.

Hutton's depiction of geological time did represent an advance on the biblically determined age of 6000 yr. However, he ignored the unique element of history within his model of geological time, in that he believed that the forces shaping the Earth's surface in the past were the same as those that shape it in the present (Rudwick, 1985; Gould, 1977, 1987; Goldman, 1982; Laudan, 1987). With such perfect, repeating cycles operating, there was no room for true change or progression.

Not surprisingly, given the philosophical tenor of the time, a major factor in Hutton's denial of historical progression was Sir Isaac Newton's model of a mechanical universe (Laudan, 1987). Such a universe was ruled by a system of laws in which the planets eternally circled the Sun in timeless perfection. This influence was so great that Hutton copied Newton's theoretical language when writing about the balanced set of forces that drove his geological cycles (Laudan, 1987).

Hutton's theory attracted relatively few followers amongst fellow geologists because they rejected both his interpretation of forces, as well as the "entirely causal" nature of his model (Laudan, 1987, p. 134), which argued against the historical nature of Earth's development. Indeed, Hutton showed little interest in historical geology; this is corroborated by the fact that he gave almost no attention to the fossils, which were becoming important in unraveling the progression of Earth history (Gould, 1987).

Nonetheless, Hutton's theory became widely disseminated through John Playfair's (1802) publication, *Illustrations of the Huttonian Theory of the Earth*. As a physicist, Playfair treated Hutton's theory as a branch of Newtonian physics, while eliminating its theological implications (Laudan, 1987; Dean, 1992; Rudwick, 1998). As we have noted previously, Newtonian principles cast a long shadow over many Enlightenment ideas about the natural world, so Playfair's adoption of them specifically within geology was natural. Playfair's treatment of Hutton was especially attractive to Charles Lyell (1797–1875), who incorporated Hutton's ideas in one of the most important works of nineteenth-century geology, *The Principles of Geology* (Lyell, 1830–1833).

In *The Principles*, Lyell provided a methodological outlook for geological questions (labeled the doctrine of uniformitarianism by philosopher William Whewell [1794–1866]) that demanded that geologists assume (a priori) that actual causes observed in the present were wholly adequate to explain the geological past, not only in kind but also degree (Rudwick, 1998). Based on this view, Lyell saw Earth as a dynamically balanced, steady-state system, in which change was gradual and continuous, but led nowhere (Rudwick, 1970, 1985; Gould, 1987; Burchfield, 1998). Thus, Lyell had a vague notion that geological time was vast, but "his notion of the earth's dynamics was curiously atemporal" (Burchfield, 1998, p. 139). In contrast, most geologists favored a progressive Earth history based on the overwhelming evidence of fossiliferous strata, which were systematically being classified during the nineteenth century (Bartholomew, 1976; Toulmin and Goodfield, 1965).

Lyell required such a restrictive methodological outlook because he believed that the way to avoid inconsistency in geology was through a strict adherence to logic. Specifically, this meant the adoption of the two scientific principles of Vera Causa and enumerative induction (Laudan, 1987; Baker, 1998; Rudwick, 1998). The source of the former, not surprisingly was Newton, and his mathematical treatise *Principia*, in which he argued that in science one must refer only to those existing causes that are sufficient to produce an effect. In the case of the latter, enumerative induction is a pattern of scientific reasoning in which the collection of facts takes precedence, unsullied by any theoretical presuppositions, from which theory might then emerge (Hull, 1973; Laudan, 1977). G.B. Greenough, the first president of the Geological Society of London, urged his members to adopt this strict form of induction, as it was "unassailably scientific" (Laudan, 1987, p. 168).

Lyell's adoption of these two principles was his response to geologists who referred to catastrophic events as forces that shaped Earth's past. Such catastrophism was an anathema to Lyell because it implied that geology relied upon unknown causes, thus violating the logical principle of simplicity (which states that the best scientific explanations are those that consist of the fewest assumptions). Lyell believed that the a priori application of uniformity (based upon Vera Causa) was necessary, if geology, like physics was to be considered a valid, logical science (Baker, 1998, 2000).

William Whewell attacked Lyell's adoption of such principles as unsuitable for a science such as geology. Whewell (1837, v. 3, p. 618) believed that geology was concerned with "the study of a past condition, from which the present is derived by causes acting in time." Thus it was inappropriate to apply Vera Causa toward specifying the nature of those causes, a priori. Moreover writing about Lyell's inductive logic, Whewell (1837, v. 3, p. 617) noted:

> (Lyell's) 'earnest and patient endeavour to reconcile the former indication of change', with any restrictive class of causes—a habit which he (Lyell) enjoins— is not the temper to which science ought to be pursued. The effects must themselves teach us the nature and intensity of the causes which have operated.

Simply put, Whewell was denying that the kind of induction advocated by Lyell, which he had borrowed from physics, was appropriate to a science such as geology (Baker, 1998).

Nonetheless, Lyell's uniformitarian view has had a deep effect on geology in the modern age (Ager, 1981; Hsu, 1994; Baker, 1998). In this chapter, we will briefly document two controversies that appear to clash with this notion of Lyellian uniformitarianism:

1. Based on uniformitarian logic, it has been proposed in the past that during the last ice age many landforms in North America and Eurasia were formed exclusively by the slow, gradual action of glaciers. Thus in 1923 when Bretz (1923) proposed that a catastrophic flood was responsible for the origin of the Channeled Scabland region of eastern Washington (state), it ignited a vehement controversy in the geological community that extended over decades. Indeed, it was not until the late 1960s that enough evidence had accumulated for this hypothesis to become acceptable to many geologists; the discovery of features, such as giant ripple marks, as well as the identification of the source of the floods themselves—the Late Wisconsin glacial Lake Missoula—caused many to rethink their opposition to a catastrophic flood as the ultimate origin of the Scablands (Bretz, 1969; Baker, 1978; Pardee, 1940, 1942). A subsequent chapter to this debate was added by Wait in 1985 when he established that glacial Lake Missoula drained periodically as scores of colossal jökulhlaups (glacier outburst floods), based on his discovery of more than 40 successive flood-laid rhythmites, which had accumulated in back-flooded valleys in southern Washington. More recently, in 1996, researchers working

in Iceland actually witnessed such jökulhlaups in action, while documenting their effects on the surrounding landscape (Bjornsson, 1998; Roberts et al., 2001). Certainly such evidence should convince those who adhere to Lyell's interpretation of uniformitarianism that such catastrophic flooding was both a strong and persistent influence on ice-age landforms.

2. Although more controversial, the debate concerning the mass extinction at the end of the Mesozoic has also exposed (at least according to some earth scientists) the flaws with (Lyellian) uniformitarian thinking (Hsu, 1994; Gould, 1986; Glen, 1994). For some earth scientists, the idea that such extinction was due to the impact of a massive extraterrestrial body is impossible because it violates their a priori prejudice against large-scale catastrophic events, which have not been documented in the present day. However, there is increasing geological evidence supporting this theory. The Chicxulub crater discovered in Yucatan, Mexico in 1981 appears to be contemporaneous with the Mesozoic extinctions, and is evidence of an impact that appears to have been forceful enough to have caused a major environmental calamity (Hildebrand et al., 1991). Moreover, such impacts are not as rare as once thought. Approximately 150 craters have now been documented on Earth, most of which are less than 200 million years old (Grieve et al., 1995), with at least some of these impacts arriving as multiple events (e.g., Spray et al., 1998). Most importantly, as with our example of catastrophic flooding, evidence for the effects of such impacts have been now been witnessed in real time, as seen in the dramatic collision of massive fragments from comet Shoemaker-Levy 9 with Jupiter in 1994 (Orton et al., 1995).

These two examples emphasize that a key part of understanding causal process in geology is found by interpreting the landforms, structures, and rocks that make up the Earth (Baker, 1998, 2000; Turner, 2000). In simple terms, the student of geology will find his answers in the concrete historical materials of the field. As Ager (1981), Baker (1998), and Hsu (1994) argued, Lyell's interpretation of uniformitarianism with its emphasis on creating a logically valid science of geology may be a historical relic with little place in modern earth sciences. Nonetheless, Lyell's interpretation of uniformitarianism still influences many geologists today; thus, Hsu (1994, p. 218) noted that a study he himself conducted on ocean chemistry was met with skepticism by many of his colleagues because, as they said, it "contradicts Lyell's uniformitarianism, the fundamental principle of geology."

CURRENT STATE OF AFFAIRS IN SCIENCE EDUCATION

The neglect of the earth sciences (and other historical sciences) is also reflected within the modern school curriculum. To understand how this developed, we will briefly focus on the history of the earth sciences in the (American) school system.

Prior to the twentieth century, geology was an intrinsic part of the high school curriculum for college-bound students in the United States. In part, this reflected the fact that geologists held preeminent roles in American science and wielded their political power accordingly. However, by 1910 such courses had low enrollment, and geology had effectively become an elective (Orion et al., 1999). The conventional wisdom of the time regarded physics and chemistry as having greater social importance than geology because they aided students in developing problem-solving skills (Bybee and DeBoer, 1994).

In the early 1960s, the domination of the physical sciences within the American education system was bolstered by the supposed national security threat posed by the Soviet space program. Science education focused on "the logical structure of the sciences and the processes of the sciences" (Bybee and DeBoer, 1994, p. 373) with less emphasis on its personal and social applications. Thus, the sciences that were emphasized, physics and chemistry, were those needed to maintain the United States' (military and) technological advantage over the Soviet Union (Mayer and Kumano, 2002).

Toward the very end of the 1960s, a program in the earth sciences reappeared in the American school system, the ESCP (Earth Science Curriculum Project) (American Geological Institute 1967), with a second program following in the early 1970s, CEEP (Crustal Evolution Education Project). In theory, the implementation of such curriculum projects suggested that the earth sciences had achieved equal status with biology, chemistry, and physics. However, this was not the case; although the ESCP received positive evaluations (Champlin, 1970), it seemingly has not made a lasting impact in the American secondary school system. CEEP was specifically designed to incorporate the new paradigm of plate tectonics, but was never successfully implemented in part due to "a lack of interest in the topic" (Orion et al., 1999).

Concurrently, these units gave the somewhat distorted image that the focus of geology was on the physical rather than the historical. This trend has continued until today. Both the *Activity Sourcebook for Earth Science* (Mayer et al., 1980) and later *Earth Science Investigations* (Oosterman and Schmidt, 1990) contain material found in the ESCP and CEEP, and the majority of the activities are strongly weighted toward the physical side of the earth sciences. This is all the more puzzling when one considers the fact that "these collections are the most widely accepted examples of what scientists and science teachers through their professional organizations have felt important to use in teaching earth science problem solving" (Ault, 1994, p. 270).

In other words, even amongst many professional earth scientists and earth science educators, there is a bias toward a geology that is strongly physical, rather than historical. However, if this is truly the case, one might question why it is necessary to teach the earth sciences, if it simply replicates many physics-based experiences?

In the last decade, a major movement for change in science education began; this movement is not only affecting the earth sciences, but the entire pre-college science curriculum. One of the key changes called for in these reforms concerns the style of learning done in the classroom, with a major focus on learning materials that emphasize inquiry. (Pre-college, this includes the American Association for the Advancement of Science's well-known Project 2061; at the college level, this includes National Science Foundation [NSF] grant 96-139, "Shaping the Future of Undergraduate Education.") There are many definitions of this term, but for our purpose, inquiry-based materials are those that more closely reflect the type of investigations that are pursued in authentic science environments. The understanding is that by replicating such environments, students will not only learn more content, but will also develop the necessary critical thinking skills to pursue independent work in science.

This call for new education materials is partly a reaction to the typical experience of pre-college students who often experience rote memorization in their science lessons. Moreover, if they experience any other learning environment, aside from lecture, it is usually a cookbook laboratory experience in which the results are predetermined. We might add that such practices have often emphasized the prevailing myth amongst both students and teachers that the experimental method is the single universal method of science, because it is rare for students to venture beyond their classroom into the field, where most historical sciences are pursued.

However, the recent reforms proposed in the national standards documents (American Association for the Advancement of Science, 1990, 1993; National Research Council, 1996) call upon teachers to convey the diversity of scientific methods, including the historical method. This is a positive step in that at least some of the student population touched by such reforms might be more attracted to historical sciences, rather than their experimental counterparts. This has certainly been the case with some students in Israel, where a program in the geosciences (at the high school level) has been offered nationally since the late 1990s. If one of the goals of science education is to increase scientific literacy amongst future citizens, then offering such choice today is an excellent policy move.

Further, many historical sciences, such as the earth sciences, have an advantage in that they integrate the conceptual skills of the other major sciences; this reflects a general trend in the sciences toward more interdisciplinary cooperation between different fields and practitioners. So again, if the goal is for students to experience authentic science environments, then being exposed to an interdisciplinary field such as the earth sciences has strong pedagogic value.

Finally, it might be noted that another goal of the current reform movement in science education is to create materials that are relevant to the lives of today's students. One important topic that fits this goal is the deepening environmental crisis. As both Turner (2000) and Frodeman (1995) have argued, the systemic and historical methodology of the earth sciences has much to contribute toward educating students about how human activity has impacted the natural environment and how to solve such environmental problems.

Currently, the design of new curriculum materials to meet the needs of the reforms is in its first stage of development. Thus, it is still too early to evaluate what effect such reforms will have on both the perception and teaching of the earth sciences within the pre-college science curriculum (Orion et al., 1999). If present experience is any indicator, there is much work to do to overcome the ingrained prejudices that educators have against historical science in general and earth science specifically. For example, even today, the guidelines for many science-fair projects (a mandatory school requirement in many states) require the use of the experimental method, and thus naturally exclude many projects of a historical nature, including the earth sciences.

GEOLOGY AS A HISTORICAL SCIENCE: A RECONSIDERATION

Recently, a growing group of philosophers, scientists, and educators have become skeptical about the existence of a single method for all of science (Cleland, 2001, 2002; Cartwright, 1999; Cooper, 2002, 2004; Diamond, 1999; Gould 1986; Hacking, 1983, 1999; Mayr, 1985; Rudolph and Stewart, 1998). It is now recognized that experimental methods and evidential reasoning can play different roles in different sciences (Hacking, 1983). Nonetheless, as Cleland (2001, 2002) noted, (most) philosophers have been reluctant to make large-scale comparisons concerning methodology across different disciplines. The ultimate result is that many outside the philosophy of science are often left with the mistaken impression that historical science is lacking when compared to experimental science.

While details of approaches and focus differ among these different researchers, a broad outline of the difference between experimental and historical sciences may be given. Our formulation here considers four interrelated fundamental dimensions categorizing this difference (modified from Diamond, 1999, p. 421–424):

1. Is evidence gathered by manipulation or by observation?
2. Is research quality measured by effective prediction or explanation?
3. Is the goal of the research to find general laws or statements or ultimate (and contingent) causes?
4. Are the objects of study uniform entities (which are interchangeable) or are they complex entities (which are each unique)?

Experimental science, as is well known, gathers knowledge by controlled experimentation, in which natural phenomena are manipulated in order to test a theory. The quality of such a theory is measured by consistency of its predictions with such experiments, and ideally, such a theory expresses a general causal law or universal statement that is applicable to a wide variety of phenomena in many contexts. Finally, the form of such research is dictated in large part by the study of uniform entities, either singly or in assemblage; the fact that such entities (atoms, molecules, genes) are identical, or nearly so, makes the formulation of general laws possible in principle, and experimental reproducibility a reasonable requirement in practice.

Historical science, on the other hand, investigates ultimate causes that often lie very deep in the past, and the effects of which are observed only after very long and complex causal chains of intervening events. Consequently, evidence is gathered by observation of naturally occurring traces of phenomena, since manipulation is impossible (e.g., we cannot wait millions of years for the results of a hypothetical geological experiment!). Comparison of similar phenomena has thus developed as a key analytical technique, as typified by the kind of "natural experiment" (described by Diamond, 1999) where systems differing in a key variable are compared in order to estimate the effect of that variable on other system characteristics.

This focus on investigating past causation further implies that the ultimate test of quality in historical science is explanatory adequacy, because the phenomena under investigation are unique and contingent, and so cannot be usually expected to repeat in the historical record. The methodology of such explanatory reasoning derives from what Cleland (2002) called the "asymmetry of causation," which is that effects of a unique event in the past tend to diffuse over time, with many effects being lost and others muddled by other intervening factors. Making sense of this complexity requires, therefore, "synthetic thinking" a lá Baker (1996), in which one fits together complex combinations of many pieces of evidence to form arguments for and against competing hypotheses.

In addition to sorting through this great causal complexity, historical scientists must also deal with the complexity of the individuals under study. Unlike (subatomic) particles (for example), which are all uniform, the entities studied by historical scientists—people, species, strata—are all unique (though often similar) individuals, which have precise details of configuration and function that are not always recoverable, in practice or even in theory. This eliminates the possibility of formulating universal laws of behavior, allowing only statistical statements of relative likelihoods at best—it is very difficult to rule a specific possibility out entirely, but rather arguments for and against hypotheses must be made on the preponderance of the best evidence. Thus, reasoning about the relative likelihood of different assertions is endemic to historical science's synthetic thinking.

STUDYING SCIENTIFIC COMMUNICATION STYLES

As we have seen, despite the historic downgrading of historical methodology in science, strong arguments can now be made that the historical sciences have, and indeed require, a different type of methodology from that used in the experimental sciences, such as physics. Clearly understanding these methodological differences will be the key to effectively increasing the role historical sciences such as geology play in secondary school and university science curricula. However, gaining such an understanding requires empirical investigation of how scientists actually do science in practice, and one major element of doing science is how scientists communicate; the ways in which scientists reason, make discoveries, and persuade their colleagues are all reflected in how they communicate with one another.

This empirical approach differs radically from more traditional methods of studying scientific methodology based on either scientists' own introspection (such as Karp, 1989) or philosophical-historical analysis of scientific discovery (for example Kuhn, 1962; Popper, 1959). Here the aim is to study what scientists say or write while doing science, in order to understand what sorts of cognitive and reasoning structures they actually use in practice, not in rationally reconstructing what they did.

The study of communication as a way to investigate scientific cognition has been most recently addressed in the experimental sciences, from the perspective of cognitive science by, among others, Dunbar and colleagues, in studies of research activities in molecular biology laboratories (Dunbar, 1995; Dunbar, 1999; Dunbar and Blanchette, 2001), and from an anthropological-linguistic perspective by Ochs and Jacoby (1997) and Ochs et al. (1994), in their studies of physicists' talk in the classroom. However, little work has been done on how historical scientists communicate, and no research, to our knowledge, has addressed possible differences between communication modes in historical and experimental sciences. We contend that such empirically based studies are essential to properly understand the characteristic communication and reasoning modes of the historical sciences (in comparison with the same in experimental sciences).

There are a number of different types of communication between scientists (in any field), which can be roughly classified by the mode of communication (speech or formal/informal writing) and by audience for that communication (research collaborators, other colleagues, and students), as laid out in Table 1.

The study of speaking patterns in scientists requires videotaping and transcription, as a prelude to linguistic discourse analysis. This is expensive and time-consuming, though, and generally precludes working with very large data sets. Written material, when available in electronic form, is often easier to work with for analysis, however, since automated tools can more easily be brought to bear. This is particularly true for formal written texts, such as journal articles or textbooks. While analysis of such formal written texts cannot give us direct insight into

TABLE 1. TYPES OF COMMUNICATION BETWEEN SCIENTISTS AND THEIR AUDIENCES

Types of communication	Audience		
	Collaborators	Colleagues	Students
Speech	Lab meetings, field research	Conference talks	Lectures
Writing			
Informal	Research notes	Correspondence	Lecture notes
Formal	Lab reports	Published articles	Textbooks

how scientists reason while doing historical-based field work, or developing arguments for or against a theory, they do give a unique window into how scientists *present* their ideas, i.e., what underpinning conceptual structures they see as essential to communicating their ideas with their peers.

Our key idea here is that many aspects of language style directly reflect how people organize ideas, argue for or against a position, or explain new concepts. Specifically, in scientific communication, we hypothesize that different scientific methodologies should imply concomitant differences in how scientists organize their discourse, and that these differences in turn will be reflected in their use of language. Thus, while textual analysis can say little to any epistemological concerns, differential analysis of scientific language use may provide us with empirical evidence for and against different proposals for describing scientific methodology in different fields. Furthermore, if such evidence is positive, showing meaningful linguistic differences between fields with different posited methodologies, the linguistic characteristics specific to each particular field may then provide useful guidance to educators in teaching and evaluating language and reasoning skills in that field.

To make this concrete, for the case of experimental and historical sciences, consider again the dimensions of methodological difference discussed in the previous section (Geology as a Historical Science), which together generate the following basic hypotheses regarding variation in language use between scientists in historical and experimental sciences:

First, we expect historical science's posited focus on observation and explanation to be expressed by language containing more explicitly comparative language than that of experimental science. On the other hand, since experimental science is posited to rely more on manipulation of variables in nature and is focused on consistency with prediction, we would expect its language to more often qualify assertions as to their predictive value or consistency with predictions.

Second, the focus of historical science on explanation in order to find ultimate causes implies that its argumentation will involve combinations of multiple lines of evidence of differing validity and generality, due to the complexity of the phenomena and the asymmetry of causation (Cleland, 2002). This further implies that historical science will use more complex and explicit qualifications of likelihood. In experimental science, on the other hand, we expect to see this less, since arguments will tend to be more narrowly constructed around a specific causal phenomenon; however, we might expect to see in experimental science qualifications related to possibility (can it happen?) or necessity (must it happen?).

Third, the fact that historical scientists study complex and (ultimately) unique entities and systems by observation and comparison implies that they would need to express many separate pieces of information linked together by contextual or comparative links. For example, think of a geologist describing a particular site—connections between adjacent statements are likely to be geographical ("…and adjacent to that is…") or temporal ("when

that process completed, then…"). Conversely, since experimental science focuses on deep causal descriptions of essentially uniform entities, we expect a more "unifocal" prose, where links between assertions are based on tight causal, conditional, or temporal links (e.g., "X causes Y whenever Z").

We are currently developing a methodology for performing linguistic analysis of scientific texts (currently written, but we intend to later consider spoken interaction as well) that combines state-of-the-art computational techniques with systemic functional linguistics (Halliday, 1994), to find support for our hypotheses. Systemic functional linguistics treats grammar as a structured set of options for realizing meanings via language in context; hence, it is a useful theory for relating language structures to the rhetorical needs of the writer and reader. In our case, we wish to find out in what ways historical and experimental scientists structure their discourses differently, and to relate such linguistic phenomena back to the several dimensions posited to describe methodological variation between fields.

During the current phase of this research project, we analyzed language use from a collection of peer-reviewed journal articles from both historical science and experimental science. The detailed composition of the corpus is summarized in Table 2.

Our main goal is to find stylistic features of language use that reliably distinguish articles in one type of science from articles in the other. Stylistic features are often subtle features of word use (including syntax) related to the "connotation" of a text, rather than its more overt specific topic. For example, the frequency of a word like "of" gives a partial cue as to how a text modifies nouns, and hence how the author describes things (detail on relevant stylistic variables in our study is given in the following sections).

To obtain empirical evidence for methodological variation between the two fields under study, our stylistic analysis must answer the following two questions:

Question 1. Can experimental science articles be reliably distinguished from historical science articles purely on the basis of stylistic features of the text? If they can, then we have prima facie evidence for differences in language use that may reflect methodological differences.

Question 2. If they can be distinguished, what stylistic features are consistently significant for such classification? What structural properties of the text are indicated by these differing styles, and how do those relate to possible differences of methodology between the two fields (as expressed in the four fundamental dimensions categorizing historical and experimental sciences, mentioned previously)?

We reiterate here that we are not assuming that such a relationship between methodology and language exists, but rather we are testing such a hypothesis empirically, by analyzing original scientific texts.

QUESTION 1. DISTINGUISHABILITY

For our current corpus, we can answer the question of distinguishability between experimental and historical sciences in

TABLE 2. JOURNALS INCLUDED IN THE CORPUS-BASED STUDY

Science type[†]	Field	Journal	No. of articles	Average words/article
Experimental				
	Physics	Physics Letters A	132	2339
		Physical Review Letters	114	2545
	Organic Chemistry	Heterocycles	231	3580
		Tetrahedron	151	5057
	Physical Chemistry	Journal of Physical Chemistry A	121	4865
		Journal of Physical Chemistry B	71	5269
Historical	Geology	Journal of Geology	93	4891
		Journal of Metamorphic Geology	108	5024
	Evolutionary Biology	Biological Journal of the Linnean Society	191	4895
		Human Evolution	169	4223
	Paleontology	Paleontologica Elec.	111	4132
		Quaternary Research	113	2939

Note: All articles in this corpus are from 2003.
[†]The authors classified the journals into their science type (historical or experimental) prior to the computer-aided investigation.

the affirmative, based on a computational study we recently conducted (Argamon and Dodick, 2004, 2005a, 2005b) on the corpus described previously. We used a computer implementation of machine-learning techniques, which enabled efficient processing of large numbers of documents to find combinations of linguistic features (from a large predefined list) that give the most accurate discrimination between different document groups (articles from different journals). (An excellent introduction to the field of machine learning is Mitchell [1997].) For those familiar with statistical analysis techniques, the methods we use have some similarity to discriminant analysis—though machine-learning techniques have properties that are more desirable for our application here.

In brief, we defined a set of 93 relevant stylistic features (based on Matthiessen's [1995] systemic functional linguistics grammar of English), which could be effectively extracted automatically from the article texts. Each article was then processed and represented by a vector of 93 numbers, where each one represented the relative frequency of a feature in that article. Once such "feature-vectors" were created for the articles, we used the popular machine-learning technique of support vector machines (Joachims, 1998) to find models for distinguishing articles in each journal from each other journal, based on these features. In our use of the method, the system constructs a linear weighting of feature values that distinguishes between two classes of training data. Accuracy of such learning was measured by the standard technique of 10-fold cross-validation, in which models are trained and tested on disjoint sets of the data. If experimental science writing is distinguishable from that in the historical sciences, we would expect classification effectiveness to be higher for pairs of journals in different kinds of sciences than for pairs in the same kind, which we would expect to be higher than for pairs of journals in the same specific field.

Figure 1 plots classification effectiveness (measured by cross-validation accuracy) for four classes of journal pairs: two journals in the same field, different fields in either experimental or historical sciences, respectively, and journals in two different kinds of sciences (historical and experimental). As the plot clearly shows, the greatest classification effectiveness (on average) is obtained for journals from different kinds of science, with intermediate effectiveness for journals from different fields in the same kind of science. Journals covering the same scientific field (more or less) are the least distinctive, as expected.

QUESTION 2. FEATURES, STRUCTURE, AND METHODOLOGY

We now turn to the question of which features are most relevant to stylistic differences between experimental and historical science writing. The stylistic features of a text that we consider here are drawn from three main categories based on Matthiessen's (1995) English grammar, which uses principles of systemic functional linguistics (Halliday, 1994). Each kind of feature we consider is connected to how scientists structure communication and relates to different propositions, as follows:

Cohesion refers to how language can connect to its larger context (both within the text and outside of it, in the "real world"). The way in which cohesion resources are used in a text expresses how the author organizes ideas and relates them to each other. A key grammatical structure that contributes to textual cohesion is *conjunction*, which describes different kinds of textual features that serve to link clauses together causally or logically. The first of the three main types of conjunction is *extension*, which links clauses giving different information together, realized by words such as "and," "but," and "furthermore." The second type is *enhancement*, which qualifies information in one clause by another (e.g., "similarly..." or "therefore..."). Third is *elaboration*, which deepens a clause by clarification or exemplification (e.g., "in other words..." or "more precisely...").

Modality qualifies events or assertions in the text according to their likelihood, typicality, or necessity. There are two main types: *modalization*, which quantifies levels of likelihood or

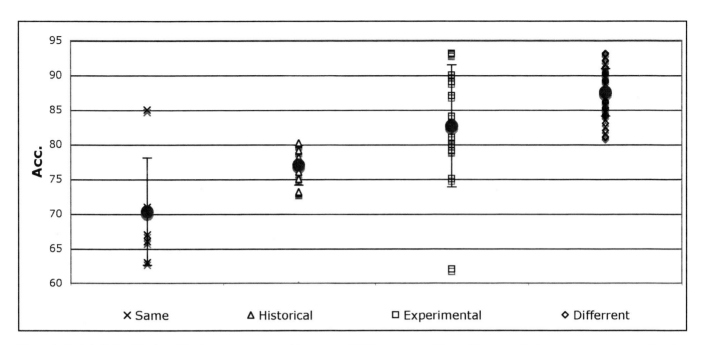

Figure 1. A plot of classification effectiveness as measured by cross-validation accuracy (Acc.). The open circles represent mean classification accuracies in a specific category (same, historical, experimental, and different), and the small squares represent measurements for each pair of journals compared in a specific category.

frequency (e.g., "probably," "might," "usually," "seldom"), and *modulation*, which quantifies ability or necessity of performance (e.g., "ought to...," "should...," "allows...," "must...").

Comment qualifies assertions in the text according to their rhetorical relation to the context. Eight types of comment are described by Matthiessen (1995): admissive (clause is an admission: honestly...), assertive (vigorous assertion: positively...), presumptive (relates clause to presumptions: evidently...), desiderative (relates to desirability: fortunately..., unluckily...), tentative (clause is tentative: honestly...), validative (scope of clause's validity: generally speaking..., in some cases...), evaluative (evaluation of actors: foolishly..., justifiably...), predictive (relates clause to predictions: as expected..., surprisingly...).

Detailed analyses of the features we found most indicative of experimental and historical science writing are given in Argamon and Dodick (2004, 2005a, 2005b); our main findings may be summarized as follows.

Within *conjunction*, we found *enhancement* to be a consistent indicator for experimental science articles, while *extension* was a consistent indicator for historical science articles. This is consistent with our hypothesis that experimental scientists will tend to hew more closely to enhancing a single story line, while historical scientists are more likely to discuss a greater variety of separate information elements (since observational methodology requires more detailed consideration of context).

Next, within *modality*, we found *modulation* to be a consistent indicator for experimental science articles, while *modalization* was a consistent indicator for experimental science articles.

This is consistent with our hypothesis that experimental scientists will focus on the possible and the necessary, while historical scientists will more often explicitly qualify assertions by likelihood and frequency, due to the complex combination of multiple uncertain lines of evidence.

Finally, within *comment*, we found *predictive* comments to be consistent indicators for experimental science articles, while *validative* comments were consistent indicators for historical science articles. This is consistent with our hypothesis that experimental scientists will tend to structure their arguments around consistency of observations with theoretical predictions, while historical scientists will be more concerned with properly defining the scope of validity of various pieces of evidence and claims.

We thus see how examination of variation in features of language use between articles in different scientific fields may be used to support hypotheses about how scientists in these fields present their research and argue for (or against) scientific positions. Clearly, historical scientists are not merely attempting to copy experimental scientists, but rather are pursuing a different agenda, and for good reason. Beyond this basic point, though, these results suggest specific areas for educators to focus on when teaching students to read and write in the earth sciences. Explicit attention should be paid to how writers link descriptions of disparate elements of a landscape (say) into a synchronic or diachronic panorama, by use of conjunctions (both explicit and implied). The distinction between extensive and enhancing conjunctions can be brought out, to help students see the different functions of different kinds of clausal linkages. Furthermore, educators can show the need for caution in evaluating the validity of evidence, by drawing attention to writers' use of *modality* and *comment*.

CONCLUSIONS

Geology, as well as other historical sciences, has in the course of history, sometimes been treated as a derivative science by scientists, philosophers, and educators. We contend that this image is misguided because it does not take into account the unique defining characteristics of such disciplines. In contradistinction to the experimental sciences, which tend to be predictive and reductionist in orientation, historical sciences, such as geology, are descriptive and systems-oriented. To a large degree, such defining characteristics are dictated by the types of phenomena that historical scientists, such as geologists, study, as well as the kind of reasoning that must be brought to bear to understand such phenomena. As we have shown, such reasoning is embedded and reflected in the end products of earth-science research–scientific communication (as seen in professional journal articles).

Due to the large number of variables associated with geological phenomena, geologists rely on an interpretive and narrative form of logic, which is used to reconstruct such phenomena (Frodeman, 1995; Raab and Frodeman, 2002; Turner, 2000). Such retrospective thinking often requires the geologist to make a meticulous survey of present conditions, which might then be used to explain phenomena of the past. Such historical and comparative explanations emphasize the differences between historical sciences, such as geology, and experimental sciences, such as (experimental) physics, which primarily focuses on establishing time invariant laws or universal statements.

The discovery of geological time is a perfect example of this working methodology, in that it required the patient unraveling of uncounted numbers of fossil-bearing strata in the field, before science recognized deep time's full implication. Through such efforts, the earth sciences have provided a true sense of Earth's historical development through the creation of a heuristic geological time scale. A single quantifiable number derived in the laboratory and describing the magnitude of Earth's age, although important to this story, could never have established this historical narrative of Earth's development. The revolution of deep time emphasizes geology's key role in reconstructing an image of the past. The environmental crisis, with its large collection of interconnected variables, emphasizes that the holistic, systemic, and historical methodology of the earth sciences has much to contribute in future to both science specifically and the welfare of the planet in general.

Scientists who downgrade the historical methodology of the earth sciences have constructed an unnecessarily limited definition of science. Moreover, this definition has also meant that within education, students are necessarily limited to the dominant paradigm of the experimental sciences, with little chance to experience the unique retrospective logic of the historical sciences. This ultimately affects their understanding of subject areas outside of geology, including evolution, ecology, and astronomy, which by definition require an understanding of temporally related changes. It also limits students' chances of being scientifically literate (a stated goal of current educational reforms).

To help rectify this situation, we follow in the footsteps of those scientists and philosophers and historians of science, including Baker, Cleland, Diamond, Frodeman, and Gould, who elucidated specific hypothesized methodological differences between historical and experimental sciences, tracing these differences to the evidentiary requirements of the questions different scientists ask and the kinds of data they work with. We have taken their analysis a bit further to examine, empirically, the conceptual underpinning of scientists' understanding of their science. As our analysis of journal articles has shown, comparative linguistic analysis of peer-reviewed journal articles can lend empirical weight to such philosophical arguments by showing how posited methods and conceptual structures are reflected in scientific language. We thus can refine and give more precise characterizations of the kinds of methodological reasoning used in different scientific fields.

Our use of automated machine-learning techniques in computational stylistics enabled analysis of potentially large collections of scientific texts. The continuation of this work will involve analysis of larger collections of texts from a wider variety of fields. Educational relevance will be gained by longitudinal studies of student-written texts at different educational levels (secondary, undergraduate, graduate) as well as textbooks and journals. Such work has therefore the potential to influence the education process by providing curriculum designers and education researchers the tools to better design new learning materials that are consonant with the calls for learning experiences that reflect the methodological diversity of all of the sciences. In this way, students not only learn the skills of specific sciences, but also the "nature" of the specific sciences (a much-desired component of modern curricula), which will also serve to banish the misconception that the historical sciences are derivative or inferior to the experimental sciences. The ultimate result is that greater options will be offered to students who enjoy the field-based methods of historical sciences, such as geology. We believe that our research program for developing precise characterizations of how scientific language use develops over time, and differs between fields, will provide a concrete basis for elucidating conceptual issues in scientific methodology.

Moreover, such research could help create a new generation of assessment tools that will permit better evaluation of students at all levels of the education process by focusing on how and when they develop the necessary writing skills to participate in inquiry-based science, which replicates a more authentic research-based learning experience. Indeed, the development of alternative forms of assessment, which go beyond simple "pencil and paper" tests that often examine memorization skills, is a major component of the current educational reforms (American Association for the Advancement of Science, 1993; National Research Council, 1996). Thus, the insights we gain into scientific communication will not only aid the cause of the historical sciences, but will in fact serve the purposes of all subjects in the science curriculum.

APPENDIX: DETAILED ANALYSIS OF SELECTED TEXT EXCERPTS

To illustrate more precisely how systemic functional linguistics features are realized in real texts, and how they indicate relevant aspects of the text that relate back to methodological variation, we consider here two sample passages, shown in Figures A1 and A2. The passages chosen are the "Conclusion" sections of a physical chemistry (PhysChem) and a paleontology (Paleo) journal article, respectively. Each text has been analyzed (by hand) by breaking it into its component clauses, and marking the following components, following Halliday (1994):

1. Topical themes are underlined; the theme expresses the topic of a clause, i.e., what it is "about." Identity or simi-

larity of theme is a strong mechanism for achieving coherence, while analysis of thematic progressions can show how a text "moves" along a story line or through a set of related ideas.

2. Conjunctions, which give the logical/causative relations between assertions, are in boldface.

3. Nesting relations between clauses are depicted by level of indentation.

4. Modal assessments, which directly quantify levels of likelihood, usuality, or necessity, are in italics.

5. Projective verb groups, the syntactic objects of which are nested assertions (clauses) and which often express modality in a sort of grammatical metaphor, are in bold italics.

Theme

First, consider thematic development in the two passages. In the PhysChem article (Fig. A1), the topic of the passage is

The adsorption of several simple methylamines on the Si-(100)-(2x1) surface has been investigated using Auger electron spectroscopy (AES), thermal desorption spectroscopy, and lowenergy electron diffraction.
Both methylamine and dimethylamine ***appear***
to undergo mostly dissociative adsorption on this surface at room temperature,
although
trapping into a molecular adsorption well ***appears***
to occur to a limited extent for both molecules, as observed by detection of a parent desorption channel in the 410-430-K temperature range.
The major desorbing thermal decomposition product for both of these species ***seems***
to come from a -hydrogen elimination-like reaction of a surface-bound $NH_x(CH_3)_{2-x}$ ($x = 1$ or 0) to form an imine, a reaction
that is *likely* to be analogous to the formation of ethylene from surface-bound ethyl groups.
This **also** results in formation of molecular hydrogen, the other main desorbing product observed for both of these species.
Trimethylamine, **however**, ***appears***
to undergo mostly molecular adsorption on this surface.
By comparison to the AES results from the adsorption of methyl iodide on Si(100), it ***was concluded that***
the initial surface saturation coverage of trimethylamine on Si(100) is 0.26 monolayers,
while
both methylamine and dimethylamine ***appear***
to saturate at about 0.48 monolayers.
The difference in saturation coverage in the case of trimethylamine ***appears to be***
because
The molecule is stuck in the physisorption well.
This results in blocking of adjacent bonding sites, *most likely* by delocalized surface electronic accommodation of the trimethylamine-silicon dative bond
and
leads to a coverage approximately half of that observed for methylamine and dimethylamine.
Ab initio and density functional calculations, even at relatively low levels, ***seem***
to capture the energetics of these surface reactions within about 15% (about 15-25 kJ/mol) compared to kinetic modeling (using computed and standard frequency factors) of thermal desorption results.

Figure A1. The conclusion section from April J. Carman, Linhu Zhang, Jason L. Liswood, and Sean M. Casey (2003), "Methylamine Adsorption on and Desorption from Si(100)," *Journal of Physical Chemistry*, ser. B, Materials, Surfaces, Interfaces, & Biophysical, v. 107, p. 5491–5502. The text is split into individual clauses, with topical themes underlined, conjunctions in boldface, modal finites and adjuncts in italics, and projective verb groups in bold italics. Indentation indicates hierarchical organization of clauses and subclauses.

set in the first clause, which talks about "adsorption" of several kinds of "methylamine." This theme then splits into two substories, the first about "methylamine and dimethylamine" (which are similar), and the second about "trimethylamine." Except for the last clause in the section (which seems to be a justification of the methodology of the study), all topical themes refer either to the several methylamines studied, reactions that they participated in, or products of those reactions. This gives a strong sense of cohesion, especially in that both story lines roughly follow parallel scripts of "chemical—reaction—result" (although the trimethylamine story contains an explicit comparison to the previous one, which also enhances cohesion).

Thematic development in the Paleo excerpt (Fig. A2), by contrast, shows a multifocal organization. The section begins talking about the "faunal record," then focuses in on "types… of…mammals" with a shift to "the extinction of…mammals," then contrasting "abundances of … mammals" in the initially focal "Camels Back Cave" with "Homestead Knoll." There is then a geographic shift to focus on Homestead Knoll and its geographical and climatic situation. Continuity is maintained throughout while panning over this landscape by keeping transitions small, either in semantic terms ("fauna" and "mammals" in the first four themes) or geographically (shifting between the two main locales). At the end of the passage, these multiple foci

The early faunal record at Camels Back Cave provides data on early Holocene environments and mammalian responses to middle Holocene desertification in the Bonneville Basin.

This record adds to the growing body of data on small mammal histories in the Great Basin

and

may prove useful in modern wildlife management issues (e.g., Lyman, 1996), especially those concerning the potential impacts of future climatic change on mammal populations in the arid west.

The types and variety of early Holocene mammals ***suggest that***

> the Camels Back Ridge vicinity was cool and moist
>
> and
>
> supported grasses and stands of *Artemisia* (likely *A. tridentata*),

and

the extinction of small mammals adapted to mesic contexts just prior to 8000 14C yr B.P. attests to the extreme aridity of the middle Holocene.

The relative abundances of these early Holocene mammals are less than those at Homestead Cave

and

It ***appears that***

> areas surrounding Camels Back Cave were not quite as cool.

This is not surprising **however**,

Since

> Homestead Knoll is 120 km to the north
>
> and
>
> areas immediately south of the cave encompass a more upland setting than southern Camels Back Ridge.

Moreover,

Homestead Cave is adjacent the Great Salt Lake (e.g., Madsen *et al.*, 2001, Figure 3)

and

> as
>
> Pacific storm systems make their way across the area,

the "lake-effect" enhancement of these storms has *probably always* come into play,

and

It is *likely* that

> this lake-edge context has *always* been wetter and slightly cooler than the southern Great Salt Lake Desert.

Regardless of these subtle differences, faunas from both caves strongly ***suggest that***

> middle Holocene desertification brought forth significant changes in regional plants and animals, including a rather rapid transition to xerophytic shrub communities dominated by *Sarcobatus vermiculatus* and *Atriplex* sp. and an overall decline in mammalian taxonomic richness.

These biotic communities have dominated the Camels Back Cave vicinity for the last ca. 8000 14C years

and

probably were similar to the native desert habitats surrounding Camels Back Ridge today.

Figure A2. The conclusion section from Dave N. Schmitt, David B. Madsen, and Karen D. Lupo (2002), "Small-Mammal Data on Early and Middle Holocene Climates and Biotic Communities in the Bonneville Basin, USA," Quaternary Research, v. 58, p. 255–260. The text is marked up as in Figure A1.

are brought together in the final two sentences, which suggest generalizations that apply to "faunas from both caves" and referring to these faunas as a single entity, "these biotic communities," Cohesion is thus achieved in this text by combining continuity (logical and geographic) of focal shift, with a concluding "tying together" of the multiple strands of the argument.

Conjunction and Nesting

In the PhysChem passage, the sense of a single (though complex) story line is strengthened by the kinds of conjunctions used, which are all enhancing, except for the nested "also" and a single "and" near the end. Enhancing conjunctions link clauses together as part of a single information unit by means of a logical ("although," "however") or causal ("because") link, and thus create a logically and causally coherent story-line linking the assertions. Similarly, the use of a small number of focal points for the story is also seen by the comparatively deep nesting of clauses throughout the passage.

The Paleo passage uses very different conjunctions; its multi-focal nature (noted previously) is also seen in the fact that nine out of eleven conjunctions are extensive—eight "and" and one "moreover." The contrast with the PhysChem passage is most strikingly seen by comparing clause nesting (shown by indentation) in the two passages—the Paleo passage is nearly flat, while the PhysChem passage has quite a complex hierarchy of nested clauses. We suggest that the flatness of the Paleo passage gives it a sort of "panoramic" text style, with an effect of looking around at a geographic/conceptual landscape, rather than following a single causally determined story line as in the PhysChem passage.

Modality

We now consider how the two passages relate to the likelihood and typicality of the phenomena and results they describe. Noteworthy in the PhysChem passage is the almost exclusive use of apparently stereotypical projective clauses to hedge on certainty ("appear," "seems"). The uniformity of phrasing argues that such usages constitute predefined templates in the genre, and do not substantially contribute to the argument being made in the passage.

Modal assessment in the Paleo passage differs, however, in the way it is expressed. About half of the modal assessments in this passage are implicit, realized by modal adjuncts, such as "probably," "always," and "likely," rather than by projective verbs such as "appear"; the greater variety of modal structures argues that they are more semantically significant in constructing the argument. For example, the double modal "probably always" establishes universality for the "lake-effect," softened for plausibility by the "probably." This is essential to drawing the conclusion that "this lake-edge contrast has always been wetter...." This illustrates that clear assessments of likelihood and typicality are needed for historically based scientific argumentation.

REFERENCES CITED

Ager, D.V., 1981, The nature of the stratigraphic record (2nd edition): London, Macmillan Press, 122 p.

Albritton, C.C., 1980, The abyss of time: New York, Farrar and Strauss, 256 p.

American Association for the Advancement of Science, 1990, Science for all Americans: New York, Oxford University Press, 418 p.

American Association for the Advancement of Science, 1993, Benchmarks for science literacy: New York, Oxford University Press, 272 p.

American Geological Institute, 1967, Investigating earth systems: Boston, Houghton-Mifflin Co.

Argamon, S., and Dodick, J.T., 2004, Linking rhetoric and methodology in formal scientific writing, *in* Proceedings, 26th Annual Meeting of the Cognitive Science Society, Chicago, Illinois, August 2004: http://www.cogsci.northwestern.edu/cogsci2004/sessions.html.

Argamon, S., and Dodick, J.T., 2005a, The languages of science: A corpus-based study of experimental and historical science articles, *in* Proceedings, 27th Annual Meeting of the Cognitive Science Society, Stresa, Italy, August 2005: http://www.cogsci.northwestern.edu/cogsci2004/sessions.html.

Argamon, S., and Dodick, J.T., 2005b, A corpus-based study of scientific methodology: Comparing the historical and experimental sciences, *in* Shanahan, J.G., Qu, Y., and Wiebe, J., eds., Computing attitude and affect in text: Dordrecht, Netherlands, Springer.

Ault, C.R., 1994, Research on problem solving: Earth science, *in* Gabel, D.L., ed., Handbook of research on science teaching and learning: New York, Macmillan Publishing, p. 269–283.

Baker, V.R., 1978, The Spokane flood controversy and the Martian outflow channels: Science, v. 202, p. 1249–1256.

Baker, V.R., 1998, Catastrophism and uniformitarianism: Logical roots and current relevance in geology, *in* Blundell, D.J., and Scott, A.C., eds., Lyell: The past is the key to the present: Geological Society [London] Special Publication 143, p. 171–182.

Baker, V.R., 1996, The pragmatic roots of American Quaternary geology and geomorphology: *Geomorphology, v.* **16**, p. 197–215.

Baker, V.R., 2000, Conversing with the earth: The geological approach to understanding, *in* Frodeman, R., ed., Earth matters: The earth sciences, philosophy and the claims of the community: Upper Saddle River, New Jersey, Prentice Hall, p. 2–10.

Bartholomew, M., 1976, The non-progress of non-progression: Two responses to Lyell's doctrine: British Journal for the History of Science, v. 9, p. 166–174.

Bjornsson, H., 1998, Hydrological characteristics of the drainage system beneath a surging glacier: Nature, v. 395, p. 771–774, doi: 10.1038/27384.

Bretz, J.H., 1923, The Channelled Scablands of the Columbia plateau: The Journal of Geology, v. 38, p. 617–649.

Bretz, J.H., 1969, The Lake Missoula floods and the Channelled Scablands: The Journal of Geology, v. 77, p. 505–543.

Burchfield, J.D., 1998, The age of the Earth and the invention of geological time, *in* Blundell, D.J., and Scott, A.C., eds., Lyell: The past is the key to the present: Geological Society [London] Special Publication 143, p. 137–143.

Bybee, R.W., and DeBoer, G.E., 1994, Research on goals for the science curriculum, *in* Gabel, D.L., ed., Handbook of research on science teaching and learning: New York, Macmillan Publishing, p. 357–387.

Carman, A.J., Zhang, L., Liswood, J.L., and Casey, S.M., 2003, Methylamine adsorption on and desorption from Si(100): Journal of Physical Chemistry, ser. B, Materials, Surfaces, Interfaces, & Biophysical, v. 107, p. 5491–5502.

Cartwright, N., 1999, The dappled world: A study of the boundaries of science: Cambridge, Cambridge University Press, 247 p.

Champlin, R.F., 1970, A review of the research related to the ESCP: Journal of Geological Education, v. 18, p. 31–39.

Cleland, C., 2001, Historical science, experimental science, and the scientific method: Geology, v. 29, p. 987–990, doi: 10.1130/0091-7613(2001)029<0987:HSESAT>2.0.CO;2.

Cleland, C., 2002, Methodological and epistemic differences between historical science and experimental science: Philosophy of Science, v. 69, p. 474–496, doi: 10.1086/342455.

Cooper, R.A., 2002, Scientific knowledge of the past is possible: Confronting myths about evolution and the nature of science: The American Biology Teacher, v. 64, p. 476–481.

Cooper, R.A., 2004, Teaching how scientists reconstruct history: Patterns and processes: The American Biology Teacher, v. 66, p. 101–108.

Dean, D.R., 1992, James Hutton and the history of geology: Ithaca, New York, Cornell University Press, 303 p.

Diamond, J., 1999, Guns, germs and steel: The fates of human societies: New York, W.W. Norton, 480 p.

Dodick, J.T., and Orion, N., 2003, Geology as an historical science: Its perception within science and the education system: Science & Education, v. 12, p. 197–211, doi: 10.1023/A:1023096001250.

Dunbar, K., 1995, How scientists really reason: Scientific reasoning in real-world laboratories, *in* Sternberg, R.J., and Davidson, J., eds., Mechanisms of insight: Cambridge, Massachusetts, Massachusetts Institute of Technology Press, p. 365–395.

Dunbar, K., 1999, The scientist in-vivo: How scientists think and reason in the laboratory, *in* Magnani, L., Nersessian, N., and Thagard, P., eds., Model-based reasoning in scientific discovery: New York, Plenum Press, p. 89–98.

Dunbar, K., and Blanchette, I., 2001, The in-vivo/in-vitro approach to cognition: The case of analogy: Trends in Cognitive Sciences, v. 5, p. 334–339, doi: 10.1016/S1364-6613(00)01698-3.

Emig, J., 1988, Writing as a mode of learning, *in* Tate, G., and Corbett, E.P.J., eds., The writing teachers' source book (2nd edition): New York, Oxford University Press, p. 85–93.

Frodeman, R., 1995, Geological reasoning: Geology as an interpretive and historical science: Geological Society of America Bulletin, v. 107, p. 960–968, doi: 10.1130/0016-7606(1995)107<0960:GRGAAI>2.3.CO;2.

Glen, W., 1994, On the mass extinction debates: An interview with Stephen J. Gould, *in* Glen, W., ed., The mass extinction debates: How science works in a crisis: Stanford, California, Stanford University Press, p. 253–267.

Goldman, S.L., 1982, Modern science and western culture: The issue of time: History of European Ideas, v. 3, p. 371–401, doi: 10.1016/0191-6599(82)90002-X.

Gould, S.J., 1977, Ever since Darwin: Reflections in natural history: New York, W.W. Norton and Company, 285 p.

Gould, S.J., 1986, Evolution and the triumph of homology, or why history matters: American Scientist, v. 74, January-February, p. 60–69.

Gould, S.J., 1987, Time's arrow, time's cycle: Myth and metaphor in the discovery of geological time: Cambridge, Massachusetts, Harvard University Press, 222 p.

Grieve, R.A.F., Rupert, J., Smith, J., and Therriault, A., 1995, The record of terrestrial impact cratering: GSA Today, v. 5, p. 189–196.

Hacking, I., 1983, Representing and intervening: Introductory topics in the philosophy of the natural sciences: Cambridge, Cambridge University Press, 287 p.

Hacking, I., 1999, The social construction of what?: Cambridge, Massachusetts, Harvard University Press, 261 p.

Halliday, M.A.K., 1994, An introduction to functional grammar (2nd edition): London, Edward Arnold, 434 p.

Hildebrand, A.R., Kring, D.A., and Boynton, W.V., 1991, Chicxulub crater: A possible Cretaceous/Tertiary boundary impact crater on the Yucatan peninsula: Geology, v. 19, p. 867–881, doi: 10.1130/0091-7613(1991)019<0867:CCAPCT>2.3.CO;2.

Hsu, K.J., 1994, Uniformitarianism vs. catastrophism in the extinction debates, *in* Glen, W., ed., The mass extinction debates: How science works in a crisis: Stanford, California, Stanford University Press, p. 217–229.

Hull, D., 1973, Darwin and his critics: The reception of Darwin's theory of evolution by the scientific community: Cambridge, Massachusetts, Harvard University Press, 473 p.

Joachims, T., 1998, Text categorization with support vector machines: Learning with many relevant features, *in* Nedellec, C., and Rouveirol, C., eds., Proceedings of ECML-98, Tenth European Conference on Machine Learning, Lecture Notes in Computer Science 1398, Springer, p. 137–142.

Karp, P.D., 1989, Hypothesis formation as design, *in* Shrager, J., and Langley, P., eds., Computational models of discovery and theory formation: San Francisco, Morgan Kaufmann, p. 275–315.

Kitcher, P., 1993, The advancement of science: New York, Oxford University Press, 421 p.

Klein, B., and Aller, B.M., 1998, Writing across the curriculum in college chemistry: A practical bibliography: Language and Learning across the Disciplines, v. 2, p. 25–35.

Kuhn, T.S., 1962, The structure of scientific revolutions (1st edition): Chicago, The University of Chicago Press, 172 p.

Laudan, R., 1977, Ideas and organizations in British geology: A case study in institutional history: Isis, v. 68, p. 527–538, doi: 10.1086/351872.

Laudan, R., 1987, From mineralogy to geology: The foundations of a science, 1650–1830: Chicago, The University of Chicago Press, 278 p.

Locke, D., 1992, Science as writing: New Haven, Yale University Press, 237 p.

Lyell, C., 1830–1833, Principles of geology (1st edition): London, Murray.

Matthiessen, C., 1995, Lexicogrammatical cartography: English systems: Dallas, Tokyo, Taipei, and Dallas, International Language Sciences Publishers, 975 p.

Mayer, V., and Kumano, Y., 2002, The philosophy of science and global science literacy, *in* Mayer, V., ed., Global science literacy: Dordrecht, Netherlands, Kluwer Academic Publishers, p. 37–49.

Mayer, V.J., Champlin, R.A., Christman, R.A., and Krockover, G.H., 1980, Activity sourcebook for earth science: Columbus, Ohio, Education Resources Information Center's Science Mathematics and Environmental Education Clearinghouse, 249 p.

Mayr, E., 1985, How biology differs from the physical sciences, *in* Depew, D.J., and Weber, B.H., eds., Evolution at the crossroads: The new biology and the new philosophy of science: Cambridge, Massachusetts, Massachusetts Institute of Technology Press, p. 43–46.

Mitchell, T., 1997, Machine learning: New York, McGraw Hill, 414 p.

Moore, R., 1993, Does writing about science improve learning about science?: Journal of College Science Teaching, v. 12, p. 212–217.

National Research Council, 1996, The National Science Education standards: Washington, D.C., National Academy, 262 p.

Ochs, E., and Jacoby, S., 1997, Down to the wire: The cultural clock of physicists and the discourse of consensus: Language in Society, v. 26, p. 479–506.

Ochs, E., Jacoby, S., and Gonzales, P., 1994, Interpretive journeys: How physicists talk and travel through graphic space: Configurations, v. 1, p. 151–171.

Oosterman, M.A., and Schmidt, M.T., eds., 1990, Earth sciences investigations: Alexandria, Virginia, American Geological Institute, 231 p.

Orion, N., King, C., Krockover, G.H., and Adams, P.E., 1999, The development of the earth sciences and the status of earth science education: A comparison of three case studies: Israel, England and Wales, and the United States: Part II, International Council of Associations for Science Education, v. 10, p. 13–23.

Orton, G., A'Hearn, M., Baines, K., Deming, D., Dowling, T., Goguen, J., Griffith, C., Hammel, H., Hoffmann, W., and Hunten, D., 1995, Collision of comet Shoemaker-Levy 9 with Jupiter observed by the NASA infrared telescope facility: Science, v. 267, p. 1277–1282.

Pardee, J.T., 1940, Ripple marks in glacial Lake Missoula: Geological Society of America Bulletin, v. 51, p. 2028–2029.

Pardee, J.T., 1942, Unusual currents in glacial Lake Missoula, Montana: Geological Society of America Bulletin, v. 53, p. 1569–1599.

Playfair, J., 1802, Illustrations of the Huttonian theory of the Earth: London, Cadell and Davis, 528 p.

Popper, K.R., 1959, The logic of scientific discovery: London, Hutchinson, 479 p.

Raab, T., and Frodeman, R., 2002, What is it like to be a geologist? A phenomenology of geology and its epistemological implications: Philosophy and Geography, v. 5, p. 69–81, doi: 10.1080/10903770120116840.

Roberts, M.J., Russell, A.J., Tweed, F.S., and Knudsen, O., 2001, Controls on englacial sediment deposition during the November 1996 jokulhlaup, Skeidararjokull, Iceland: Earth Surface Processes and Landforms, v. 26, p. 935–952, doi: 10.1002/esp.236.

Rudolph, J.L., and Stewart, J., 1998, Evolution and the nature of science: On the historical discord and its implication for education: Journal of Research in Science Teaching, v. 35, p. 1069–1089, doi: 10.1002/(SICI)1098-2736(199812)35:10<1069::AID-TEA2>3.0.CO;2-A.

Rudwick, M.J.S., 1970, The strategy of Lyell's *Principles of Geology*: Isis, v. 61, p. 4–33, doi: 10.1086/350576.

Rudwick, M.J.S., 1985, The meaning of fossils (2nd edition): London, MacDonald, 287 p.

Rudwick, M.J.S., 1998, Lyell and the *Principles of Geology*, *in* Blundell, D.J., and Scott, A.C., eds., Lyell: The past is the key to the present: Geological Society [London] Special Publication 143, p. 3–15.

Schmitt, D.N., Madsen, D.B., and Lupo, K.D., 2002, Small-mammal data on early and middle Holocene climates and biotic communities in the Bonneville Basin, USA: Quaternary Research, v. 58, p. 255–260, doi: 10.1006/qres.2002.2373.

Schumm, S.A., 1991, To interpret the world: Ten ways to be wrong: Cambridge, Cambridge University Press, 133 p.

Sober, E., 1993, Philosophy of biology: Boulder, Colorado, Westview Press, 231 p.

Spray, J.G., Kelley, S.P., and Rowley, D.B., 1998, Evidence for a Late Tri-
    assic multiple impact event on earth: Nature, v. 392, p. 171–173, doi:
    10.1038/32397.
Toulmin, S., and Goodfield, J., 1965, The discovery of time: New York, Harper
    and Row, 280 p.
Turner, C., 2000, Messages in stone: Field geology in the American West, *in*
    Frodeman, R., ed., Earth matters: The earth sciences, philosophy and the
    claims of the community: Upper Saddle River, New Jersey, Prentice Hall,
    p. 51–62.

Wait, R.B., 1985, Case for periodic colossal jokulhlaups from Pleistocene glacial
    Lake Missoula: Geological Society of America Bulletin, v. 96, p. 1271–
    1286, doi: 10.1130/0016-7606(1985)96<1271:CFPCJF>2.0.CO;2.
Whewell, W., 1837, History of the inductive sciences: London, John W. Parker.

MANUSCRIPT ACCEPTED BY THE SOCIETY 21 MARCH 2006

Geological Society of America
Special Paper 413
2006

Understanding and enhancing visualizations: Two models of collaboration between earth science and cognitive science

David N. Rapp

Educational Psychology, 211 Burton Hall, 178 Pillsbury Drive, S.E., University of Minnesota,
Minneapolis, Minnesota 55455, USA

David H. Uttal

Department of Psychology and School of Education and Social Policy,
Northwestern University, Evanston, Illinois 60208, USA

ABSTRACT

Geoscience visualizations are commonplace; they appear in television news programs, classroom lectures, conference presentations, and internet hypermedia. But to what degree do individuals who view such visualizations actually learn from them, and if so, why? As visualizations become more commonplace in school, laboratory, and entertainment settings, there has been a concurrent interest in considering the effectiveness of such presentations. How can we build effective collaborations that address pedagogical questions in the earth sciences while also informing theories about the cognitive processes that underlie visualization experiences? In this chapter, we contend that only through directed, collaborative projects between earth scientists and cognitive scientists will significant advances in visualization research take place. We describe two specific models of such collaboration, the advisory model and the reciprocal model, and argue that a reciprocal model presents a more effective framework for addressing important questions about the nature of visualization experiences. Such a model will inform both the design of effective visualizations for teaching complex geoscience topics, as well as provide insight into the processes that underlie learning from visualizations.

Keywords: visualizations, mental representations, cognitive science, earth science, symbolic development, conceptual change.

INTRODUCTION

Computer-driven visualizations have become commonplace in earth science classrooms. In a variety of situations, instructors use these visualizations to teach theories and concepts that are critical to earth science coursework (Edelson et al., 1999). Visualizations are also used as tools for communicating in the field. Visualizations thus can provide impressive models and demonstrations of scientific concepts. They are often not just nice, but also necessary, particularly when a topic is challenging to present because of pragmatic (e.g., how do we view geologic activity in real time?), financial (e.g., how do we pay for a class to travel to an actual volcano site?), or even motivational issues (e.g., how do we get students engaged in a lecture on seismic activity?). For all of these reasons, we predict that these types of visualizations will continue to enjoy increased usage in the classroom into the foreseeable future.

Rapp, D.N., and Uttal, D.H., 2006, Understanding and enhancing visualizations: Two models of collaboration between earth science and cognitive science, *in* Manduca, C.A., and Mogk, D.W., eds., Earth and Mind: How Geologists Think and Learn about the Earth: Geological Society of America Special Paper 413, p. 121–127, doi: 10.1130/2006.2413(09). For permission to copy, contact editing@geosociety.org. ©2006 Geological Society of America. All rights reserved.

As the basic implementation of geoscience-based visualizations continues to increase, so does continued interest in basic research that addresses how students and scientists use, comprehend, produce, and learn from visualizations (Ploetzner and Lowe, 2004). In other words, there is focused interest in the design and assessment of visualizations as educational methodologies. Such work can provide an indication as to the situations in which visualizations will be most effective; it can additionally suggest ways in which visualization experiences can result in successful learning. Up until this point, much of this work has traditionally concentrated on the ways in which computer-driven presentations can appropriately convey educational topics, the acquisition of skills necessary to design and use visualizations, and to a lesser extent, the cognitive underpinnings of visualization learning processes (e.g., Hegarty et al., 2002; Maki and Maki, 2002; Mayer, 2001; Renshaw et al., 1998; Slocum et al., 2001). The goal of our future work should be to empirically validate claims about the definite benefits, rather than the potential gains, of visualizations. The stakeholders interested in these efforts, specifically earth scientists (cutting across geoscientific research areas) and cognitive scientists (cutting across domains including psychology, computer science, and education), are now prepared to systematically hypothesize, build, test, and evaluate visualization systems and their impact on human cognition.

The purpose of this chapter is to contribute to the development of interdisciplinary work that links, as the title of this book implies, the sciences of the earth with the sciences of the mind. Our overarching belief is that only through direct collaboration among earth scientists and cognitive scientists can we hope to make strides in the assessment, application, and understanding of visualizations (as tools for data exploration, hypothesis testing, scientific communication, and learning). Unfortunately, at this point, much of the work on visualizations in the earth sciences, with a few exemplary exceptions, has proceeded in largely a multidisciplinary rather than an interdisciplinary manner. Thus, we argue that the field will best progress as a function of mutually beneficial scientific interactions. These activities can address many important research questions that cut across fields, informing both theoretical and practical issues associated with visualizations. But what form should these interactions take, and what can we do to make them most effective?

In line with this view, we contend that a *reciprocal model* of collaboration will result in productive, interactive relationships between the geosciences and cognitive sciences. In this case, geoscientific questions about the use or understanding of visualizations are directly related to fundamental, theoretical issues in the cognitive sciences. That is, visualization tools can be used to assess underlying cognitive processes (including learning), and the findings of these studies can provide insight into effective educational design (Rapp et al., 2003). This kind of collaborative approach benefits both the geoscience and cognitive science communities. This model contrasts quite starkly with the more traditional interdisciplinary model, which we call an *advisory model*. In this mode of collaboration, cognitive scientists work to improve the quality of visualizations and students' resulting understanding of them by providing suggestions in line with psychological principles of organization. In this case, cognitive scientists serve essentially in an advisory capacity, offering geoscientists design suggestions based on findings from, for example, the vision sciences, human factors research, and educational technology.

We believe that in the long run the field of visualization is more likely to benefit from a reciprocal model rather than from one-sided, advisory interactions in which cognitive scientists serve as consultants to geoscientists or vice versa. We also argue that grounding these partnerships with respect to theoretically driven questions about knowledge acquisition will result in robust research programs that can directly inform the use of visualizations. To make this case, we provide examples of visualization issues organized around these two types of collaborative models. We begin by describing some research questions that fit with current usage of the advisory model, in which cognitive scientists are asked to help improve geoscience visualizations. We discuss the types of situations these questions are meant to address. Next, we describe the broader scope and utility of the preferred reciprocal model. To expand on this issue, we also describe two sample topics that could be effectively addressed by this model. These topics provide an opportunity for considering important research questions of interest to both geoscientists and cognitive scientists. We close with an optimistic view toward the future of visualization and the nature of effective, robust collaborations among visualization researchers.

THE ADVISORY MODEL OF COLLABORATIVE RESEARCH

Question: How Do We Make Visualizations Look Better?

Broadly speaking, many visualization researchers are interested in the optimal methods for designing a system's visual and functional presentation. This includes establishing the best ways to design a simulation, the appropriate colors to use for attracting attention, the types of controls that will help users navigate a database, and various other surface characteristics associated with a visualization. These questions will, necessarily, be related to other issues that arise in visualization assessment. However, this category of questioning tends to be driven by aesthetic concerns rather than deeper inquiries into the nature of learning.

Although we believe that this type of research can indeed lead to the development of more effective visualizations, we contend that exploring this issue in an extended way will not lead to new insights into how people understand and learn from visualizations. For example, studying the most effective placements for pictures and texts will not inform our comprehension of visualization experiences. This is not meant as a controversial statement; the visual appearance of a presentation is essential from a design point of view, but extended focus on appearances for appearances' sake fails to describe the important ways in which individuals interact and potentially learn from visualizations. There are several popular texts that attempt to answer these types of questions by providing useful suggestions for improving the surface appearance and impact of visual presentations (e.g., Harris, 2000; Tufte, 2001). But critically, the more educationally valid question as to whether the system will lead to learning is ignored because the focus is on what looks best. At heart, visualization researchers are likely interested in the deeper question of whether and how the visualization improves learning. The advisory model pushes away from this important line of questioning.

In no way should we downplay the importance of the surface qualities of visualizations. Certainly, visualizations should be designed to promote effective (and pleasing) visual experiences; their strength, after all, is that they can make opaque concepts visually perceptible and, consequently, tractable. Perhaps focusing on the question of effective visual design is a necessary first step in developing collaborations between geoscientists and cognitive scientists. But we hope that this sort of research is just that—a first step rather than an end in its own right.

Question: Does a Particular Visualization Improve (or Hurt) Learning?

A second category of research questions to which cognitive science could contribute, but would not specifically advance research in cognitive science per se, concerns the effects of specific visualizations on learning in specific educational settings (e.g., a single earth science class or topic). Visualizations are designed for a variety of reasons, but one of the most popular is for educational purposes (be it for the student, scientist, or layperson). If visualizations are designed for conveying information, one important question to be asked before they are implemented is whether the visualizations actually facilitate learning (Rapp, 2005; Rapp and Kendeou, 2003; Rapp et al., 2004). Many designers of visualizations are interested in finding out whether their particular visualizations "work." That is, they want to know whether their design increases overall learning or facilitates learning in a particular domain or for a particular test topic.

Addressing this question is certainly of interest to some cognitive scientists. Nevertheless, we have classified the question of whether a *particular* visualization "works" as an example of collaboration aligning with the advisory model. The reason for this is that these sorts of questions focus on the specific visualization, rather than on the *process* of learning. Cognitive scientists are prepared to answer the question of whether a visualization works, and doing so is certainly an important contribution, but answering such a question does not in itself contribute to the cognitive agenda of understanding underlying mental processes. Thus, the question of whether a *particular* visualization is effective is, we believe, still derived from the advisory model. A cognitive scientist can make an important contribution to answering this question, but doing so will rarely make an important contribution to the broader geoscience community or cognitive science in general (but see Mayer [2001] for descriptions of work that

generalizes findings to a broader array of learning situations and cognitive processes).

This section has briefly described two kinds of questions that can be answered by one-sided collaborations between cognitive scientists and geoscientists. In answering these questions, the cognitive scientist serves in an advisory role, as a reference source for addressing issues of interest specifically to geoscientists and their visualization designs. In the next section, we provide examples of collaborations that promote a more interactive relationship between cognitive science and the geosciences.

THE RECIPROCAL MODEL OF COLLABORATIVE RESEARCH

Traditional issues of interest to cognitive scientists have included not only the ways in which stimuli (such as visualization presentations) influence thought and behavior, but also the underlying processes involved in those thoughts and behavior. For visualizations, then, analogous concerns would assess whether visualizations lead to comprehension by examining the underlying causes of any presumed benefits. While visualization researchers profess interest in the ways that visualizations influence learning, comprehension, and performance, they have traditionally, although not uniformly, been less interested in the underlying causes of those processes. We contend that a consideration of the underlying mechanisms of learning and memory provides theoretical grounding for addressing the implications of visualizations in a variety of settings. In fact, evaluating these processes directly will lead to the development of more valid answers to the questions posed even by the advisory model.

There are a variety of theories that attempt to account for the underlying processes of comprehension. We now present some examples of this work. Researchers have described the structure and contents of memory (e.g., Baddeley, 1992; Jacoby, 1991; Roediger, 1990). Some have contended that long-term memory involves the encoding of declarative facts, procedural activities, and episodic experiences. By detailing the types of information that are stored in memory, these researchers also seek to outline how to best facilitate the acquisition and retrieval of knowledge. Extensive research has also examined the effects of learning contexts on comprehension (e.g., Jonassen, 1999; Linderholm and van den Broek, 2002; Cordova and Lepper, 1996). This work describes how student goals, motivation, and background knowledge influence the acquisition of information into long-term memory, and its later application in a variety of situations. Cognitive psychologists have additionally examined how individuals process multimedia stimuli, by assessing the benefits that accrue as a function of simultaneously studying various stimuli types, including text, pictures, and other media formats (e.g., Brunyé et al., 2004; Hegarty and Just, 1993; Mayer, 2001; Stemler, 1997). Across these domains (and they are but a sample of relevant projects), researchers have developed testable hypotheses that not only contribute to a better understanding of human functioning, but also have been used to enhance qualities of everyday experience (e.g., in educational interventions, see Fuchs and Fuchs, 1998; in functional object design, see Norman, 1988). Additionally, it should be clear that each of these topics has potential implications for the use of visualizations.

Geovisualizations, then, provide an excellent case example for assessing the cognitive processes that underlie multimedia learning experiences. And based on this research, findings should be useful for conceptualizing the features and characteristics necessary for developing effective visualizations (Rapp et al., 2003). As we have suggested, a concern for the underlying causes of thought and behavior can provide the theoretical underpinnings for thinking about the impact of visualizations on learning. Given what we know about the basic functioning of the human mind, any group of researchers assessing visualizations will be better equipped to make appropriate design decisions and develop visualization applications if they organize their questions around issues of higher-order cognitive functioning.

To better illustrate reciprocal interactions in line with this framework, we next focus on two examples of potential collaborative topics. These topics necessitate the evaluation of underlying mechanisms of cognition, an extended consideration of the ways in which individuals learn, and an overarching interest in the practical application of findings to educational experiences. The topics assess underlying processes involved in learning (of interest to cognitive scientists) and the ways in which learning can be facilitated through geovisualizations (of interest to earth scientists).

SAMPLE RECIPROCAL TOPIC ONE

What does Visualization Use Reveal about Symbolic Development?

This topic illustrates very well the reciprocal, collaborative model that we have in mind. Research on students' understanding of visualizations may prove to be relevant to an issue that cognitive scientists typically call *symbolic development*. Work on symbolic development has tended to focus on how children develop an understanding of symbolic representations and the fundamental knowledge that one thing can stand for another. Examples include research on children's understanding of the relation between maps or scale models and actual spaces (DeLoache, 1995, 2000; DeLoache et al., 2003; Uttal, 2000) or between written text and spoken language (Bialystok and Martin, 2003; Bialystok et al., 2000; Tolchinsky, 2003).

An important finding from this work is that young children often have difficulty grasping the symbolic nature of representations that seem ostensibly simple to adults. For example, children younger than 3 cannot use a simple scale model as a tool for finding a toy hidden in a room (DeLoache, 1987, 2000). In addition, even when symbolic understanding does emerge, children are often highly reliant on iconic representations; they believe that the symbol should look exactly like or otherwise perfectly resemble what it represents in the world. For example, one child observed that a red line on a map could not represent a road (when in fact it actually did represent a road) because there are no red roads in the world (Liben, 1999). Another child contended that the line was not a road because it was too narrow to fit a car. Likewise, when learning about text, preliterate children may believe that written words must resemble in some ways (e.g., length or size) the spoken words that they represent (Bialystok, 1992).

A related challenge for children involves dealing with the dual nature of symbols (Uttal et al., 1997). All symbols are both representations of something else and objects in their own right. For example, a scale model is both a representation of a particular space and an object itself. Most adults know to focus on the representational aspects of the symbol and to ignore the nonsymbolic properties. As you read the words on this page, for example, you take for granted the characteristics of the text and the paper on which it is printed. You know that the meaning is conveyed by the arrangement of the letters to form words; hence, the particular font that is used, or the quality of the paper, becomes much less important. However, young children do not share this understanding. They tend to focus on the symbol as an object itself rather than as a representation of something else. Experimental manipulations that have increased or decreased the salience of objects in their own right have led to changes in children's understanding of the symbolic properties of those objects. For example, encouraging children to play with a scale model actually makes it harder for them to use the model as a guide for finding a hidden toy in a room. Conversely, putting the model behind a pane of glass so that children cannot interact with it makes it easier for them to use the model as a symbol (DeLoache, 2000).

What does research on young children have to do with older students learning to use geoscience visualizations? At first glance, the two might not seem related, but discussions with geoscience colleagues suggest otherwise. There may be an underlying similarity between children's struggles in understanding representations in general, and the understanding of geoscientific concepts that are well-known to experts but are difficult for novices to understand (or visualize). Several geoscience colleagues have told us that their students have difficulty grasping even the basic notion that a complex visualization is a representation (that is, that it stands for something in the world). Instead, they sometimes interpret features and items in the visualization in terms of their properties as objects in their own right, rather than as representations of something else. The students seem to lose track of the representational nature of the complex visualizations, focusing instead on the colors (rather than on what the colors represent) or the shape of the objects. They may see, for example, red or yellow blobs (the surface features), rather than patterns of heat distribution below the Earth's surface (the underlying concepts). These problems strike us as remarkably similar to those that young children face when first learning about symbolic relations. Is it the case that adults, when faced with a new symbol system, must deal yet again with the dual nature of symbols? Is symbolic development ever really "over," or does it continue or begin anew when we encounter new types of symbols?

This is a fascinating and potentially fruitful area for the kind of reciprocal collaboration that we envision. The geosciences provide a wonderful testing ground for investigating whether principles of symbolic development continue to apply in adulthood. At the same time, the geosciences would benefit from detailed, theoretically motivated studies of the cognitive and perceptual bases of the processing of visualizations. Pursuing such a question benefits both disciplines, and hence, the issue of symbolic development and geoscience visualization can lead to truly reciprocal collaborations.

SAMPLE RECIPROCAL TOPIC TWO

What do Visualization Experiences Reveal about Processes of Conceptual Change?

Science learning involves the construction of accurate explanations for concepts and principles in particular domains. Traditionally, students come to classrooms with prior knowledge within these domains. This prior knowledge, in the best of all possible worlds, is correct, coherent, and amenable to change as students learn new facts and concepts. However, evidence demonstrates that students often possess incorrect views or misconceptions for scientific topics, and that these incoherent beliefs are highly resistant to updating (Guzzetti et al., 1993; Kendeou and van den Broek, 2005). This occurs in scientific domains including earth science, physics, and chemistry, and these misconceptions are not specific to particular age groups (Pace, et al., 1989). Unfortunately for most instructors, this means that not only do they have to be concerned about presenting the appropriate material to their students, they also need to worry about refuting their students' existing, inaccurate models.

Work on the updating of mental representations in terms of knowledge acquisition for scientific concepts has focused on *conceptual change* (Hynd and Guzzetti, 1998; McCloskey, 1983; Vosniadou, 2003). Conceptual change is the process of restructuring earlier incorrect beliefs with modified, correct information. According to this work, representations in long-term memory are updated when newly experienced information is inconsistent with prior knowledge. The nature of these processes has been studied in a variety of domains including text processing (e.g., Avraamides, 2003; O'Brien et al., 1998; Rapp et al., 2001; Zwaan and Radvansky, 1998), spatial cognition (e.g., Franklin and Tversky, 1990; Klatzky, et al., 1998; Waller et al., 2002), and science learning (e.g., Diakidoy et al., 2003; diSessa, 1982, 1993; Posner et al., 1982; Smith et al., 1993). This work has specified strategies that align with cognitive functioning that are potentially effective in helping students revise their misconceptions (e.g., Alvermann and Hynd, 1989; Dole and Smith, 1989). For example, a mental representation or belief is more likely to be updated when prior information is explicitly refuted as incorrect, an explanation is

provided as to why that information cannot be correct, and an indication is given as to what the correct model should look like (see Kendeou et al., 2003, for a discussion of these issues).

Thus, cognitive scientists and educational psychologists have attempted to outline not only the processes by which information is updated from a mental representation, but also the situations that most effectively lead to successful updating. Much of this work has focused specifically on text information, investigating the use of expository texts, narrative refutation materials, and detailed examples as tools for initiating the updating of misconceptions (e.g., Linderholm et al., 2000). However, computer-based presentations such as visualizations are beginning to replace these source materials in many earth science courses. Thus, the research issue should be readily apparent—can visualizations provide an effective means for updating student misconceptions, and if so, what do these visualizations tell us about the nature of prior knowledge?

Consider the case of a student with a misconception about the interior of Earth (Vosniadou and Brewer, 1992, 1994). Some children possess the belief that the interior of Earth is actually hollow, and that it is possible to walk inside Earth as on the surface. A verbal or text description of why this is wrong would not provide the best opportunity for instantiating revision processes in the student; a visualization might be more effective because it can graphically display the appropriate framework, illustrate why the inappropriate framework could not be plausible, and detail some of the underlying processes at work under Earth's surface. That is, an appropriately designed visualization can convey the important concepts in a way that requires students to update their misconceptions and undergo conceptual change. The use of particular visualizations, and their effectiveness, can provide insights into the nature of students' mental representations (e.g., their mental models of the concepts; Rapp, 2005), the construction and updating processes of those representations, and the most effective techniques for revising misinformation. In other words, this research can inform theories about the processes and products of memory and comprehension.

Consider a second case example intended to highlight the importance of visualizations for conceptual change under different circumstances. Visualizations are often used by scientists to analyze information and consider existing data sets, maps, and object arrays in different ways. Geoscientists who discover novel findings through the use of such visualizations are indeed going through a similar process of conceptual change. That is, their existing knowledge about a topic area is now being informed, and potentially revised, as a function of their experiences. Thus, the question of how visualizations might best offer opportunities for engaging in processes of conceptual change need not be limited to student experiences. Instead, they may underlie a variety of situations for which visualizations provide new perspectives on data.

Clearly then, this area of research holds much potential for addressing issues of interest to cognitive scientists and geoscientists. Evaluating how visualizations can promote conceptual change can help outline the appropriate design features for developing visualization lessons, the conceptual frameworks that define mental representations, and the underlying cognitive processes that guide the construction and application of knowledge. Based on these two examples, from the research areas of symbolic understanding and conceptual change, it is readily apparent that reciprocal, collaborative research can benefit our understanding of geoscience visualization comprehension at a variety of levels and for a variety of questions.

CONCLUSION

Earth science visualization, and science visualization in general, has progressed steadily in a relatively short time (particularly from a geologic viewpoint). Researchers, theorists, and instructors from a variety of areas have become intrigued at the prospect of presenting data from novel perspectives, and implementing graphics and animation to illustrate complex ideas. The field is now at a critically important stage; researchers in core domains (cognitive science, the natural sciences, educational technology, etc.) are moving beyond pure visualization development, as they begin to address how visualizations work and whether they have any educational impact. In this chapter, we have focused on frameworks of collaboration as a prime concern for accomplishing these goals. We have attempted to describe two models of collaboration, detailing the types of questions that each model most effectively addresses. In addition, we have made a case for relying on the reciprocal model as a framework for establishing collaboration between earth scientists and cognitive scientists. We have described the reciprocal model to support ongoing, effective research programs that directly inform the study of geovisualizations, as well as informing theories of human cognition. Of course, we do not simply dismiss the types of questions that fit into the advisory framework; we simply contend that those questions are less likely to promote long-term collaboration that informs theory across disciplines at the intersection of earth and mind.

We remain optimistic for the future of visualization research. The potential for using visualizations both to understand how we process information and for developing valid techniques that facilitate learning are well worth the effort of establishing strategic collaborative programs. We must make sure not to squander the opportunities that visualization research potentially affords for assessing a variety of questions beyond "does this look good." Visualization research has much to tell us about how the mind works, how people learn, how we understand geoscientific data, and how to build more effective educational experiences in the geosciences.

ACKNOWLEDGMENTS

We thank Cathy Manduca, Steve Reynolds, and two anonymous reviewers for their comments on earlier versions of our manuscript. This chapter is based on work supported by a Research and Development in Molecular Visualization minigrant awarded by the National Science Foundation and a Faculty Summer Research Fellowship from the Office of the Dean of the Graduate School of the University of Minnesota, both awarded to the first author.

REFERENCES CITED

Alvermann, D.E., and Hynd, C., 1989, Effects of prior knowledge activation modes and text structure on nonscience majors' comprehension of physics: The Journal of Educational Research, v. 83, p. 97–102.

Avraamides, M.N., 2003, Spatial updating of environments described in texts: Cognitive Psychology, v. 47, p. 402–431, doi: 10.1016/S0010-0285(03)00098-7.

Baddeley, A.D., 1992, Working memory: Science, v. 255, p. 556–559.

Bialystok, E., 1992, Symbolic representation of letters and numbers: Cognitive Development, v. 7, p. 301–316, doi: 10.1016/0885-2014(92)90018-M.

Bialystok, E., and Martin, M.M., 2003, Notation to symbol: Development in children's understanding of print: Journal of Experimental Child Psychology, v. 86, p. 223–243, doi: 10.1016/S0022-0965(03)00138-3.

Bialystok, E., Shenfield, T., and Codd, J., 2000, Languages, scripts, and the environment: Factors in developing concepts of print: Developmental Psychology, v. 36, p. 66–76, doi: 10.1037/0012-1649.36.1.66.

Brunyé, T., Rapp, D.N., and Taylor, H.A., 2004, Building mental models of multimedia procedures: Implications for memory structure and content, *in* Proceedings of the 26th Annual Meeting of the Cognitive Science Society: Hillsdale, New Jersey, Erlbaum (CD-ROM).

Cordova, D.I., and Lepper, M.R., 1996, Intrinsic motivation and the process of learning: Beneficial effects of contextualization, personalization, and choice: Journal of Educational Psychology, v. 88, p. 715–730, doi: 10.1037/0022-0663.88.4.715.

DeLoache, J.S., 1987, Rapid change in the symbolic functioning of very young children: Science, v. 238, p. 1556–1557.

DeLoache, J.S., 1995, Early understanding and use of symbols: Current Directions in Psychological Science, v. 4, p. 109–113, doi: 10.1111/1467-8721.ep10772408.

DeLoache, J.S., 2000, Dual representation and young children's use of scale models: Child Development, v. 71, p. 329–338, doi: 10.1111/1467-8624.00148.

DeLoache, J.S., Pierroutsakos, S.L., and Uttal, D.H., 2003, The origins of pictorial competence: Current Directions in Psychological Science, v. 12, p. 114–118, doi: 10.1111/1467-8721.01244.

Diakidoy, I.N., Kendeou, P., and Ioannides, C., 2003, Reading about energy: The effects of text structure in science learning and conceptual change: Contemporary Educational Psychology, v. 28, p. 335–356, doi: 10.1016/S0361-476X(02)00039-5.

diSessa, A., 1982, Unlearning Aristotelian physics: A study of knowledge-based learning: Cognitive Science, v. 6, p. 37–75, doi: 10.1016/S0364-0213(82)80005-0.

diSessa, A., 1993, Toward an epistemology of physics: Cognition and Instruction, v. 10, p. 105–225, doi: 10.1207/s1532690xci1002&3_2.

Dole, J.A., and Smith, L.C., 1989, Prior knowledge and learning from science text: An instructional study, *in* McCormick, S., and Zutell, J., eds., Cognitive and social perspectives for literacy research and instruction: Thirty-eighth yearbook of the National Reading Conference: Chicago, Illinois, The National Reading Conference, Inc., p. 345–352.

Edelson, D.C., Brown, M., Gordin, D.N., and Griffin, D.A., 1999, Making visualization accessible to students: GSA Today, v. 9, no. 2, p. 8–10.

Franklin, N., and Tversky, B., 1990, Searching imagined environments: Journal of Experimental Psychology, General, v. 119, p. 63–76, doi: 10.1037/0096-3445.119.1.63.

Fuchs, D., and Fuchs, L.S., 1998, Researchers and teachers working together to adapt instruction for diverse learners: Learning Disabilities Research and Practice, v. 13, p. 126–137.

Guzzetti, B.J., Snyder, T.E., Glass, G.V., and Gamas, W.S., 1993, Promoting conceptual change in science: A comparative meta-analysis of instructional interventions from reading education and science education: Reading Research Quarterly, v. 28, p. 117–159.

Harris, R.L., 2000, Information graphics: A comprehensive illustrated reference: New York, Oxford University Press, 448 p.

Hegarty, M., and Just, M.A., 1993, Constructing mental models of machines from text and diagrams: Journal of Memory and Language, v. 32, p. 717–742, doi: 10.1006/jmla.1993.1036.

Hegarty, M., Narayanan, N.H., and Freitas, P., 2002, Understanding machines from multimedia and hypermedia presentations, *in* Otero, J., Leon, J.A., and Graesser, A.C., eds., The psychology of science text comprehension: Hillsdale, New Jersey, Lawrence Erlbaum Associates, p. 357–384.

Hynd, C., and Guzzetti, B.J., 1998, When knowledge contradicts intuition: Conceptual change, *in* Hynd, C., ed., Learning from text across conceptual domains: Mahwah, New Jersey, Lawrence Erlbaum Associates, p. 139–164.

Jacoby, L.L., 1991, A process dissociation framework: Separating automatic from intentional uses of memory: Journal of Memory and Language, v. 30, p. 513–541, doi: 10.1016/0749-596X(91)90025-F.

Jonassen, D., 1999, Designing constructivist learning environments, *in* Reigeluth, C.M., ed., Instructional-design theories and models: A new paradigm of instructional theory, Volume II: Hillsdale, New Jersey, Lawrence Erlbaum Associates, p. 215–239.

Kendeou, P., and van den Broek, P., 2005, The role of readers' misconceptions on comprehension of scientific text: Journal of Educational Psychology, v. 97, p. 235–245, doi: 10.1037/0022-0663.97.2.235.

Kendeou, P., Rapp, D.N., and van den Broek, P., 2003, The influence of readers' prior knowledge on text comprehension and learning from text, *in* Nata, R., ed., Progress in education: New York, Nova Science Publishers, Inc., p. 189–209.

Klatzky, R.L., Loomis, J.M., Beall, A.C., Chance, S.S., and Golledge, R.G., 1998, Spatial updating of self-position and orientation during real, imagined, and virtual locomotion: Psychological Science, v. 9, p. 293–298, doi: 10.1111/1467-9280.00058.

Liben, L.S., 1999, Developing an understanding of external spatial representations, *in* Sigel, I.E., ed., Development of mental representation: Theories and applications: Mahwah, New Jersey, Lawrence Erlbaum Associates, p. 297–321.

Linderholm, T., and van den Broek, P., 2002, The effects of reading purpose and working memory capacity on the processing of expository text: Journal of Educational Psychology, v. 94, p. 778–784, doi: 10.1037/0022-0663.94.4.778.

Linderholm, T., Everson, M.G., van den Broek, P., Mischinski, M., Crittenden, A., and Samuels, J., 2000, Effects of causal text revisions on more- and less-skilled readers' comprehension of easy and difficult texts: Cognition and Instruction, v. 18, p. 525–556, doi: 10.1207/S1532690XCI1804_4.

Maki, W.S., and Maki, R.H., 2002, Multimedia comprehension skill predicts differential outcomes of web-based and lecture courses: Journal of Experimental Psychology, Applied, v. 8, p. 85–98, doi: 10.1037/1076-898X.8.2.85.

Mayer, R.E., 2001, Multimedia learning: Cambridge, UK, Cambridge University Press, 222 p.

McCloskey, M., 1983, Intuitive physics: Scientific American, v. 248, p. 114–122.

Norman, D.A., 1988, The design of everyday things: New York, Doubleday, 272 p.

O'Brien, E.J., Rizzella, M.L., Albrecht, J.E., and Halleran, J.G., 1998, Updating a situation model: A memory-based text processing view: Journal of Experimental Psychology: Learning, Memory, and Cognition, v. 24, p. 1200–1210, doi: 10.1037/0278-7393.24.5.1200.

Pace, A.J., Marshall, N., Horowitz, R., Lipson, M.Y., and Lucido, P., 1989, When prior knowledge doesn't facilitate text comprehension: An examination of some of the issues, *in* McCormick, S., and Zutell, J., eds., Cognitive and social perspectives for literacy research and instruction: Thirty-eight yearbook of the National Reading Conference: Chicago, Illinois, The National Reading Conference, Inc., p. 213–224.

Ploetzner, R., and Lowe, R., 2004, Dynamic visualizations and learning: Learning and Instruction, v. 14, p. 235–240, doi: 10.1016/j.learninstruc.2004.06.001.

Posner, G., Strike, K., Hewson, P., and Gertzog, W., 1982, Accommodation of a scientific conception: Toward a theory of conceptual change: Science & Education, v. 66, p. 211–227.

Rapp, D.N., 2005, Mental models: Theoretical issues for visualizations in science education, *in* Gilbert, J.K., ed., Visualization in science education: Dordrecht, Kluwer Academic Publishers, p. 43–60.

Rapp, D.N., and Kendeou, P., 2003, Visualizations and mental models—The educational implications of GEOWALL: San Francisco, California, Paper presented at the annual fall meeting of the American Geophysical Union.

Rapp, D.N., Gerrig, R.J., and Prentice, D.A., 2001, Readers' trait-based models of characters in narrative comprehension: Journal of Memory and Language, v. 45, p. 737–750, doi: 10.1006/jmla.2000.2789.

Rapp, D.N., Taylor, H.A., and Crane, G.R., 2003, The impact of digital libraries on cognitive processes: Psychological issues of hypermedia: Computers in Human Behavior, v. 19, p. 609–628, doi: 10.1016/S0747-5632(02)00085-7.

Rapp, D.N., Culpepper, S., Kirkby, K., and Morin, P., 2004, Stereo visualization and map comprehension: San Francisco, California, Paper presented at the annual fall meeting of the American Geophysical Union.

Renshaw, C.E., Taylor, H.A., and Reynolds, C.H., 1998, Impact of computer-assisted instruction in hydrogeology on critical-thinking skills: Journal of Geoscience Education, v. 46, p. 274–279.

Roediger, H.L., III, 1990, Implicit memory: Retention without remembering: The American Psychologist, v. 45, p. 1043–1056, doi: 10.1037/0003-066X.45.9.1043.

Slocum, T.A., Blok, C., Jiang, B., Koussoulakou, A., Montello, D.R., Furhmann, S., and Hedley, N.R., 2001, Cognitive and usability issues in geovisualization: Cartography and Geographic Information Science, v. 28, p. 61–75.

Smith, J.P., diSessa, A.A., and Roschelle, J., 1993, Misconceptions reconceived: A constructivist analysis of knowledge in transition: Journal of the Learning Sciences, v. 3, p. 115–163, doi: 10.1207/s15327809jls0302_1.

Stemler, L.K., 1997, Educational characteristics of multimedia: A literature review: Journal of Educational Multimedia and Hypermedia, v. 6, p. 339–359.

Tolchinsky, L., 2003, The cradle of culture and what children know about writing and numbers before being taught: Mahwah, New Jersey, Lawrence Erlbaum Associates, 232 p.

Tufte, E.R., 2001, The visual display of quantitative information (2nd ed.): Cheshire, Connecticut, Graphics Press, 197 p.

Uttal, D.H., 2000, Seeing the big picture: Map use and the development of spatial cognition: Developmental Science, v. 3, p. 247–286, doi: 10.1111/1467-7687.00119.

Uttal, D.H., Scudder, K.V., and DeLoache, J.S., 1997, Manipulatives as symbols: A new perspective on the use of concrete objects to teach mathematics: Journal of Applied Developmental Psychology, v. 18, p. 37–54, doi: 10.1016/S0193-3973(97)90013-7.

Vosniadou, S., 2003, Exploring the relationships between conceptual change and intentional learning, *in* Sinatra, G.M., and Printrich, P.R., eds., Intentional conceptual change: Mahwah, New Jersey, Lawrence Erlbaum Associates, p. 377–406.

Vosniadou, S., and Brewer, W.F., 1992, Mental models of the earth: A study of conceptual change in childhood: Cognitive Psychology, v. 24, p. 535–585, doi: 10.1016/0010-0285(92)90018-W.

Vosniadou, S., and Brewer, W.F., 1994, Mental models of the day/night cycle: Cognitive Science, v. 18, p. 123–183, doi: 10.1016/0364-0213(94)90022-1.

Waller, D., Montello, D.R., Richardson, A.E., and Hegarty, M., 2002, Orientation specificity and spatial updating of memories for layouts: Journal of Experimental Psychology: Learning, Memory, and Cognition, v. 28, p. 1051–1063, doi: 10.1037/0278-7393.28.6.1051.

Zwaan, R.A., and Radvansky, G.A., 1998, Situation models in language comprehension and memory: Psychological Bulletin, v. 123, p. 162–185, doi: 10.1037/0033-2909.123.2.162.

Manuscript Accepted by the Society 21 March 2006

Helping Students Learn

In this section, we hear from geoscience educators who bring together geoscience expertise with educational research methods to apply what we know about geoscience and learning in their teaching. These writings demonstrate the difficulty of teaching complex geoscience concepts well, the range of misunderstandings that students can bring to or develop during instruction, and the techniques that these educators use in developing effective instruction. Taken together the four chapters outline a rigorous approach to (1) understanding the specific goals of instruction and the particular aspects of the content that are challenging to students, (2) designing activities that are guided by research on learning, and (3) testing these activities to make sure that learning is occurring as expected.

We begin with work by Danny Edelson and his colleagues from the School of Education and Social Policy at Northwestern University and Aha! Interactive. These education researchers outline a framework for thinking about the design of teaching activities grounded in cognitive and educational research. They then develop a geoscience example and demonstrate how it can be tested through interviews that determine the match between the design assumptions and the student experience. This chapter provides a framework for thinking about the design and development of geoscience teaching materials. Mike Taber (Colorado College) and student Kristin Quadracci use Edelson's design framework and tools to explore learning by elementary education students. As future teachers, it is particularly important that these students develop a strong understanding of and comfort with geoscience concepts. Taber uses interviews and classroom products to understand the obstacles to students' development of a working understanding of temperature and climate. He then modifies his teaching activities and demonstrates significant improvement. This chapter demonstrates how we can learn to improve our teaching by collecting important observational data of what students do and what they know.

Stephen Reynolds and his colleagues at Arizona State University combine a similar design framework with the development of a technologically enabled virtual world to address the challenges of teaching students to visualize Earth structures in three dimensions. This chapter demonstrates the interplay between educational research on learning in the geosciences and the development of tools that facilitate specific aspects of student learning. The educational research described in this chapter sheds light on the fundamental issues of spatial cognition and shows how basic visual skills can be enhanced with appropriate geoscience instruction.

Finally, we return to complex systems in a chapter by David Bice (Pennsylvania State University and Carleton College). Bice lays out the ways in which quantitative modeling can be used to develop students' understanding of the behavior of complex systems. Implicit in his instructional method is a major emphasis on models and their role in geoscience. This chapter reflects the development of educational materials in close communication with students, a less formal mechanism for obtaining the insights on learning that are common to all four chapters in this section.

This section of the book demonstrates the intentionality and skill of good instruction. Excellent geoscience education, particularly when serving a diverse student population, is not an accident. It brings together careful thinking about the goals of instruction (geoscience content and skills), conscious investigation of students' understanding and learning, and application of research on teaching and learning. Modern technology and access to geoscience data provide new opportunities to enhance teaching, including mechanisms for addressing issues as disparate as difficulty in visualizing in three dimensions, understanding global variations of fundamental variables, and development of intuition regarding the behavior of complex systems. New technologies combined with an improved understanding of geoscience learning and a rigorous approach to geoscience education position us to make major strides in enhancing geoscience learning for all students. The same methodologies that are illustrated here for geoscience education could also be applied to studying learning by and communication among researchers with a similar improvement in our ability to collectively learn about Earth.

Geological Society of America
Special Paper 413
2006

Engineering geosciences learning experiences using the Learning-for-Use *design framework*

Daniel C. Edelson
Virginia M. Pitts
School of Education and Social Policy, Northwestern University, Evanston, Illinois 60208, USA

Christina M. Salierno
AHA! interactive, Inc., 53 West Jackson Blvd., Suite 1135, Chicago, Illinois 60604, USA

Bruce L. Sherin
School of Education and Social Policy, Northwestern University, Evanston, Illinois 60208, USA

ABSTRACT

In this chapter, we consider the design of learning experiences in the geosciences. Recognizing that too often, educational experiences do not lead to understanding that the learner can draw on when it is relevant, we focus on learning that leads to usable understanding. We use the analogy of engineering research and development to describe the way we have applied findings from cognitive science research to the design of geosciences curricula. We present a design framework based on research in cognitive science that offers guidelines for the design of learning activities that motivate learning and provide learners with opportunities to apply what they are learning. We illustrate the design framework with an example of a middle school curriculum that focuses on the relationship between physical geography and climate. We also present strategies for conducting formative evaluations of curriculum and describe how we use them to iteratively refine a design.

Keywords: instructional design, motivation, design research, learning sciences.

INTRODUCTION

Learning is the interface between Earth and mind. Both scientists and others develop conceptions about Earth through learning processes. Scientists use research techniques to expand understanding at the forefront of human knowledge, while others apply their own learning skills to expand their personal understanding. In this chapter, we are concerned with the challenges of fostering geosciences learning in formal educational settings. We view education as an applied science akin to engineering. Education has its own knowledge base and practices, but it rests on the sciences of learning and of the domains that make up the curriculum. Addressing the educational challenges of the earth sciences calls for an engineering approach that applies both the cognitive and earth sciences.

Sound engineering proceeds through an iterative process of systematic design and evaluation. Both design and evaluation involve the application and extension of theory. As design researchers (Cobb et al., 2003; Design-Based Research Collective, 2003; Edelson, 2002) in the learning sciences, we are particularly interested in the application and development of scientific theories of learning and education. Our objective in this chapter is to present a demonstration of how that engineering process can be carried out in the geosciences and to describe a particular framework that we have used to guide our own design and evaluation processes.

Edelson, D.C., Pitts, V.M., Salierno, C.M., and Sherin, B.L., 2006, Engineering geosciences learning experiences using the *Learning-for-Use* design framework, *in* Manduca, C.A., and Mogk, D.W., eds., Earth and Mind: How Geologists Think and Learn about the Earth: Geological Society of America Special Paper 413, p. 131–144, doi: 10.1130/2006.2413(10). For permission to copy, contact editing@geosociety.org. ©2006 Geological Society of America. All rights reserved.

In the work we describe in this chapter, we are concerned with engineering learning experiences in the geosciences to address two substantial educational challenges that are not adequately addressed by traditional instructional approaches: (1) motivating learners to learn (not just engage), and (2) ensuring that learners develop knowledge that they can access and apply when it is relevant.

Regardless of the nature of the learning activities that students participate in, if they are not sufficiently and appropriately engaged, they will not attend to those activities in ways that will foster learning. Likewise, if students do not construct knowledge in a manner that supports subsequent retrieval and application of that knowledge, it remains inert. Inert knowledge (Whitehead, 1929) is understanding that exists in an individual's memory in some form but not in a form that leads it to be retrieved or applied when it is useful. For example, a student might be able to recite a principle in an exam without being able apply that principle in a real world problem-solving context. We use the term "usable knowledge" to describe the opposite of inert knowledge. Usable knowledge and skills are stored in an individual's memory in a form that supports retrieval and application when relevant.

To address the challenges of engagement and inert knowledge, we developed the *Learning-for-Use* design framework (Edelson, 2001). The *Learning-for-Use* framework draws on contemporary research in cognitive science to provide guidance for the design of learning activities that foster usable understanding. In the first part of the chapter, we present *Learning-for-Use* as a framework for the design of geoscience learning activities. To illustrate the *Learning-for-Use* framework, we present an example of a curriculum unit that we designed using the framework. This unit, called *Planetary Forecaster*, is a 6 wk middle school unit on climate modeling.

In the second part of the chapter, we focus on evaluation. In the process of engineering learning experiences, the role of evaluation is to understand how well the design is achieving the goals that have been established for it and why it may be falling short. The evaluation should generate results that can inform the revision of the design and allow the designers to determine when they have reached their goals. In the work we present here, we are specifically concerned with ascertaining how well a curriculum unit is achieving the goals of *Learning-for-Use* and how shortcomings that are identified can be addressed through iterative redesign. In the latter sections of this chapter, we describe research methodologies that we have employed to assess how well units designed with the *Learning-for-Use* framework are achieving their goals, and we present examples from studies of *Planetary Forecaster* in public school classrooms.

Thus, our discussions of design and evaluation have dual goals—to demonstrate how a systematic process of curriculum engineering can proceed from theory to practice and to describe a particular approach to the engineering of geosciences curriculum based on cognitive science research.

LEARNING FOR USE

The *Learning-for-Use* design framework provides guidance to instructors and curriculum developers on how to design learning activities that foster engagement and useful understanding. It is based on research from cognitive science (e.g., Bransford et al., 1999) that describes how people develop usable knowledge.[1]

The Development of Usable Knowledge

The foundation of the *Learning-for-Use* design framework consists of four robust findings from contemporary learning research. These are (Edelson, 2001):

1. Constructivism: Learning takes place through the construction and modification of knowledge structures.
2. Goal-directed learning: Knowledge construction is a goal-directed process that is guided by a combination of conscious and unconscious understanding goals.
3. Situated learning: The circumstances in which knowledge is constructed and subsequently used determine its accessibility for future use.
4. Inert knowledge: Knowledge must be constructed in a form that supports use before it can be applied.

In developing the *Learning-for-Use* design framework, we drew on these findings to build a model of learning that could distinguish between experiences that lead to the development of usable knowledge and experiences that either lead to no significant learning or lead to the development of inert knowledge. The result is a description of a process that characterizes experiences that lead to usable knowledge. This description represents the theory of learning on which the *Learning-for-Use* framework is built. This process model consists of three stages: (1) motivation to learn, in which the learner experiences the need for new understanding based on its usefulness; (2) knowledge construction, in which the learner builds new knowledge structures in memory based on experiences in the learning environment; and (3) knowledge organization, in which knowledge structures are connected, transformed, and reinforced to support future use.

Motivation

The first step in the development of usable knowledge is recognizing and feeling the need for new knowledge or skills.[2] The motivation step generates the goal of developing new understanding. In this context, we are using "motivate" in a very specific sense. It describes the motive to develop specific

---

[1]To enhance readability, we often use the terms *knowledge* and *understanding* to refer to both conceptual knowledge and skills. The fact that we do not always use the term *skills* does not mean we place less emphasis on them.

[2]While the first step in the *Learning-for-Use* model is called *motivation*, this phase is only concerned with a small portion of what is normally thought of as motivation in education. Addressing the broader motivational challenges of engaging students in schooling is critical to, but beyond the scope of, the *Learning-for-Use* model.

knowledge or skills. This motivation to develop specific understanding is distinct from two other forms of motivation. First, it describes the motivation to learn, rather than the motivation to engage in a particular set of activities. Second, it describes the motivation to learn specific knowledge or skills, rather than a more general attitude or disposition toward learning in a particular context. To lead to usable knowledge, it is important that the motivation be grounded in the learner's recognition of the usefulness of the knowledge. If students are motivated to learn based on how the designers want them to be able to use that knowledge in the future, then their goals will lead them toward development of that knowledge in a usable form. If students are motivated to engage rather than learn or they are motivated to learn by goals other than how the designers want them to be able to use the knowledge, then they will not be motivated to develop the knowledge in a usable form. So, for example, if they are motivated by the goal of reciting knowledge in a testing situation, they will not necessarily be motivated to learn how to apply it. Edelson and Joseph (2004) refer to this motivation to acquire specific knowledge or skills for their usefulness "interest-based in usefulness."

Knowledge Construction

The second step in the development of usable knowledge is the construction of new knowledge structures in memory. Current models of learning describe the construction of new knowledge as the addition of new concepts to memory, subdivision of existing concepts, and the creation of new connections between concepts. The "raw material" from which a learner constructs new knowledge can be firsthand experience, communication from others, or a combination of the two. This step in the *Learning-for-Use* model recognizes incremental knowledge construction as the fundamental process of learning.

Knowledge Organization

The third step in the development of usable knowledge is the organization of knowledge for use, which addresses the need for accessibility and applicability of knowledge. In the organization step, knowledge is reorganized, connected to other knowledge, and reinforced in order to support its future retrieval and use (Anderson, 1983). To be retrieved when it is relevant, knowledge must be indexed by features of situations in which that knowledge applies that will cause that knowledge to be activated in those situations (Chi et al., 1981; Glaser, 1992; Kolodner, 1993; Schank, 1982; Simon, 1980). One form of organization for use is the development of those indices and retrieval cues. Organization of knowledge for use can also take the form of reinforcement, which increases the strength of connections to other knowledge structures through the traversal of those structure and increases the likelihood that those connections between knowledge structures will be found in the future. To support the application of knowledge once it is retrieved, knowledge must be stored in a form that supports its application. Therefore, a third form of organization for use is the transformation of declarative knowledge into a procedural form that supports the application of that knowledge (Anderson, 1983).

While there is an inherent ordering among these three steps, this ordering does not preclude overlaps or cycles. For example, knowledge construction and organization may be simultaneous, and knowledge construction or organization can create motivation to address gaps in current understanding. Because of the incremental nature of knowledge construction, it can require several cycles through various combinations of the steps to develop an understanding of complex content.

The theory behind the *Learning-for-Use* framework is that all three of these steps are critical to the development of usable knowledge. The motivation step is necessary to provide students with goals that will guide and sustain the knowledge construction and organization required to develop usable knowledge. The knowledge organization step is essential to prevent students from constructing understanding that remains inert. While this model of learning represents a synthesis of existing research, it is designed to support the engineering of learning experiences that develop usable knowledge by focusing attention on the importance of all three steps in the learning process. We believe this is important because, despite the findings in cognitive science research that underlie this model, a great deal of current curriculum design, including that which draws on cognitive science research, continues to focus on knowledge construction, without commensurate attention to motivation and knowledge organization.

The *Learning-for-Use* Design Framework

Based on this model of learning, we have developed the *Learning-for-Use* design framework. This framework provides guidelines for the design of activities that will lead to the development of robust, useful understanding. The model of learning described previously poses the hypothesis that for each learning objective a designer must create activities that effectively achieve all three steps in the learning-for-use model. The design framework provides guidelines and recommendations for achieving all three steps.

The *Learning-for-Use* design framework describes different design strategies that meet the requirements of each step (Table 1). The different design strategies for each step can be treated as alternative or complementary ways to complete the step. In the case of rich content, however, several learning activities at each step involving both of the processes for that step may be necessary. In particular, we have found that a balanced combination of different kinds of knowledge construction activities is most effective at achieving the goals of the knowledge construction step.

Because it is based on the same contemporary research as other design frameworks that have been developed in recent years, the *Learning-for-Use* design framework shares many qualities with them. For example, knowledge integration environments (Linn, 2000), goal-based scenarios (Schank et al., 1993, 1994), and anchored instruction (J. Bransford et al., 1990) are all consistent with the learning-for-use approach. The goal of the

TABLE 1. OVERVIEW OF THE LEARNING-FOR-USE DESIGN FRAMEWORK

Step	Name	Description	Desired Effect
Motivate	Create task demand	Students are presented with a task that requires new understanding	Create a perceived need for new knowledge or skills.
	Elicit curiosity	Students are placed in a situation that *elicits curiosity* by revealing an unexpected gap in their understanding	Student becomes aware of limits of knowledge and need for new knowledge to address those limits.
Construct	Direct experience	Students are provided with *direct physical experiences or observation* of phenomena	Students construct knowledge structures encoding the attributes and relationships that describe the phenomena.
	Indirect experiences	Students hear about, view, or read about phenomena	
	Modeling	Students observe another person performing a task	Students construct knowledge structures that encode the elements of a practice.
	Instruction	Students are told or read about how to perform a task	
	Explanation	Students are provided with explanations of phenomena or processes	Students construct knowledge structures that encode causal information behind the relationships among phenomena or elements of a process.
	Sense making	Students engage in explanation or synthesis activities	
Organize for use	Practice	Students use components of new understanding outside of motivating context	Students construct procedural representations from declarative representations, reinforce understanding, and expose limitations and need for further knowledge construction.
	Apply	Students *apply* understanding in context	Students develop indices for retrieval, construct procedural representations from declarative, reinforce understanding, and expose limitations and need for further knowledge construction
	Reflect	Students articulate what they have learned and what the boundaries of that understanding are	Students re-index Knowledge for retrieval, expose limitations and need for further knowledge construction.

Learning-for-Use design framework is to capture the elements of these effective designs at a level of generality that can encompass the full range of effective approaches to developing usable knowledge. The contribution of the framework is that it describes the elements that are, at least partially, responsible for the effectiveness of these approaches and grounds them in research. For designers developing new approaches and activities, it is designed to draw attention to the importance of all three steps in the development of usable knowledge and to provide suggestions for how to achieve them. The *Learning-for-Use* framework has proven useful for both designing learning activities and analyzing existing activities.

In an analysis of specific research-based knowledge integration and anchored instruction environments, we found that the strengths of the designs and the differences among them were captured in terms of the *Learning-for-Use* framework (Edel-

son and Bang, 2003). In science, the "Learning Cycle" that was developed in the 1960s as a way to engage students in learning through authentic inquiry (Abraham, 1998; Karplus and Thier, 1967; Lawson, 1995; Renner and Stafford, 1972) and its modern variants, such as the BSCS 5E design approach (Bybee, 2002) are consistent with learning-for-use, as is Krajcik et al.'s (1999) project-based approach.

In our own work, we focused on a specific form of learning-for-use that we call scenario-based inquiry learning. Scenario-based inquiry learning combines elements of goal-based scenarios and project-based science. In scenario-based inquiry learning, the same task is used to create demand for new understanding (motivate) and to enable learners to apply that understanding (organize for use). As in goal-based scenarios, the task comes from the scenario that provides students with a role and a goal. As in project-based science, a substantial portion of the knowledge construction in scenario-based inquiry learning occurs through firsthand scientific inquiry (guided or open-ended) on the part of students.

Learning-for-Use in the Geosciences

The *Learning-for-Use* design framework can be used both to develop new learning activities and analyze existing learning activities. In either case, the first step is to identify the learning goals for the activities. The process that follows goal identification typically involves cycles of identifying possible ways to motivate those learning objectives for the target audience of students, activities that would support knowledge construction for them, and activities that would give students the opportunity to reorganize their new understanding for use. As with any complex design process, selecting a coherent and effective combination of activities to achieve each stage requires designers to balance numerous tradeoffs to achieve the best practical combination.

So, the first step in applying *Learning-for-Use* in the geosciences involves selecting learning objectives to address. In recent years, a number of reports have argued for the importance of geoscience education for an educated populace and have described specific geoscience knowledge and skills that students from elementary school through college should master (American Association for the Advancement of Science [AAAS], 1994; Barstow and Geary, 2001; Ireton et al., 1996; Manduca et al., 2002; National Research Council [NRC], 1996). Three themes that receive significant attention in these documents are: (1) the need for students to understand earth science from a systems perspective, (2) the centrality of field work and direct observation in the geosciences, and (3) the interpretation of historical data.

Having selected learning objectives, a designer must identify candidate activities for motivating those learning objectives, and constructing and organizing knowledge for use. In considering motivation, a designer might consider specific techniques that might be useful in the geosciences for eliciting curiosity or tasks that create demand for geosciences knowledge and skills. A common way to elicit curiosity is to present a surprising phenomenon to students. In the geosciences, that might be achieved by giving students the opportunity to directly observe surprising phenomena in the field or in data. In considering how to create demand through a task, it is often helpful to look at the way that geosciences knowledge and skills are used by expert practitioners, for example, in oil exploration, weather forecasting, or environmental policy making.

In knowledge construction, it is also important to look at the ways that geoscience concepts can be experienced, demonstrated, and explained. For example, some geosciences processes can be directly observed in the field, while others take place at scales of time or space that make them impossible to observe directly. In that case, evidence for the process may be perceptible in the field or in data, or processes can be demonstrated through dynamic processes. In general, it is inefficient and often unrealistic to expect students to "discover" scientific concepts. For that reason, providing students with direct experience and observation of scientific phenomena should generally be combined with offering them explanations and representations. The specialized representations that geoscientists use for describing and characterizing processes can be helpful to learners in developing their own understanding of those processes. In general, learners benefit from learning about concepts using multiple representations, models, or analogies, where the different approaches capture different essential features of the target content.

In organization for use, it is important to provide students with the opportunity to both *practice* using new skills and knowledge in simple contexts and to *apply* skills and knowledge in realistic contexts. Just as with motivation, tasks from authentic professional practices can be very effective contexts for applying new understanding. In helping students to reflect on what they have learned, it can be helpful to focus on the specific forms of explanation and argumentation that are used in the field. For example, if students were learning about an explanation for a phenomenon that is based on a historical record, it might be helpful to have them reflect on the structure of that kind of geoscience explanation and how the evidence supports the conclusion.

PLANETARY FORECASTER[3]

Planetary Forecaster is a middle school curriculum unit for earth systems science that we developed using the *Learning-for-Use* design framework. It combines computer-supported investigations of geospatial data with hands-on laboratory activities in which students observe and measure the phenomena under study. The *Planetary Forecaster* curriculum unit is the product of an ongoing iterative development effort that involves teachers both directly, as members of design teams, and indirectly, as implementers who are observed or provide feedback. The curriculum has been through three revision cycles based on three cycles of classroom implementation.

Unit Scope and Sequence

The content goal for the unit is for students to understand how physical geography influences temperature at a climatic time scale. The premise of the curriculum unit is that students have been asked by a fictional space agency to identify the portions of a newly discovered planet that are habitable given information about the planet's topography, water cover, and the tilt of its axis. For simplicity, the planet has the same atmospheric makeup as Earth, is orbiting around a star with the same intensity as the sun, and has an orbit with the same radius as Earth's. This mission is designed to create a demand for understanding of the curriculum's target content.

---

[3]Planetary Forecaster is a redesign of the *Create-A-World* activity that was described in Edelson (2001).

There are four major relationships that students must understand to complete the task. They are:

Curvature: The effect of a planet's curved surface on the intensity of the solar radiation received at each point and the length of the day.

Tilt: The effect of the tilt of a planet's axis of rotation on intensity of solar radiation and length of day at different times of year.

Land/Water heat capacity: The effect of surface cover (land versus water) on the temperatures at different locations due to differences in specific heat capacity and reflectivity.

Topography: The effect of surface elevation on the temperatures at different locations.

Understanding these relationships requires an understanding of fundamental scientific concepts that are commonly found in national, state, and local standards documents, such as the Earth-Sun relationship, radiative energy transfer, conservation of energy, heat, and temperature, specific heat capacity, and the ideal gas law.

The curriculum is divided into seven sections that take from one to five class periods each:

1. Setting the stage. In this section, students conduct an exercise in articulating prior conceptions in which they draw color maps showing their current conceptions of global temperatures. They then compare their maps with actual data from Earth and formulate initial hypotheses about the factors that influence temperature.

2. Getting the task. Students learn about their mission of identifying habitable regions on a newly discovered planet, *Planet X*. They do an exploration of habitable regions on Earth. (For the purposes of this unit, habitable is defined as having minimum temperatures above 25 °F and maximum temperatures below 80 °F.) Students are assigned to investigate the four factors listed (shape, tilt, surface cover, and elevation) for their influence on temperature. They are told that they will receive data about the shape, tilt, surface cover, and topography of Planet X that will help them to develop a map predicting the distribution of temperature on Planet X.

3. Investigating shape. Students investigate the effect of angle of incidence of solar energy on surface temperature through hands-on laboratory exercises and explorations of global incoming solar energy data for Earth. They create an initial temperature map for Planet X that shows variation of temperature with latitude.

4. Investigating tilt. Students investigate the effect of a tilted axis of rotation on temperature at different times of year through explorations of incoming solar energy data for Earth. They observe how the bands of incoming solar energy shift with seasons. They modify their temperature map for Planet X to account for seasonal differences.

5. Investigating surface cover. Students investigate the effect of land versus water on temperatures through hands-on laboratory exercises looking at specific heat

of water and soil and explorations of global surface temperature data for Earth. They modify their temperature map for Planet X to account for differences in temperature over land and water.

6. Investigating elevation. Students investigate the effect of elevation on temperature through explorations of global surface temperature data for Earth. They modify their temperature map for Planet X to account for differences in temperature at different elevations.

7. Final recommendations. Students identify habitable areas by looking at maximum and minimum temperature values in their temperature maps for Planet X. They present their findings and their recommendations for colonization.

The curriculum materials place a special emphasis on forming and revising hypotheses and include journaling activities that ask students to record their hypotheses together with evidence and explanations. At each stage of the curriculum, students are asked to describe the factors that they believe affect temperature, how they affect temperature (i.e., the direction of the effect), and why (i.e., the underlying causes). They are also asked to provide any evidence they might have for these hypotheses and any open questions. They first record their hypotheses about the factors that affect temperature during the initial "setting the stage activity." During the portions of the unit where they investigate individual factors, they record their initial hypothesis about how each factor affects temperature before they do their investigations, and then they record their revised understanding following the investigation. It is this revised description of the relationship between a particular factor and temperature that they use when they construct their temperature maps for Planet X.

Planetary Forecaster *as an Example of* Learning-for-Use

Planetary Forecaster is an example of scenario-based inquiry learning. In the case of *Planetary Forecaster*, students adopt the role of a scientist and the goal of identifying areas that are suitable for colonization in the fictional scenario of a newly discovered planet. As a scenario-based inquiry learning unit, *Planetary Forecaster* incorporates seven strategies from the *Learning-for-Use* design framework to achieve all three steps in learning for use.

Motivate. The curriculum creates a demand for understanding through the mission of determining habitable areas on Planet X. This mission requires that they model temperatures for Planet X based on the data provided about the planet, which in turn demands that students understand the relationships between physical geography and temperature that comprise the content learning objectives for the unit. It also elicits curiosity through the stage-setting activities, which ask students to articulate their prior conceptions about the content and confronts them with the limitations of their understanding. After trying to create temperature maps for Earth based on their prior understanding, students become curious about what the actual temperature patterns are and why they are that way.

Construct. Students learn about the relationships between physical geography and temperature through a combination of hands-on laboratory exercises, computer-based investigations of earth science data, readings, lectures, and discussions. The hands-on labs provide them with direct experiences with the phenomena and relationships they are learning about. The computer-based investigations provide them with indirect experiences of these same relationships at a scale that they cannot experience directly. The readings, lectures, and discussions provide them with explanations of the phenomena and relationships from which they can construct understanding and give them opportunities for sense-making.

Organize for use. The process of constructing temperature maps for Planet X gives students the opportunity to apply their understanding of the relationships between physical geography and temperature as they are developing it. Classroom discussions and the journaling activities where students record their hypotheses encourage students to reflect upon their developing understanding.

EVALUATING *LEARNING-FOR-USE* CURRICULA

The engineering of effective learning environments requires an iterative cycle of design and evaluation. In this section, we move from the question of how to design learning environments for the geosciences to how to design evaluations that can inform their improvement, a process known as formative evaluation. The concern for motivation, knowledge construction, and knowledge organization in *Learning-for-Use* raises specific questions for formative evaluation. The first question one must ask is whether the designs for each of the stages in the learning-for-use model are functioning as intended. For example, are the motivation activities actually eliciting curiosity or creating a demand for new understanding? The second question one must ask is whether the individual elements of the design are working together to enable students to develop usable knowledge—knowledge that they can retrieve and apply in authentic contexts.

In this section, we describe the design of studies that we have constructed to conduct formative evaluations of *Planetary Forecaster*, together with some illustrative examples of findings from these studies. These studies were designed to show how models of learning and design frameworks, such as the ones presented in the previous section, can guide evaluation.

Studying Motivation: Role and Goal Adoption

A critical issue for a scenario-based inquiry learning unit like *Planetary Forecaster* is: do the students "buy-in" to the scenario sufficiently to create a motivation to learn the target learning objectives? To investigate this question, we developed a methodology for investigating the extent to which students adopt the role and goal associated with a scenario. This methodology was developed as part of a larger research program investigating differences in role and goal adoption across students, differences in

individual students' buy-in over time and across different types of activities, and the impact of these differences on engagement and learning (Pitts and Edelson, 2004).

This research design is based on several assumptions. First, expectancy-value theory developed by Eccles and colleagues (1998) predicts that students are likely to adopt a role and goal when they see the role and goal as being consistent with some aspect of their identity (who they want to be, what they like to do) and believe they are capable of playing the role and achieving the goal . However, their role and goal adoption is likely to be influenced by their understanding of the role and goal, which will generally evolve over the duration of a curriculum unit. Finally, a student's engagement in the context of any specific activity will be influenced, not just by the nature of their role/goal adoption, but by their perception of the relationship between that day's activity and the role and goal.

Thus, to study role and goal adoption, it is necessary to understand some relatively stable traits about students, such as their attitudes and beliefs about the role and goal in the unit, including both desirability and perceived abilities. For example, do students view the role of scientist as a desirable role, or do they feel they are capable of conducting extended scientific investigations? It is also necessary to understand how these beliefs and attitudes evolve over the course of a unit, and how they are influenced by their perceptions of the relationship of specific activities to the overall role and goal. For example, does a student's level of goal adoption increase over time, or does he or she feel that certain activities are not authentic to the practices of scientists? Finally, it is necessary to understand the nature and level of students' engagement over the period of a unit and their learning outcomes. For example, do students find the scientific investigations compelling or boring, and have they mastered specific learning objectives by the end of the unit?

To collect this information, we designed a diverse array of data collection methods that were selected to create as complete a picture of role and goal adoption and engagement as possible. Data collection included: (1) presurveys on students' attitudes and beliefs about school, the role and goal associated with the curriculum, and about their abilities; (2) classroom observations; (3) daily minisurveys about students' engagement, perceived level of role and goal buy-in, and perceived fit of each day's activity to the role and goal; (4) periodic extended interviews to understand students' perceptions of the role, goal, and specific activities in depth; and (5) pre- and post-tests.

Each of these sources of data provides a different perspective on student motivation and engagement. The presurveys provide us with a baseline understanding of a students' stable attitudes with respect to science, school, their self-confidence, and interests. It also provides us with shallow data about their initial reaction to the scenario in the unit. Classroom observations provide us with a record of classroom activities, including whether and how the teacher connects individual activities to the scenario context. They also enable us to gather observational data about student engagement. The daily minisurveys

(1 min multiple-choice questionnaires) provide a picture of how students' engagement and perception of the relationship of the activity to the goal and role vary from day to day and. This data can be used to see how the nature of the activity interacts with the students' level of overall buy-in to the scenario, which influences both: (1) the engagement in a given day and (2) their subsequent buy-in to the scenario. For example, if a student does not perceive a fit between the activity and either the role or the goal, he or she is not likely to be motivated by the scenario to engage in that activity. In that case, the demand created by the scenario will not effectively motivate the knowledge construction or organization activities that day. On the other hand, if the activity of a particular day changes the student's understanding of the role or goal in a way that makes it more appealing, then the student's overall buy-in to the scenario will increase. In looking for these effects, we also must attend to the influence of self-confidence and other variables that may be influencing their engagement on a given day and their overall buy-in. The extended interviews provide a richer picture of students' interests, buy-in, and perceptions of specific activities. In these interviews, students are asked indepth questions about their interests, attitudes about the scenario, and responses to specific activities. In these interviews, we ask students to list days when they felt particularly engaged and when they felt particularly motivated by the scenario, and when they felt least engaged and least motivated by the scenario. This helps us to understand how students' understand the scenario and the activities and how those understandings interact with their stable attitudes and interests. The pretest and post-tests measure student content learning and are compiled to see if there are correlations between patterns of motivation and engagement and learning outcomes.

We have collected this data in the context of several scenario-based inquiry units over a two year period, including one enactment of *Planetary Forecaster*.

A Study of Motivation and Role and Goal Adoption in *Planetary Forecaster*

In this section, we report on a pilot study of role and goal adoption conducted in an eighth grade all-girl science classroom in a Chicago public school. In this study, we collected and analyzed student interviews. Since the time of this study, we have completed studies using the full range of data collection methods described previously, but in the context of other scenario-based inquiry units. Additional studies of *Planetary Forecaster* are planned.

In this study, eight students were selected for interviews based on their presurveys. The sample was selected to include some students who reported that they liked science and some who reported that they didn't; some who preferred challenging task and were curiosity-driven, and some who preferred easier tasks and were more extrinsically motivated; some students who believed they had a high ability in science and some who

didn't. We report findings about interest and role adoption, which correspond to the strategies of eliciting curiosity and creating task demand in the *Learning-for-Use* framework.

Interest

Seven of eight students interviewed reported that they were interested in the content of *Planetary Forecaster*. In particular, they expressed interest in its connection to their own weather: "I think it's interesting 'cause you're wondering about the weather, you wonder why it's so cold in October, but in other places it's hot…." "I like learning about the weather 'cause I'm usually talking about the weather, and I'm interested in it."

Role Adoption

Five of six students liked the idea of taking on the role of scientist. "Oh, I love it. I really do. Because you want to get it from another person's perspective. So I'm in a science perspective right now…you wonder how scientists feel, learning about new ideas, and discovering and having new strategies." However, the majority (5 out of 7) students saw themselves as more of a student than a scientist when they did the curriculum. For the most part, reasons for "seeing themselves as a scientist" (or not) had to do with the extent to which the task characteristics matched their idea of a scientist, specifically:

1. The extent to which they were learning (like a student) versus the extent to which they knew what they were doing (like a scientist). For example, "I'm kinda in the middle … I'm still learning, (so) I feel like a student, the teacher is still explaining things to me, but I do feel like a scientist 'cause I know a lot to kinda make a prediction."
2. The extent to which the activities they were doing were those a scientist would engage in. For example, "More as a scientist, because, um, the activity that we did when we pointed the light, that was something that not a lot of students would actually do."
3. The extent to which they were thinking on their own. "… when we were coloring what we thought the temperature was, I kind felt like a scientist." (When asked why:) "Because I was on my own, and I was putting what I thought."

One student talked about becoming more of a scientist as she really started "getting into" what they were talking about. She said, "At first I think of myself as a student, but then when I start getting into what they're talking about, it changes, that's when we start researching and stuff …."

One of the surprising results of this study was that one student did not realize that the scenario was fictitious. In fact, she told the researcher that she was beginning to suspect that it was not real and was going to be angry with her teacher if it turned out to be made up. We have found similar students in subsequent studies of other units, and it has raised questions about how to present scenarios to students in scenario-based inquiry learning in such a way that it engages students in the role and pursuit of the goal because of their plausibility without misleading them about their realism. In ongoing curriculum design work, we are exploring ways to present scenarios to students as fictitious while still helping them to understand how adopting the role and goal can help to contextualize their learning

The overall impression we gained from this study about *Planetary Forecaster*'s effectiveness at eliciting curiosity and creating task demand is that it was sufficiently effective at both. It successfully channeled students' interests in weather variation into curiosity about climate, and it provided students with an opportunity to play a desirable role. However, there were clear limits to the extent to which students adopted the role in the curriculum. In ongoing research, we are looking at the effect on student role and goal adoption of the prominence of the role and goal in the curriculum materials and the teacher's statements. We also are studying the relationship between role and goal adoption and learning outcomes.

Studying Learning: Students' Conceptions

In conducting a formative evaluation of a *Learning-for-Use* curriculum, it is also important to understand to what extent students have developed usable understanding—understanding that they can retrieve and apply in context. While a traditional written test can be helpful in assessing students' understanding, we have found it more helpful to conduct extended interviews of students, which enable us to expose not just the correctness but the nature and structure of their understanding.

In order to assess the impact of *Learning-for-Use* curriculum units on student understanding and track the development of that understanding over time, we developed a data collection methodology that involves several elements: (1) written pre- and post-tests consisting of multiple choice and short answer, which allow us to assess student understanding efficiently for a large number of students; (2) clinical interviews before, during, and following the enactment of a unit, which allow us to assess student understanding in-depth for smaller numbers of students; (3) classroom observations, which allow us to understand the way that the unit was implemented by the teacher and to track in-class experiences of specific students; and (4) collection of student work, which allows us to understand how students performed work that was assigned and to assess the understanding that was called for by those assignments.

The goal of combining all these elements is to put together as complete a picture as possible of what students have learned and how this learning is explained by the students' experiences as part of the unit. Ideally, they can be done in a way that sheds light on the value of specific knowledge construction and knowledge organization activities, to see both the independent and combined impacts.

A Study of Students' Conceptions during *Planetary Forecaster*

In this section, we describe a study of *Planetary Forecaster* that implemented many of the elements described above. As with the previous study, this was a pilot study that was designed mostly as a way to test the evaluation methods.

Context

This study was conducted in a fifth-grade classroom of 27 students in a Chicago public school with a diverse, urban population. Classroom observations indicated that the teacher, Martha (a pseudonym), successfully created an inquiry-based learning environment in which students investigated phenomena rather than simply receiving information about it. She repeatedly told her students, "I'm not going to tell you all the answers, you'll have to come up with them yourselves." Martha had high expectations of her students, and the discourse was at times above a typical fifth-grade level; for example, these fifth-graders referred to times when they had to be "metacognitive," or, "think about [their] thinking." Class sessions generally involved significant discussion among Martha and the students. Finally, Martha structured her science class so that her students paralleled scientists. When students were confused about anomalous data in a laboratory exercise, she would ask them what real scientists do in this situation, to which they would respond "recollect the data," and, time permitting, would do just that. Overall, the classroom environment was excellent for the implementation of an inquiry-based curriculum such as *Planetary Forecaster*.

Methods

Data were collected via pre- and postinterviews of selected students, written pre- and postassessments, student work, and classroom interactions with students. Five participants were interviewed individually before beginning the curriculum and again near the end. The purpose of the interviews was to elicit more in-depth explanations from the students by probing their understanding of involved concepts in a way that could not be done on a paper-and-pencil test. The teacher selected students based on the interviewer's request to include students of varying academic abilities who were capable of articulating their thoughts fairly well.

The interviews were designed with the intention of examining not only what students think happens in temperature-related phenomena, but also why or how they think that event happens. The content of the pre-interview included all four factors covered in the curriculum. A main question for each of the four content areas was generated, and, based on prior research and expected student responses, follow-up questions contingent on the response were included in the script. Students were asked to draw pictures to aid their verbal explanations, especially for the questions involving the Earth-Sun relationship and the seasons. The mid-point interview discussed here focused primarily on the Earth-Sun relationship and effect of the curvature of Earth on intensity of sunlight. It also touched on the seasons, a topic that the class had partially covered.

The pre-test was administered at the start of the curriculum and the post-test was administered several weeks after the teacher completed her enactment of the curriculum. The written assessment was designed with the objective of getting a greater breadth of data than could be obtained from the interviews alone. The test consisted of multiple choice, short answer, and true/false questions. The answer options for the multiple choice questions often contained "lure" choices; that is, misconceptions that had been previously demonstrated by other students, such as "In the winter, the Earth is farther away from the sun, and in the summer, the Earth is closer to the sun." Similarly, four of the six true/false questions were lure statements. Exams were scored on the basis of whether a student answered the question correctly, answered the question incorrectly by giving or selecting a lure answer, or answered the question incorrectly without giving or selecting a lure.

The class was observed two to three times a week throughout the duration of the curriculum. During lecture and whole-class sessions (approximately half of the classes were run in this format), the researchers sat in the back of the classroom and recorded field notes. During group work sessions, they occasionally worked with various small groups in the same manner as the teacher—facilitating discussion, attaining a grasp on student understanding, answering questions, etc. Additionally, student work completed either in class or as homework assignments was collected for analysis. Many of the assignments were completed in small groups of three to five students in class.

The study focused on the portion of the curriculum in which students investigated the effect of Earth's spherical shape and the tilt of its axis of rotation on the intensity of the incoming solar energy at different latitudes at different times of year. Students engaged in several hands-on and computer-based activities to support their construction of knowledge about this content. All the activities were designed around a conceptual model of incoming solar energy as parallel "rays" of light. We selected this model of insolation in the design of the curriculum because it was sophisticated enough to explain variation in heating at different latitudes but simple enough to be accessible to middle school students. In the portion of the unit on the effects of curvature, students engaged in two knowledge construction activities. In the first one, they conducted a hands-on laboratory exercise where they used a penlight to represent the Sun and measured the area of the light beam from the penlight as it appeared on the paper at different angles. Each angle of the paper represented a different angle of incidence of sunlight from the equator to the poles. This laboratory exercise was designed to demonstrate that with increasing angles (as you move toward the poles), the same amount of light spreads out over a larger area, resulting in a lower amount of energy per unit of area. The second activity allowed the students to see data visualizations of measured incoming solar energy showing the same decrease in energy intensity at a global scale that they viewed in their hands-on exercise. In the section on tilt, students conducted a hands-on investigation with globes and penlights, in which they processed the globe around the light source observing which portion of the globe received the most and least direct sunlight at the equinoxes and solstices. This activity, too, was accompanied by a computer activity, in which students compared visualizations of Earth's incoming solar energy at each season.

Selected Findings

In the following paragraphs, we present a case study of the evolution of an individual student's conceptions over a portion of the *Planetary Forecaster* unit. We include it here to show the value of a detailed picture of a students' understanding for formative evaluation. Because our goal in this chapter is to illustrate rather than report complete findings, we are only presenting one of three case studies that we developed as part

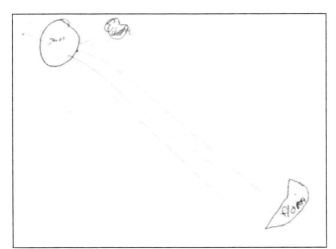 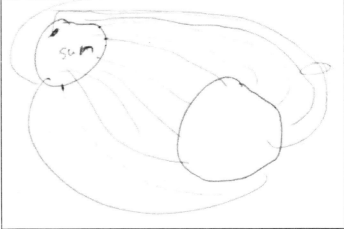

Figure 1. Drawings from Alice's pre-interview. On the left is her drawing showing the longer sun rays reaching Florida and shorter sun rays reaching Alaska. On the right is her more general drawing of how the rays of the sun reach Earth. The dark spot on the Sun was drawn to indicate a particularly warm portion of the Sun.

of this study. Salierno et al. (2005) presented all three cases and a detailed analysis of the misconceptions relevant to *Planetary Forecaster*. In this case study, we present a detailed description of the state of Alice's (a pseudonym) understanding of the differential heating of Earth at different latitudes due to the angle of incidence of solar radiation. We describe her understanding as demonstrated before the unit, followed by a description of our observations of Alice during the unit, and then her understanding as demonstrated in the interview following the segment of the unit dealing with curvature of Earth's surface and angle of incidence of solar radiation.

Before the unit. Alice presented an intriguing case because she revealed initial conceptions that were not documented in prior research. When asked why Florida is warmer than Alaska, she indicated that different parts of Earth are heated by different parts of the sun, and that Florida receives its sunlight from a warm part of the sun. She drew a picture showing Florida receiving longer sun rays than Alaska (Fig. 1), and explained in answer to the question, "Does the way sunlight hits Earth have to do with temperature at different places?" that the strength of a ray of sunlight is determined both by its length and the part of the sun from which it originates. In answer to both questions, she indicated that longer rays carry more heat, although it was not clear whether she meant that rays that travel farther through space carry more heat, or she was simply using length to indicate strength in her written representation. Alice also drew rays of sunlight that curve, including some that curved around Earth to reach portions of the globe that were facing away from the sun (Fig. 1).

Alice's description of the causes of temperature change with the seasons was very disjointed. She knew that it is winter in the Southern Hemisphere when it is summer in the Northern Hemisphere. However, she was unable to explain why, and she presented several partial arguments about the spinning of Earth on its axis, the movement of Earth around the Sun, and "maybe because of the atmosphere." In answer to a question asking why it was cold on the day of the interview (a winter day) even though it was sunny, she said that the sunlight is somehow different. Her pre-test was consistent with the interview. She missed three of the eight questions about the Earth-Sun relationship, giving answers that were consistent with the explanations she gave in her interview.

During the unit. Despite being talkative in her interviews, Alice spoke very little during class discussions and group work. However, researchers did observe her on two occasions make comments or draw diagrams that were consistent with her pre-interview statements about the sun's rays. Both her statements within her group and her answers to the reflection questions in the penlight laboratory exercise revealed that she observed that the area covered by the penlight increased as the angle became more acute, however, she did not recognize that the brightness of the light decreased. Making this observation is probably critical to understanding that the increase in area results in a decrease of intensity. The likelihood of a student understanding the relationship between angle and intensity in the absence of this concrete observation is diminished because the student must instead apply the abstract principle of conservation of energy. Alice, in fact, did not demonstrate in her exercise write-up that she understood the relationship between angle and intensity.

Following the unit. In the postinterview, Alice correctly explained that the equator is the warmest part of Earth because it is almost at a 90 degree angle to incoming sunlight and therefore receives the most direct light. She did not mention differences in length of rays or refer to rays that originate in different parts of the sun. In answer to the questions about Florida and Alaska, she said:

Researcher: Last time we talked about…Florida and Alaska…why again would it be warmer in Florida than Alaska?

Alice: I think it was because Florida would get part—part sunlight, part direct, but it's not really direct, it's like at a slanted angle, but it would be at ninety degree.

Researcher: Okay, so it would be more slanted than ninety… What kind of sunlight does Alaska get?

Alice: I don't think Alaska gets that much light.

Researcher: Okay, so they just get less? Do you know why they might get less than Florida?

Alice: Less direct sunlight.

However, when asked directly about the relationship between angle of incident light and intensity, Alice had the relationship reversed. She stated consistently that heat and light intensity increase with area, claiming that the same amount of light spread out over a larger area has more heat and greater intensity than it would spread out over a smaller area. In addition, while she had mostly eliminated curved rays from her drawings, when asked about the difference between temperatures at the equator and the poles, she explained that at the poles it is cooler because the light has to curve to get there, and she drew curving lines of light arriving at the poles. In the post-test Alice actually scored worse than on the pre-test, missing four rather than three questions. The lack of improvement[4] appears to be due to the fact that she still did not understand the relationship between angle and intensity.

Discussion of Results

Alice was typical of the students that we studied in that she had fragmented and mostly incorrect conceptions initially. Like the other two students that we interviewed, significant misconceptions that appeared in her pre-interview were no longer apparent in the postinterviews (although additional assessments would be necessary to verify that they did not reappear at a greater interval following the curriculum). In their postinterviews, all three students understood the central relationship of this portion of the

---

[4]The additional incorrect answer was a question on seasons that the class had not covered yet. The answer she gave was consistent with what they had learned about curvature, but did not reflect the additional effect of tilt.

curriculum: that temperatures decrease with increasing latitudes. However, none of them was able to bring together all the pieces that the section was trying to teach in order to connect angle of incidence to intensity of sunlight (via conservation of energy) and to use this relationship to explain differences in temperature. Based on the detailed information about these three students and the post-test results of the other students in the class, we concluded that the curriculum was making a difference in these students' abilities to retrieve and apply relevant knowledge, but the unit was not fully achieving the goals of its designers.

We have several hypotheses for why the students were not achieving a better level of understanding of the target concepts. The first is that fifth-grade students are not developmentally ready for the abstract reasoning that this unit requires. There is evidence for this in the fact that they were able to understand directly observed relationships, such as the relationship between angle and area, but not able to extend this via an abstract principle, such as conservation of energy, to understand the relationship between angle and intensity. In fact, the curriculum was targeted at sixth to eighth graders. Another hypothesis for why students did not achieve the desired depth of understanding is that there is important prerequisite understanding that the curriculum did not address directly. To understand the implications of angle of incidence and tilt for temperature, students must understand the "ray" model of light and must understand the Earth-Sun relationship, including the shape of Earth's orbit, period of Earth's revolution around Sun, and period of Earth's rotation around its axis, well enough to overcome common misconceptions. The curriculum assumes that students understand these concepts or that they will pick them up as a result of their experiences with the curriculum. In fact, there is some evidence that students do "pick them up." For example, Alice mostly abandoned her theory of curving rays of sunlight, despite the fact that there was no activity that directly addressed the nature of these rays, just numerous representations of sunlight using straight arrows to represent sunlight. Presumably, the curriculum could be more effective if it were to target these important prerequisite concepts and if it were to include activities that directly addressed problematic misconceptions, such as those documented here.

Our final hypothesis raises questions about *Planetary Forecaster* as an implementation of the *Learning-for-Use* design framework. In fact, the task that students were asked to do did not demand that they understand the reasons that latitude and seasons effect temperature. It simply demanded that they know what the relationships are. In the end, the task that students were being asked to do was to apply their understanding *that* temperature varies with latitude and *how.* It did not clearly require that they be able to explain *why.* In fact, all three students demonstrated in their class work, in their postinterviews, and their post-tests that they did know that temperature decreases as you move away from the equator. It is possible that a redesign of the curriculum that placed a greater demand on explaining why the four factors affect temperature would be more effective. On the other hand, it is also possible that students are not sensitive enough to the actual demands of the task—that their learning of the *that* and the *how* but not the *why* is the result of the knowledge demands of the task.

Reflections on Evaluating *Learning-for-Use* Curricula

In this section, we have described methods for evaluating two different critical aspects of *Learning-for-Use*: (1) the extent to which a particular unit instilled the goal of achieving its learning objectives (motivation), and (2) the extent to which it fostered the development of its target understanding (knowledge construction).

We also presented cases of how these methods have been applied in formative evaluations of the *Planetary Forecaster* curriculum. The lesson of both of these studies is that the unit is at least partially successful in achieving its goals. In the motivation study, students found the goal interesting and the role of scientist appealing. However, they reported that for the most part, they did not feel that they were playing the role very much of the time because they did not find the activities to be consistent with their understanding of a scientist's activities. This finding has important implications both for the design of activities and for the need to help students understand how specific activities fit into the role. In the student conceptions study, students' conceptions showed evidence of change toward the target understanding, but they did not demonstrate the complete understanding that the designers of the curriculum were targeting. This result requires further study, but it has led us to consider several implications for the design of the unit, including the possibility that the task does not create demand for the depth of understanding that we were seeking.

The studies we described in this chapter were designed to look at effectiveness of an individual unit, rather than assessing the effectiveness of the general approach. In order to evaluate the general approach, it would be necessary to conduct investigations across multiple units. It would also be necessary to conduct comparative studies that looked at the impact of removing elements of the *Learning-for-Use* framework. In future work, we hope to be able to do this research. For example, to look at the effect of the motivation strategy of creating task demand, we would like to conduct a study that will compare *Planetary Forecaster* with a unit that contains all of the same knowledge construction, reflection, and application activities, but without the contextualizing scenario. Similarly, to investigate the role of application, we would like to conduct a study of a unit that contains the same motivation and knowledge construction activities without the opportunity to reflect on or apply what the students have learned in context.

LEARNING-FOR-USE IN THE GEOSCIENCES

Recent reports have called for reform in geoscience education, including an emphasis on a systems approach and the techniques of geoscience inquiry and explanation (American Association for the Advancement of Science [AAAS], 1994;

Barstow and Geary, 2001; Ireton et al., 1996; National Research Council [NRC], 1996). If these reform efforts based on contemporary trends in the geosciences are to have a positive impact, they must be implemented in accordance with contemporary understanding of how people learn. The *Learning-for-Use* design framework has been developed to encode that understanding in a set of design guidelines. The development and research efforts described in this chapter are intended to serve as a model of how these guidelines can be implemented and evaluated in a geosciences context. However, significant additional research remains to be done on learning in the geosciences (Manduca et al., 2002) and on *Learning-for-Use* applications.

In closing, we feel it is important to emphasize the critical need for disciplinary expertise in developing effective curriculum units. *Planetary Forecaster* is one of several scenario-based inquiry learning units in the geosciences that have been developed by the Geographic Data in Education (GEODE) Initiative at Northwestern University. In every case, geoscientists have played critical roles in identifying appropriate scenarios, clarifying the learning goals, developing knowledge construction and application tasks, developing scientific explanations, verifying the scientific accuracy of curriculum materials, and developing assessment. We have been successful in creating partnerships between curriculum developers, teachers, technologists, and geoscientists by developing common ground around goals and strategies. The *Learning-for-Use* framework and its implementation in the form of scenario-based inquiry learning have provided an important part of that common ground by giving individuals with diverse expertise a shared vocabulary for discussing curriculum design.

ACKNOWLEDGMENTS

The authors would like to express their gratitude to the many teachers and researchers in the Center for Learning Technologies in Urban Schools and Center for Curriculum Materials in Science who contributed to this research. This material is based upon work supported by the National Science Foundation under grants REC-9730377, REC-9720663, REC-0087751, and ESI-0227557. Any opinions, findings, and conclusions or recommendations expressed in this material are those of the authors and do not necessarily reflect the views of the National Science Foundation.

REFERENCES CITED

Abraham, M.R., 1998, The learning cycle approach as a strategy for instruction in science, *in* Fraser, B.J., and Tobin, K.G., eds., International handbook of science education: Dordrecht, Netherlands, Kluwer Academic Publishers, p. 513–524.

American Association for the Advancement of Science (AAAS), 1994, Benchmarks for science literacy: New York, Oxford University Press, 448 p.

Anderson, J.R., 1983, The architecture of cognition: Cambridge, Massachusetts, Harvard University Press, 345 p.

Barstow, D., and Geary, E., eds., 2001, Blueprint for change: Report from the National Conference on the Revolution in Earth and Space Science Education: Cambridge, Massachusetts, TERC, 97 p.

Bransford, J., Sherwood, R., Hasselbring, T., Kinzer, C., and Williams, S., 1990, Anchored instruction: Why we need it and how technology can help, *in* Nix, D., and Spiro, R., eds., Cognition, education, and multimedia: Hillsdale, New Jersey, Erlbaum, p. 115–141.

Bransford, J.D., Brown, A.L., and Cocking, R.R., eds., 1999, How people learn: Brain, mind, experience, and school: Washington, D.C., National Academy Press, 379 p.

Bybee, R.W., 2002, Scientific inquiry, student learning, and the science curriculum, *in* Bybee, R.W., ed., Learning science and the science of learning: Arlington, Virginia, NSTA Press, p. 25–37.

Chi, M.T.H., Feltovich, P.J., and Glaser, R., 1981, Categorization and representation of physics problems by experts and novices: Cognitive Science, v. 5, p. 121–152.

Cobb, P., Confrey, J., diSessa, A., Lehrer, R., and Schauble, L., 2003, Design experiments in educational research: Educational Researcher, v. 32, no. 1, p. 9–13.

Design-Based Research Collective, 2003, Design-based research: An emerging paradigm for educational inquiry: Educational Researcher, v. 32, no. 1, p. 5–8.

Eccles, J.S., Barber, B.L., Updegraff, K., and O'Brien, K.M., 1998, An expectancy-value model of achievement choices: The role of ability self-concepts, perceived task utility and interest in predicting activity choice and course enrollment, *in* Hoffman, L., Krapp, A., Renninger, A., and Baumert, J., eds., Interest and learning: Proceedings of the SEEON Conference on Interest and Gender: Kiel, Germany, Institute for Science Education (IPN) at the University of Kiel, p. 267–279.

Edelson, D.C., 2001, Learning-for-use: A framework for the design of technology-supported inquiry activities: Journal of Research in Science Teaching, v. 38, no. 3, p. 355–385, doi: 10.1002/1098-2736(200103)38:3<355::AID-TEA1010>3.0.CO;2-M.

Edelson, D.C., 2002, Design research: What we learn when we engage in design: Journal of the Learning Sciences, v. 11, no. 1, p. 105–121, doi: 10.1207/S15327809JLS1101_4.

Edelson, D.C., and Bang, M.E., 2003, Integrating technology-supported activities and non-technology activities in support of conceptual learning: A design survey: Paper presented at the Annual Meeting of the American Educational Research Association, April 21, 2003, Chicago, Illinois, as part of a symposium entitled "Teaching Complex Scientific Ideas: Teachers Using Technology To Support Student Understanding."

Edelson, D.C., and Joseph, D.M., 2004, The interest-driven learning design framework: Motivating learning through usefulness, *in* Kafai, Y.B., Sandoval, W.A., Enyedy, N., Nixon, A.S., and Herrera, F., eds., Proceedings of the Sixth International Conference of the Learning Sciences, Santa Monica, California, June 22–26, 2004: Mahwah, New Jersey, Erlbaum, p. 166–173.

Glaser, R., 1992, Expert knowledge and process of thinking, *in* Halpern, D.F., ed., Enhancing thinking skills in the sciences and mathematics: Hillsdale, New Jersey, Erlbaum, p. 63–75.

Ireton, M.F.W., Manduca, C.A., and Mogk, D.W., eds., 1996, Shaping the future of undergraduate earth science education: Innovation and change using an earth system approach: Washington, D.C., American Geophysical Union, http://www.agu.org/sci_soc/spheres/ (accessed June 2006).

Karplus, R., and Thier, H.D., 1967, A new look at elementary school science: Chicago, Rand McNally, 204 p.

Kolodner, J.L., 1993, Case-based reasoning: San Mateo, California, Morgan Kaufmann, 612 p.

Krajcik, J., Czerniak, C., and Berger, C., 1999, Teaching children science: A project-based approach: Boston, McGraw-Hill, 356 p.

Lawson, A.E., 1995, Science teaching and the development of thinking: Belmont, California, Wadsworth, 624 p.

Linn, M., 2000, Designing the knowledge integration environment: International Journal of Science Education, v. 22, no. 8, p. 781–796, doi: 10.1080/095006900412275.

Manduca, C.A., Mogk, D.W., and Stillings, N., 2002, Bringing research on learning to the geosciences: Northfield, Minnesota, Science Education Resource Center, Carleton College, 34 p.

National Research Council (NRC), 1996, National science education standards: Washington, D.C., National Academy Press, 274 p.

Pitts, V.M., and Edelson, D.C., 2004, Role, goal, and activity: A framework for characterizing participation and engagement in project-based learning environments, *in* Kafai, Y.B., Sandoval, W.A., Enyedy, N., Nixon, A.S., and Herrera, F., eds., Proceedings of the Sixth International Conference of the Learning Sciences, Santa Monica, California, June 23–26, 2004: Mahwah, New Jersey, Erlbaum, p. 420–426.

Renner, J.W., and Stafford, D.G., 1972, Teaching science in the secondary school: New York, Harper and Row, 370 p.

Salierno, C., Edelson, D.C., and Sherin, B.L., 2005, Development of student conceptions of the Earth-Sun relationship in an inquiry-based curriculum: Journal of Geosciences Education, v. 53, p. 422–431.

Schank, R.C., 1982, Dynamic memory: Cambridge, Cambridge University Press, 272 p.

Schank, R.C., Fano, A., Bell, B., and Jona, M., 1993/1994, The design of goal-based scenarios: The Journal of the Learning Sciences, v. 3, no. 4, p. 305– 346, doi: 10.1207/s15327809jls0304_2.

Simon, H.A., 1980, Problem solving and education, *in* Tuma, D.T., and Reif, R., eds., Problem solving and education: Issues in teaching and research: Hilldale, New Jersey, Erlbaum, p. 81–96.

Whitehead, A.H., 1929, The aims of education: Cambridge, Cambridge University Press.

MANUSCRIPT ACCEPTED BY THE SOCIETY 21 MARCH 2006

Geological Society of America
Special Paper 413
2006

Building geoscience vocabularies using a data visualization tool (WorldWatcher)

Michael R. Taber[†]
Colorado College, Colorado Springs, Colorado 80903, USA

Kristin Quadracci[†]
Front Range Community College, Brighton, Colorado 80601, USA

ABSTRACT

Tools for visualizing data provide an opportunity for students to build useful understanding of geoscience vocabularies. Edelson's (2001) *Learning-for-Use* framework serves as an instructional model for designing an experience for students in which they can learn fundamental geoscience concepts. This paper presents results from an experiment on project-based learning with three cohorts (in subsequent semesters) of preservice elementary teachers. The context for the experiment was a capstone science course for preservice elementary teachers. The project consisted of six steps in which students were instructed to create a paleotemperature map of the Late Jurassic. Students made their decisions based on their constructed knowledge about factors that influence near-surface air temperature: latitude (axial tilt and curvature), topography and subsequent lapse rate, atmospheric effect, and surface cover (albedo). Analyses of reflection papers and classroom observations from each step in the project indicated improvement in content knowledge for all student cohorts. However, regarding the ability to perform complex analysis, only students who successfully built new geoscience vocabularies performed better on predicting and defending their final temperature maps. This is attributed to their ability to *use*, not just define the geoscience vocabularies contained in the project.

Keywords: inquiry, constructivism, paleoclimate, pedagogy, preservice.

INTRODUCTION

This paper provides insights into the use of WorldWatcher data visualization software (http://www.worldwatcher.org) to teach basic climate (temperature) concepts via an inquiry-based project. Preservice elementary teachers were the subjects of an experiment in which two questions were addressed:

1. Can students understand the relationship(s) among two or more variables by analyzing data using WorldWatcher, a data visualization software?

2. Can students develop the capacity (i.e., useful vocabularies) to make predictions from the application of real data?

Preservice elementary teachers enrolled in a capstone science course for interdisciplinary liberal arts majors at the University of Northern Colorado (UNC) were the subjects in this experiment. This particular group of students was selected because of their significant deficiency in science education. When asked, nearly 80% of these students could not recall a moment in their K–12 education when science was "fun and

[†]mike.taber@coloradocollege.edu; kristinquadracci@yahoo.com.

Taber, M.R., and Quadracci, K., 2006, Building geoscience vocabularies using a data visualization tool (WorldWatcher), *in* Manduca, C.A., and Mogk, D.W., eds., Earth and Mind: How Geologists Think and Learn about the Earth: Geological Society of America Special Paper 413, p. 145–155, doi: 10.1130/2006.2413(11). For permission to copy, contact editing@geosociety.org. ©2006 Geological Society of America. All rights reserved.

exciting." Approximately 95% of the students didn't even recall doing science (beyond simple "phases of water") in elementary. Essentially, we want these preservice teachers to not only teach science in elementary school, but to do so in a manner that persuades their students to pursue science. A seemingly unbreakable circle exists, where most elementary teachers are not only afraid to teach science, but have no general idea of what science is all about, and therefore, their students are discouraged with science.

This experiment attempted to gain insight into why preservice elementary teachers were generally unable to "do science." While students can easily define new geoscience vocabularies (regurgitated on weekly quizzes), they often struggle with using the new vocabularies in the context of "research" or "doing science." Thus, if students are given the opportunity via an inquiry-based project, will they properly use their new vocabularies?

The context for the experiment is the course project, *Jurassic Jacuzzi*, where students use their knowledge about factors that effect temperature at the surface of Earth to predict Earth's surface temperature 150 million years ago.

Edelson (2001) provided a framework for the pedagogical design of inquiry-based, project activities used in the experiment. The *Learning-for-Use* framework consists of three components: motivate the learning objectives; build knowledge; and refine and apply the new knowledge. In contrast, the traditional model for undergraduate instruction is to spend most of the course on learning through lecture, with minimal motivation and almost no opportunities to apply the knowledge or build useful vocabularies. Unfortunately, the lecture method is comfortable for both the lecturer and the passive student. During lecture, the student faces no mental challenges and the instructor can simply convey information at her predetermined pace. Even in most laboratory settings, the laboratory is contrived with known outcomes. Students know there is a "right answer" in the exercise and are merely trying to find the best method to replicate the answer. Thus, in both lecture and laboratory, the student does not have the opportunity to use their newly acquired vocabularies by applying them to new situations.

Data presentation and analysis software, such as World-Watcher, provide an opportunity for students to use data in order to build geoscience vocabularies. If students are asked to make predictions, test their predictions, and refine their goals, then the students are presented with an opportunity to build their capacity for useful vocabularies.

DESIGN OF THE EXPERIMENT

The interdisciplinary liberal arts (IDLA) major at UNC is required to take four science courses, three with laboratory components: earth science (lab), physical science (lab), and biology (lab). The capstone course is a nonlaboratory course titled, "Principles of Scientific Inquiry: Finding Order in Chaos" (SCI 465). The course is designed to give students an experience with some

of the major discoveries in the major science disciplines. For instance, the earth science focus is on plate tectonics and modeling of climate change.

The IDLA major must concentrate (18 semester credit hours) in one of nineteen disciplines. The majority of the IDLA majors in this experiment were concentrating in Speech Communications (Table 1). Of the 97 students in this research, only 6% concentrate in science and 7% in math. All but seven students were female, and five were sophomores, taking the course synchronously with at least one prerequisite course.

The SCI 465 course at UNC utilizes Gregory Derry's Book, *What Science Is and How it Works* (1999) as thematic framework for teaching about inquiry in the context of science. For example, in discussing Wegener's idea of continental drift, Derry describes the inquiry process as rich in methodical observation. Derry's presentation of *how science works* illustrates several characteristics of *doing* science, such as the identification of patterns as explanation for repeatable observations for the basis of prediction. In the course, students are asked to explore the electromagnetic spectrum, atomic theory, Mendeleyev periodic table, and evolution and ecology in such a manner as follows *What Science Is and How it Works*.

This experiment consisted of a three cohorts (in consecutive semesters) of students completing an inquiry-based project based on plate tectonic and climate concepts. The project activities utilized the *Learning-for-Use* framework outlined by Edelson (2001). The third cohort of students completed the project, but an additional activity on collecting temperature data was added.

NATURE OF THE STUDENT EXPERIENCE

Jurassic Jacuzzi Project Overview

The Jurassic Jacuzzi project is based on "Planetary Forecaster," developed by Edelson et al. (see Edelson et al., this volume, chapter 11). *Jurassic Jacuzzi* focuses on determining the global mean temperature of Earth during the Late Jurassic, 150 million years ago. Students, working in teams of two or three, predict paleotemperatures via the use of conceptual, database

TABLE 1. DISTRIBUTION OF INTERDISCIPLINARY LIBERAL ARTS (IDLA) MAJOR CONCENTRATIONS FOR STUDENTS IN ALL COHORTS

IDLA concentration	Percentage ($n = 97$)
Speech communications	26
English	19
Fine arts	17
History	9
Math	7
Ethinic and gender studies	7
Bilingual education	4
Earth science	4
Environmental studies	3
Geography	2
Physics	1
Biology	1

modeling in WorldWatcher. During the project, the instructor does not lecture on any of the concepts. Rather, students explore factors that effect temperature via activities, which are conducted in class. The instructor does occasional conduct discussions in class, particularly when a group discovers something significant. There are six steps to the *Jurassic Jacuzzi* project.

Step One: Thinking about Temperature

Students were first asked to create a mean temperature data set for July using WorldWatcher and compare their data set with actual mean July temperatures. (Edelson [2001] describes this activity in more detail.) The goal of this activity was to expose the student's prior knowledge and subsequent gaps in knowledge. Achieving this goal proved to be extremely motivating to the students. Many of the students remarked that their knowledge about the spatial distribution of temperature was severely lacking. None of the students could explain the spatial and temporal distribution of temperature beyond "seasons" or "temperature is generally colder in the mountains." The main vocabularies stressed during this activity were Kelvin temperature, spatial, temporal, and mean.

Step Two: Constructing Knowledge about Spatial and Temporal Distribution of Temperature

Students began step two with the examination of temperature data sets in order to refine their knowledge about spatial temperature variation. Students used WorldWatcher to explore the role of curvature and axial tilt (Fig. 1) and greenhouse gases in the atmosphere. The objective of step two was for students to understand that there are multiple factors influencing temperature. However, students were asked to ponder which factor(s) were most influential. Aside from the Sun, students recognized that atmosphere plays a major role (when compared to temperature without an atmosphere), as well as topography and major biomes (tropics, desert, etc....). In addition to the atmospheric effect, students completed step two with the motivation to examine the effects of elevation and surface cover.

In step two, students were again provided opportunities to build their knowledge about certain vocabularies: spatial, temporal, atmospheric effect, topography, and biomes.

Step Three: Constructing Knowledge about Temperature versus Elevation

Cohort 3 students began step three with collecting temperature profiles using Vernier Probes and Palm 550 Handhelds over two different surfaces on campus (snow and open grass or sidewalk). The purpose of this activity was to (1) provide students with a sense of where temperature data comes from and (2) show students that temperature varies with height. The previous two cohorts did not have any idea of where temperature came from or even what temperature is. When asked to "sketch a picture of temperature," nearly 98% of the students in cohorts 1 and 2 drew a picture of a thermometer.

All students used data in WorldWatcher (Fig. 2) to estimate the moist adiabatic lapse rate (~6.0 K km^{-1}). Students used the synchronized mouse and selection tools in WorldWatcher to graph changes in temperature versus changes in elevation at 33.5°N latitude in the Himalayas. Students were asked to "define" their observations. Most students suggested, "air temperature cools with height" as their definition. The concept of lapse rate was then introduced via discussion.

When students revisited their mean July temperature maps created in step 1, approximately half of the students did use the words "lapse rate" to describe their failure to account for cooler temperatures at higher elevations. Step three introduced "lapse rate" and "variation" as new vocabularies, and continued building the students' understanding of "mean."

Step Four: Influence of Surface Cover on Temperature

In step four, students again used WorldWatcher to identify patterns that describe the relationship of surface cover and temperature. One objective of step 4 was for students to learn about data control. In this case, students learned to control the factor of incoming solar radiation by looking for changes along constant latitude (to avoid temporal and spatial changes due to curvature, tilt, and day of year).

A second objective in step four was to provide experience in making predictions based on data. For some biomes (tundra, for example), the relationship between temperature and the major surface cover was unclear and inconsistent spatially. For others (dry, warm desert and tropical humid, for example), the relationship was more clearly defined. Students had to judge the weight of influence each surface cover had on temperature. Students were asked to compare the annual mean temperature of the biome as compared to the global mean. For example, when selecting major northern deserts, the mean temperature for the selection is 293 K as compared to the global mean of 288 K. Students were asked to decide on the two most influential biomes. Most students chose dry, warm deserts and tropical humid biomes. "Data control," "data-based predictions," and "weighing factors" were new vocabularies introduced in step 4. By the end of step 4, students had a firm understanding and use of the vocabulary word "mean."

Step Five: Applying Large-Scale Plate Tectonics to Create a Topographic Map

Students were introduced to plate tectonics by first visualizing the distribution of earthquakes using the Discover Our Earth (http://atlas.geo.cornell.edu/education/) interactive data mapping software developed at Cornell University. The motivation was simple; "How long does it take before a global earthquake pattern emerges?" Students were amazed that in less than four months, most of the plate boundaries were mapped by earthquake activity.

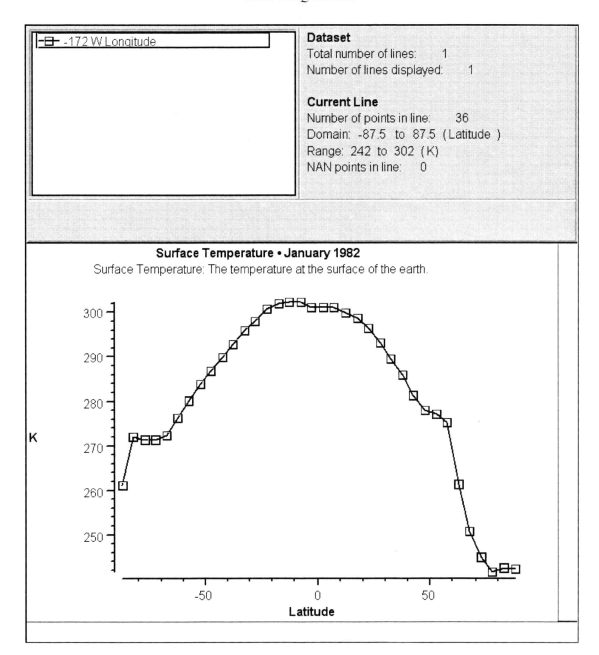

Figure 1. Temperature versus latitude for January 1982 created using WorldWatcher's line plot tool. (WorldWatcher Software: http://www.worldwatcher.org.)

Next, students mapped earthquakes, elevation, and bathymetry data sets using WorldWatcher to describe patterns in topography (mountain ranges) and bathymetry (trenches) associated with earthquakes and volcanoes (Figs. 3A and 3B).

Students then applied their knowledge about plate tectonics to determine the breakup of Pangaea and resulting topography. Students used visualizations from the PALEOMAP project (http://www.scotese.com) and the Ocean Drilling Stratigraphic Network's plate tectonic reconstruction model (http://www.odsn.de/odsn/) to estimate the location of continents and mountains on Earth 150 million years ago.

The actual elevations of Late Jurassic mountains are unknown. Therefore, students estimated the mean mountain elevation as 3000 m, using WorldWatcher as a model for exploring data about current mountain elevations. Young volcanoes due to Late Jurassic divergence were not considered in determining topography. The remaining nonmountainous elevation was estimated as 500 m, resulting in a topography data set for the Late Jurassic (Fig. 4).

The expectation was that students would have the skills to estimate values, based on mean values obtained from analysis of elevation and bathymetry. For example, students already could

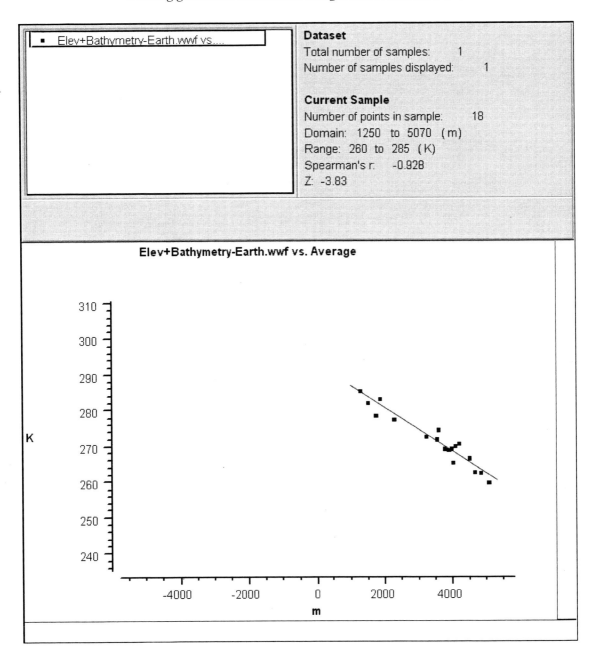

Figure 2. Temperature change with elevation based on synchronized selection of elevation data (Fig. 1) and average climatic temperature data. This graph was used to estimate the moist adiabatic lapse rate (~6 K km⁻¹).

use the selection tool in WorldWatcher to determine the mean of a selected biome (from step 4). When surveyed, students indicated that they did not know the direction of thinking to take in determining how high to map paleomountains. Some students simply mapped all mountains as 5000 m (upper end of current mountain heights). Only 8% of the student actually determined how high to map paleomountains based on the mean value of current mountains.

Students could define the word "mean" as an average for numbers. Students also could use the selection tool in World-

Watcher without any problems. Students could even read the statistic, "mean," from the WorldWatcher visualization window. However, very few students could use "mean" as a basis for predicting the heights of paleomountains.

Step Six: Applying Knowledge about Temperature to Create a Temperature Map

The final phase of the project required students to combine their knowledge about temperature variation with latitude,

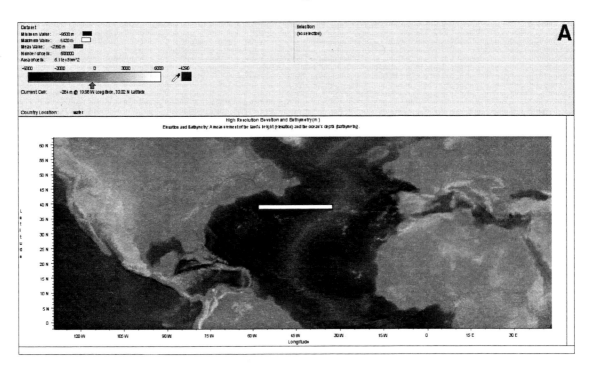

Figures 3. (A) Selection of data along the Mid-Atlantic Ridge used in generating a topographic profile (B, facing page).

elevation, atmospheric effect, and surface cover in order to estimate a mean global temperature for their 150 million year old Earth (Fig. 5). The order in which they developed their final temperature map is described by

First, they constructed a base temperature map by converting absorbed energy at Earth's surface. Students assumed no topography (landmass at uniform 1 m) and no change in the solar constant in the past 150 million years.

Second, they constructed a temperature map with current atmospheric effects.

Third, they constructed a temperature map based on their elevation map (Fig. 4) using knowledge about moist adiabatic lapse rate.

Next, students conducted a comparison of their estimated mean global temperature with 6–7 K temperature increase estimated by Royer et al. (2001). Based on the comparison, students were asked to conclude if their temperature maps were wrong and why, or conclude that Royer et al. (2002) were wrong and why, or make corrections to their temperature map and defend their decisions by systematically adjusting elevation estimates and/or atmospheric effect (due to increased CO_2 levels) in order to achieve a mean global temperature ~6 K warmer than it is today.

A graduate student periodically conducted observations (cohort 1 only), using a modified version of the Horizon Research Inc. Classroom Observation protocol, which was developed for the National Science Foundation's Local Systemic Change program. Students in all cohorts were also interviewed throughout the project and asked to write reflection essays in order to

understand the type of decisions they were making. Data from postactivity interviews and analysis of project summaries were also collected.

DISCUSSION

Classroom Observations, Reflection Essays, and Interviews

Students in all cohorts were able to easily grasp knowledge about the mechanics of using WorldWatcher, such as zooming and selecting subsets of data. Students also were able to interpret graphical data. For example, in Figure 2, students wrote the line as "a straight line and therefore temperature gets colder as elevation gets higher." However, despite the ability to "read the graph," students in the post-test failed to recognize the line for what it represented: lapse rate. Student reflection essays offer some insight into the problem. Students could explain what the graph illustrates (straight line), but they could not defend why they were graphing the temperature with elevation data. Making the connection between the mechanics of working with data and the underlying reasons "why" was found to be a constant frustration for students.

The problem was a student's lack of vocabulary related to the graphical display of data. As simple as it sounds, students in a pretest prior to the project start did not use the words "axis," "linear," "increase," and "decrease" when explaining graphical data. In addition, when looking at temperature variation with latitude (an early exercise in step 1), many students had difficulty in equating the negative numbers on the *x* axis with south latitude (Fig. 1).

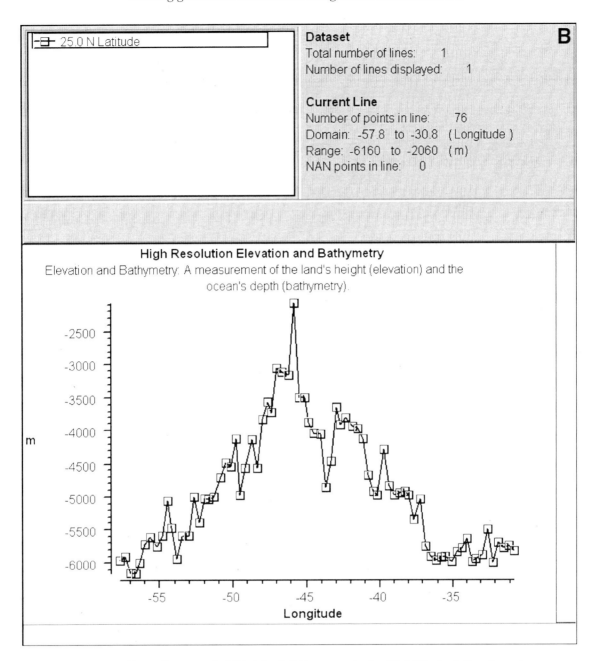

Figure 3, continued. (B) Topographic profile across the Mid-Atlantic Ridge created using WorldWatcher's line plot tool.

By step 5, however, many of the students were beginning to use vocabularies in analyzing data sets. For instance, students were comfortable with determining the mean temperature of a biome and articulating what the mean value represented, in the context of the minimum and maximum values. Interestingly, though, students in cohorts 1 and 2 were completely unable to explain why some of their temperature values were unrealistic (e.g., 80 K for Antarctica). In postproject interviews, the students posed two interesting questions to the instructor: "What is temperature?" and "What are ridges?"

What is Temperature?

Despite a lengthy project on working with factors that influence temperature, students in cohorts 1 and 2 did not know what temperature meant or even where temperature data originates. Some students thought the visualization of temperature data represented the tangible surface of Earth, such as a hot parking lot or a cold snow surface. The students did not know that the temperature data was an estimate of the air temperature near the ground based on multiple sources (stations, buoys, satellites, etc....). Second, students did not

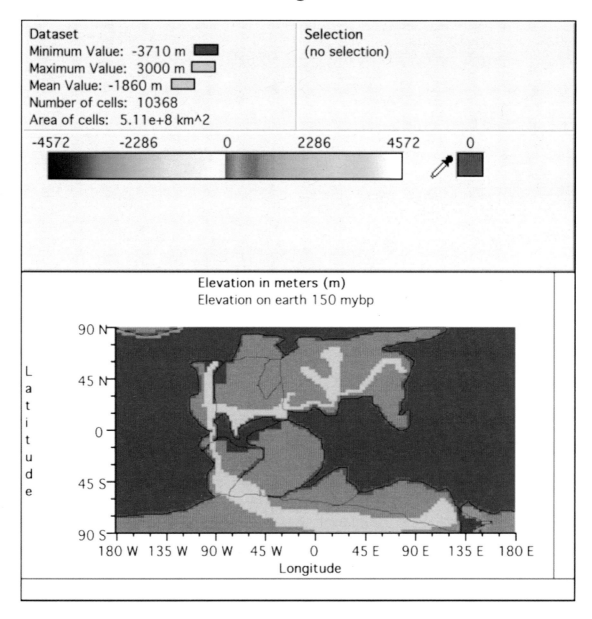

Figure 4. Estimated continent and mountain locations derived from the PALEOMAP project (http://www.scotese.com/) and the Ocean Drilling Stratigraphic Network (http://www.odsn.de/odsn/). White regions represent the approximate locations of mountains.

know that annual global mean temperature meant the annual, day and night, average of all the grid cells in the data set. Most instructors (including the lead author on this paper) would have simply never addressed this issue, as the assumption is made that students know the accurate definition of temperature. Yet, it is very clear that the students' lack of understanding of temperature leads to their inability to conduct the necessary reasoning to make defendable temperature maps. As a result of this insight, a new activity on collecting near-surface temperature was introduced in step 3 for cohort 3. Students in cohort 3 proceeded through the project after the experience of collecting temperature data and knowing Earth is the source of the data.

What are Ridges?

When graphing the Mid-Atlantic Ridge (Figs. 3A and 3B), most students were surprised to discover the ridge topography. On the pretest activity, students explained that divergent boundaries created canyons. Interviews with students revealed the misconception as divergence leading to the separation of plates and subsequent void or "Grand Canyon."

Due to the visual representation of student-selected data, however, the misconception about topography along plate boundaries was then graphically dismissed. This was evident when students were asked to speculate about the topography on convergent boundaries (students then thought about the mechanics of convergence)

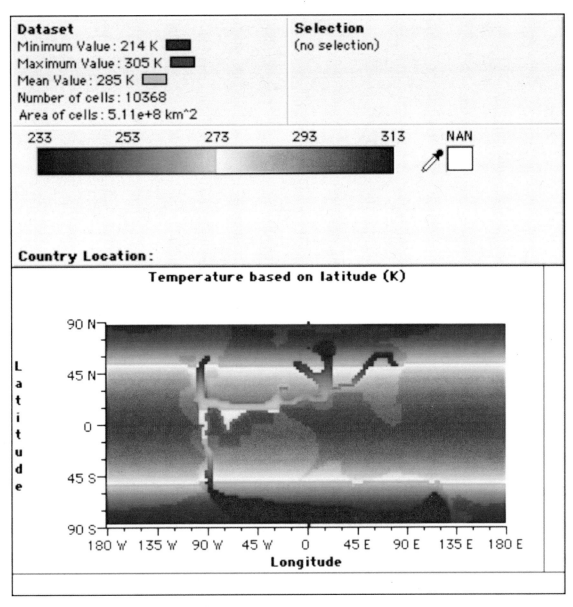

Figure 5. Annual mean temperature of the Late Jurassic as determined from variation in latitude, moist adiabatic lapse rate, and location of deserts. The mean temperature of the data set is 285 K, compared to 286 K today.

and confirm their speculation by using WorldWatcher to create a line graph of topography data across a convergence boundary.

Pushing Their Inquiry Skills: Decisions Regarding the Final Temperature Map

Determining a method for conducting an investigation to understand why the global mean temperature maps were ~6 K less than Royer et al. (2001) proved to be very difficult for students. The instructor provided no guidance on how to conduct the comparison or even how to interpret the results. Most students simply concluded that the global mean temperature in the Late Jurassic would be similar to today's at 286 K (Fig. 5), but could not offer an explanation as to why the estimated mean temperature did not agree

with Royer et al. (2001). Students previously examined the influence of greenhouse gases on temperature by comparing Earth's temperature without an atmosphere to temperature with an atmosphere. Despite the conclusion from Royer et al. (2001) that the Late Jurassic had 3–5 times more CO_2, 80% of the students in cohort 1 (40% in cohort 3, a major improvement) failed to investigate the influence on temperature due to increased greenhouse gases (Fig. 6). Why?

Student Deficiencies

Some students indicated that any errors in calculating temperatures must be in their choice of mathematical operator (i.e., add instead of subtract) in using a mathematical operation in World-

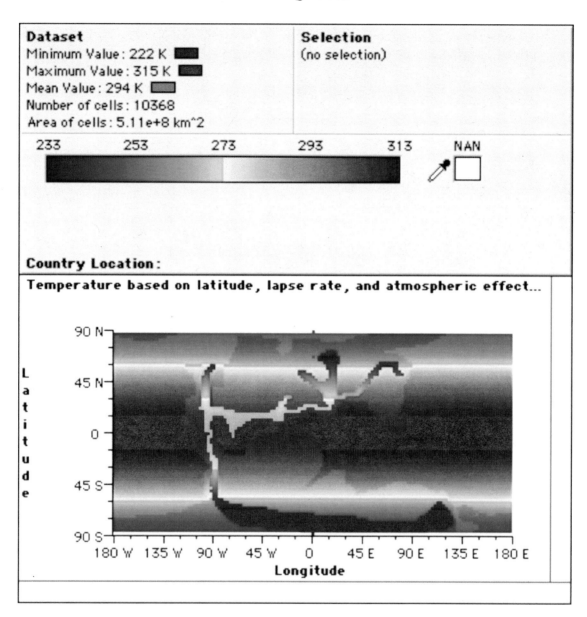

Figure 6. The resulting temperature data set estimated by a 3% atmospheric effect and subsequent increase in global mean temperature due to a doubling of CO_2, based on paleo-CO_2 estimates of Royer et al. (2001).

Watcher or that WorldWatcher had a programming error. The salient questions are: why were the students wrong in this thinking? Why were they unable to determine the cause of their error?

Further evaluation of student responses in interviews and analysis of student project summaries led to the discovery of three major deficiencies on the part of the students. First, students were uncertain about the estimation of data. Students failed to constitute the boundaries of what data was "real." Students were unable to determine if their estimates of temperature were "correct." Students continually sought reassurance from the instructor regarding their predicted temperatures.

The second deficiency was in evaluating causality. Indeed students did recognize changes in value of the numbers while conducting "trial and error" experimentation with data. However, students were generally unable to use content vocabularies to explain why changes occurred (i.e., the lapse rate problem). Students offered simple explanations, such as "I subtracted [this amount]," rather than "an increase in elevation is correlated with a decrease in temperature due to the lapse rate."

A third deficiency was in quantitative reasoning. When interviewed, students indicated one reason they may not have calculated a percent increase in the atmospheric effect with their temperature data is that they did not understand the *impact* of a "3 percent increase" (Fig. 6). Again, students knew mechanically how to do the calculation in WorldWatcher, they just didn't know when to apply the skill.

Each of these deficiencies presents a "teaching moment" for the instructor. The key is recognizing the need to build new vocabularies and provide students with the opportunity to apply the vocabularies. In the scope of this research project, only cohort 3 benefited from teaching moments. As a result, students in cohort 3 indicated in postinterviews that they were more comfortable in their decisions made during steps 5 and 6. Indeed, more students (60% versus 20% for cohorts 1 and 2) were successful in defending their decisions about why the global mean temperature was 6 K warmer during the Late Jurassic. Inadvertently, some students (5%) in cohort 3 actually doubled temperatures due to the doubling of CO_2. Analysis of reflection essays was inconclusive as to why students did not recognize this error.

SUMMARY

Classroom observations, analysis of student reflection papers, and analysis of student project summaries revealed that the occurrence (in writing) of both content and science process vocabularies increased as the course project progressed. However, students struggled with the understanding of the vocabularies, often resulting in their nonuse or misuse. Intervention of an activity where students collected near-surface temperature data focused on the meaning of temperature and improved the students' understanding of temperature when completing their final temperature map. Continued pedagogical intervention on additional content and science process vocabularies was necessary, albeit time consuming.

Analyses of reflection papers from each step in the project indicated improvement in content knowledge for all cohorts. However, regarding the ability to perform complex analysis, which was evaluated in steps 5 and 6, students in cohort 3 performed better on predicting and defending their final temperature maps. Exact reasons for this are speculative. The temperature data collection activity introduced in cohort 3 certainly could have helped, but further research is needed to identify key interventions during class by the instructor, which collectively may have had a greater impact on student success in *using* geoscience vocabularies. In addition, further research is needed to determine the longitudinal impact of the course project on the students' ability to use geoscience vocabularies in the proper context.

ACKNOWLEDGMENT

Research presented in this paper was funded by the National Science Foundation, GEO-0122026.

REFERENCES CITED

Derry, G.N., 1999, What science is and how it works: Princeton, New Jersey, Princeton University Press, 311 p.

Edelson, D.C., 2001, Learning-for-use: A framework for the design of technology-supported inquiry activities: Journal of Research in Science Teaching, v. 38, no. 3, p. 355–385.

Edelson, D., Pitts, V., Salierno, C., and Sherin, B., 2006, this volume, Engineering geosciences learning experiences using the *Learning-for-Use* design framework, *in* Manduca, C., and Mogk, D., eds., Earth and Mind: How Geologists Think and Learn about the Earth: Geological Society of America Special Paper 413, doi: 10.1130/2006.2413(11).

Royer, D.L., Berner, R.A., and Beerling, D.J., 2001, Phanerozoic atmospheric CO change: Evaluating geochemical and paleobiological approaches: Earth-Science Reviews, v. 54, p. 349–392, doi: 10.1016/S0012-8252(00)00042-8.

MANUSCRIPT ACCEPTED BY THE SOCIETY 21 MARCH 2006

Geological Society of America
Special Paper 413
2006

The Hidden Earth—Interactive, computer-based modules for geoscience learning

Stephen J. Reynolds
Michael D. Piburn
Debra E. Leedy*
Carla M. McAuliffe*
James P. Birk
Julia K. Johnson
Arizona State University, Tempe, Arizona 85287-1404, USA

ABSTRACT

Geology is among the most visual of the sciences, and spatial reasoning takes place at various scales and in various contexts. Among the spatial skills required in introductory college geology courses are spatial rotation (rotating objects in one's mind) and spatial visualization (transforming an object in one's mind). Geologic curricula commonly require students to visualize Earth in many ways, such as envisioning landscapes from topographic maps, the interaction of layers and topography, and the progressive development of geologic features over time.

To facilitate learning in introductory college geology laboratories, we created two geologic modules—*Visualizing Topography and Interactive 3D Geologic Blocks.* The modules were developed as learning cycles, where students explore first, are then introduced to terminology and concepts they have observed, and finally apply their knowledge to different, but related problems. Both modules were built around interactive QuickTime Virtual Reality movies that contain landforms and geologic objects that students can manipulate on the computer screen. The topography module pairs topographic maps with their three-dimensional (3D) representations on the same screen, which encourages students to visualize two-dimensional maps as three-dimensional landscapes and to match corresponding features on the map and 3D perspective. The geologic blocks module permits activities that are not possible with normal paper-based curricula, such as interactively rotating, slicing into, eroding, and faulting the blocks. Students can also make the blocks partially transparent to reveal the internal geometry of layers, folds, faults, intrusions, and unconformities. Both modules encourage active participation by having students describe, draw, and predict, and both modules conclude with applications that require the students to extend and apply key concepts to novel situations. Assessment of the modules using control and experimental groups shows that the modules improved student performance on a geospatial test, that general spatial ability can be improved via instruction, and that differences in performance between the genders can be eliminated by a semester-long laboratory.

*Current address, Leedy: Glendale Community College, 6000 W. Olive Avenue, Glendale, Arizona 85302, USA. Current address, McAuliffe: TERC, 2067 Massachusetts Avenue, Cambridge, Massachusetts 02140, USA.

Reynolds, S.J., Piburn, M.D., Leedy, D.E., McAuliffe, C.M., Birk, J.P., and Johnson, J.K., 2006, The Hidden Earth—Interactive, computer-based modules for geoscience learning, *in* Manduca, C.A., and Mogk, D.W., eds., Earth and Mind: How Geologists Think and Learn about the Earth: Geological Society of America Special Paper 413, p. 157–170, doi: 10.1130/2006.2413(12). For permission to copy, contact editing@geosociety.org. ©2006 Geological Society of America. All rights reserved.

"To go out into the field with a geologist is to witness a type of alchemy, as stones are made to speak. Geologists imaginatively reclaim worlds from the stone they're trapped within."
–Frodeman (1996, p. 417).

Keywords: geoscience education, visualization, topographic map, geologic structure.

INTRODUCTION

Geology is arguably the most visual of the sciences. Visualization by geologists takes place at a variety of scales, ranging from the region to the outcrop to the thin section. Many geologists have the ability to mentally transport themselves rapidly from one scale to another, using observations at one scale to constrain a problem that arises at another scale. Observations from the outcrop are used to construct a regional geologic framework, which in turn guides what features are looked for and recognized at the outcrop (Frodeman, 1996). Observations at two spatially separate outcrops may lead the geologist to visualize a major, regional anticline, along with its hidden subsurface geometry, its eroded-away projections into air, and perhaps even a causative thrust fault at depth.

Spatial skills can be challenging for some students, but our experience has shown that several education strategies help alleviate these challenges. The first strategy is use of a learning-cycle approach in introducing new concepts. A typical learning cycle has three phases (Lawson, 1995): an exploration phase, a term- and concept-introduction phase, and an application phase. In the initial, exploration phase, students have the opportunity to observe and explore concepts and phenomena, unencumbered by an overemphasis on technical terms. Once the students have personal experience with the topics, the instructor guides students in acquiring meanings of terms and understandings of concepts (term and concept introduction). Finally, in the application phase, the students apply their new experiences, conceptual knowledge, and terminology to different, but related problems.

A second strategy is structuring curricula so that students interact with each other and have a chance to explore and discuss topics in a nonthreatening, peer-to-peer setting (Macdonald and Korinek, 1995). Such interactions require students to verbalize their thinking as they attempt to solve problems, allowing students to more thoroughly express and explore uncertainties and to gain confidence via peer-to-peer feedback, mediated by the instructor.

SPATIAL VISUALIZATION IN GEOLOGY

Practicing geologists engage in many kinds of spatial-visual activities. Much of classical geology is concerned with understanding the distribution, both on the surface and at depth, of geologic units, geologic structures, and natural resources. To help them visualize these distributions, geologists have developed various kinds of maps, diagrams, and other graphical representations of geologic data (Rudwick, 1976; Davis and Reynolds,

1996). Geologists use these types of illustrations to help them visualize landscapes, surficial and subsurface geology, and geologic changes over time.

Geologists use topographic maps to visualize the shape of the land surface from contours. To do this, a geologist must mentally transform the abstract, two-dimensional map, with its squiggly contour lines, into a three-dimensional landscape. Geologists perform a similar spatial transformation by visualizing the landscape from a two-dimensional aerial photograph. In this case, geologists use visual clues from the aerial photo, such as shadows, the typical appearance of streams and other features, and a mental picture of what the landscape "ought to look like."

Geologists rely extensively on geologic maps, which show the types and ages of rock units exposed on the surface, as well as faults, folds, and other geologic structures. Most geologic maps incorporate a topographic base map so that geologic features can be referenced to their actual elevation and location on the map. A geologist examining a geologic map will alternately focus on the geology and the topography to construct a mental picture of how the two are related. This mental process is a type of selective focus or disembedding, in which one aspect is mentally isolated from a multifaceted context. Geologists disembed when they look at landscapes, outcrops, or thin sections, isolating and focusing on the important aspects and paying less attention to the background noise present in every geologic scene.

From a geologic map, geologists may construct an interpretive geologic cross section or a three-dimensional portrayal of the geologic architecture. Geologists use cross sections to visualize the subsurface geology, to reconstruct the geologic history, and to explore for natural resources by determining the depth to a specific coal-bearing layer, copper deposit, or oil field. This ability to visualize the geometry of rock bodies within the solid, opaque Earth is essential to practicing geologists, and has been recognized by visualization researchers as an aptitude called visual penetrative ability (Kali and Orion, 1996). Beginning geology students have great difficulty visually penetrating geologic objects, such as those portrayed on block diagrams. Many students simply cannot envision the three-dimensional geometry from the two-dimensional clues on the sides and tops of geologic blocks.

Geologists also construct a sequence of diagrams to illustrate successive geologic changes in an area. Many geologic processes require so much time that humans are not around long enough to observe any significant changes in the landscape. To approach this problem, geologists have developed the technique of "trading location for time." By this we mean that geologists look at several present-day areas and mentally arrange these into a sequence interpreted to represent an evolutionary sequence through time. A narrow deep canyon, for example, is interpreted to be a younger phase of landscape development than an area that has been eroded down into a series of low, subdued hills.

SPATIAL VISUALIZATION IN GEOLOGY COURSES

One of the main goals of a geology course is to teach students how to visualize geology in a way similar to practicing geologists. When the Laboratory for Introductory Geology at our university was redesigned, we decided to restrict the course to those aspects that are most important to real geologists and that best exemplify geologic problem solving. Students now learn how to:

- construct, read, and visualize topographic and geologic maps;
- visualize geology in the subsurface;
- visualize and reconstruct past environments from rocks and minerals;
- reconstruct geologic history from rocks, minerals, and maps; and
- understand the implications of geology for society.

Most of the laboratory course was designed to be a situated-learning environment, where learning takes place in the context of a large, complex problem. In this case, we created a virtual world called *Painted Canyon*, which is imaginary but closely modeled after the geology of the Southwest United States, where our campus is located. Most learning about maps, minerals, rocks, geologic structures, and reconstructing geologic history is centered on trying to understand the geology of Painted Canyon (Fig. 1), with a final goal of determining where to site a hypothetical human colony and acquire the natural resources needed to build and sustain a colony. This approach is very different than that of a traditional laboratory exercise, where learning about topographic and geologic maps is commonly decoupled from study of minerals and rocks, and the map-mineral-rock knowledge is not later applied to solve a problem.

To help students understand and visualize topographic maps, students construct a contour map by successively filling with water a plastic box containing a plastic mountain and drawing a map of the shoreline at each water level. After they have used such concrete manipulatives, the students interact on the computer with a module entitled *Visualizing Topography*. This

Figure 1. Perspective view of *Painted Canyon*, a virtual three-dimensional (3D) world within which student learning is situated.

experience is reinforced by having students use topographic maps throughout the semester to locate rock and mineral samples and decide which areas have safe slopes for situating a colony.

To help students better visualize the three-dimensional geometries of geologic structures, students interact with another computer-based module entitled *Interactive 3D Geologic Blocks*. This module helps students explore how geologic structures, such as inclined layers, will intersect the top and sides of 3D geologic blocks.

To help students understand and visualize geologic maps, they construct their own geologic map, on a topographic base, from three-dimensional perspectives of Painted Canyon (e.g., Fig. 1). To complete this map, students need to (1) recognize how geology and topography interact, (2) draw lines on the topographic map that correspond to boundaries between geologic units on the perspectives, and (3) reconstruct the order in which the rock units and geologic structures were formed. The students then use this geologic map to construct a cross section of the units in the subsurface and to determine the impacts of geology on the colony they must site.

After studying Painted Canyon, students have a chance to apply these skills to several interesting and real places in the Southwest. They use, in an integrative way, topographic maps, geologic maps, and rock samples from these places to reconstruct the geologic history.

The last several weeks of the laboratory are devoted to having students use geologic information to solve other geologic problems, such as identifying the source of groundwater contamination. For these exercises, students again use contour maps, but this time of the elevation of the water table, to determine the direction of groundwater flow. Students also go on a local field trip to make their own observations in the field and use a topographic base map to construct a geologic map and cross section. Finally, the students visit the map library to use topographic and geologic maps to write a report on the geology of their hometown. The field and library assignments give the students an opportunity to apply what they have learned throughout the semester.

VISUALIZATION MODULES IN GEOLOGY

These two comprehensive modules, described in the previous section, were created to address specific learning problems common among introductory geology students. The purpose of these modules was to enhance students' spatial-visualization skills in the context of real problems presented to geologists. The skills specifically targeted were spatial visualization, spatial orientation, visual penetrative ability (Kali and Orion, 1996), and the ability to reconstruct the sequence of geologic events. Both modules were constructed using a learning-cycle approach where students explore a concept, are introduced to the term or concept discovered during exploration, and then apply the concept in a new situation.

In both modules, virtual 3D objects were created, animated, and rendered using the program *Bryce* (1999) and exported as

QuickTime Virtual Reality (QTVR) files. *Bryce* uses sophisticated rendering techniques, such as ray tracing, to create the illusion of three-dimensional objects by using depth perception and varying lighting and shading. Contour maps of hills, valleys, and other real geologic features were draped over digital topography, using *Bryce*, to create the appearance of three-dimensional topography while simultaneously showing contour lines.

Movies were created to rotate around various axes depending on the purpose of a module's section. All QTVR movies were created by rendering image sequences in *Bryce* and importing them into an Apple QTVR object movie. The layout of images in a QTVR object movie is like a grid or matrix (Fig. 2), with rows and columns. In a QTVR object movie, clicking and dragging horizontally moves from image to image in a row, whereas clicking and dragging vertically moves within a column. In our case, a row generally consisted of images depicting a type of motion, such as rotation or slicing, while moving within a column allowed further rotations (about another axis) or changing aspects such as shading, rotations, transparency, deposition of layers, erosion, and the amount of faulting.

Both modules were designed to be interactive, to promote active learning, and to avoid mindless screen-turning. Students progressing through the modules in an active way should retain more information and understand more content than would students passively reading a series of screens or watching a series of noninteractive animations. During initial piloting of the modules, we quickly discovered that students would stop and read two lines of text, but would be more likely to skip the text entirely as its length increased. As a result, most text in the modules was shortened to one or two lines.

Worksheets were designed to maximize interactivity by requiring active involvement, such as sketching, predicting, and describing. In addition, students worked in pairs and were asked at specific places in the modules to discuss their observations and predictions with one another. To encourage such discussion, most questions were open-ended questions or asked students to observe, interpret, and draw features they have seen on screen. The worksheets served as a focus of discussion between students.

Visualizing Topography Module

The first module, called *Visualizing Topography* (http://reynolds.asu.edu/topo_gallery/), focused on the skills required to visualize, understand, and use topographic maps and contour lines, such as identifying key features, identifying elevation changes, recognizing correspondence between the map and 3D perspectives, wayfinding, and constructing topographic profiles. Students' difficulties arose from an inability to understand three-dimensional perspectives depicted by two-dimensional representations. Students were given topographic maps with four unique movie types, which (1) controlled the amount of shading in a black and white contour map draped over digital topography, (2) rotated colored contour maps draped over landscapes to gain a top view or side view, (3) raised and lowered virtual water levels on 3D terrains, and (4) sliced

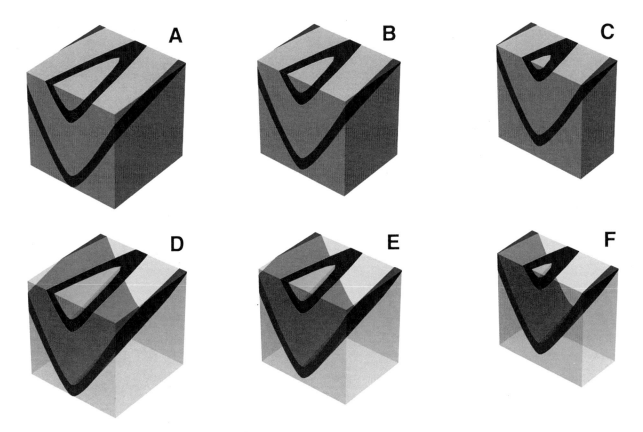

Figure 2. Matrix arrangement of images in a QuickTime Virtual Reality (QTVR) object movie, where clicking and dragging horizontally moves from image to image in a row, whereas clicking and dragging vertically moves within a column. In both rows, the user can slice into a block to reveal its internal geometry, but the block is partially transparent in the bottom row.

into terrains to show how topographic profiles relate to spacing of contour lines and elevation changes. Figures 3, 4, 5, and 6 show a simple hill landscape represented by each mode, respectively. This module was designed to cover three simple landscapes (hill, valley, and cliff) commonly encountered when reading and interpreting topographic maps. These three landscapes were presented with the four movie types to encourage the visualization of simple features in three dimensions.

Movies were created to show the three-dimensionality of landscapes. The shading movies, both black and white and colored, were given the appearance of shadows using a proper direction of illumination in *Bryce* (Figs. 3B and 4B). Students could directly compare a flat, two-dimensional map with a three-dimensional map to draw a parallel between specific points and features on the two maps. The ability to see valleys and peaks in terms of shade and light allowed to students to discover the relationship between shapes of contour lines and the topographic features they represent.

The first few pages of the module define the terms "topography" and "topographic maps," and provide navigation suggestions. Then, the module illustrates the different types of movies users will see within the module (e.g., movies that play auto-

matically versus those that require student action). This module grouped similar types of movies and visualization issues, so that students adapted to each type of movie and became familiar with the way in which each type of movie allowed them to inspect the landscape. This also allowed discussion questions to focus on the important aspects depicted by an animation and enabled students to compare and contrast the different landscape features (e.g., hill versus valley).

Most screens in the module are shown in a split-screen mode where the left half of the screen is a topographic map of the landscape being studied and the right half contains one of the movies. Figures 3A and 3B appear on one screen together. Both images on these split screens begin in identical orientations and scales so students can compare the contour lines. As the user clicks and drags the mouse upward in the movie on the right, the amount of shading increases as the sun angle changes. Students immediately notice the appearance of hills, valleys, or cliffs, as well as high- and low-elevation points.

The second type of movies shows colored topographic contours in which the movie rotates both vertically and horizontally, providing students with top, side, and oblique views of the shaded landscape (Fig. 4). Students are then asked open-ended

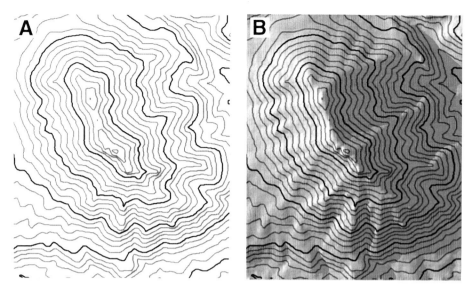

Figure 3. (A) Two-dimensional topographic map of a simple hill. (B) Shading movie where users click and drag the mouse up and down to increase and decrease the amount of shading.

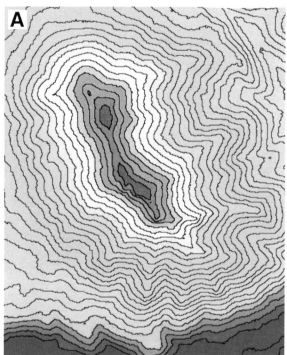

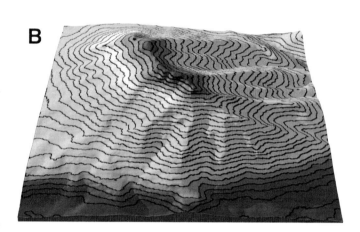

Figure 4. (A) Two-dimensional topographic map with color-coded elevations. (B) Rotating and shading movie. Clicking and dragging the mouse up and down rotates vertically while changing the amount of shading. The landscape can be rotated horizontally by dragging sideways.

discussion questions that require observation and interpretation. The questions below represent the types of questions asked about a still image of each landscape.

- Can you now envision what this terrain looks like based on the map?
- What is the hill's overall shape?
- What are some of the finer details of its shape?
- Is it the same steepness on all sides?
- Is it aligned in some direction?

After seeing several such movies, students can discuss details in depth and modify any answers that were debated or unresolved. Students are then asked to write, on their worksheet,

a clear verbal description for someone who has never seen each feature. They are provided suggestions as to how to describe a landscape and ultimately are shown a sample description written by a field geologist.

The next type of movie for visualizing three-dimensional features is one in which terrain is flooded with virtual water (see Fig. 5A). By clicking and dragging vertically in the movie, users can raise and lower the virtual water level, which is parallel to the contour lines. The correspondence of the horizontal water plane and a contour reinforces the idea that each contour line represents a single elevation. Also, seeing the interaction of water and terrains helps students isolate and visualize basic features within an

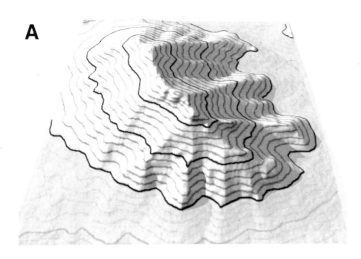

Figure 5. (A) Flooding movie. Users change the water level by clicking and dragging up and down. (B) Slicing terrains movie. Users change the depth of cut by clicking and dragging up and down.

overall landscape. This interactive section allows students to set the water level at a contour line that might have previously been confusing for them. For example, students that do not understand how closely spaced contour lines can represent a cliff can come to understand this concept when they can alter the water level themselves. After students interact with each feature, they are again asked to describe how the water flooded the area, using the questions below:

- Where does it flood first? Where does it flood last?
- What pattern does the water make when it is halfway up the slopes?

After interacting with several flooding movies, students are asked to verbally describe how the land would flood over time. This verbal description marks the end of the exploration phase of a learning cycle. This is followed by a section of the module that defines contour lines and index contours and that represents the term- and concept-introduction phase of the learning cycle.

The last type of movie consists of topographic profiles produced when students click and drag to slice into the virtual terrain (Fig. 5B). Then, students are shown a two-dimensional representation of a landscape with a line drawn on it and are asked to show an elevation profile that corresponds to that path (Fig. 6). Several types of movies (showing increasing shading, rotating colored topographic maps, or slicing into terrains) are provided to help students determine the correct profile.

The computer-based module is followed up by a complex, map-based problem that students must solve with their topographic map skills. Using the contour map of Painted Canyon, students must (1) design a road up a hill, ensuring that the road nowhere exceeds a 10% grade, or (2) determine the optimal location for an aqueduct to drive a power plant. This part of the module represents the application phase of the learning cycle and guides the student into solving a problem with real-world applications.

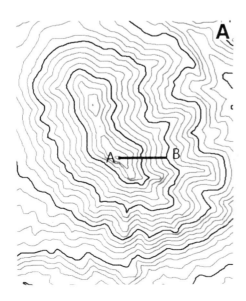

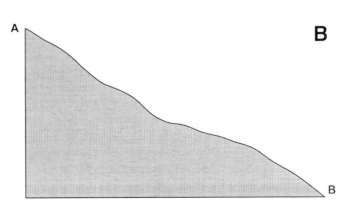

Figure 6. In the application phase of the learning cycle, students are asked to predict what profiles across the three featured landscapes would look like if they were to hike along indicated paths.

During the course of the module, students have interacted with different types of movies (e.g., shading versus flooding) for each type of landscape feature (e.g., hill, valley). We believe, but have not specifically assessed, that having students observe and interact with such multiple representations helps students build a more complete mental image of each type of feature.

Interactive 3D Geologic Blocks Module

The interactive blocks module focused on developing students' visual penetrative ability, which is essential for the process of reconstructing the structural geometry and geologic history of an area. A crucial step in understanding the geologic history of an area requires the ability to reconstruct the sequence of events from oldest to youngest. This involves interpreting and visualizing the order of different events, such as layer deposition, folding, faulting, and intrusion. In nature, many geologic features are buried beneath the surface leaving only partial structures on which to base conclusions. The blocks module was designed to help students visualize how geologic features exposed on the surface

would continue into the subsurface. Animation techniques used to accomplish this include the rotation of blocks, making blocks partially transparent, slicing into blocks, offsetting faults, eroding the tops and sides of blocks, depositing layers, and revealing unconformities.

The 3D blocks Web site (http://reynolds.asu.edu/blocks) contains the module the students used, as well as links to instructional information such as (1) pages that list individual movies to allow instructors and students to access movies without entering the module, and (2) links to Word and PDF files of the worksheets that accompany the module. A worksheet was developed for each of the five main sections in the module (Fig. 7).

In the introduction to the module, students receive instruction on navigation, examples of the different types of movies, and how the faces of blocks will be labeled (front, back, left, right, top, and bottom). After this introduction, students can explore any of five types of geologic structures: layers, folds, faults, intrusions, and unconformities. Students are informed that the topics are easiest to cover in the order presented in the menu (layers, then folds, faults, intrusions, and unconformities), but if

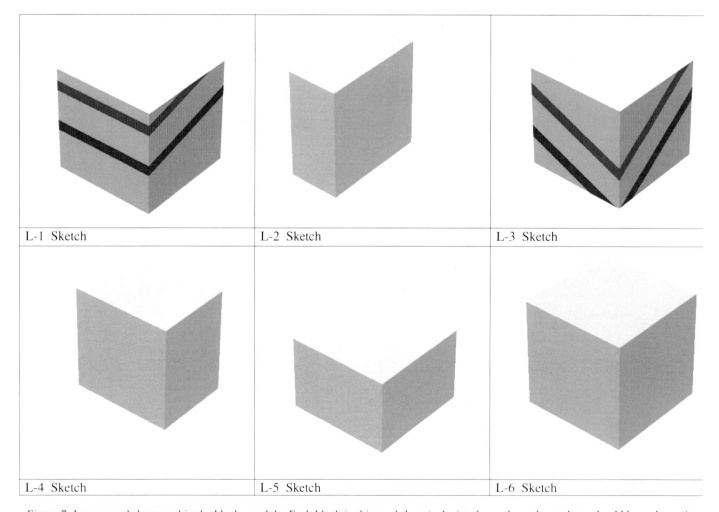

Figure 7. Layers worksheet used in the blocks module. Each block in this worksheet is depicted exactly as the students should have drawn it, such as showing their prediction of what a block would look like if it were sliced in half.

one section has already been covered or is too simplistic, it can easily be skipped.

For this module, 3D block models were constructed within *Bryce* using Boolean operations, such as showing a layer only if it was contained within a block. Boolean subtraction allowed one block to slice into another and through any geologic structures. A master animation file contained steps with all the possible depictions, such as rotating the block in 10-degree increments, both for an opaque block and a transparent one, hiding each visible face with a white plane, and slicing into the block from two sides and the top. This animation file rendered a sequence of 206 images for each geologic block, and these images were then combined in various ways into a QTVR matrix. One-row movies commonly permit the user to rotate a block or slice into a static block, whereas multirow movies allow other combinations, such as rotations and changing transparency. This format permits students to interactively control the type and speed of changes that occur, allowing students to learn at *their* optimal rate.

For each type of geologic structure, the module has movies for different orientations of this kind of structure. For example, the layers part of the module includes layers with horizontal, gentle, moderate, steep, and vertical dips. For each orientation, students are commonly asked to make a prediction, such as to predict how the layers continue from visible to hidden faces of the block. Alternatively, students are shown a block with a "cutting plane" intersecting it and are asked to sketch how the block would appear if it was cut along this plane (Fig. 8C). The purpose of a cutting plane is to cut into a block and understand how features are configured within the block. In various movies, students can cut left to right, right to left, or top to bottom to fully understand orientations of features inside the blocks. Figure 8 shows examples of blocks for horizontal layers. To check their predictions, students have access to various types of movies, such as those which rotate, change the transparency of, or slice into a block.

Online quizzes are integrated into the module at the end of each section so students can immediately apply what they have learned and receive feedback as they proceed. Quizzes include a variety of questions, including multiple choice, sketches, and prediction, closely aligned to the types of questions asked through-

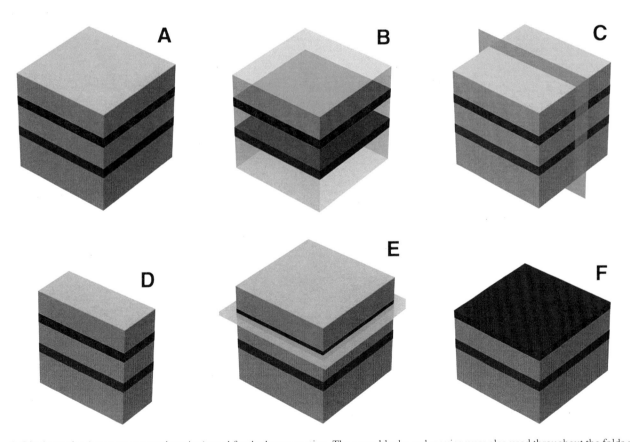

Figure 8. Block movies (transparency and cutting) used for the layers section. The same blocks and movies were also used throughout the folds section. (A) Opaque block with horizontal layers students can rotate. (B) Same block as in A that students can rotate and change transparency. (C) Left cutting plane. Students are instructed to cut into the block from left to right. (D) Left cutting plane movie. The block has been cut into 2/3 of the way. (E) Top cutting plane. Students can cut into the block from top to bottom. (F) Top cutting plane movie. The block has been cut into 1/3 of the way.

out each section. Where possible, feedback is given for questions and follow-on movies allow students to verify their own answers. The last question in each quiz asks students to draw a block that would be consistent with a given series of geologic events. In the laboratory exercises, this question certainly elicited the best discussions within teams and clearly assessed if students could visualize geologic features and a sequence of events.

The folds section proceeds exactly as the layers section—with the same progression of screens and the same types of movies: rotations, transparency, cutting side to side and top to bottom. Movies are included for horizontal and plunging anticlines and synclines.

The faults section consists of several subsections: types of faults, faulted layers, and faulted folds. The types-of-faults subsection contains images and movies of dip-slip, strike-slip, and oblique-slip faults. Subsequent movies permit taking a fault-containing block and progressively rotating it, changing transparency, increasing the offset on faults, and eroding into the block (Fig. 9).

The next section of the module covers intrusions. The main types of movies are rotations, changing transparency, and cutting from top to bottom in a block. These movies are intended to help students see that plutons are irregular, whereas dikes and sills are more planar, and to understand how the level of erosion influences the map view of each type of intrusion (Fig. 10). The questions in this section's quiz are integrative, focusing on having students reconstruct geologic histories from a series of

events, including formation of layers, folds, faults, and intrusions. Students use rotating blocks with complex geologic histories to reconstruct the sequence of events in the order in which they must have occurred.

The last section covers unconformities, in combination with other geologic structures seen earlier in the module. For example, a block might contain faulted folds that were eroded and then overlain by new layers. Students can click and drag the mouse to remove the layers above the unconformity and observe the geometry of the underlying structures. At the end of this section, and thus the end of the blocks module, students take an integrated quiz. Questions ask students to reconstruct a geologic history, predict what an unconformity will look like, sketch a block for a sequence of events, and interpret geologic events from an image taken in the field (Fig. 11). The application phase of the module includes the integrated quiz and having students apply their "blocks knowledge" to geologic maps and cross sections for a real area in the Southwest United States.

EVALUATION

The complete details of the evaluation of the Hidden Earth project have been described in separate publications (Piburn et al., 2002, 2005). Consequently, we will include here only the most important details and results.

The evaluation was completed in four introductory geology laboratory sections taught during a summer session. Two were

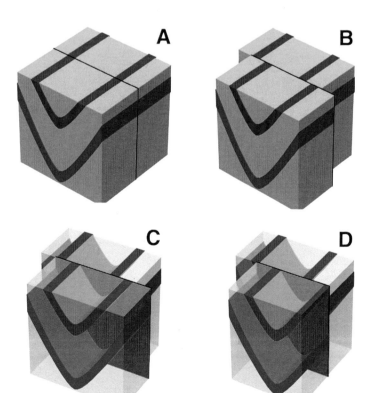

Figure 9. Four blocks showing the progressive types of movies covered in the faults section of the blocks module. These four blocks specifically show a horizontal syncline offset by a left-lateral strike-slip fault. (A) Original image of opaque block with horizontal syncline folds in faults section. (B) Same block as in A now offset by a strike-slip fault. (C) Same block as in B now made partially transparent. (D) Same block as in C now eroded on the front right side to make that face even.

scheduled from 7 to 9 a.m. and two from 11 a.m. to 1 p.m. Each section was taught by a different teaching assistant. One section from each time was chosen as a control group, and the other as an experimental group.

Students were pretested with two measures of spatial ability and with a geospatial test that was created to match the contents of the introductory laboratory manual. The experimental group experienced the topographic map and geologic block computer modules, while the control group did related, noncomputer-based exercises. At the end of the five week summer session, students in both the control and the experimental groups were tested again with all three instruments.

Both control and experimental groups improved in their mastery of the laboratory material as evidenced by their scores on the geospatial test. However, there was a significant difference between those students who had completed the Hidden Earth modules and those who had not, with the performance of the experimental group exceeding that of the control group.

One indication of the difference between these groups is a comparison of normalized gain scores. Normalized gain is computed by dividing the amount of improvement (post-test minus pretest) by the total room for improvement (total score minus pretest). Mean gain scores in the experimental group were 60%, while those in the control group were only 45%.

There were also important differences between the performance of males and females in the laboratories. There were significant initial differences between the genders on all instruments on the pretest, with males beginning with higher scores than females. However, by the end of the experiment, scores of the two groups were identical. When gain scores were compared for all students, females improved by 56%, while males only improved by 48%.

The spatial measures used in this study were the Cube Comparisons Test and the Surface Development Test, both taken from the Kit of Factor-Referenced Cognitive Tests published by Educational Testing Service (Ekstrom et al., 1976). In the first test, students were asked to rotate in their mind a cube with symbols on the sides. It is a measure of spatial orientation. In the second test, they were asked to fold a planar view of a figure into a three-dimensional figure. It is a measure of spatial visualization.

The Hidden Earth modules had no demonstrable effect on performance on the Cube Comparisons Test. However, there was a significant difference between control and experimental groups on the Surface Development Test, with the experimental group improving significantly over the control group. In a regression equation that included both measures, the Surface Development Test alone explained a significant portion of the increased performance of the experimental group on the geospatial test.

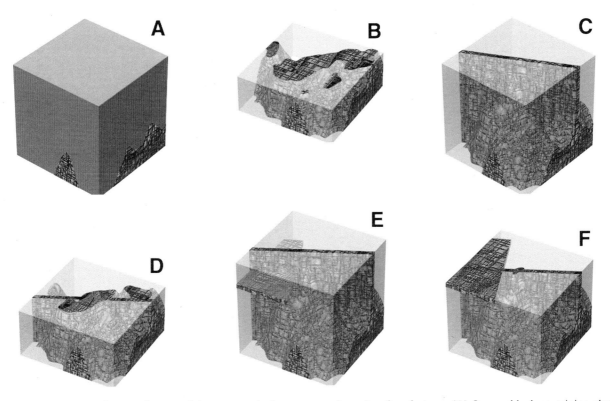

Figure 10. Blocks in intrusions section containing progressively more complex subsurface features. (A) Opaque block containing pluton. (B) Partially transparent block cut from top to reveal pluton. (C) Partially transparent block of pluton and dike. (D) Partially transparent block of pluton and dike cut from top to reveal intersection. (E) Partially transparent block of pluton, dike, and sill. (F) Partially transparent block of pluton, dike, and sill, cut from the top.

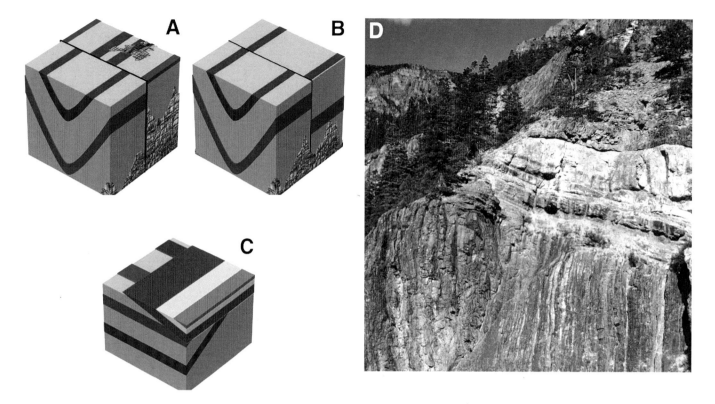

Figure 11. Integrative quiz questions given at the end of the intrusions and unconformities sections. (A) Integrative quiz question asking students to place the events (faulting versus intrusion) in the order they must have happened. (B) Integrative quiz question asking students to place the events (faulting versus intrusion) in the order they must have happened. (C) Integrative quiz question asking students to place events (tilting of layers, erosion, or unconformity) in the order they must have happened. (D) Field-related question asking students to identify the key events that occurred to form this feature and the order in which they occurred.

DISCUSSION

"Reform of science education must be predicated on research on learning and teaching materials and practices that are developed from that research."

–Geoscience Education Working Group (1997)

This project demonstrated that a curriculum based on interactive visualizations can improve spatial ability, lead to improved learning about spatial aspects of geology, and eliminate differences in performance between the genders. To achieve these gains, we began by determining what we wanted students to be able to do and redesigning the entire laboratory from scratch to emphasize these goals and objectives. Next, we used results from education and cognitive research, along with our experience in such laboratories, to anticipate the spatial aspects with which students would have the most difficulty. We then created a set of innovative, computer-based materials, built around interactive QuickTime Virtual Reality movies that portrayed the 3D nature of geology. We imbedded these visual materials into multimedia-based curricula structured as learning cycles, where students undertook explorations before receiving formal terms and concept explanations. Each learning cycle culminated in an appli-

cation of the learned concepts and skills to realistic problems. The materials are available on the web (http://reynolds.asu.edu), have been distributed via optical media to colleges and universities from Arizona to Papua New Guinea, and form the core of a K–12 curriculum on topographic maps (http://www.terc.edu). Instructors have the flexibly of using the QTVR movies in a fully tested module or as stand-alone visualizations in a laboratory, web-based, or even lecture setting, to suit their own pedagogical objectives and philosophies.

The effectiveness of these materials has been demonstrated using intact laboratory sections as control and experimental groups. In this study, students improved their spatial-visualization skills (as measured by the Surface Development Test), but evidently not their spatial-orientation abilities. Spatial visualization is a significant predictor of the amount of spatially related geologic content learned, and visualization and prior knowledge had equal power in a regression equation in predicting postinstruction geospatial test scores. This demonstrates the importance of spatial ability, especially the ability to transform an image, in the learning of geology.

Many questions linger about the nature of spatial orientation and visualization and how these interact with learning. Other spatial factors, such as disembedding and visual penetrative ability (Kali and Orion, 1996), are extremely important to geologists, but were not directly specifically assessed by our study. We have developed materials that specifically address each of these abilities, but these have not yet been implemented in a carefully controlled research experiment. For example, our geologic block movies, with the ability to make a block partially transparent, directly support improvement of visual penetrative ability, but only a few questions on the geospatial test assess this ability. The entire suite of spatial abilities, with the possible exception of spatial orientation, has an important influence on learning in geology courses and should be considered when teaching geology and designing geologic curricula.

In general, technology is expensive and difficult to use, and not clearly superior to more traditional methods of instruction. It is our opinion that the superiority of computer-based education only becomes evident in cases where it is not possible to deliver the instruction by any other means.

A case in point is the *Visualizing Topography* module in this study. The geology department at our university for years has been using the "volcano in a box" laboratory, which originated many years ago with the Earth Science Curriculum Project. However, a wide range of landforms that students could explore in the same way is not available. We are able to render virtually any topographic feature in the world into a three-dimensional, terrain that can be manipulated and flooded with virtual water. In addition, we have been able to create many new ways for students to manipulate these images that are not possible with a physical model.

The same is true for the geologic blocks module. A teaching laboratory typically has only one or two types of three-dimensional blocks for students' perusal. We have been able to produce dozens of interactive 3D geologic blocks with an exceptionally wide variety of features. These virtual blocks allow students to do things, like making the blocks transparent, that are impossible (or at least prohibitively expensive) to do with physical models.

Our modules illustrate how such computer-based instructional materials may be implemented in a constructivist context and assessed in a controlled experiment. Using the modules, students first have the opportunity to observe various images and fully explore the interactive movies. In accordance with constructivist principles, the modules were designed for small-group learning, although use by a solitary student is also possible. The modules ask students to create mental representations and discuss these with their partner(s) in their own words. By asking students to describe what they envision, we hope to help students become better at using multiple representations and at transforming one type of representation (e.g., a mental spatial one) into a different mode of representation (e.g., a verbal one).

One of the characteristics of science curricula since the reform movement of the 1960s has been their attempt to accurately portray the nature of science. This was commonly expressed as a concern for the structure of the discipline (Bruner, 1960). Initially, this took form as something approximating what is usually described as the "scientific method," and curricula taught students to observe, infer, and test hypotheses. More recently, science educators have recognized significant differences among scientists working under different paradigms, and have come to see that there may be many structures of this discipline we call science.

We have been trying to emphasize what we believe is a structure of the discipline of geology that is especially important, and perhaps more so in this case than in other sciences. Geologists use time and space to construct theories about Earth. While the more traditional processes of science remain important, they are to some extent subordinated to the temporal-spatial reasoning that we think is characteristic of geology.

We believe that instruction should be anchored in authentic contexts and faithful to the structure of the geological sciences. Unfortunately, introductory courses at the college and university level are often disconnected collections of topics with no apparent coherence, and the tasks given to students in the laboratory bear little resemblance to the work of practicing scientists. We have tried to create a single unifying structure in which we situate instruction. Painted Canyon, a computer-generated terrain, is the context within which our students learn geology. We try to represent the thought process of the geologist through series of tasks for students that are similar to those being undertaken by practicing geologists.

This study challenges some conventional methods of teaching science. We suggest that students need to be engaged actively in realistic settings that are like those experienced by geologists themselves. Student learning about maps, geologic structures, and other topics should be imbedded in a realistic context rather than as a series of unrelated, out-of-context lessons. Rather than dealing entirely in verbal forms of learning, student should engage all of their mental faculties, including, but not limited to, spatial visualization. We further suggest that having students construct multiple representations of geologic features will allow them to better create mental constructs of prototypical features (e.g., hills, valleys, synclines) and employ these in solving real geologic problems.

Finally, engaging in situated activities helps students to develop a set of intellectual skills that are demonstrably important to the learning of science and to the practice of geology, and it gives them some sense of what it is like to be a geologist. That, it seems to us, is among the most important goals of any course in laboratory science.

ACKNOWLEDGMENTS

This material is based upon work supported by the National Science Foundation under grants EAR-9907733 and DUE-0127595. Any opinions, findings, and conclusions or recommendations expressed in this material are those of the author(s) and do not necessarily reflect the views of the National Science Foundation. We thank Ann Bykerk-Kaufman, Kim Kastens, and Steven Semken for helpful reviews, and Dave Mogk and Cathy

Manduca for organizing a number of workshops and symposia where we have interacted with and learned from our cognitive, educational, and geologic colleagues.

REFERENCES CITED

Bruner, J., 1960, The importance of structure, *in* The process of education: Cambridge, Massachusetts, Harvard University Press, 97 p.

Bryce4 [Computer Software], 1999, Toronto, Corel Corporation.

Davis, G.H., and Reynolds, S.J., 1996, Structural geology of rocks and regions (2nd ed): New York, John Wiley & Sons, Inc., 776 p.

Ekstrom, R., French, J., Harman, H., and Dermen, D., 1976, Manual for Kit of Factor Referenced Cognitive Tests: Princeton, New Jersey, Educational Testing Service.

Frodeman, R.L., 1996, Envisioning the outcrop: Journal of Geoscience Education, v. 44, p. 417–427.

Kali, Y., and Orion, N., 1996, Spatial abilities of high-school students and the perception of geologic structures: Journal of Research in Science Teaching, v. 33, p. 369–391, doi: 10.1002/(SICI)1098-2736(199604)33:4<369::AID-TEA2>3.0.CO;2-Q.

Lawson, A., 1995, Science teaching and the development of thinking: Belmont, California, Wadsworth, 624 p.

Macdonald, R.H., and Korinek, L., 1995, Cooperative-learning activities in large entry-level geology courses: Journal of Geological Education, v. 43, p. 341–345.

Piburn, M.D., Reynolds, S.J., Leedy, D.E., McAuliffe, C., Birk, J.E., and Johnson, J.K., 2002, The Hidden Earth: Visualization of geologic features and their subsurface geometry: Paper accompanying presentation to national meeting of National Association of Research in Science Teaching (NARST), New Orleans, Louisiana, 47 p., with CD-ROM.

Piburn, M., Reynolds, S., McAuliffe, C., Leedy, D., Birk, J., and Johnson, J., 2005, The role of visualization in learning from computer-based images: International Journal of Science Education, v. 27, p. 513–527.

Rudwick, M.J.S., 1976, The emergence of a visual language for geological science 1760–1840: History of Science, v. 14, p. 149–195.

MANUSCRIPT ACCEPTED BY THE SOCIETY 21 MARCH 2006

Geological Society of America
Special Paper 413
2006

STELLA modeling as a tool for understanding the dynamics of earth systems

David M. Bice[†]

Department of Geosciences, Pennsylvania State University, University Park, Pennsylvania 16802, USA

ABSTRACT

Earth system science represents an important new way of looking at our planet, but it is difficult to help students learn, in an experiential mode, about the complex dynamics of earth systems. Here, I describe how the computer program STELLA can be used to construct and then experiment with a variety models to illustrate some important concepts of systems dynamics. A very simple model of a bath tub with a faucet and a drain serves to illustrate a wide range of systems concepts including residence time, response time, lag times, and feedback mechanisms. Variations on the bath tub model provide examples that illustrate the problem of model complexity versus simplicity. A more complicated model of the global carbon cycle is used to demonstrate one means of model validation, testing the model against the historical record of CO_2 buildup in the atmosphere, using as input the historical record of fossil fuel emissions and land use changes.

Keywords: STELLA, modeling, carbon cycle, dynamic systems, systems concepts.

INTRODUCTION

One of the most important recent developments in the earth sciences has been the move toward looking at Earth as a large, complex, interconnected system. This field of study, earth system science, is exciting not just because it is new (in fact, it is not that new—see the appendix of Strahler and Strahler, 1989), but because it deals with relevant issues such as global climate change and also because it is highly integrative. Conversations with undergraduates at Carleton College have revealed, perhaps not surprisingly, that societal relevance and integration of different disciplines are characteristics students desire in their education. For these and other reasons, earth system science is an attractive new emphasis in many undergraduate earth science and geology courses. Moreover, the systems approach to understanding whole earth dynamics was identified as the major objective for the future of the earth sciences by the National Research Council (NRC, 1993).

But how does one go about teaching modeling in earth system science? Regardless of how you choose to incorporate earth system science into geology classes, you face challenges associated with reviewing and/or learning the relevant physics, chemistry, biology, and meteorology that are needed to understand global systems such as the carbon cycle or the global climate system. Other challenges arise when you search for ways to go beyond the passive description of how various earth systems are constructed and how they operate. Although dynamic systems surround us, we are generally not very good at understanding and predicting their behavior without the aid of some type of model that allows experimentation and observation. In this paper, I describe—in the form of several examples—how the computer program STELLA can provide an effective means for enabling students to understand and explore the dynamics of earth systems. This amounts to developing the "systems" part of earth system science.

The task of using computer models to explore the dynamics of earth systems is made much easier through the use of

[†]E-mail: dbice@geosc.psu.edu.

Bice, D.M., 2006, STELLA modeling as a tool for understanding the dynamics of earth systems, *in* Manduca, C.A., and Mogk, D.W., eds., Earth and Mind: How Geologists Think and Learn about the Earth: Geological Society of America Special Paper 413, p. 171–185, doi: 10.1130/2006.2413(13). For permission to copy, contact editing@geosociety.org.

a program called STELLA (High Performance Systems, Inc., http://www.hps-inc.com/), which runs on both Macs and PCs. STELLA is essentially a graphical programming environment that is specifically designed for modeling systems that can be described by a series of differential equations. Users construct graphical representations of systems and then enter values and expressions corresponding to the components of the system. The program uses this information to construct a set of differential equations that are integrated over time using standard numerical techniques. The algorithms used in STELLA are the same used by most programmers to carry out the numerical integration of differential equations. STELLA models seem to be extensively used in ecology and economics (Hannon and Ruth, 1994), but relatively few earth scientists (Mayer, 1990; Moore and Derry, 1995) have made use of this program in teaching and research. This is somewhat surprising given the extensive use of box-models in geochemistry (Garrels et al., 1973; Walker, 1991; Richter and Turekian, 1993) and the obvious possibilities for modeling systems such as the rock cycle, the water cycle, and the carbon cycle, among others.

It is of course possible to understand how a system like the global water cycle works without modeling, but this understanding is largely static and qualitative. Modeling provides a means for deepening this understanding by exploring the dynamics in a quantitative manner. For example, one could look at a typical depiction of the global water cycle and think about the consequences of groundwater withdrawal, irrigation, and reservoir building on the whole system. This thinking cannot progress too far beyond some qualitative conjecture without the aid of a numerical model; but armed with a model, one can understand quantitatively the impacts of these changes on global sea level and others parts of the system.

INTRODUCTION TO THE MODELING PROCESS WITH STELLA

In order to illustrate some fundamental aspects of modeling with STELLA, we begin with a very simple system—a bath tub of water with a faucet and drain. Details for constructing the model can be found at http://www.geosc.psu.edu/~dbice/DaveSTELLA/ modeling/ch2.3.html.

From Real World to Conceptual Model to Computer Model

The first step in modeling is to define and consider the system as it exists in the real world. This involves identifying the components of the system, the material or entity that is moving through the system, the major processes involved in moving this material or entity, and the other quantities that these processes depend on. This step necessarily involves simplifying the real world because it is obviously impossible to model the full complexity of nature. Drawing a cartoon of the system, as shown in Figure 1, is an important part of this process. When possible, constructing an actual physical model of the system is very helpful (Moore and Derry, 1995) in understanding the dynamics of the system as well as the connection between the physical model and the STELLA model.

Schematic Drawing of BathTub System

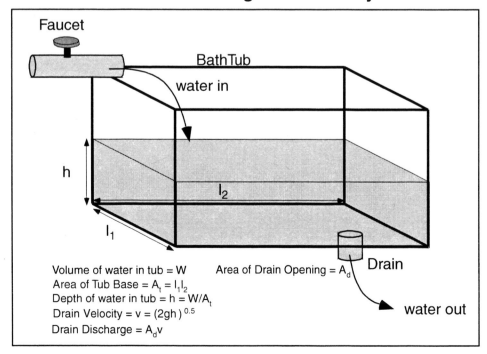

Figure 1. A simple sketch of the water bath tub system, consisting of a faucet, a drain, and bath tub that contains water. The faucet flow rate is independently controlled, but the rate of flow through the drain is a function of the water depth and the area of the drain opening.

Volume of water in tub = W
Area of Tub Base = $A_t = l_1 l_2$
Depth of water in tub = $h = W/A_t$
Drain Velocity = $v = (2gh)^{0.5}$
Drain Discharge = $A_d v$

The next step in the modeling process involves representing the various inflows and outflows in the form of equations. The two flow processes in this case are represented by the faucet and the drain. The faucet flow is simply an adjustable constant; the drain flow is instead a function of the size of the drain opening and how much water is in the bath tub, because the weight of the water overlying the drain determines the amount of pressure that is forcing the water through the drain. A more precise description of this dependence is provided by Torricelli's law, which states that the velocity of water flowing out of a drain is given by:

$$v = \sqrt{2gh} \, , \tag{1}$$

where v is velocity, g is gravity, and h is the water depth. The velocity is then multiplied by the area of the drain opening to give a discharge in volume of water per unit of time.

Figure 2 shows how this system is represented in STELLA using the four building blocks of systems—reservoirs, flows, connectors, and converters (nomenclature of HPS Inc., the authors of STELLA). The connector arrows represent dependence; the depth of water is dependent on the amount of water in the bath tub and the area of the bath tub base. The converters represent either constants or variables defined by equations or graphs. Note that the two flows have cloud symbols at the ends away from the bath tub, indicating that this is an open system, drawing water from some unspecified source, and sending it to an unspecified sink at the other end.

The system described in Figure 2 is essentially a simple differential equation that has the general form of:

$$\frac{dW}{dt} = F - kW \, . \tag{2}$$

Here, W is the volume of water in the bath tub, F is the faucet flow rate, and k is a constant that incorporates the bath tub dimensions, the drain dimensions, and gravity (combination of equations shown in Fig. 1).

The STELLA model depicted in Figure 2 is complete and ready to run after we specify the initial amount of water in the bath tub, the inflow rate, the length of time of the simulation, and the increments of time (the time step, or dt of the calculations) over which the program does the calculations. The user can also specify different integration techniques, with the default being Euler's method. The time step (adjustable via a program menu) is critically important, and before any model results can be seriously considered, it is important to try varying the time step to see how the model results change—if the results do not change significantly when you decrease the time step by one-half, then the time step is at an acceptable value; otherwise, the time step must be reduced to smaller values.

Using the Model to Illustrate Systems Concepts

There are a number of important concepts of dynamic systems behavior that can be illustrated with this simple bath tub

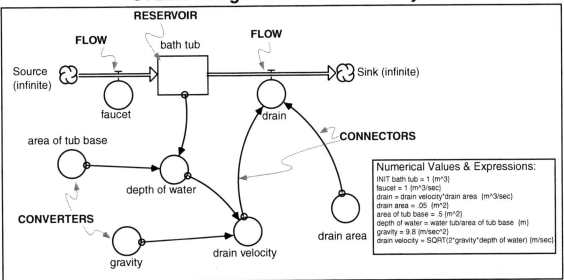

STELLA Diagram of the BathTub System

Figure 2. The bath tub system as represented in STELLA. The reservoir, flows, and converters all have numerical values associated with them; hidden in this view, they can be seen and changed by double-clicking on each symbol. If no numerical value or expression is associated with a symbol, the program shows a question mark to prompt the modeler to enter a value or equation. The numerical values and expressions used in this model are given in the box. INIT stands for the initial amount of water in the bath tub; comments enclosed in {brackets} are used to help keep track of units; note that the time units here are seconds.

model. These concepts are useful in understanding all dynamic systems, even very complicated ones, such as the global climate system.

Steady State

Running the model for 100 s (Fig. 3) reveals some interesting changes as the system evolves toward a steady state, where the amount of water in the bath tub stays constant. The inflow stays constant over time, but the outflow undergoes an exponential change, increasing until it approaches the same value as the inflow. Initially, the inflow is greater than the outflow, and so the amount (and depth) of the water in the tub increases, thus increasing the drain velocity and the outflow; this continues until the inflow and outflow match, at which point water continues to move through the system, but the amount of water in the tub remains the same.

Residence Time

When the system is in steady state, we can define another concept—the residence time. The residence time is effectively the average length of time that an entity—in this case a water molecule—remains in a reservoir. It is really only meaningful for a reservoir that is at or near a steady-state condition. By definition, the residence time is the amount of material in the reservoir divided by either the inflow or the outflow (they are equal when the reservoir is at steady state). If there are multiple inflows or outflows, then we use the sum of the outflows or inflows to deter-

mine the residence time. For the water bath tub system shown here, the residence time is:

$$t_{residence} = \frac{\text{amount in tub}}{\text{outflow}} = \frac{10.16\text{m}^3}{1\text{m}^3\text{s}^{-1}} = 10.16\text{s} . \quad (3)$$

If we increase the flow rate, the water moves through the reservoir faster, so the residence time decreases. It is possible, then, to calculate any of the above three parameters (residence time, reservoir amount, and inflow or outflow) if the other two are known and if we assume the system is in a steady state. For instance, if we assume that the water cycle is in a steady state and we know how much water is in the atmosphere and the global rainfall, then we can calculate the residence time of water in the atmosphere. Residence time is an important concept in problems of pollutants in groundwater or surface-water reservoirs, and also in understanding the long-term effects of greenhouse gases added to the atmosphere.

Response Time

A closely related concept is that of the response time of a system, which measures how quickly a system recovers and returns to its steady state after some perturbation. This concept can be illustrated by running several simulations in which the starting amount of water in the reservoir is varied while the inflows and outflows remain unchanged. The results, shown in Figure 4, are somewhat surprising; regardless of how great the initial departure from the ending steady state, this system gets to steady-state at about the same time.

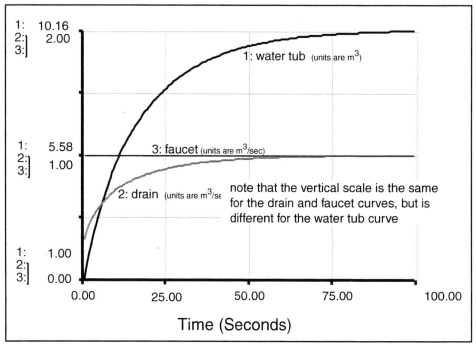

Figure 3. Results of running the bath tub model for 100 s using the initial conditions given in Figure 2. After ~75 s, the system is in a steady state.

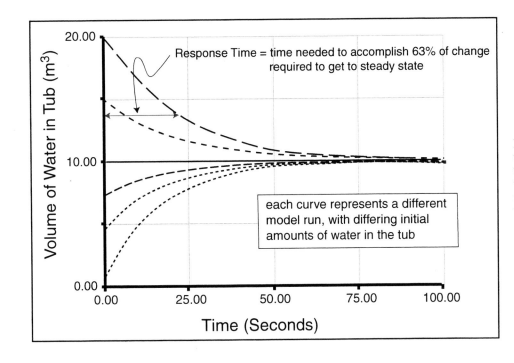

Figure 4. Results of running the bath tub model five different times, varying the initial amount of water in the bath tub. In each case, the system returns to its steady state in ~75 s, with a response time of around 20 s.

The concept of response time can be more clearly illustrated by an even simpler system, consisting of one reservoir (W) and one outflow (D) defined as a simple fraction (k) of the amount in the reservoir (W) such that at each instant in time,

$$D = kW . \qquad (4)$$

In this case, the response time is defined as $1/k$—this turns out to be the time needed for the system to accomplish 63% ($1/e$) of the return to its steady state. Also note that in a very simple system, the residence time and the response time are numerically the same, even though they are mathematically and conceptually different (the former reflects a steady state, the latter reflects a transient state). The response time is a very useful concept because if it is known (or hypothesized), we can make some predictions about how quickly the system will respond to a change in the amount in the reservoir. Alternatively, if we change one of the inflow or outflow processes, we can predict how that will affect the response time of the system. The concept of response time is important in understanding the future of the global carbon cycle—if we halt the anthropogenic alterations to the carbon cycle, the response time of the system tells us how long it would take for the carbon cycle to return to a more natural state.

A more detailed discussion of the concepts and mathematical formulation of residence time and response time can be found in Rodhe (1992) or at http://www.geosc.psu.edu/~dbice/ DaveSTELLA/modeling/ch2contents.html.

Another important observation to be made here is that the system evolves to the same steady state in each case, so the steady state of a system (along with the response time) is primarily determined by the nature of its inflows and outflows.

Feedback Mechanisms

This particular system returns to a steady state because it contains a negative feedback mechanism in the connection between the drain flow rate and the amount of water in the bath tub. A negative feedback mechanism is a controlling mechanism, one that tends to counteract some kind of initial imbalance or perturbation. A familiar example of another negative feedback mechanism is a simple thermostat in a home that responds to changes from the steady state, returning the home to a specified temperature. Note that the word negative, as used here, means that this mechanism acts to reverse the change that set it into operation. If our bath tub is in its steady state, knocking the system out of its steady state by suddenly dumping in more water will cause a response—the drain will increase its flow rate, thus decreasing the amount of water in the bath tub, bringing it back toward the steady-state value. If we instead decrease the amount in the tub, the negative feedback associated with the drain will force the amount of water in the bath tub to increase until the steady state is returned. The important thing to remember is that negative feedback mechanisms tend to have stabilizing effects on systems.

In contrast, a positive feedback mechanism is one that exacerbates some initial change from the steady state, leading to a runaway condition—it acts to promote an enhancement of the initial change. One way to modify the simple bath tub system to create a positive feedback system is to alter the system (Fig. 5) so that the inflow depends on how much water is in the bath tub.

This system has one possible steady state, where the initial amount of water in the bath tub is 5 m³; any departure from this value, however slight, leads to runaway behavior, and the amount of water in the tub follows an exponential curve of the form:

Positive Feedback Leads to Runaway Behavior

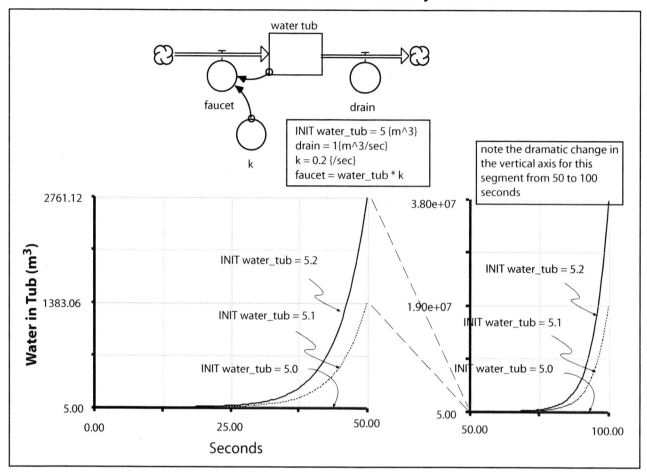

Figure 5. Modified bath tub system that illustrates a positive feedback mechanism. In this case, the faucet is defined such that its rate of inflow increases as the amount in the bath tub increases, while the drain is defined as a constant (physically unreal, of course). The model was run three times with different initial amounts of water; initial values greater than 5.0 triggered the positive feedback mechanism, leading to runaway behavior that follows an exponential curve. Comparing the reservoir values at 50 s and 100 s shows the impressive increases that result from exponential growth—38 million m^3 of water in the case where the initial value is 5.2 m^3.

$$W(t) = \frac{d}{k} + \left(W_0 - \frac{d}{k} \right) e^{kt}, \qquad (5)$$

where $W(t)$ is the amount of water in the bath tub at any time, d is the drain constant (1 m^3 /s in our case), k is the faucet rate constant (0.2), W_0 is the initial amount of water in the bath tub (variable in the three model runs shown in Fig. 5), and t is time. A useful thing to remember with exponential growth is that the doubling time can be easily calculated (after some manipulations of the above equation):

$$t_{doubling} = \frac{0.693}{k}. \qquad (6)$$

Here, the doubling time works out to be 3.465 s.

If this model is run with an initial water bath tub value of less than 5 m^3, another important lesson is learned, which is: in

the real world, there are limits to exponential change, regardless of whether that change leads to growth or decline. In this case, the limit is reached when there is no more water left in the bath tub. In the case of population growth, the limit to exponential growth is reached when the carrying capacity of the ecosystem is approached—then the population growth decelerates and gradually approaches the carrying capacity (with reference to the human population, see Cohen [1995] and Meadows et al. [1992] for detailed discussions).

Positive feedback mechanisms, like negative feedback mechanisms are not necessarily good or bad. Epidemics and infections have positive feedback mechanisms associated with them, but so does the growth of money in a bank account with compounded interest. Earth contains a wide variety of both positive feedbacks and negative feedbacks, and, depending on the conditions, either kind of feedback may dominate. But—and this is very important—the mere fact that we exist, the fact that our planet has water and an atmosphere is compelling evidence to suggest that ultimately, our earth system is dominated by negative feedback mechanisms (see Kasting [1989] or Lovelock [1988] for more discussion of this). However, it is equally important to realize that human time scales are much shorter than the history of Earth, and over periods of time that interest humans, positive feedback mechanisms may be very important; they have the potential to produce dramatic changes.

Lag Time

We next consider a slightly more complex system to illustrate the concept of lag time. In Figure 6, two water bath tubs have been connected such that the drain from one flows into the adjacent bath tub. Here, the drains have been simplified greatly—all of the drain parameters in our first model are represented by rate constants labeled k_1 and k_2; these rate constants get multiplied

by the amount in the reservoir at any time to give the volumetric rate of flow out of the drain. Next, we take advantage of a useful feature of STELLA—the ability to define various parameters as graphical functions of other system variables or time. In this case, I want to show how the system responds to a sudden spike in the faucet flow rate, so I first define the faucet rate as being equal to time, then click on a button in the dialog box and a graph appears, enabling you to define the nature of this graphical relationship. The faucet in this case starts out with a value of 1 m³/s, which puts the system in a steady state to begin with, then increases to a peak value of 4 m³/s, and then quickly returns to 1 m³/s again and stays there for the duration of the experiment.

The response of the system is shown in Figure 6. The first bath tub reaches its peak 1 second behind the peak in the faucet—it lags behind the faucet. The second bath tub peaks at a lower value and much later than the first—the perturbation is buffered by the first water bath tub. Note that both bath tubs return to their steady state after variable amounts of time and that the total area

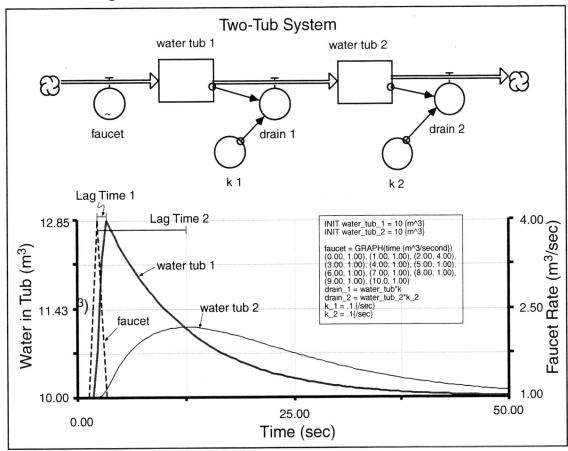

Figure 6. A system with two bath tubs connected by a drain illustrates the concept of lag time. Here, both bath tubs start out with the same amount, and the drains have identical rate constants; the faucet is defined as a graphical function of time, starting at a value of 1 m³/s, then jumping up to 4 m³/s at time = 2, then returning to 1 m³/s for the duration of the time. Water bath tub 1 peaks at a value of 12.85 m³ at time = 3, so this reservoir has a lag time of 1 s; tub 2 peaks much later, at time = 12, so its lag time is 10 s behind the faucet peak, and 9 s behind the "upstream" reservoir.

under the two curves is equal—meaning that the same volume of water moved through each reservoir. The pulse of extra water, propagating through the system is very similar to the pulse of water moving down a stream system, with the lag time in this analogy being the time between the peak in the rainfall and the flood peak along a certain reach of the stream. The concept of lag time is also relevant to systems such as the global carbon cycle—anthropogenic additions of CO_2 into the atmosphere are similar to the faucet here; the climatic response involves a certain lag time. This lag time means that if we halt emissions today, the climate will continue to warm—a fact that many policy-makers and citizens should be aware of.

MODEL SIMPLICITY VERSUS COMPLEXITY

Models are clearly meant to represent simplified versions of the real world, yet they should be complex enough capture the essence of the real system. So, what is too simple, and what is simple enough? One way to understand this is by way of three variations on the water bath tub model, shown in Figure 7. In the simplest version of this system, the faucet and drain flows are simple constants—they do not change over time. The more realistic model uses Torricelli's law to express the rate of flow out of the drain. The intermediate model simply represents the drain flow as the product of a rate constant times the volume in the bath tub. From the results (Fig. 7), it is clear that the simplest model does a poor job of representing the real behavior of this system; it drops off at a constant rate and does not achieve a steady state except in the special case where the inflow is set equal to the outflow. This simple system does not have any negative feedback associated with it either. So, this is a good example of a model that is too simple. In contrast, the intermediate model does a remarkably good job of matching the behavior of the more complex model. It is fair to say, then, that the intermediate model is simple enough and yet not too simple—it captures the essence of the more complex model using a more parsimonious mathematical representation. Nevertheless, the simple model is valuable as a starting point in the modeling process; its shortcomings provide suggestions for improvements and added complexity.

It is worth noting that even the more complex model shown in Figure 7 is not overly complex. An overly complex model might, for instance, try to represent the friction, viscosity, and three-dimensional turbulent flow in the water, which would clearly represent overkill in this case.

INCREASED MODEL COMPLEXITY

Natural systems are usually more complicated than our simple water bath tub model, so it is important to explore some aspects of the dynamics of more complex systems. In the following discussion, we will pay particular attention to how the response time of the system changes with increasing complexity.

To begin with, imagine adding another drain flow to our simple water bath tub model. If we represent the two drain flows in the manner of the intermediate model of Figure 7, each with its own rate constant k, we could show that the resulting response time of the model would be $1/(k_1 + k_2)$, which is less than the response time with just one drain ($1/k_1$). The implication is that a system with more flows has a shorter response time—it can react to changes faster and moves to its steady state faster. As we will see, this is not always the case in systems with connected reservoirs.

More complex systems consist of numerous reservoirs, linked together by various flows. In order to understand the effect of these connections, consider the case shown in Figure 8, where two isolated reservoirs with simple drain-like flows are then connected to each other such that the outflow of one reservoir becomes the inflow of the other reservoir, but the flows are mathematically the same, and the starting amounts in the two reservoirs are also the same. The result of connecting these reservoirs is to decrease the response time of the system to $1/(k_1 + k_2)$, as shown in Figure 8. Another way of saying this is that the connected system is more responsive than the disconnected system.

This last point is often true, but only to a certain point, as illustrated in the next example in which four reservoirs with drain-like flows are connected (Fig. 9). We can imagine this system in its disconnected state and consider the response times of the individual reservoirs with their draining flows; these response times, given in Figure 9, range from 1.67 to 5 yr. If we were to simply extend our analysis of the rate constants, we might hypothesize that for this four-reservoir model, the response time of the whole system would be given by:

$$\tau_{connected} = \frac{1}{k_{12} + k_{23} + k_{34} + k_{41}} = \frac{1}{1.5} = 0.67 , \qquad (7)$$

where k_{12} represents the rate constant for the flow between reservoirs 1 and 2, etc. When we test this hypothesis by running the model, we find that the real behavior is more complex, and the overall response time of the system is difficult to define, but if we focus on the reservoir labeled M2, which appears to be the slowest to respond, we can estimate that the response time of the whole system is in the range of 4–5 time units. Obviously, our simple mathematical prediction of the response time was wrong; when faced with a more complex system, it is better to define the response time of the whole system by direct observation.

Figure 7. Three variations of the bath tub model, with varying degrees of complexity. The simplest model has a constant drain, while in the more realistic model, the drain flow rate is calculated using Torricelli's law. The model of intermediate complexity just represents that drain flow as a rate constant multiplied by the amount of water in the bath tub. Comparison of the models shows virtually no difference between the intermediate complexity model and the more realistic one. The intermediate model is thus an acceptably simple model, though not so simple that it fails to capture the essence of the system.

Three Versions of the Bathtub Model

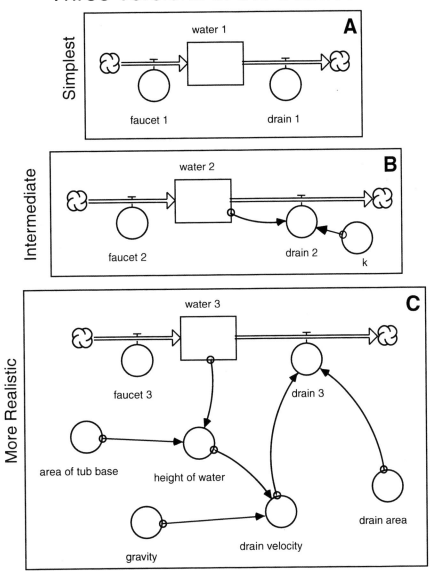

A — Simplest

water 1
faucet 1
drain 1

B — Intermediate

water 2
faucet 2
drain 2
k

C — More Realistic

water 3
faucet 3
drain 3
area of tub base
height of water
gravity
drain velocity
drain area

Comparison of Three Bathtub Models

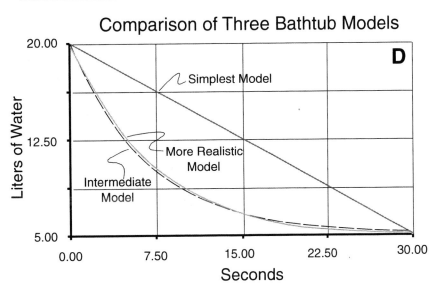

Simplest Model

More Realistic Model

Intermediate Model

Liters of Water

20.00

12.50

5.00

0.00   7.50   15.00   22.50   30.00

Seconds

D

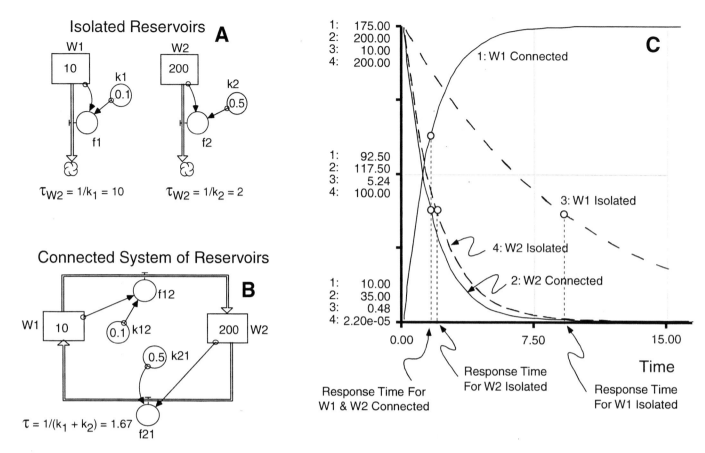

Figure 8. Here, two reservoirs with typical draining flows involving rate constants k_1 and k_2 are shown in a disconnected system (A) and in a connected system (B). The performance of these two systems (C) illustrates the effect of increased connectedness; the connected system shows a shorter response time, given by $1/(k_1 + k_2)$.

By studying the evolution of this system, we can see that the reservoirs tend to overshoot their eventual steady-state values, delaying their arrival at steady state. Why do they overshoot? One way of understanding this behavior is to study the apparent response times of each outflow, noting that they are not all the same and they alternate between short and long response times. The reservoir labeled M3 is initially furthest from steady state, and it has a shorter response time than M2, the next reservoir downstream, with the result that material piles up in M3 faster than it can adjust, moving it far away from its steady state. If we apply a similar analysis to the other pairs of reservoirs, we can better understand why this system overshoots. Note that in this case, the response time of the whole system is significantly greater than the response times of some of the reservoirs considered in the disconnected state. Recall from our examination of the simple two-reservoir system that this was not the case—the two-reservoir system had a shorter response time than either of the reservoirs considered in the disconnected state. So, in larger systems, the overall response time of the system may be significantly greater than the response times of the separate parts of the system.

Figure 9 also shows the effect of adding more flows to this four-reservoir model—this amounts to increasing the connectedness of the system. Our simple analysis would lead us to believe that making this change will decrease the response time of the system, and in fact when we run this model, we find that such is the case. This further supports the idea that increased connectedness, which amounts to increased complexity, decreases the response time.

VALIDATION AND THE SIGNIFICANCE OF COMPUTER MODELS

The purpose of a model is not to replicate the real world—it is clearly impossible to put the complexity of the real world into a computer. Instead, the goal is usually to understand something about the behavior of a system, including how the system responds to changes. We create and use these models because their real-life versions are so complex, large, and often slow that we cannot generally understand them without some kind of controlled experimentation. But, the obvious simplification of models commonly leads to skepticism that ranges from complete

Response Times in Larger, More Complex Systems

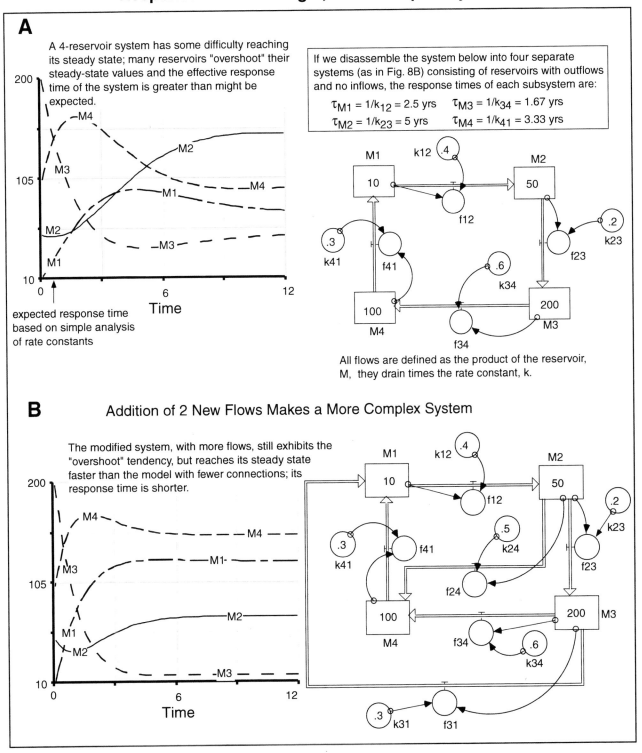

A A 4-reservoir system has some difficulty reaching its steady state; many reservoirs "overshoot" their steady-state values and the effective response time of the system is greater than might be expected.

expected response time based on simple analysis of rate constants

If we disassemble the system below into four separate systems (as in Fig. 8B) consisting of reservoirs with outflows and no inflows, the response times of each subsystem are:

$$\tau_{M1} = 1/k_{12} = 2.5 \text{ yrs} \qquad \tau_{M3} = 1/k_{34} = 1.67 \text{ yrs}$$
$$\tau_{M2} = 1/k_{23} = 5 \text{ yrs} \qquad \tau_{M4} = 1/k_{41} = 3.33 \text{ yrs}$$

All flows are defined as the product of the reservoir, M, they drain times the rate constant, k.

B Addition of 2 New Flows Makes a More Complex System

The modified system, with more flows, still exhibits the "overshoot" tendency, but reaches its steady state faster than the model with fewer connections; its response time is shorter.

Figure 9. Two versions of a larger system. The upper system shows that the response time of larger systems is not as easily predicted as in the case of smaller, two-reservoir systems. In larger systems, some reservoirs may overshoot their eventual steady-state levels, thus delaying their eventual arrival at steady state. The lower version (B) is identical to the upper system (A), with the exception of the addition of two new flows; the resulting behavior shows that increasing the connectedness of a large system decreases the overall response time.

rejection of anything the model reveals to a milder form in which the results are accepted as a good possibility for the way the real world behaves. So, how does one develop a sophisticated, nuanced appreciation for the significance of model results?

Computer models such as the ones shown in this paper are nothing more than a set of differential equations that are integrated over time. The significance of the model results is therefore dependent on the nature of the equations. Just as there is a range in the quality of equations from highly abstract to highly realistic, there is a range in the significance of the model results. If the equations were pulled out of thin air, then the results would not be significant relative to any real world system (but they would nevertheless be meaningful in a purely mathematical sense). If the equations were designed to express the general relationships of a real-world system (e.g., the intermediate model of Fig. 7), the model results might be only qualitatively meaningful. If the equations were designed and tested such that they mimicked the important processes of the real-world system, then the model results may be quantitatively significant, and the model might have some important predictive capabilities. A model such as this last type could be tested against known histories of the real-world system; models that pass these tests are validated, and

their results can be considered to be reliable, at least within a certain range of conditions.

The task of model validation is simple in some cases. For instance, the water bath tub model is easily tested by constructing a real version of the model (see Moore and Derry, 1995) and collecting some real data to compare with the computer model results. If this succeeds, then the model is validated, and we could say that it captures the essence of the system; if not, then we must examine the model carefully, make revisions, and then retest. Torricelli's law, used to construct the more realistic version of the water bath tub model in Figure 7, has been tested and generally gives quite reliable results.

But for larger systems, such as the global carbon cycle (Fig. 10), the process of model validation is a bit trickier—you clearly cannot create a laboratory version of such a vast, global-scale model. Instead, we have to rely on some kind of natural experiment in which we have some knowledge of an imposed change and some record of the model's performance or state over time. Unwittingly, humans have been conducting such an experiment, and the state of the carbon cycle is partly available in the form of instrumental measurements since the late 1950s and ice-core records of atmospheric CO_2 concentrations before then (Fig. 11).

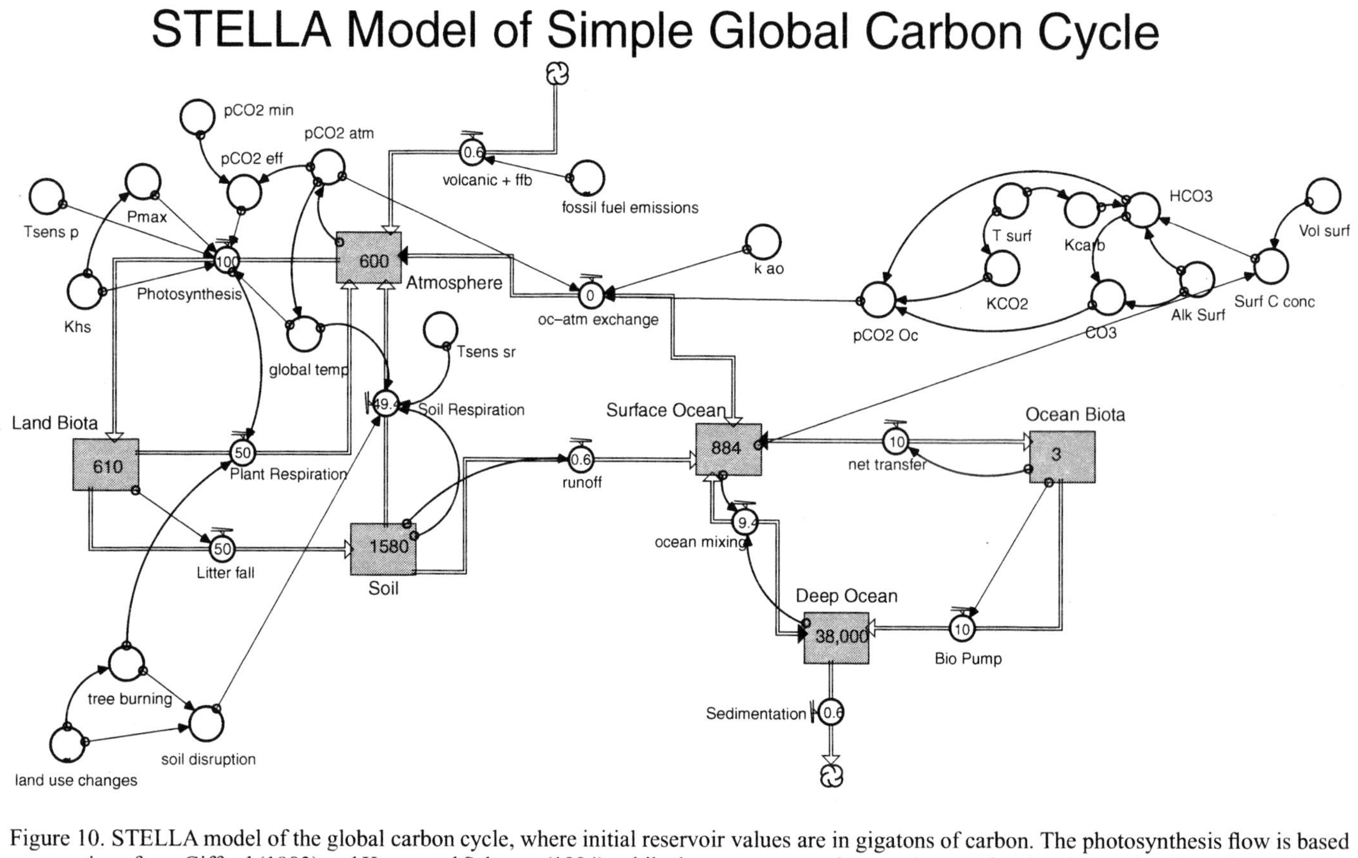

STELLA Model of Simple Global Carbon Cycle

Figure 10. STELLA model of the global carbon cycle, where initial reservoir values are in gigatons of carbon. The photosynthesis flow is based on equations from Gifford (1993) and Kwon and Schnoor (1994), while the ocean-atmosphere exchange of carbon is based on Broecker and Peng (1993) and Walker (1991). Most of the other flows are simple draining flows; some also include a temperature sensitivity factor.

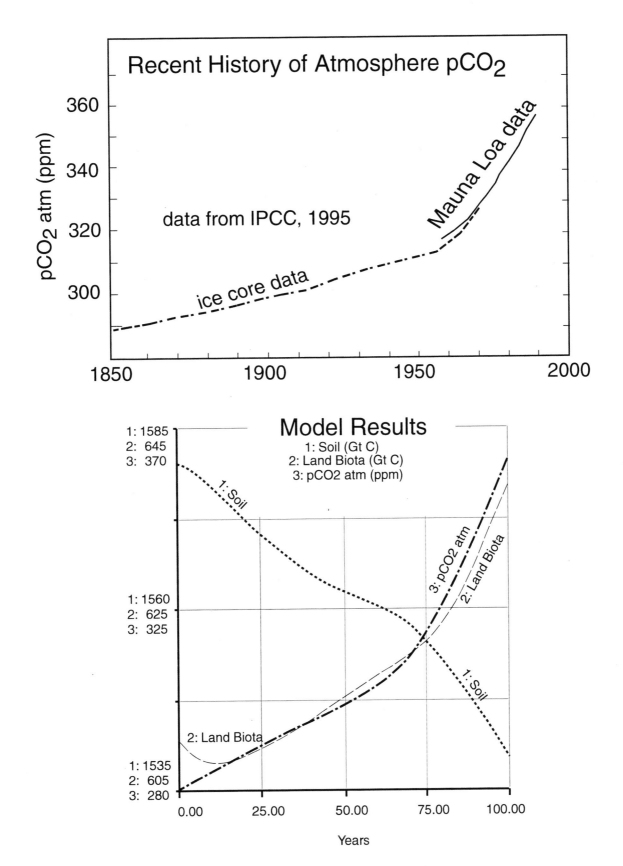

Figure 11. The results of running the STELLA model of the global carbon cycle with the history of fossil fuel emissions and land-use changes (from Table 1) compare fairly well with the observed record of atmospheric CO_2 buildup over the same time period. The model is thus validated (in a relatively simple, first-order sense), meaning that the model's results are potentially meaningful in a quantitative sense.

Figure 10 shows a STELLA diagram of a simple global carbon cycle that can be tested by adding in the anthropogenic carbon additions given in Table 1. This model incorporates the best estimates of reservoir sizes and mathematical representations of the major processes, including a fairly detailed carbonate chemistry scheme and a detailed photosynthesis scheme. For details on constructing the model and downloadable versions, see Bice (2006). The anthropogenic effects are added by making three changes to the system. The fossil fuel emissions, varying as a graphical function of time, are added straight to the atmosphere. The land-use changes represent carbon transfer from burning trees (75% of the total at each point in time) and through accelerating soil respiration (the remaining 25% of the total at each point in time). These transfers are represented by adding two new flows that go from the land biota and soil reservoirs to the atmosphere reservoir (not shown in Fig. 10). As can be seen in Figure 11, the model results match the observed record of atmospheric CO_2 fairly closely, and so, to a first approximation, this model passes a validation test. This means that models such as this—very similar to the one used by the Intergovernmental Panel on Climate Change (IPCC) in their exploration of the effects of various future emissions scenarios (IPCC, 1995)—generate results that are quantitatively meaningful. This successful validation does not make this carbon cycle a perfect predictor of the future performance of the real global carbon cycle, but it probably does give a pretty good estimate of what will happen, so long as there is not some complex nonlinear aspect of the system that kicks in once we stray too far from the states experienced in the past hundred years. In other words, the initial validation of the model earns it a status of cautious respectability.

CONCLUSIONS

Computer modeling offers the possibility of developing a deep understanding of the dynamics of earth systems. While numerous computer programs could be used to this end, STELLA is particularly well-suited, especially for beginning students because of the ease of use relative to other programming languages. Simple models are easily created, modified, run, and observed, providing a superb tool for experiential learning. Experimenting with these models, making changes, and trying to predict the response, followed by comparing predictions with actual performance leads to the development of a fairly sophisticated, almost intuitive sense of system dynamics.

A surprisingly complete range of systems dynamics concepts can be illustrated through modifications of a very simple system that represents flow of water in and out of a bath tub. Although these models are far removed from the complexity of real earth systems, they are simple to create, modify, and understand; in fact, more complex systems are often so challenging to understand that simple concepts may be obscured.

At one level, experimentation with computer models might have as its goal the development of general, abstract systems concepts. In this case, there is no need to consider the relation

TABLE 1. HISTORY OF ANTHROPOGENIC CARBON ADDITIONS TO THE ATMOSPHERE

Year	Fossil fuel (Gt C/yr)	Land use (Gt C/yr)
0	0.365	0.6
10	0.548	0.6
20	0.837	0.65
30	1.030	0.65
40	1.046	0.7
50	1.190	0.7
60	1.620	0.8
70	2.543	1.1
80	4.006	1.3
90	5.172	1.25
100	5.941	1.5

Note: Sources: Andres et al. (2000) and Houghton (2000). Year 0 corresponds to calendar year 1890.

between the model results and the real world—the model is significant in and of itself, making no claims to represent the behavior of a real-world system. But inevitably, students of earth system science will want to explore systems with greater relevance to the real world, and this raises the question of whether or not the model captures the essence of the real-world system. Various model validation approaches can help answer this question; for instance, the global carbon cycle model shown here did a fairly good job of matching the system response to the anthropogenic alterations over the past 100 yr, and therefore seems to warrant a level of cautious acceptance.

ACKNOWLEDGMENTS

This work represents the result of an ongoing collaboration in learning with the many outstanding students at Carleton College. In addition, I thank my colleagues in the Geology Department, especially Cathy Manduca, for their insight and encouragement. Much of this work was made possible through a grant from Carleton College.

REFERENCES CITED

Andres, R.J., Marland, G., Boden, T., and Bischof, S., 2000, Carbon dioxide emissions from fossil fuel consumption and cement manufacture, 1751–1991, and an estimate of their isotopic composition and latitudinal distribution, *in* Wigley, T.M.L., and Schimel, D.S., eds., The carbon cycle: Cambridge, UK, Cambridge University Press, 292 p.

Bice, D.M., 2006, Modeling the carbon cycle, http://www.geosc.psu.edu/~dbice/DaveSTELLA/Carbon/c_cycle_models.htm#top (July 2006).

Broecker, W.S., and Peng, H.-S., 1993, Greenhouse puzzles: New York, Eldigio Press, 251 p.

Cohen, J.E., 1995, How many people can the Earth support?: New York, Norton, 532 p.

Garrels, R.M., McKenzie, F.T., and Hunt, C., 1973, Chemical cycles and the global environment: Los Altos, California, W. Kaufmann, 206 p.

Gifford, R.M., 1993, Implications of CO_2 effects on vegetation for the global carbon budget, *in* Heimann, M., ed., The global carbon cycle: North Atlantic Treaty Organization (NATO) ASI Series, v. 115, p. 159–200.

Hannon, B., and Ruth, M., 1994, Dynamic modeling: New York, Springer-Verlag, 248 p.

Houghton, R.A., 2000, Emissions of carbon from land-use change, *in* Wigley, T.M.L., and Schimel, D.S., eds., The carbon cycle: Cambridge, UK, Cambridge University Press, 292 p.

Intergovernmental Panel on Climate Change (IPCC), 1995, Climate change 1994: Cambridge, Cambridge University Press, 339 p.

Kasting, J., 1989, Long-term stability of the Earth's climate: Global and Planetary Change, v. 1, p. 83–97, doi: 10.1016/0921-8181(89)90017-9.

Kwon, O.-Y., and Schnoor, J.L., 1994, Simple global carbon model: The atmosphere–terrestrial biosphere–ocean interaction: Global Biogeochemical Cycles, v. 8, p. 295–305, doi: 10.1029/94GB00768.

Lovelock, J., 1988, The ages of Gaia: New York, Norton, 325 p.

Mayer, L., 1990, Introduction to quantitative geomorphology; an exercise manual: Englewood Cliffs, New Jersey, Prentice Hall, 380 p.

Meadows, D.H., Meadows, D.L., and Randers, J., 1992, Beyond the limits: Post Mills, Vermont, Chelsea Green Publishing, 300 p.

Moore, A., and Derry, L., 1995, Understanding natural systems through simple dynamical systems modeling: Journal of Geological Education, v. 43, p. 152–157.

National Research Council, 1993, Solid-earth sciences and society: Washington, D.C., National Academy Press, 46 p.

Richter, F., and Turekian, K., 1993, Simple models for the geochemical response of the oceans to climatic and tectonic forcing: Earth and Planetary Science Letters, v. 119, p. 121–131, doi: 10.1016/0012-821X(93)90010-7.

Rodhe, H., 1992, Modeling biogeochemical cycles, *in* Butcher, S.S., Charlson, R.J., Orians, G.H., and Wolfe, G.V., eds., Global biogeochemical cycles: San Diego, Academic Press, 379 p.

Strahler, A.N., and Strahler, A.H., 1989, Physical geography (4th ed.): New York, John Wiley and Sons, 562 p.

Walker, J.C.G., 1991, Numerical adventures with geochemical cycles: Oxford, Oxford University Press, 192 p.

MANUSCRIPT ACCEPTED BY THE SOCIETY 21 MARCH 2006

An Agenda for the Future

This publication demonstrates the power of collaborations among geoscientists, educators, and cognitive scientists in understanding the nature of the geosciences, the fundamental cognitive processes that are particularly well developed in geoscientists, and the strategies and techniques for developing geoscience expertise in students of all types. It builds on and grows from a number of activities and discussions bringing together geoscientists, educators, and cognitive scientists (http://serc.carleton.edu/research_on_learning/).

At the highest level, these discussions have uniformly resulted in four major conclusions that provide a strong motivation for continued collaboration:

Geoscience education can be substantially enhanced by the use of research on learning in the design of learning environments and experiences. A clear articulation of what geoscience students should be able to do is needed and can guide the design and implementation of new instructional practices that are informed by learning science. Research into what it means to be a geoscience expert and how learning in geoscience is accomplished will illuminate these goals as well as the pathways to achieving them.

Several aspects of geoscience provide unique challenges to learning that require new research. Example areas include geologic time, understanding Earth as a complex system, the use of visualization by geoscience experts and students, and the nature of scientific reasoning employed in studying natural, open systems and their impact on humanity. These areas provide exciting opportunities for fundamental research into how people think and learn that will provide a much-needed foundation for instructional design in the geosciences.

Research that will improve education in the geosciences must be coupled with mechanisms to bring those findings into widespread practice. This will require that basic research on cognition, research on effective educational practice, curriculum and materials development, faculty professional development, and national dissemination all proceed hand-in-hand in an integrated fashion. The opportunities for coupled research and development projects that engage collaborative work by geoscientists and cognitive scientists are the most exciting aspects of the discussions to date.

The geosciences present a favorable environment for systematic research in the learning sciences. Geoscience educators are receptive to research partnerships with the learning sciences. Their interest stems, in part, from their awareness that there has been a lack of research on geoscience learning that would correspond to that done in chemistry, physics, and other sciences. The geosciences are an exceptionally rich cognitive domain that offers both interesting parallels to, and differences from, other scientific fields. In addition, geoscience education reaches a very large and diverse student population with a curriculum that offers accessible opportunities for student inquiry that is enlivened by numerous policy issues.

Together geoscientists, educators, and cognitive scientists recognize that collaborative research (as described by Rapp and Uttal) is needed in three fundamental areas.

Geoscientific cognition. Studies of the nature of geoscientific knowledge and the cognitive processes involved in the practice of the geosciences at the expert level provide a foundation for research on geoscience education and illuminate how communication and learning within the research process could be improved. Studies could focus on how geoscientists frame questions and organize information, how they make, defend, and evaluate arguments or scientific claims, and the role of visualization in these activities. The roles of observation, historical thinking, and analysis of complex systems are pivotal in this work.

Learning the geosciences. Research on how geoscientific concepts and methods are learned supports both the understanding of geoscientific cognition and the development of new learning environments and instructional strategies for the field. Studies in this area would involve a strong focus on learning about complex systems and complex data, geologic time, and visualization, which are recognized as critical and challenging areas for developing geoscience understanding.

Geoscience education. Research on cognition and learning should be pursued in dynamic interaction with the development and assessment of new instructional methods, materials, and technologies for geoscience education. Educational research must not only be informed by evolving theories of cognition and learning but geoscience instructional environments must also be sites for research on cognition and learning. This work plays the dual role of enhancing studies of learning and cognition and testing their practical application in the classroom. Studies like those described in "Helping Students Learn" are of high interest because they provide a methodology that tests both our understanding of learning and our strategies for teaching. The roles of field work, data exploration, and computer-assisted visualization are of particularly high interest.

This framework exploits the synergies apparent among studies of experts, students, and children for illuminating the development of cognitive processes and of geoscience expertise. Studies of learning situated in geoscience research and educational environments will ensure that research is focused on learning that both geoscientists and cognitive scientists recognize as important with results that will be of use in geoscience research, geoscience education, and education and cognition more broadly.

Successful implementation of this research agenda depends upon the development of researchers who are interested in and qualified to do this work in the geosciences, education, and cognitive science communities. Creating this workforce will require substantial capacity development in all three areas. For geoscientists, this will require recognition of the importance of such research and the value of applying its results to geoscience education and research. For educators and cognitive scientists, it will require a growing understanding of geoscience, its importance in our society, and the opportunities such research provides for enhancing fundamental understanding of cognition and improving education. Professional development opportunities that bring together geoscientists, educators, and learning scientists are a fundamental aspect of this capacity building, as are opportunities for faculty to develop their capacity to observe student learning and design and evaluate their teaching practices.

Lastly, this research will not reach its potential impact without recognition of its use and value. Faculty bodies nationwide are undergoing a change in their approach to teaching, recognizing that it is an activity that requires scholarship. Geoscience faculty are well positioned to be leaders in the scholarship of teaching and learning as it requires the same observational and synthesis skills described in this volume as the characteristics of geoscience expertise. Like Earth, the subjects of study, individual learners and classrooms, are complex systems. Dissemination of existing research on learning in formats that reach and speak to geoscientists is an essential step in building our ability to bring research on learning to the geosciences.

This publication is a step in this direction; it demonstrates how three different groups approach understanding geoscience thinking and the application of that knowledge to geoscience teaching. We hope that by bringing these papers together in one volume, we will catalyze the imagination of researchers in all areas and help prepare the ground for widespread collaboration.